AMERICAN SPORTS EMPIRE

HOW THE LEAGUES

BREED SUCCESS

Frank P. Jozsa, Jr.

PRAEGER

Westport, Connecticut
London

Library of Congress Cataloging-in-Publication Data

Jozsa, Frank P., 1941–
    American sports empire : how the leagues breed success / Frank P. Jozsa, Jr.
        p. cm.
    Includes bibliographical references.
    ISBN 1-56720-559-3 (alk. paper)
    1. Professional sports—United States. I. Title.

GV583.J65 2003
796'.0973—dc21   2002029759

British Library Cataloguing in Publication Data is available.

Library of Congress Catalog Card Number: 2002029759
ISBN: 1-56720-559-3

First published in 2003

Praeger Publishers, 88 Post Road West, Westport, CT 06881
An imprint of Greenwood Publishing Group, Inc.
www.praeger.com

Printed in the United States of America

The paper used in this book complies with the
Permanent Paper Standard issued by the National
Information Standards Organization (Z39.48-1984).

10 9 8 7 6 5 4 3 2 1

In memory
of
John J. Guthrie, Jr., Ph.D.

Contents

Preface

Most fans become infatuated with and entertained by professional team sports at an early age. Generally, this experience occurs for kids when professional games are broadcast on cable and television networks or when a child accompanies his parents on game day to a ballpark for minor or major league baseball, an arena for basketball, a stadium for football or an ice rink for hockey. For me, this kinship with and addiction to professional sports began when my father drove us each year from Terre Haute, Indiana, to St. Louis, Missouri, to root for the baseball Cardinals. After the game ended, time was devoted to seek the autograph of the team's star and my favorite player, Stan "The Man" Musial. In the late 1940s and early 1950s, it was fun to record game statistics and cheer when great ballplayers such as the Brooklyn Dodgers' Roy Campanella and the New York Giants' Willie Mays competed against Musial and his teammates in a doubleheader at Sportsman Park—renamed Busch Stadium—on a hot Saturday afternoon in July.

After an early initiation to big-time sports, the dream of some teenagers and young adults is to diligently practice and eventually become a player for a professional team. Even though the probability of joining the Cincinnati Reds, Indiana Pacers, Chicago Bears or New York Rangers is infinitesimal, a skilled athlete normally participates on elementary, middle and high school teams to earn a college scholarship or attract the attention of a professional scout. After moderate success as a catcher/pitcher from Little League through college, it was my ambition to play professional baseball. Because of injuries and other factors besides luck, this opportunity faded. Nevertheless, when my career switched to academics, professional team sports became a challenge to research and study from a business and economic perspective.

The ongoing effort to combine academics and sports resulted in *Relocating Teams and Expanding Leagues in Professional Sports: How the Major Leagues Respond to Market Conditions,* which was published in 1999 by Quorum Books. As the book's co-author, it was gratifying to reflect and write about how a sports franchise owner decides when and where to move his club and how the leagues make business decisions to approve or deny the entry of new teams. The genesis of that book was the topic of my Ph.D. dissertation, "An Economic Analysis of Franchise Relocation and League Expansion in Professional Sports, 1950–1975," which was completed at Georgia State University in 1977. Twenty-five years later, my second book will further contribute to the literature about the behavior, conduct and history of this unique industry in America.

American Sports Empire is a title that will appeal not only to avid and casual sports fans, but also to coaches, managers and players, business journalists and historians and to the administrators and owners of minor and major league professional sports franchises in the United States and elsewhere. Essentially, the book's seven chapters emphasize and highlight how the various leagues—American and National Leagues in Major League Baseball, National Basketball Association, National Football League and National Hockey League—became the organizational models and prominent parent groups in professional team sports.

Related to how each sports league originated, matured and prospered as described in Chapter 1, Chapters 2 through 7 focus, respectively, on the distinctive features and roles of teams, owners, players, the media industry, fans and governments. To support the historical background and analysis of sports, athletes, events and organizations between the late 1800s and 2002, selected chapters in *American Sports Empire* contain tables that measure the performances of teams and players, the strategies of owners and the media, and the commitment and loyalty of fans. The majority of the tabled data, facts and other information was extracted from government sources, from sports articles in books, magazines, newspapers and research studies, and from the current World Wide Web sites of leagues and teams. Generally, wherever appropriate the sports events, player and team performances, and respective seasons varied based on which issue or topic was discussed.

In *American Sports Empire,* several important issues and problems that involve professional team sports are revealed and updated. Based on the seasons studied, these matters include whether competitive imbalance or parity existed within each sports leagues, which clubs and players excelled, how businessmen as franchise owners fail and succeed, what salaries players earned, why the media industry promotes and strengthens professional sports, what player- and team-specific attributes fans admire and dislike, and which governments and taxpayer groups subsidized the construction of arenas and stadiums. In sum, according to the research performed for this book the future business prospects, entertainment value and growth of each league in the twenty-first century will depend on the leadership of the respective commissioners and franchise owners, and on interteam competitiveness, player performances, media companies, fan loyalties and government decisions.

Three well-regarded sports books were extensively used as references. The authors, titles and publishers were Roger G. Noll, ed., *Government and the Sports Business* (Washington, DC: The Brookings Institution, 1974); James Quirk and Rodney D. Fort, *Pay Dirt: The Business of Professional Team Sports* (Princeton, NJ: Princeton University Press, 1992); James Quirk and Rodney D. Fort, *Hard Ball: The Abuse of Power in Pro Team Sports* (Princeton, NJ: Princeton University Press, 1999).

An assortment of colleagues and friends assisted, guided and supported me during the development of this book. Pfeiffer University's Dean of the Undergraduate College, Dr. Bettie Starr and the former head of the School of Business, Professor Toby Poplin, agreed to adjust my teaching schedule at the Misenheimer Campus in the 2001–2002 academic year. Because of their confidence and trust in my scholarship, there was sufficient opportunity and time for me to successfully complete the manuscript. Frank Chance, Pfeiffer's director of information support services and assistant professor of library science at the Charlotte Campus, informed me about databases. Furthermore, he forwarded me numerous articles on professional sports that appear in the book's Selected Bibliography. Frank's comments and viewpoints about teams, owners and players were insightful, practical and thought-out. Indeed, this book improved because of his input. Librarians Norman Wilson and Lara Little at the Misenheimer Campus loaned me materials such as *The World Almanac and Book of Facts* and various sports books. Their contributions reduced research time and expense. The Charlotte Campus's assistant dean for student services, Michael Utsman, is a computer whiz who assisted in the preparation of the tables and listened to my progress reports on each chapter. Mr. Utsman never hesitated to help me. For that, he earns my gratitude and respect. My close friend Maureen Fogle allowed me to use her personal computer and home office to produce the manuscript. Despite the mess created from documents and paperwork scattered about her office to accomplish the research and write, Maureen freed me from housekeeping chores to focus on the task of meeting the publisher's deadline date. Besides the forenamed individuals, former Pfeiffer University MBA student and ex-employee of the Carolina Panthers and San Francisco 49ers Martha Robinson mailed me a league-specific resource and media guide, the *NFL 2001 Record & Fact Book*. Her gift is appreciated. Finally, Quorum Books' Senior Editor Hilary D. Claggett, Greenwood Press's Senior Production Editor Heidi L. Straight and Thistle Hill Publishing Services' Editorial Director Angela Williams Urquhart cooperated with me to ensure the transformation of the manuscript into *American Sports Empire*.

The late Dr. John J. Guthrie, Jr., co-author of *Relocating Teams and Expanding Leagues in Professional Sports,* was the inspiration for this book. While a college professor, John edited and wrote several books and numerous articles.

He motivated his students in economics and history courses and cared about each student's education and well-being. Considered a top competitive runner in the Daytona Beach area in the 1980s and 1990s, one of his former students said, "Professor Guthrie is good at what he does. He's funny and we [students] learn something at the same time." Well short of the finish line he deserved, on February 22, 2000, John died in his sleep. This book is dedicated to his memory.

Introduction

Since the late 1800s, professional team sports have become increasingly deep-rooted and popular as an entertainment choice for Americans. Irrespective of age, ethnicity, gender, political affiliation, race and socioeconomic environment, there are millions of children, teenagers and adults who idolize and emulate the athleticism and hustle of their favorite ballplayers. Some sports fans, for example, attempt to duplicate the home run swing of San Francisco Giants outfielder Barry Bonds, the thunderous dunks of Los Angeles Laker center Shaquille O'Neal, the pinpoint passes of Green Bay Packers quarterback Brett Favre, and the power plays of Pittsburgh Penguins center and owner Mario Lemieux. Other fans collect and exchange sports cards, host tailgate parties before and after home games, manage a team in fantasy sports, participate in local campaigns and convince voters to adopt an arena or stadium referendum, purchase a club seat and Personal Seat License, read the sports section of the daily hometown newspaper, visit a sport's Hall of Fame and watch the Entertainment Sports Programming Network (ESPN) at a downtown sports bar. Consequently, professional team sports are a frequent and significant leisure activity for a vast segment of the U.S. population.

While employment and production in the U.S. manufacturing and service industries fluctuated during the business cycles that occurred between 1900 and 1950, American professional sports leagues tended to flourish. In Major League Baseball (MLB), the American League of Professional Baseball Clubs (AL) and National League of Professional Baseball Clubs (NL) were fixed in size with each league composed of eight teams per season. Meanwhile, as alternatives to the AL and NL, three viable nonbaseball leagues emerged. The National Hockey League (NHL) was formally established in 1917, the National Football League (NFL) in 1922 and the National Basketball Association (NBA) in 1946. Indeed, despite the challenges and threats from competitive sports organizations since the early 1900s, for various demographic, economic, financial and geographic reasons these five leagues survived to become the most prosperous groups of teams in big-time sports during the twentieth century.[1]

The ethical, legal, political, racial and social realities aside, from the early 1970s the business, economic and marketing aspects and problems within the professional sports leagues rose to prominence and became newsworthy topics in America. As such, sports-related issues were identified and then studied by an array of academics, historians, and sports industry journalists, practitioners and reporters. A sample of their publications reveals how teams, owners, players, the media, fans and government officials jointly contribute to the longevity and prosperity of the eminent American sports leagues in professional baseball, basketball, football and hockey. Listed in a chronological sequence by discipline is a mixture of engaging sports books and articles that has evolved from reputable business, economics and marketing sources. This literature will be summarized first and then followed by a synopsis of selected readings embodied in sports law and ethics. After these titles and articles are reviewed, the purpose, thesis and organization of this book are presented as a guideline to prepare the reader for the topics that will be discussed in Chapters 1 through 7.[2]

SPORTS LITERATURE

Because of a unique hierarchy and infrastructure, for at least three decades the business, operations and strategies of American sports leagues and teams have been fertile research subjects for economists. For instance, in two theoretical papers published in the early 1970s, the California Institute of Technology's James Quirk and University of Kansas's Mohamed A. El-Hodiri predicted that when the percentage of championships and games won, total metropolitan population, and the quality of franchises abandoned or moved are explanatory variables, big cities with high drawing potential, such as Chicago and New York, have stronger teams than those located in small cities with low drawing potential, such as Cincinnati and Kansas City. Therefore, these economists verified that the existing rules structure of professional sports leagues, including the player reservation system, was an inadequate system to balance playing strengths and team performances.[3]

Lance E. Davis, a former colleague of Quirk's at the California Institute of Technology, in 1974 examined the self-regulation of organized baseball from the 1909 to 1971 seasons inclusive. Because MLB is organized and operated as an economic cartel, and cartels limit competition and divide markets, Davis advocated a total repeal of baseball's antitrust exemption that would benefit team players and the general public. After modeling the economic structure of baseball in his article, Davis wrote, "In general, it appears that the commonly held opinion that the pre-1920 cartel was ineffective is probably correct, that the post-

1945 behavior has been even less effective than was supposed, and that the [cartel's] performance during the Landis regime, while better than what preceded and followed it, was not as effective as is generally believed."[4]

Similar to the behavioral and structural models developed by Quirk, El-Hodiri and Davis, throughout the 1980s and 1990s other academicians portrayed the American professional sports leagues as cartels or as monopolies that restrict the entry of potential competitors and thereby financially harm fans and taxpayers, and limit players' freedom. Given those outcomes, in a 1991 article historian Stephen F. Ross made three compelling proposals about the control and power of professional sports. First, he justified the application of antitrust suits to league organizations that had adopted player reservation systems. Second, Ross approved a government investigation of internal sports league business decisions that involved broadcast rights, expansion, franchise relocation and revenue sharing. Third, to provide more sports market competition and consumer choice, he supported the creation of rival leagues to challenge the entrenched AL, NL, NBA, NFL and NHL. Despite these proposals, Ross admitted that insufficient data existed to fully explain each league's anticompetitive expansion practices and other polices that prevailed in the professional sports industry.[5]

In sum, to the late 1990s many renowned economists and historians suggested that the federal government initiate legislation to redirect the resources of the professional sports markets. Based on their models, these researchers say public policies are needed to increase parity or the playing strengths between teams. Thus, legislation is required first, to adopt more liberal formulas that govern the allocation of broadcast and gate revenues among league teams; second, to force leagues to expand in large-city markets and in high-growth metropolitan areas; and third, to prohibit league rules that grant member clubs the right to exclude the broadcasts of visiting teams from the home clubs' territory. If these legislative initiatives are passed by Congress and enforced by the Justice Department, economists and historians who have studied the sports industry believe that the mandates would restore competitive balance and allow revenues and profits to be distributed more equitably among member teams within each sports organization.

After 1991, four intriguing and provocative business/economics sports books were published. Each title provided further empirical evidence and theories that economic resources were being misallocated within the professional sports markets because of the monopolistic practices of leagues. Basically, the authors revised and updated the previous studies mentioned earlier and introduced some unresolved issues that focus on and influence specific communities, franchise owners and leagues, team players and the general public. A recap of each book reinforces those perspectives.

In *Pay Dirt: The Business of Professional Team Sports* (1992), James Quirk and University of Washington economist Rodney D. Fort evaluated the distinctive features of professional sports arenas and stadiums, competitive balance within sports leagues, tax sheltering as practiced by team owners, history of the reserve clause, demographic characteristics of markets for franchises, factors that affect salary determination in baseball and the failure of rival sports leagues. Based on anecdotes about players and owners, and given the research about league histories, sports lore and tradition, and team statistics, authors Quirk and Fort arrive at three arguable yet reasonable conclusions. First, the most important economic benefit a team provides to a city is a common identification symbol, which is something that unifies the city's citizens. The value of this benefit, however, is difficult to calculate and quantify in money terms. Second, the best possible solution to stop the abuse of monopoly power by the dominant professional sports leagues is not government regulation. Rather, it is the creation of competitive professional sports markets that consist of two or more independent leagues, with roughly equal drawing potential, and with all franchises located in a megalopolis. Third, based on accepted accounting practices each preeminent sports league in America operates with a significant degree of competitive imbalance no matter how the inequity is measured. Because of these conclusions, therefore, Quirk and Fort infer that microeconomic theory does not agree with or support team owners who claim that the reserve-option clause and other league rules are needed to restore and maintain competitive balance. According to author, columnist, pundit and sports fan George Will, "Quirk [and Fort] demonstrate that decisions made in the executive offices of sports franchises can be as fascinating as, and can influence, what happens in the games."[6]

In 1994, then Ernst & Young consultants Jerry Gorman and Kirk Calhoun, along with contributing sportswriter Skip Rozin, authored *The Name of the Game: The Business of Sports.* This title provides a rationale for how the major sports leagues evolved, how their growth was fueled by the broadcast media, and how skyrocketing player salaries put pressure on teams to generate more income during games from club seats, concessions, corporate sponsorships, in-house advertising, luxury suites, merchandise sales, parking fees, permanent seat licenses, and from taxpayers who subsidize the construction of modern arenas and stadiums. Although these and other revenue sources are familiar to sports industry analysts, authors Gorman, Calhoun and Rozin further assess the innovative marketing gimmicks and schemes that club owners use to attract fans and gain their loyalty. Finally, in their book the trio also discuss other business activities within professional sports such as the financial rewards from merchandising club logos, the economic realities of trading a superstar such as Wayne Gretsky, and the monetary investment required to place a team on the court, field or ice for a season. According to one reader, however, *The Name of the Game* covers many well-researched sports issues and topics rather than examines the problems that are controversial and difficult to explain.[7]

Subsequent to the elegant models and well-regarded case studies and theories that appeared in *Pay Dirt*, in 1997 two notable sports economics professors—Stanford University's Roger G. Noll and Smith College's Andrew Zimbalist—edited *Sports, Jobs and Taxes: The Economic Impact of Sports Teams and Stadiums.* The book's first part examines four relationships. They are the economic impact of new stadiums and local employment, of professional sports clubs and local government subsidies, of the politics required to attract and retain teams, and of stadium design and community development. The book's second part consists of case studies that involved the construction and operation of major league sports facilities in various cities. Essentially, in *Sports, Jobs and Taxes* Noll and Zimbalist arrive at three overriding conclusions. They declare that, one, public investments in sports franchises and facilities are not a major impetus to communities' economic growth and employment. Two, in the majority of case studies a sports stadium's or team's net subsidy exceeds its financial benefit. And three, that selected cities subsidize teams' facilities because professional sports are popular and because of the advantage and leverage teams enjoy from the monopolistic policies and practices of their respective leagues. In sum, professional sports teams and the facilities they occupy are not economically beneficial to local economies, create only minor employment opportunities, and obligate taxpayers with long-term debt from the subsidy. Thus, in part the conclusions of Noll and Zimbalist resemble those stated in previous studies conducted by Quirk, Davis, El-Hodiri, Fort and Ross.[8]

Given the thesis that franchise owners are foremost obsessed with their team's cash flows, market bases and profits, and not with fan loyalties, game strategies and winning league championships, in 1999 professors Quirk and Fort authored their second sports book, *Hard Ball: The Abuse of Power in Pro Team Sports*. This title explores how, in recent years the superior major sports leagues—AL, NL, NBA, NFL and NHL—have restructured. In effect, the balance of economic power has shifted overwhelmingly from communities, fans and taxpayers to the league monopolies, and to a lesser extent, to the other professional sports industry entities such as the franchise owners, players, the media and player unions. More specifically, the book addresses how players, taxpayers, team owners and the television networks are affected by and respond to the monopoly power of leagues. Similar to policies proposed by Noll and Zimbalist in *Sports, Jobs and Taxes*, to restore a competitive environment Quirk and Fort maintain that the U.S. Justice Department should file suit under the antitrust laws to break up the five existing monopoly leagues into several independent professional leagues. Consequently, because of the competition from new leagues there will be more clubs located in medium-to-large U.S. cities, less taxpayer subsidies committed to the construction of arenas and stadiums, an increase in game broadcasts on the nation's cable, satellite and television networks, and a decrease in the growth of franchise market values, player salaries, team profits and ticket prices. Basically, the authors contend that competition would unleash market forces, which eventually would shift control and power from league owners, players and player unions to communities and fans. In *Hard Ball*, unfortunately, Quirk and Fort fail to consider whether sports leagues are natural monopolies. Furthermore, they feebly justify the economic and social benefits that would result from increased competition and the entry of additional sports leagues and teams. Notwithstanding, these flaws in the book are minor yet difficult to ignore in an analysis of professional sports markets. *Hard Ball* completes the literature review on the economics of sports. A summary of the marketing publications that amplify and relate to the professional sports industry and markets follows next.[9]

Sports marketing is the specific application of marketing principles and processes to sports products and services and to the promotion of nonsport goods that are associated with sport. One key element in the marketing communications process is television, which is defined as a channel or medium. To improve the business environment, sports marketers attempt to reach the mature or adult market by broadcasting games on cable, satellite and television networks. In turn, this activity increases the demand for and boosts the income of professional sports leagues and the teams, coaches, managers, owners, and players.

Because of unique product qualities and national exposure, for decades the premier professional sports leagues have succeeded in obtaining government approval to pool offerings of national broadcasting packages. Furthermore, these organizations have implemented blackouts and enforced territorial restrictions to prevent competition for local broadcast rights. Indiana University Professor Ira Horowitz discussed this public policy issue in his 1974 article, "Sports Broadcasting," which appeared in Noll's *Government and the Sports Business*. There is weak justification, according to Horowitz, for nationwide broadcasting collusion among the [sports] cartel members. Instead, he preferred that each member club be granted the authority and responsibility to negotiate and regulate its own broadcast activities in local, regional and perhaps national markets. As a result, this strategy would permit each league to nationally promote its sport and allow each team the freedom to focus on and penetrate its local and regional media market. Furthermore, as a marketing ploy to generate cash inflows, clubs would be authorized to compete for and sell arena or stadium naming rights to enterprising corporate sponsors who may be geographically dispersed. The experience of the 1960s, in Horowitz's view, suggests " ... that the major-league broadcast cartels, in particular, produce higher rights fees for all their members and higher sponsor's fees paid either directly to the clubs for local rights, or to the networks for commercial time."[10]

Especially since the early 1990s, the promotion and sales of sports athletic clothing, merchandise, memorabilia and team logos have exceeded the expectations of marketing managers in the professional sports industry. The value of this business has been documented, critiqued and itemized in various publications. Besides the specialized articles that have appeared in issues of *Advertising Age, ADWEEK, Brandweek, Consumer Behavior, Daily News Record, Journal of Advertising, Journal of Marketing, Marketing* and *Sporting Goods Business*, sports marketing books that contain new models and applications are increasingly being produced for practitioners and college/university students who major in sports administration, management and marketing. For example, in 1999 Northern Kentucky University's associate professor of marketing, Matthew D. Shank, published the first edition of *Sports Marketing: A Strategic Perspective*. In his book, Professor Shank presents a framework for franchises to explicitly organize and implement a strategic sport marketing process. The textbook includes many applications of marketing principles and processes to the professional sports industry and its elements, which include fans, leagues, the media, owners, players, vendors and teams. Inevitably, sports consultants and entrepreneurs, marketers and marketing firms will read this book and other publications for concepts, methods and techniques to promote events and to sell the branded products of and those designed for professional sports athletes, leagues and teams. Other than the economics and marketing models, in the literature there is another subject area that significantly impacts the business and operation of the professional sports industry. This topic is concerned with the practices and theories of sports law and ethics.[11]

An overview of the publications in sports law discloses that the primary policy instrument used by the federal government to minimize the abuse of power, as practiced by the professional sports leagues, is antitrust action. A lawyer and legal scholar, Steven R. Rivkin, published the seminal research on antitrust action in editor Noll's book, *Government and the Sports Business*. In 1974, an article written by Rivkin titled, "Sports Leagues and the Federal Antitrust Laws," appeared as Chapter 11 in Noll's book. In his piece, Rivkin analyzes three legal issues. They are the history of antitrust action in sports, antitrust precedents established in other industries that might apply to professional team sports, and whether future antitrust suits are likely to reduce the anticompetitive practices of the unregulated sports industry. After a thorough investigation of cases that involved antitrust actions and sports, Rivkin recommends three interdependent approaches to the external or government control of professional sports leagues. In his view, the federal government should first, enact restrictions on specific key aspects of league activity such as the draft and player retention system. Second, the federal government should impose legislative guidelines about the judicial disposition of antitrust suits. Third, the U.S. Congress should appoint a federal or National Sports Commission to regulate the rules structure as established by the professional sports leagues. In retrospect, although Rivkin's recommendations are appropriate and worthwhile according to several legal scholars, the oversight of professional sports organizations has remained basically free and unrestrained from federal government intrusion.[12]

Other than the applied and theoretical business, economic and marketing articles and titles written about the professional sports industry, in the 1990s two books and one article cited here were published that relate to the legal aspects of sports. In 1999, University of Massachusetts at Lowell's Associate Professor Michael E. Jones authored *Sports Law*. This book was written primarily for undergraduate and graduate students who are enrolled in a college or university sports law course or program, and for lay persons who are interested in how sports and law intermingle in contemporary society. The title is an inside look at the legal components of the professional sports industry, which includes controversial issues such as labor and antitrust remedies, league and franchise contracts, and player-to-agent relationships and torts as applied to sports. In detail,

a discussion of such matters as the business elements of bylaws and league con-
stitutions, team admission standards to enter various leagues, territorial restrictions of member clubs, and the relocation of franchises are contained in the
text. In Chapter 7, "The Business of Sports: Leagues, Teams, Relocations, and
Building Stadiums," Professor Jones foresaw three significant trends that involved the professional sports business and sports law. One, he claimed there
would be an increase in the corporate ownership of sports teams, especially by
the large media and entertainment companies. Two, Jones predicted a profusion
of taxpayer-subsidized sports arenas and stadiums. And three, he wrote that the
sport leagues will fear losing "Raiders-style" antitrust lawsuits. In sum, Jones
motivates *Sports Law* readers to ponder and answer four controversial legal
questions: "Is the NFL Green Bay Packers' community-based ownership the
appropriate model for other sports teams? Would you propose that the U.S.
Congress grant the professional sports leagues limited antitrust immunity on
stadium finance when franchise owners threaten to move their team unless taxpayers pay for the construction of a new facility? What reforms, if any, could
leagues voluntarily initiate to match the supply and demand for professional
sports teams and thereby avoid conflicts that occur when communities raise the
ante on stadium deals? Finally, what steps should be taken, and by whom, to
protect local fans from the relocation of their home team?"[13]

In 2000, another well-known sports scholar, Harvard University Law Professor Paul C. Weiler authored *Leveling the Playing Field: How the Law Can Make
Sports Better for Fans.* Since economic, social and technological forces inter-
mittently and unpredictably disrupt the goal of evenly balanced professional
sports games, Professor Weiler argues that the law is an essential tool to level
the playing field among leagues, owners, and players and ultimately among fans
and taxpayers. After analyzing an assortment of economic and moral issues that
arise in competitive sports, he examines why the current proposals to dissolve
the dominant professional leagues and create new organizations are impractical
and unrealistic recommendations. According to Weiler, to reduce the monopoly
power of sports leagues Congress should pass legislation that: first, modifies the
federal law that allows cities to issue tax-exempt bonds for stadium construction; second, bans the use of public funds for building stadiums; and third, expands antitrust law to require leagues to approve the entry of a new franchise
whenever a qualified owner or community can make a case for it. Weiler's critics, however, contend that each professional sports league should be free to serve
its customers with internal policies and rules that keep franchises stable and
player talent dispersed. Moreover, his critics claim there is insufficient evidence
to prove that consumers overpay for sports events because of the anticompetitive and unreasonable practices of leagues. Thus far, Congress has allowed the
sports markets to determine arena and stadium finances and to resolve expansion and relocation issues.[14]

Besides antitrust action against sports leagues and the regulation of sports
markets, there exist other issues, practices and problems that involve sports law

and ethics. These topics include but are not limited to: the ethics of corporate sponsorship to support franchises and players; league ownership restraints; multiteam collective bargaining contracts; the power of player agents; and league policies regarding player infractions such as alcohol abuse, domestic violence, unprescribed drug consumption, gambling, robbery, sexual harassment and other crimes and illegal activities. A superb reference to research the cases that involve league, player and team ethics is *Sports Ethics in America: A Bibliography, 1970–1990*, which was authored in 1992 by Drew University Professor of Social Ethics Donald G. Jones. This comprehensive, multidisciplinary bibliography cites nearly 2,800 books and articles printed in journals, magazines and newspapers that have been published generally in the United States since 1970. The three primary environments of sports that are listed in the bibliography include the team, game or contest, and society. *Sports Ethics* was designed to be a research tool for sports scholars and for undergraduate and graduate college and university students. It also serves as a source of practical information that has applications for college and university administrators, athletes, athletic directors and coaches, and for professional sports agents and union officials. In sum, the study of sports law and ethics contains complex and sensitive legal and social issues for officials in sports organizations at all levels of competition to consider.[15]

In part, the accounting and finance results determine how the decisions arrived at by professional sports league executives, team owners and player unions will impact communities, fans and taxpayers. To excite fans and general readers, therefore, sports commentators and economists, and media journalists publish business articles that contain accounting statistics and other financial information about several aspects of the professional sports industry. If reported, the data include arena and stadium construction costs, present and future franchise values, league and team broadcasting contracts negotiated with various radio and television networks, distribution effects of luxury taxes imposed on high payroll clubs, and the escalation of player salaries and team expenses, revenues, profits and ticket prices. Frequently, the business-related articles dominate the headlines and columns of local newspaper sports pages and appear in nonsports journals and magazines such as *Business Week, Forbes* and *Fortune*. Other than the publication of financial statistics about leagues, owners and players, people in a community and especially sports fans seemingly demand more information about the business success of their home team(s). After a review of the relevant literature, two readable sports books were selected that focus primarily on sports fans, economics and finance. Written with passion, each author proposes some practical reforms that professional leagues should implement to preserve the integrity of sports and make games more affordable, competitive and entertaining for spectators.

In 1995, economist Thomas Kruckemeyer published *For Whom the Ball Tolls: A Fan's Guide to Economic Issues in Professional and College Sports*. His clearheaded and realistic analysis of the economics and finance issues that plague team sports poses five questions that should interest professional sports fans.

First, do the enormous salaries that are paid to professional players always result in higher ticket prices? Second, are franchise owners primarily trying to win division titles and league championships or to earn excess profits from their sports investments? Third, should public money be used to build sports arenas and stadiums to attract expansion clubs and to discourage home teams from relocation? Fourth, should the professional leagues continue to expand and perhaps saturate the sports markets? And fifth, should teams that incur financial losses each season and accumulate debt be free to fold, merge or relocate?[16]

Besides the measures of team performance such as regular season wins, win-loss percentages and the number of postseason berths and playoff victories, there are tables in Kruckemeyer's book that contain financial statistics for teams in selected years. This data includes franchise expansion fees and market values, player salaries, team expenses and revenues, total sport payrolls, and a club's financial impact on a local economy. This information is used by the author to justify how and why leagues need to initiate reforms. In MLB, for instance, Kruckemeyer would terminate binding salary arbitration, adopt league-wide sharing of local broadcast revenues, liberalize free agency and permit prudent league expansion. Conversely, he would adamantly oppose any system of government control and the regulation of leagues as that performed for the utility industry. Essentially, *For Whom the Ball Tolls* directly and explicitly discusses these and other controversial topics that should arouse the curiosity and intellect of average sports fans.[17]

If interpreted from a fan's perspective, Emmy Award–winning television sportscaster Bob Costas is ambivalent about the current status and future of professional sports. He deplores the attitude and insensitivity of superstar players who, after one or a few productive seasons, selfishly abandon their communities and teammates for a larger salary with a competitive team in the sport. According to Costas, in professional baseball the designated hitter rule, interleague play, wild card system, and the payroll disparities between small-to-medium and large market teams are surmountable league problems. Published in 2000, Costas' book *Fair Ball: A Fan's Case for Baseball* addresses these issues and presents common sense, albeit radical and untested solutions for their implementation.[18]

If appointed as MLB commissioner, Bob Costas would unilaterally and if necessary abolish the designated hitter rule, adopt comprehensive revenue sharing, eliminate interleague play and wild-card games, and institute player salary caps and floors that would restrict the range of salary differences between league clubs. Despite the book's cogent arguments and pleas for various reforms, after evaluation Commissioner Bud Selig, team owners and the players union would unanimously reject these proposals. Indeed, without the authority to implement reforms and to participate in owner-player collective bargaining meetings, Costas's well-intentioned book is merely a statement of baseball's ills and a rallying cry for the sport's fans. In brief, *Fair Ball* argues for reforms that may or may not improve the sport and its leagues or teams, or benefit communities, fans and taxpayers.[19]

This completes the literature review of selected articles and books on the professional sports industry and its elements. The next section of the Introduction presents an overview of *American Sports Empire: How the Leagues Breed Success,* and the basis of the book's thesis and organization. Then, the chronological arrangement of the chapters and their selected topics are discussed.

BOOK OVERVIEW

American Sports Empire essentially demonstrates and depicts how the five major sports leagues and their member clubs, franchise owners, team players, the media and government organizations collaborate and cooperate to create entertainment value, enthuse fans and ensure a prominent role for the professional sports industry in American society. Rather than focus entirely on long-standing and well-researched theoretical and empirical issues, such as league-player union relations and case illustrations of league expansion or team relocation, this title applies business, demographic, economic, financial and sports-related data and facts to reveal the key opportunities and strategies that confer power upon and prestige to the AL and NL in MLB, and to the NBA, NFL and NHL.

In brief, the literature on big-time sports denotes that prior research studies have largely ignored the interdependence and linkage of leagues, team owners and players, and the media and governments in the marketing and supply of sports events including games, which are unique entertainment products that have been beloved and enjoyed by fans for decades. The organization, thesis and conclusion of this book, therefore, do not duplicate nor negate the previous research on the professional sports industry. The concepts, statistics, terms and theories in *Sports Empire* are discussed at a basic-to-average comprehension level. The jargon appears in the sports section of daily city newspapers and in popular sports journals and magazines. The language of sports, also, is inferred and spoken outright during broadcasts of games on radio and television, and in commentary on local sports talk radio and news programs.

A professional sport's core authority, as well as its legal and organizational structure, is the league. In part, each league seeks to maintain a competitive balance between conference and particularly division teams, control the current size and long-term growth of the sport, and initiate and implement reforms such as realignment. Furthermore, leagues negotiate labor and nationwide radio, television and World Wide Web–based contracts, promote team rivalries, and monitor the behavior of franchise owners and team coaches, managers and players. In turn, a member club's competitive strength and financial success are primarily determined by the cash inflows earned from gate receipts and local, regional and national radio and television network broadcasts; from the coaches' and general managers' decisions and the owner's strategies; from the players' skills and performances; and from the revenue streams that flow from a privately and/or publicly financed home arena or stadium.

The local and perhaps national media, meanwhile, hypes the athletic abilities, achievements and conduct of players, publicizes game highlights and reports on the team's progress. Ultimately, the media's publications and publicity impact the team's image in the community, region and nation, and consequently influences the future game attendance, operating revenue and net profit of the franchise. Simply put, the interplay of leagues with franchise owners and players, player unions, and the media and governments jointly contribute to the business fortune, marketing clout and privileged status of America's professional sports teams.

In general, this book concurs with academic economists who conclude that the AL and NL in MLB, and the NBA, NFL and NHL each operates as a cartel within an oligopoly sports market. Given this premise, Chapter 1 exposes the business functions, strategies and tactics that professional sports organizations have historically implemented to accomplish their mission. In hierarchy and structure, all professional sports leagues are, conceivably, clans. They each consist of a commissioner and his or her administrative and executive staffs, and the member team owners. Based on the recommendations of internal committees and task forces, and external consultants and business affiliates, leagues make the final decisions to realign divisions and conferences and to permit the entry of new franchises into the clan. Furthermore, leagues also approve the relocation of ill-placed and financially inferior clubs from one metropolitan area to another. Whether each league's decision process is an effective and efficient way for an organization to manage its long-term stability and to control the size and growth of its sport is explicitly evaluated in Chapter 1.

His or her other duties aside, a league commissioner represents the preferences of owners in collective bargaining with player unions and in communications with communities, fans and the media. Although the commissioner's responsibilities and tasks are meaningful and well-defined, his or her primary goals are to reach a consensus with owners to establish, implement and enforce internal policies, rules and standards that relate to competitive balance, national broadcast rights, penalties for coach, owner and player misdeeds, realignment, revenue sharing, salary minimums and caps, and other organizational matters. To clarify these goals in-depth, the chapter discusses some historic reforms that various commissioners have supervised on behalf of league owners.

Other than the aforementioned issues and topics, Chapter 1 implicitly considers why rival sports leagues failed to coexist and strengthen in America as did the AL and NL in MLB, and the NBA, NFL and NHL. Then, the chapter looks at the various reasons for the attendance boom that has occurred in baseball's minor leagues, and the formation, development and progress of the National Basketball Development League, NFL Europe League and the minor leagues in hockey. The discussion of these leagues concludes the chapter.[20]

Chapter 2 focuses on the participation, role and significance of member teams within each sports league. During a season, teams must be close-knit and cohesive organizations in order to play competitively and to support owners in their quest to win championships and earn profits. Each member club is expected to remain loyal and adhere to and enforce league policies, regulations, rules and standards. For selected seasons, in this chapter there are tables that contain the performances of league teams, and the characteristics of their location while playing in small-to-medium, medium-to-large or large markets. Factual financial and sports-related statistics and information, such as average and per game attendance, win-loss percentage, operating income, and the number of playoff appearances and titles and championships won, will be applied in this and other chapters to measure league and team performances. How, when and why certain teams win division, conference and league championships and thrive as usiness enterprises, while other teams do not, depend on the capabilities and interaction of the respective coaches, franchise owners, executive and support staffs, managers and players. In the long term, only a moderate proportion of sports franchises in each league has been disciplined and well managed, admired and enthusiastically supported by their hometown fans, and lauded by the local and national media. Chapter 2 states why, for example, this occurred for the Green Bay Packers and not the Arizona Cardinals.

In Chapter 3, the sports franchise owners who have provided leadership for their organizations are identified and profiled. Typically, team owners are successful and wealthy entrepreneurs who own and manage nonsports business enterprises. As such, they are innovators, investors and risk-takers, but perhaps not passionate about their sports clubs. Interestingly, since the mid-1980s entertainment companies, media conglomerates and other types of corporations have gradually replaced partnerships, proprietorships and syndicates as owners of professional sports clubs. The rationale for this transformation, and its consequences are explained in Chapter 3. Intuitively, franchise owners vicariously influence their team's culture, orientation and performance with their communication skill, integrity, leadership style, motivation, personality and vision. In the majority, owners retain the power to employ and replace team coaches or managers, administrative and executive staffs, and players. These decisions ultimately shape the organization's character and determine its current and future competitive and financial performances. Other than the efforts to maximize profits or minimize losses, to participate in team operations, and to set ticket prices, Chapter 3 also explains how selected team owners, with the cooperation of the local business community, media and government persuade taxpayers to finance the construction of a new or the renovation of an existing arena or stadium.[21]

In part, Chapter 4 explores how players have been affected by and contribute to the league and team conditions. The impact of salary caps and team payrolls on player performances and league standings are other important topics investigated in the chapter. Are professional athletes considered heroes and role models or prima donnas and thugs by the nation's youth and adult fans? In recent years, an increasing number of alleged and documented incidences of criminal activities, misconduct and unethical behavior, which have led to arrest and incarceration, involve professional athletes. This state of affairs is a league, team and community issue alluded to in Chapter 4. Finally, this chapter discusses the cultural, political and socioeconomic factors that have internationalized sports and examines the business rationale for team owners to employ, and for coaches to play, foreign athletes in MLB.

A variety of local, regional, national and international media enterprises inform and supply their audiences with up-to-date sports data and statistics. This information includes game highlights, player achievements and infractions, team performances during the regular season, and other sports-related matters. Given these topics, Chapter 5 discusses how, what and why the media willingly provide this information to sports fans and the general public in the interests of professional leagues and teams. This chapter also describes the business and technological implications of widely used and profitable media sources such as the Internet, pay-per-view programs, sports talk radio, and cable and satellite programming. Will these mediums increase market share and subscribers, and eventually replace the traditional media such as city newspapers, sports journals and magazines, radio stations and the prime television networks? Are fans oversaturated with sports news and statistics? Which sports are the least and most publicized and why? These questions are evaluated in Chapter 5.[22]

Chapter 6 describes the behavior, culture and motivation of sports fans. The characteristics of apathetic, casual and diehard fans, and of nonfans are differentiated. Indeed, the various research studies that have measured how fans commit to a sport are outlined. Then, the changes in annual ticket prices and fan costs for leagues and teams are tabled and discussed. To this end, Fan Cost and Sports Loyalty Indexes are presented and interpreted for selected seasons. A list of the "Best Sports Places" in America has been periodically published by *The Sporting News*. This chapter explains how *The Sporting News* assembles the list, and why certain places—areas and cities—are ranked, accordingly.[23]

Since when and why have the federal and various local and regional governments become involved with and subsidized the business and operations of professional sports leagues and teams? Chapter 7 assumes government officials are civic-minded public servants. They adopt pro-sport legislation, interact with and join the local business community to attract new or retain current sport franchises, issue bonds and raise taxes to pay the construction costs of sports facilities, and generally support the strategies of leagues and team owners. By sport and team, the chapter discusses the extent to which various governments have committed taxpayer money to build or renovate arenas and stadiums from the early 1990s to 2001 inclusive. Furthermore, Chapter 7 lists and reviews the franchises whose arenas and stadiums were subsidized.[24]

After Chapter 7, the Conclusion is presented. It provides an overview of how member teams, franchise owners, team players, the media industry and governments have collectively contributed to the progress and success of each sports league in the twentieth century. Furthermore, the Conclusion predicts which sports league(s) will flourish in the twenty-first century and whether professional team sports will contract, stagnate or expand after 2002. The book concludes with the Appendix, which contains three tables that were not contained in the chapters, as well as a Selected Bibliography and an Index.

In addition to the professional leagues' commissioners and staff, minor and major league team owners and players, and avid sports fans, *American Sports Empire* will also interest applied researchers such as private sector business economists, historians and organizations that conduct surveys. Other potential readers of the book include sports analysts, journalists and reporters; college faculty who teach sports administration, economics, ethics, law, management and marketing; and city, county and state government officials who are indirectly involved with the existence and success of professional sports franchises in their areas. The book, therefore, will appeal to a multidisciplinary and diverse group of readers, and especially to males who are aged from fifteen to sixty-five.

NOTES

1. Since 1876, six rival sports leagues have challenged MLB, two the NBA, seven the NFL and one the NHL. For an economic analysis of the strategies that motivated these rival leagues, see James Quirk and Rodney D. Fort, *Pay Dirt: The Business of Professional Team Sports* (Princeton, NJ: Princeton University Press, 1992), 294–332; Roger G. Noll, ed., *Government and the Sports Business* (Washington, DC: The Brookings Institution, 1974).

2. The literature published on the history of professional sports is abundant. For a current Selected Bibliography, see Frank P. Jozsa, Jr. and John J. Guthrie, Jr., *Relocating Teams and Expanding Leagues in Professional Sports: How the Major Leagues Respond to Market Conditions* (Westport, CT: Quorum Books, 1999). Besides that title, other literature on sport history includes books written by Benjamin G. Radar, *American Sports: From the Age of Folk Games to the Age of Spectators* (Englewood Cliffs, NJ: Prentice-Hall, 1983); Randy Roberts and James Olsen, *Winning Is the Only Thing: Sports in America Since 1945* (Baltimore: Johns Hopkins University Press, 1989); S. W. Pope, ed., *The New American Sport History: Recent Approaches and Perspectives* (Champaign: University of Illinois Press, 1997); Steven A. Riess, *Major Problems in American Sport History* (Boston: Houghton Mifflin Company, 1997); Harold Seymour, *Baseball: The Golden Age,* 2nd ed. (New York: Oxford University Press, 1989).

3. See James Quirk and Mohamed A. El-Hodiri, "An Economic Model of a Professional Sports League," *Journal of Political Economy* 79 (March/April 1975), 1302–1319; Idem., "The Economic Theory of a Professional Sports League," in Roger G. Noll, ed., *Government and the Sports Business,* 33–80. For other research on professional sports leagues, see Michael A. Flynn and Richard J. Gilbert, "The Analysis of Professional Sports Leagues as Joint Ventures," *Economic Journal* (February 2001), F27; John Vrooman, "A General Theory of Professional Sports Leagues," *Southern Economic Journal* (April 1995), 971–991.

4. The economic theories of cartel behavior, when applied to professional baseball and competition in the player and product markets, are topics that have been modeled and analyzed. See Lance E. Davis, "Self-Regulation in Baseball, 1909–71," in Roger G. Noll, ed., *Government and the Sports Business,* 349–386; Thomas A. Piraino, Jr., "The

Antitrust Rationale for the Expansion of Professional Sports Leagues," *Ohio State Law Journal* (November 1996), 1677–1729.

5. Stephen F. Ross, "Break Up the Sports League Monopolies," in Paul D. Staudohar and James A. Mangan, eds., *The Business of Professional Sports* (Champaign: University of Illinois Press, 1991), 152–173.

6. For a book that analyzes the market for sports franchises, the reserve clause and antitrust laws, the competitive balance in sports leagues, and other topics in the economics of professional sports, see *Pay Dirt* authored by James Quirk and Rodney D. Fort. To read an editorial review of the book, see George Will, "Pay Dirt: The Business of Professional Team Sports," at http://www.amazon.com cited 1 July 2001.

7. See Jerry Gorman, Kirk Calhoun and (Contributor) Skip Rozin, *The Name of the Game: The Business of Sports* (New York: John Wiley & Sons, 1994). In an editorial posted on a Web site, an unknown reviewer from Kirkus Reviews wrote an appraisal of *The Name of the Game*. The reviewer stated, " ... the authors offer once-over-lightly run-downs on the complex commercial infrastructure of the top four spectator sports, and the awesome pay gains obtained by journeyman talent in the wake of free agency, the financial rewards of astutely merchandising club logos, the sizable outlays required for player development, and the companies most likely to sponsor ads on play-by-play broadcasts." See "The Name of the Game: The Business of Sports," at http://www.amazon.com cited 26 June 2001,

8. A critic of Roger G. Noll and Andrew Zimbalist, eds., *Sports, Jobs and Taxes: The Economic Impact of Sports Teams and Stadiums* (Washington, DC: Brookings Institution Press, 1997), states: "While such examples as Minneapolis, Chicago, and Cincinnati display evidence to support the editors' theories, the repetitiveness of these chapters' points begin to wear on the reader. Still, one comes away fully understanding what is continually stressed by Zimbalist and Noll." For other reviews of the book, see "Sports, Jobs and Taxes: The Economic Impact of Sports Teams and Stadiums," at http://www.amazon.com cited 30 June 2001.

9. See James Quirk and Rodney D. Fort, *Hard Ball: The Abuse of Power in Pro Team Sports* (Princeton, NJ: Princeton University Press, 1999). In a review of this title, a customer who read *Hard Ball* remarked, " ... both economists re-describe the world of pro sports in a manner that can affect even the most opinionated. Their [Quirk and Fort] rhetoric and logic are compelling and appealing." See "Hard Ball: The Abuse of Power in Pro Team Sports," at http://www.amazon.com cited 5 July 2001.

10. For an in-depth discussion of the effects of broadcasting on team attendance, the importance of local and national broadcast rights, and the implications of sports broadcasts on sponsors, see Ira Horowitz, "Sports Broadcasting," in Roger G. Noll, ed., *Government and the Sports Business*, 275–323.

11. It is vital for sports industry marketers to comprehend and apply the principles of consumer behavior, demand management, distribution, product development, promotion mix, segmentation and the design of sponsorship programs to professional sports events, leagues and teams. To review these and other marketing concepts, see Matthew D. Shank, *Sports Marketing: A Strategic Perspective* (Upper Saddle River, NJ: Prentice-Hall, 1999); Idem., *Sports Marketing: A Strategic Perspective*, 2nd ed. (Upper Saddle River, NJ: Prentice-Hall, 2002). For other sports marketing books, see Bernard J. Mullin, Stephen Hardy, and William Sutton, *Sports Marketing* (Champaign, IL: Human Kinetics Publishers, 1993); Howard Schlossberg, *Sports Marketing* (Cambridge, MA: Blackwell

Publishers, 1996); Phil Schaaf, *Sports Marketing: Its Not Just a Game Anymore* (Amherst, MA: Prometheus Books, 1995).

12. To the mid-1970s the principal court cases on the reasonableness of controls that, as related to professional sports athletes' activities, were challenged under the Sherman Antitrust Act, include *Molinas v. National Basketball Association, Washington State Bowling Proprietors Association, Inc. v. Pacific Lanes, Inc., Deesen v. Professional Golfers' Association of America*, and the *Denver Rockets v. All-Pro Management, Inc.* For how reasonableness was interpreted and litigated in the settlement of these cases, see Steven R. Rivkin, "Sports Leagues and the Federal Antitrust Laws," in Roger G. Noll, ed., *Government and the Sports Business*, 389–395.

13. For the body of bylaws, laws, regulations, rules and standards that apply to and govern the National Collegiate Athletic Association, Global Amateur Sports, Olympic sports, player agents and unions, and professional athletes and teams, see Michael E. Jones, *Sports Law* (Upper Saddle River, NJ: Prentice-Hall, 1999). For other titles on sports law, see Robert C. Berry and Glenn M. Wong, *Law and Business of the Sports Industry* (Westport, CT: Praeger, 1993); Mark S. Levinstein, *Sports Law: Representing and Advising Athletes, Teams, Leagues, and Sports* (New York: Lawyer Media, Inc., 1998).

14. See Paul C. Weiler, *Leveling the Playing Field: How the Law Can Make Sports Better for Fans* (Cambridge, MA: Harvard University Press, 2000). There are reviews of Weiler's book that challenge his thesis and conclusion. See D.W. Miller, "Scholars Call a Foul on Pro Sports Leagues," *The Chronicle of Higher Education* (13 October 2000), A28–29; "Leveling the Playing Field: How the Law Can Make Sports Better for Fans," at http://www.amazon.com cited 28 June 2001.

15. Since the 1970s, sports ethics is a primary research topic that appears in an increasing number of scholarly studies. Moreover, a large proportion of college and university students who major in sports administration, economics, finance, law, management and marketing are required to complete at least one course in sports ethics. For a reference tool to research and teach ethics in sport-related disciplines, see Donald G. Jones and Elaine L. Daley, *Sports Ethics in America: A Bibliography, 1970–1990* (Westport, CT: Greenwood Press, 1992).

16. There is a scarcity of practical and up-to-date academic business administration, finance and marketing sports books that discuss how ticket prices and stadium costs affect the current and future attendance and expenditures of fans and households. With more information about player salaries and the amounts of franchise expenses, revenues and profits, sports fans would appreciate the actual nature and state of professional sports and perhaps demand reforms from specific leagues and team owners. To evaluate the economic problems that are detrimental to professional sports, see Thomas J. Kruckemeyer, *For Whom the Ball Tolls: A Fan's Guide to Economic Issues in Professional and College Sports* (Jefferson City, MO: Kruckemeyer Publishing Company, 1995). In a review of this book, one customer commented, "This is one of the best books I have read. It takes the mundane issues of sports and makes them easily understood and enjoyable to read." See "For Whom the Ball Tolls: A Fan's Guide to Economic Issues in Professional and College Sports," at http://www.amazon.com cited 3 July 2001.

17. Ibid.

18. Each season, the majority of baseball teams have a small chance to win a league title and qualify for the World Series. Furthermore, at ballparks there are large proportions of seats that are sold to corporations whose employees rarely attend games. See Bob

Costas, *Fair Ball: A Fan's Case for Baseball* (New York: Broadway Books, 2001) for a discussion of these issues and what baseball can do to make the game worthy of fan devotion. For editorial reviews of Costas' book, see "Fair Ball: A Fan's Case for Baseball," at http://www.amazon.com cited 2 July 2001.

19. Ibid.

20. For the status of professional minor league sports organizations, see Landon Hall, "Building Boom Brings Millions of Fans Back to Minor Leagues," at http://sports.yahoo.com cited 16 June 2001; Marjo Rankin Bliss, "Perko to Build Team in NBDL," *Charlotte Observer* (24 June 2001), 9H; "New League Has NBA Backing, Player Interest," *Charlotte Observer* (15 November 2001), 4C; "NBDL Background Information," at http://www.nba.com cited 31 July 2001; "NBDL Fact Sheet," at http://www.nba.com cited 31 July 2001; "CBA Rises to Play Its 56th Season," *Charlotte Observer* (10 August 2001), 6B; "NFL Europe: The Adventure Begins," at http://www.nfleurope.com cited 31 July 2001; "NFL Europe: From the Beginning," at http://www.cnnsi.com cited 1 June 2001; "NFL Europe: Commissioner Praises NFL Europe League," at http://www.nfleurope.com cited 3 July 2001; "World League Renamed NFL Europe," at http://www.nfl.com cited 11 March 1998; "NHL History," at http://www.nhl.com cited 30 March 2000; "NHL Hockey," at http://www.infoplease.com cited 12 April 2000; Cliff Mehrtens, "Checkers Not Lone Choice," *Charlotte Observer* (13 March 2002), 2C.

21. The decisions and the short- and long-term strategies and tactics of sports team owners are reported in various publications. For example, see Daniel Fisher and Michael K. Ozanian, "Cowboy Capitalism," *Forbes* (20 September 1999), 170–178; Richard O'Brien and Mark Mravic, "Owners You Can Trust," *Sports Illustrated* (21 December 1998), 32–33; Frank Deford, "Incompetent Owners Ruining Baseball," at http://www.cnnsi.com cited 26 July 2000; Gordon Forbes, "Owners to Kick Around Alignment," at http://www.usatoday.com cited 18 October 1998.

22. For the business deals between various media companies and professional sports leagues and teams, see Stefan Fatsis, "Yankees Holding Company Set to Form a Sports Network Valued at $850 Million," *Wall Street Journal* (11 September 2001), B4; Stefan Fatsis and Bruce Orwall, "Broadcast Bounce: NBA's Pact With AOL, Disney Puts Most Games in Cable's Court," *Wall Street Journal* (17 December 2001), B6; Mark Hyman, "Putting the Squeeze on the Media," *Business Week* (11 December 2000), 75; Anna Wilde Matthews, "NFL Nears Web-Properties Deal With AOL, Viacom, SportsLine," *Wall Street Journal* (9 July 2001), B4; Rich Thomaselli, "NHL Markets Web Site," at http://www.proquest.umi.com cited 24 September 2001.

23. The best sports areas and cities, Fan Cost Indexes, Sports Loyalty Indexes and game ticket prices are topics discussed in Chapter 6. For data and information about these issues in professional sports, see Rick Bonnell, "Charlotte Not Elite, But Not Bad," *Charlotte Observer* (5 July 1998), 2H; Bob Hille, "TSN's Best Sports Cities," *The Sporting News* (30 June 1997), 14–23; Robert Passikoff, "N.Y. Yankees Aside, Winning Isn't Only Key to Fan Loyalty," *Brandweek* (6 November 2000), 32–33; John Helyar, "Sports: Watching Football in Person Now Costs Even More," at http://www.proquestmail.com cited 19 July 2001; Don Muret, "NHL's Average Cost Up 5.5%; Bruins Top the List," at http://web4.infotrac.galegroup.com cited 18 October 2001; "The Brand Keys Sports Loyalty Index," at http://www.brandkeys.com cited 1 November 2001; "Fanatics," at http://www.cnnsi.com cited 28 March 2000; "Grading FanAntics," at http://web2.infotrac.galegroup.com cited 15 October 2001.

24. With public money, governments subsidize the construction of arenas and stadiums to benefit fans, sports leagues, team owners and players. See Kathleen Johnston, "Pacers Lease Contains Financial Guarantees," *Indianapolis Star* (5 November 1997), 16; Meg Vaillancourt, "Menino Wants High Returns on Investment in Fenway," *Boston Globe* (11 May 2000), C1, C17; Jon Talton, "Cities May be Sorry Places If Ballparks Strike Out," *Charlotte Observer* (10 May 1998), 1D; "Stadium Measure Narrowly Passes," at http://www.cnnsi.com cited 8 November 2000; Dara Akiko Williams, "Judge Rejects Effort to Put Ballpark on the Ballot," at http://sports.yahoo.com cited 28 February 2000.

Chapter 1

Leagues

The five dominant and elite leagues based in the United States, which are the focus of *American Sports Empire,* have been vigorous organizations that consist of their member teams. In 2000, for example, the regular seasons of MLB's AL and NL were, respectively, 99 and 124, while the NBA celebrated 54, NFL 78 and the NHL 83 seasons. Despite the entry of and competitive challenges from rival leagues throughout the 1900s, the business, operations and markets of the five leagues expanded especially between 1950 and 2000. As a result of the leagues' image and popularity, professional team sports has spread across the nation.[1]

To measure each league's progress, Tables 1.1 and 1.2 were designed. Table 1.1 denotes the percentage growth in the number of teams, games and regular season attendance experienced by the five sports leagues from the 1950 to 2000 seasons inclusive. Table 1.2 reflects, for six selected seasons, the trend in per game attendance of each sports league. Since regular season attendance was not available for the NBA and NHL in 1950, their initial percentage growth and per game attendance entries originated with the 1960 season. What conclusions can be derived from Tables 1.1 and 1.2 about America's premier professional sports organizations?

Despite a sluggish U.S. economy in the 1950s, domestic inflation, social turbulence and the Vietnam War in the 1960s, a recession and lackluster stock market in the 1970s, and federal budget deficits and recessions in the 1980s and early 1990s, between 1950 and 2000 each sports league realized an impressive percentage growth in teams, games and total attendance, and in the volume of per game attendance. In percentages, the NHL had the largest increase in teams and games, and the NBA was highest in total attendance (Table 1.1). In per game attendance, the AL experienced robust growth in the 1970s and 1980s, the NL in the 1950s, 1970s and 1990s, the NBA in the 1960s through 1980s, the NFL in the 1960s, and the NHL in the 1960s and 1980s (Table 1.2). In part, these trends occurred because of the leagues' decisions to expand operations and place franchises in growing cities of the U.S. South, Southeast and West, to launch risky

Table 1.1
Percentage Growth in Teams, Games and Attendance, by Sports League, 1950 to 2000

League	Teams	Percentage Growth Games	Attendance
AL	75	83	260
NL	100	110	380
NBA	71	112	1446
NFL	138	73	728
NHL	367	446	717

Note: Percentage Growth was determined by dividing the total number of Teams, Games or Attendance in 2000 by the total in 1950, subtract 1 from the result, and then convert the decimals to percentages by multiplying the product by 100.

Source: The World Almanac and Book of Facts (Mahwah, NJ: World Almanac Books, 1951, 2001); James Quirk and Rodney D. Fort, *Pay Dirt: The Business of Professional Sports* (Princeton, NJ: Princeton University Press, 1992), 479–504; Memorandums from MLB, and the NBA, NFL and NHL; *NFL 2001 Record & Fact Book* (New York: National Football League, 2001).

Table 1.2
Per Game Attendance, by Sports League, for Selected Seasons

League	1950	1960	1970	1980	1990	2000
AL	14.7	14.9	12.4	19.2	26.7	29.1
NL	13.5	17.4	17.1	21.8	25.2	30.9
NBA	n.a.	5.1	7.6	11.1	15.6	16.9
NFL	13.3	17.1	52.2	59.8	63.8	66.1
NHL	n.a.	11.0	13.1	12.5	15.0	16.4

Note: Per Game Attendance is each league's total regular season attendance in thousands divided by the total number of regular season games. The n.a. indicates that the regular season attendance is not available.

Source: See Table 1.1.

and untested marketing campaigns, to sign potentially lucrative national cable, satellite and network television contracts, and to persuade various governments and taxpayers to subsidize the construction of new sports arenas and stadiums. Grouped, these factors led to the spectacular but uneven growth rates in teams, games and attendance, especially in the 1960s through 1980s. In reflection, *Wall Street Journal* sports journalist Stefan Fatsis wrote, "The U.S. population swelled and moved south and west; TV networks and corporations became richer and more eager to bankroll games; wannabe team owners were willing to pay huge membership fees; leagues needed new revenue sources to finance rocketing player salaries." Given the numbers in Tables 1.1 and 1.2, will the momentum and upward trend in the percentage growths of teams, games and attendance continue in each sport after 2000?[2]

In general, the sports leagues have seemingly neglected to narrow the persistent and wide operating revenue disparities that exist between teams located in small-to-medium and large markets. Because of this inequality, and excessive ticket prices, exorbitant player salaries, inept league commissioners, uninvolved club owners, and periodic league lockouts and union work stoppages, an increasing number of communities, fans and taxpayers have become disillusioned with professional sports. This situation raises two questions. First, what are the current issues and future problems that confront each league? Second, what innovative rules, strategies and tactics will sports commissioners and leagues need to implement to be successful beyond 2000? In this chapter, these questions will be addressed next for the AL and NL in MLB, and then for the NBA, NFL and NHL. After the issues and problems in each major sports league are discussed, then the operations of the primary minor league organizations that exist in each sport get scrutinized.

MLB

Prior to 1950, the various MLB commissioners and team owners in the AL and NL made insightful business decisions to advance the development of major league baseball in the United States. Beginning in 1900 and grouped into ten-year spans, a few examples of these decisions are highlighted here. During 1900 to 1909, the Americans (now AL), Nationals (now NL) and a minor league group banded together into "Organized Baseball," to be ruled by a National [baseball] Commission. During 1910 to 1919, the AL and NL contributed to the termination of the Federal League (FL), after the FL demanded recognition as a major circuit and began raiding the AL and NL for players. During 1920 to 1929, the major league schedule was increased from 140 to 154 games per season, and a rule barring the spitball received unanimous league approval. During 1930 to 1939, the first night baseball game was introduced when Cincinnati played at Philadelphia in May 1935. And, during 1940 to 1949, the major leagues adopted an annuity plan for coaches, players and trainers, and Jackie Robinson became the first African-American player admitted to the big leagues.[3]

Furthermore, between 1900 and 1950 two strong-willed MLB commissioners, Judge Kenesaw "Mountain" Landis and A.B. "Happy" Chandler, were involved in controversial league incidents that would fundamentally change the future conduct of the sport. Landis, who served from 1921 to 1944 as organized baseball's first commissioner, in the mid-1910s viewed the AL and NL as a benign "trust." To encourage a comprise between the government and baseball, he delayed the FL's antitrust suit against the "trust" which pleased MLB owners. After he was elected as Judge Landis' successor in 1945, Kentucky's U.S. Senator A.B. "Happy" Chandler warned Philadelphia Phillies players, during the 1947 season, not to personally abuse or physically harm African-American player Jackie Robinson and block his appearance at games. Five years later, Commissioner Chandler was fired because the major league owners decided that

"Happy" arbitrarily misrepresented their interests regarding the creation of rules considered detrimental to baseball. In retrospect, during their reign as czars of baseball Landis and Chandler had supreme power. They would unilaterally rule, without appeal on any practice deemed damaging to the sport, and therefore were constantly in conflict with the team owners. Eventually, the opposition from the league doomed the tenures of Commissioners Landis and Chandler.[4]

After 1949, there were various overriding events and incidents that occupied the efforts and interests of MLB's commissioners and team owners. Beginning in 1950 and presented in ten-year increments are samples of these activities. In 1950 to 1959, the AL vetoed owner Bill Veeck's plan to switch his St. Louis Browns team to Baltimore, while the NL sanctioned owner Lou Perini's transfer of his Boston Braves club to Milwaukee. In 1960 to 1969, organized baseball adopted a free agent draft and an unrestricted draft package, which permitted teams the right to negotiate with high school, college and other amateur players. In 1970 to 1979, the AL adopted a designated hitter rule whereby a hitter could be assigned to bat for the starting pitcher and all subsequent pitchers in any games without otherwise affecting the status of the current pitcher in the lineup. Finally, in the 1980s and 1990s MLB's commissioners and team owners refocused their efforts. That is, they deliberated about expansion, the construction of new and renovation of existing ballparks, free agency and the escalation of player salaries, revenue sharing, national television commitments, and player union strikes that created work stoppages.[5]

As events occurred in the sport, from 1950 to 2000 inclusive the commissioners in organized baseball gradually became public spokespersons for the league owners. Relative to the dictatorial administrations of Judge Kenesaw Landis and A.B. Chandler, the majority of future commissioners commanded less authority, control and responsibility when the power base for decisions in professional baseball totally shifted to the team owners. A few commissioners such as Ford C. Frick (1951–1965), William D. Eckert (1965–1968), Bowie Kuhn (1969–1984), Peter Uberroth (1984–1988) and Bartlet Giamatti (1988–1989) attempted, but failed, to implement any radical reforms that were unpopular with the team owners. As such, the days of a commissioner who served as the final arbitrator of decisions, which could range from the suspension of a team owner to the resolution of disputes between players and clubs, had albeit ended. With their authority and power diminished, former Commissioner Francis Vincent (1989–1992) had, and current Commissioner Allan H. "Bud" Selig (1998–present) has less incentive and owner approval to unilaterally amend and enforce baseball's regulations, rules and standards as Landis and Chandler did.[6]

Before discussing the historical issues and problems that continue to plague modern baseball, it is noted that in the 1950s MLB revised its strategy regarding franchise relocation, and in the 1960s regarding the entry of new teams in the sport. In response to market conditions and lucrative opportunities in California for the owner of the Brooklyn Dodgers, Walter O'Malley, and for the pro-

Table 1.3
AL Team Relocation and Expansion, 1950 to 2000

Year	Team	From	To	Expansion
1953	Browns	St. Louis	Baltimore	
1954	Athletics	Philadelphia	Kansas City	
1960	Senators	Washington	Minnesota	
1961	Angels			Los Angeles
1961	Senators			Washington
1967	Athletics	Kansas City	Oakland	
1969	Pilots			Seattle
1969	Royals			Kansas City
1970	Pilots	Seattle	Milwaukee	
1971	Senators	Washington	Texas	
1977	Mariners			Seattle
1977	Blue Jays			Toronto
1998	Devil Rays			Tampa Bay

Note: Year is the club's first season at the relocated or expansion site.

Source: James Quirk and Rodney D. Fort, *Pay Dirt*, 399–499; Frank P. Jozsa, Jr. and John J. Guthrie, Jr., *Relocating Teams and Expanding Leagues in Professional Sports: How the Major Leagues Respond to Market Conditions* (Quorum Books, 1999), 23, 46.

Table 1.4
NL Team Relocation and Expansion, 1950 to 2000

Year	Team	From	To	Expansion
1953	Braves	Boston	Milwaukee	
1958	Dodgers	Brooklyn	Los Angeles	
1958	Giants	New York	San Francisco	
1961	Colts			Houston
1961	Mets			New York
1966	Braves	Milwaukee	Atlanta	
1969	Expos			Montreal
1969	Padres			San Diego
1993	Marlins			Florida
1993	Rockies			Colorado
1998	Diamondbacks			Arizona

Note: Year is the club's first season at the relocated or expansion site.

Source: Quirk and Fort, *Pay Dirt*, 391–399; Jozsa and Guthrie, *Relocating Teams and Expanding Leagues in Professional Sports*, 20, 49, 104; *The World Almanac and Book of Facts*, 1998–2001.

prietor of the New York Giants, Horace Stoneham, the AL and NL approved franchise relocation in the early 1950s and league expansion in the early 1960s (Tables 1.3 and 1.4). As a result, five MLB clubs moved in the 1950s, three in the 1960s and two in the 1970s. Furthermore, regarding expansion, eight teams joined MLB in the 1960s, two in the 1970s and four in the 1990s. The team movements and expansions occurred primarily to and at sites in medium and large cities in Canada and in the U.S. Southeast and West. In total, factors such as climate, market population, population growth, the availability of a new or refurbished stadium, and except for Los Angeles, Oakland, and New York, the absence of another MLB team, explain why the league approved and owners selected these specific sites to relocate an existing team or establish an expansion franchise. In sum, because of the timely team movements and league expansions in MLB, the sport grew from 16 clubs that played 1,232 games in 1950 to 30 teams that competed in 2,430 contests in 2000.[7]

Based on the recent history of games, incidents, seasons and other events that have affected professional baseball, yet to be resolved are four complex and interrelated business, economic and managerial issues that require a concerted effort by Commissioner Bud Selig and the team owners. Listed in priority order, these problems according to many sports analysts, economists, historians and practitioners are first, the competitive imbalance or the lack of parity between division and conference teams; second, the inadequate growths in attendance and television ratings; third, whether the owners should approve additional expansions and team movements; and fourth, whether the league should withdraw the charters of clubs that are inferior in performance and hopelessly unprofitable. Because these issues are interconnected, they will be discussed based on the most recent sports data that have been reported in magazines and newspapers and published in the academic literature on professional team sports and markets.

Before proceeding, however, to analyze these and other matters in this and future chapters, time-period constraints were established regarding the collection and tabling of demographic, economic, financial, and sports-specific statistics and values. That is, for selected seasons prior to 1950, a portion of sports-specific quantitative data and information relative to the characteristics and performances of professional leagues, players and teams was either inaccurately recorded or not reported. Regular season attendance, for example, is not available for the NBA and NHL before the mid-1950s, for the NFL before 1934 and for MLB prior to 1901. For our purposes, therefore, any tabled qualitative and quantitative data and/or statistics presented in *American Sports Empire* are either within or from the 1950 to 2002 seasons inclusive. In sum, for each league this book will apply demographic and sports-specific data, information and statistics about coaches, games and managers, and the performances of players and teams that appeared in reputable periodicals and other literature sources.

In reference to the primary issues in MLB, perfect competitive balance or parity in playing strengths between teams, however measured, is unattainable in the AL, NL or in any other American sports league. Based on the historical studies of professional sports, a variety of equations, formulas and mathematical methods and models have been applied to measure the inequality or imbalance in playing strengths within divisions, conferences and leagues. The measurements and statistics include the Gini Coefficient, range, standard deviation of the distribution of win-loss percentages, ratio of the actual to idealized standard deviation, and the number of clubs finishing above and below specific winning percentages. Therefore, because the empirical studies on professional sports used different qualitative and quantitative sports-specific data and demographic information, invariably these quantitative measurements provided mixed and frequently conflicting results regarding the extent of competitive balance in MLB and in the other sports leagues.[8]

Rather than evaluate or rework those analyses, to measure parity in MLB Table 1.5 was constructed. This table depicts numerically, in adjacent columns, the distribution of three performance characteristics for thirteen AL and eleven

Table 1.5
AL and NL Team Performance Characteristics, 1990 to 2000

Teams	Wins	Win-Loss Percentage	Postseason
American League			
New York Yankees	938	.540	6
Cleveland Indians	913	.526	5
Chicago White Sox	911	.525	2
Boston Red Sox	899	.518	4
Toronto Blue Jays	884	.509	3
Texas Rangers	878	.506	3
Baltimore Orioles	868	.500	2
Oakland Athletics	864	.498	3
Seattle Mariners	855	.492	3
Detroit Tigers	841	.485	0
Anaheim Angels	820	.473	0
Kansas City Royals	802	.462	0
Minnesota Twins	787	.454	1
National League			
Atlanta Braves	1020	.587	9
Cincinnati Reds	894	.515	2
San Francisco Giants	887	.511	2
Houston Astros	885	.510	3
Los Angeles Dodgers	883	.508	2
New York Mets	861	.496	2
St. Louis Cardinals	853	.491	2
Montreal Expos	843	.486	1
Pittsburgh Pirates	843	.486	3
Chicago Cubs	804	.463	1
Philadelphia Phillies	797	.459	1

Note: Wins are the total regular season wins per team for eleven years. Win-Loss Percentage is the average or mean winning percentage per team for eleven regular seasons. Postseason is the sum of division titles won and wild-card game appearances per team. The Milwaukee Brewers were excluded in Table 1.5 because in 1998 the club switched from the AL Central Division to the NL Central Division. The Tampa Bay Devil Rays in the AL and Arizona Diamondbacks, Colorado Rockies and Florida Marlins in the NL were also excluded because the four clubs entered MLB after 1990.

Source: The World Almanac and Book of Facts, 1991–2001; Worldwide web sites of each sports league at http://www.mlb.com, http://www.nba.com, http://www.nfl.com and http://www.nhl.com.

NL teams that were located at their respective sites for eleven consecutive seasons or from 1990 to 2000 inclusive. For each column of values, a mean or average and a standard deviation, which measures the dispersion or spread of the data, were calculated and applied to the AL and NL characteristics. (As reference numbers for the reader, the means and standard deviations for each league are reported in Table A.1 of the Appendix.) Given the three characteristics and the eleven seasons of team performances and statistics, what conclusions can be stated about parity in MLB?

Table 1.5 reveals that, for each characteristic, the cumulative performance of the top eight AL teams—New York Yankees to Oakland Athletics—is superior to their NL counterparts—Atlanta Braves to Montreal Expos. Furthermore, the bottom four AL teams—Detroit Tigers to Minnesota Twins—are inferior in performance to the last four clubs—Montreal Expos to Philadelphia Phillies—in the NL. In the distribution of Wins, 70 percent (9) of the AL and 73 percent (8) of the NL teams ranked within one standard deviation of 866, which were each league's mean wins. In Win-Loss Percentage, 77 percent of the AL (10) and 73 percent (8) of the NL clubs placed within one standard deviation of .500, which was each league's average winning percentage. In qualifying for Postseason play, within one standard deviation of 7.5 average postseason appearances were 62 percent (8) of the AL and 82 percent (9) of the NL teams. These percentages and number of teams for each of the variables denote that, despite the superior performances of the AL New York Yankees and NL Atlanta Braves, from 1990 to 2000 inclusive, a relatively high degree of competitive balance existed in the AL and NL. In fact, given the poor performances of the large-market AL Detroit Tigers and the NL's Chicago Cubs and Philadelphia Phillies, these distributions weaken the argument made by some researchers to increase the proportions of home gate receipts and local broadcasting revenues from the large-to-small-market franchises in order to improve equity. Otherwise, except for the top-notch performances of the AL Cleveland Indians and NL Cincinnati Reds, generally the small-market clubs ranked in the lower one-third of the distributions.

In total, for the eleven seasons the AL's Kansas City Royals, Oakland Athletics and Minnesota Twins, and the NL's Montreal Expos and Pittsburgh Pirates lost more games than they won and qualified for only eight postseason appearances. Besides the poor performances of these five clubs as indicated in Table 1.5, since expansion the AL Tampa Bay Devil Rays and NL Florida Marlins have each been inferior teams in total wins and average winning percentages, and, except for the Marlins' 1997 World Series title, in postseason appearances. Grouped, these four AL and three NL franchises accumulated more than $200 million in operating losses between 1995 and 1999. Without financial subsidies from others, therefore, the long-term outlooks of these clubs are bleak. That is, unless the respective franchise owners invest more resources in the player development and minor league programs, or the league expands revenue sharing, the average win-loss percentages of these seven teams will remain below .500 in future seasons.[9]

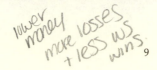

Since 1995, the Houston Astros was the only team to reach the playoffs and rank in the lower half of the NL in payroll. This occurred in 1997. Thus, in MLB, for five total seasons less than 2 percent of postseason games won were by clubs that ranked in the lower 50 percent of their league in payroll. This outcome indicates that, with respect to the distributions of team payrolls and wins, competitive balance within MLB has declined since the mid-1990s. Consequently, to reduce the payroll disparities between small- and large-market teams, in January 2000 MLB owners granted Commissioner Selig the authority to fine clubs $2 million and employees $500,000 if the "best interests" clause of the sport's constitution is violated. Furthermore, to redistribute more wealth among league teams, the owners authorized Selig's office to collect all Internet revenues and a portion of the money from radio broadcasts and potential video rights. As the league's cash inflows from the Internet expand, this policy will provide Commissioner Selig with additional money to allocate and thereby narrow the revenue differences between the small- and large-market clubs in the AL and NL. Whether the redistributed funds will be efficiently used by teams to develop more talented players or squandered by the owners for personal expenditures is uncertain.[10]

In November 2000, a blue-ribbon economic study committee made three recommendations to increase the competitiveness between MLB teams. The panel suggested that the league impose a 50 percent luxury tax on team payrolls that exceed $84 million, share 40 to 50 percent of all local broadcast revenues, and ensure that small-market clubs receive a disproportionate amount of national broadcasting and licensing revenues if the recipient franchise owners establish a minimum player payroll of $40 million per season. Moreover, the committee urged MLB to expedite the relocation of small-market clubs to address the competitive imbalance issues that are detrimental to the game and a discouragement to fans. The committee also encouraged Commissioner Selig and the leagues to expand the domestic and international promotion and multimedia advertising of the sport on the Internet and to broadcast more games on radio and television into foreign countries.[11]

If baseball's operating losses continue to average $200 million or more per year, eventually MLB owners will be forced to reform the sport. Begrudgingly, they could reach a consensus and decide to reallocate a greater proportion of the sport's annual $3 billion cash inflows to small-market franchises. For sure, the enforcement of a 50 percent luxury tax on teams with excessive payrolls and a generous redistribution of local and regional broadcast revenues will permit low-payroll teams to acquire high-price free agents and to reward their superstar players with lucrative bonuses and incentive clauses based on long-term contracts. However, whether the majority of small-market clubs will become competitive, win proportionately more games, earn division titles and qualify for wild-card appearances is unknown. In sum, with more subsidies from teams with high payrolls such as the Atlanta Braves, Boston Red Sox, Cleveland Indians, Los Angeles Dodgers and the New York Mets and Yankees, baseball "experts" such as former Senate Majority Leader George Mitchell, previous Federal Reserve Board Chairman Paul Volcker and columnist George Will predict that greater opportunities will exist for competitive balance and parity in the AL and NL.

Revenue sharing aside, to improve the sport's long-term competitiveness and business prospects Commissioner Selig and league owners revised the inter-league game schedules beginning with the 2002 season. Furthermore, these executives may decide to realign divisions, approve team movements and elim-inate the most inferior franchises. In the 2002 season, for example, division pairings were switched to promote rivalries, and, for logistical reasons, the six-game series was reduced to a three-game set. On whether to implement realignment, *Wall Street Journal* sports columnist Frederick Klein opined, "Baseball's basic problem is that it's a waltz-time game in a hip-hop era, but it's likely that large-scale realignment would turn off waltz-lovers without lur-ing hip-hoppers."[12]

For various reasons, MLB will prohibit any cash-depleted franchises from re-locating to large markets such as Chicago, Los Angeles and New York. And, in 2002 there were no medium-sized Canadian and U.S. metropolitan areas that contained a vacant, modern, single-purpose baseball stadium with abundant amenities, and the market population and corporate wherewithal to financially support a team. Even so, this situation may change soon. Organized in 1999, a Washington, D.C., baseball group has tried unsuccessfully to attract an MLB club to the nation's capital. Indeed, without a lucrative stadium deal, luxury taxes on high payroll teams, or the reallocation of broadcast revenues from large- to small-market clubs, perhaps an owner from the Florida Marlins, Minnesota Twins, Oakland Athletics or Tampa Bay Devil Rays will apply for and receive approval from Commissioner Selig and the league to relocate his or her club to the suburbs of Washington, D.C., or Northern Virginia.[13]

Coupled with the redistribution of local broadcast revenues and the freedom to move financially deficient teams, another option to increase competitive bal-ance within the AL and NL is the elimination of one or more franchises. The MLB players union and Smith College economics professor Andrew Zimbalist oppose league consolidation. According to Professor Zimbalist, "It's not a long-term solution, not a fan-friendly solution, and isn't an economically efficient solution from the standpoint of the game's public relations." Consolidation, how-ever, would remove up to fifty low-performance players from the big leagues, provide more money for the remaining clubs, and possibly reduce the revenue disparity between the richest and poorest franchises. As a business strategy, therefore, to reduce the AL and NL by one or more franchises is a reasonable alternative for teams competing before apathetic fans who are seated in obso-lete ballparks that are unnecessarily located in small markets.[14]

In 2001, MLB owners overwhelmingly authorized Commissioner Selig to begin the process of eliminating two teams before either the 2002, 2003 or 2004 season commences. The three clubs identified for disbandment were the Florida Marlins, Minnesota Twins and Montreal Expos. Because of revenue shortfalls from their local markets and stadiums, and persistent operating losses, at least two of the selected franchises will eventually fold or merge. Undoubtedly, investors and groups in Washington, D.C. and elsewhere have prepared plans to convince MLB that selected metropolitan areas are inadequate to support a major league baseball team.

Despite the woes of its parent organization, minor league baseball in the United States is robust because attendance, revenues and the number of teams have surged in recent years. This phenomenon is discussed next followed by the business conditions and internal struggles that exist in professional basketball, football and hockey.[15]

MINOR LEAGUE BASEBALL

After World War II, minor league baseball attendance surged in the United States and then peaked at forty million in 1949 when more than 400 clubs had played before capacity crowds. After the mid-1950s, however, when the Brooklyn Dodgers and New York Giants migrated to California, when the AL and NL expanded in the early 1960s, and when MLB games appeared on national television, the minor leagues retrenched and attendance remained flat at 10 million until the mid-1980s. Then, for various reasons a resurgence in attendance occurred in the minor leagues. Nationwide, 23 million baseball fans watched 164 minor league teams compete in 1989. Eleven years later, approximately 38 million spectators attended the games of 180 teams, which included the sixteen-team Mexican League. Why did this transformation in attendance occur?[16]

Since the mid-to-late 1980s, the ongoing development, growth and popularity of minor league baseball in the United States happened, in part, because of four factors. First, business-savvy minor league team owners realized that to attract casual baseball fans and other spectators to events, games must be marketed as a wholesome experience for families and a joyful adventure for kids and teenagers. This strategy succeeded. For example, to keep the crowds at minor league contests from getting bored, before games and between innings costumed mascots dance on dugouts, hug babies and race tiny tots around the bases. Furthermore, adult and miniature batting and pitching apparatuses are stationed in ballparks' open areas for hitting practice and for throwing sixty-mile-per-hour fast balls at targets. At some ballparks, prior to the first inning pitch Little League teams are identified and encouraged to take bows while the minor league players canvass the crowd to sign autographs.

Second, to give spectators a better view of games from their seats, in 1990 MLB established uniform standards for seat capacity and required other conveniences at minor league ballparks. That is, most stadiums were restructured to seat 5,000 to 10,000 people at $2 to $8 per seat. Besides chair backs for every seat and clear sight lines to the field, surrounding some of the baseball diamonds in the United States are fan amenities such as hot tubs, museums, picnic pavilions, playgrounds, swimming pools, video scoreboards and other entertainment and amusement attractions.

Third, by tapping revenue sources such as billboard advertising, club seats, corporate sponsorships and luxury suite rentals, and by scattering vendors throughout the ballpark to sell beverages, food and souvenirs, team owners would maximize their cash inflows. This meant that, for entrepreneurs the strategy to own and operate a minor league team became primarily an economic investment to be nurtured rather than a hobby, which is underdeveloped.

Fourth, to lure suburbanites downtown and recover the perceived economic and social benefits from the public's investments, several U.S. cities, municipalities and states provided taxpayer money for the construction and renovation of minor league stadiums. The Bridgeport Bluefish in Connecticut, Harrisburg Senators in Pennsylvania, Portland Beavers in New Mexico, Staten Island Yankees in New York City, and the Toledo Mud Hens in Ohio each has received taxpayer subsidies for its facilities. Besides high-profile business leaders such as multi-billionaire Warren Buffet, there are celebrities and former athletes like comedian/actor Bill Murray, Houston Astros pitching legend Nolan Ryan, and former Los Angeles Lakers superstar Magic Johnson who are co-owners of minor league teams. Indeed, their participation as owners promotes the franchises' image in the community and improves the clubs' ability to survive and earn an above-average financial return as an ongoing business venture. In general, since the mid-to-late 1980s minor league baseball has thrived and enjoyed success, while MLB and its teams has confronted a host of conflicts, issues and problems. Baseball aside, what is the business and team operating environments in professional basketball?[17]

NBA

Before the late 1930s, the prominent U.S. professional basketball leagues were located in the Northeast and Middle Atlantic states. After the four-team National Basketball League was formed in 1898 in Philadelphia, other leagues organized and established regular season schedules. They were the Philadelphia League in 1902, Central League in 1906, Eastern and Hudson River Leagues in 1909, New York State League in 1911, Western Pennsylvania League in 1912, Pennsylvania State League in 1914, Inter-State League in 1915, Metropolitan Basketball League in 1921 and the American Basketball League (ABL) in 1926. These were primitive leagues that consisted of competitive teams such as the Buffalo Germans, New York Trojans, New York Celtics (later reorganized as the Original Celtics), New York Whirlwinds and Cleveland Rosenblums. Each of these clubs played "wildcat" basketball games and staged barnstorming tours in cities and regions throughout the East and Midwest. Despite the introduction of the bounce pass, fast break, foul shot and pivot play, these teams enthusiastically played to entertain fans and show off the skills of individual players. Because of the mismatch in player's abilities, the Germans and other clubs won most games by lopsided scores against mediocre and inept amateur and professional teams.[18]

Because of dominant teams such as the Celtics, Whirlwinds and Rosenblums, games became monotonous, spectators gradually lost interest, attendance fell, and except for the ABL the professional leagues in the Northeast and Middle Atlantic areas ultimately disbanded. The ABL, which scheduled games in nine cities, ceased operations from 1929 to 1932 and then resumed play in 1933 when it chartered two outstanding teams, the New York Jewels and Philadelphia Sphas. The Jewels consisted of athletes who had played for the St. John's "Wonder Five" during their college days. The Sphas, meanwhile, emerged from the South Philadelphia Hebrew Association to be coached by Eddie Gottlieb. Unfortunately, the four-year hiatus in scheduled games had diminished the league's fan support. Thus, by the mid-1940s the ABL surrendered its recognition as a major basketball organization.

Prior to the ABL's decline, Lonnie Darling, who had started the Oshkosh All-Stars in the early 1930s, organized the National Basketball League (NBL) in 1937. Darling placed the NBL's franchises in small-to-medium midwestern cities. Although it failed to be recognized as a power among leagues, the NBL represented balanced competition and stability. As such, these qualities transformed professional basketball from casual entertainment to big business. In contrast to the exhibitions and tours of leagues that existed in the early 1900s, the formation of the NBL introduced parity in team schedules, provided a basis to compare the performances of players and teams, normalized game rules, and persuaded franchise owners to market regular season games as a conduit to winning a championship.[19]

Meanwhile, in June 1946 Boston Garden's President Walter Brown and Cleveland Arena's owner Al Sutphin met and created the Basketball Association of America (BAA), which consisted of eleven teams that were located in large U.S. cities. To encourage a fast-paced game, the clubs were not permitted to play a zone defense. Because of the competitive teams that played in the rival NBL, the BAA struggled to survive despite the addition of four franchises in 1948. The teams that had vacated the NBL included the well-respected Minneapolis Lakers. The Lakers' star, 6-foot, 10-inch George Mikan had been an All-American center at DePaul University in Chicago. In the mid-to-late 1940s, he was considered professional basketball's greatest drawing card. Mikan's migration to the BAA destabilized the nation's market for professional basketball.

Indeed, the rivalry between the BAA and NBL teams became fierce because each league competed for fans, players and national recognition. Financially, this competition was not in the best interest of the two organizations. Therefore, to streamline schedules and attract spectators to their arenas, in 1949 the BAA and NBL, along with the deteriorating ABL, merged to form a new seventeen-team circuit, the National Basketball Association (NBA). Because the majority of teams that joined the NBA had abandoned the BAA, 1946–1947 was designated as the new league's inaugural season. After the merger, a surplus of small market clubs forced NBA President Maurice Podoloff and Executive Board Chairman Ike W. Duffy to downsize the organization. Between 1950 and 1960, the

NBA shrunk from seventeen to eight franchises, and the total regular season games declined from 562 to 259. In 1960, the league's attendance was 1.3 million, or 200,000 per team, while per game attendance equaled 5,100. Remarkably, forty years later twenty-nine clubs played 1,189 games, and total attendance reached 20 million, which converted to 700,000 per team or approximately 17,000 per game.[20]

Besides aggressively expanding its membership, since 1950 the NBA has authorized the relocation of numerous clubs from unprofitable markets. In total, twenty franchise expansions and fifteen team movements occurred between 1950 and 2000. Listed chronologically beginning with the 1951–1952 season, Table 1.6 depicts thirty-five transactions that the basketball owners had initiated to meet consumer demand and to assure the league's niche in America's professional sports history. Did the NBA make prudent decisions to let teams relocate? Was expansion in the best interest of communities, fans, owners, players, teams and the sport? How successful have the NBA's expansion and relocated clubs performed at their respective sites?

In Chapter 5 of *Relocating Teams and Expanding Leagues in Professional Sports*, authors Frank P. Jozsa, Jr. and John J. Guthrie, Jr. evaluated and ranked a total of nine relocated and fifteen expansion teams that played in the NBA from 1990 to 1997 inclusive. Three performance characteristics—each club's average win-loss percentage and home attendance for eight seasons and its estimated market value in 1997—were equally weighted at .33 and assigned points based on how well the team succeeded at its site. Then, the product of the weights and assigned points were summed to determine the total points and respective ranks for each club. Because nine of the thirty-five sites in Table 1.6 were abandoned, and because two clubs joined the NBA after 1990, twenty-four teams were ranked by Jozsa and Guthrie in their book.[21]

Based on the total points assigned, three relocated teams were rated superior and three each average and inferior. Meanwhile, two expansion teams were rated superior, seven average and six inferior. Thus, 63 percent (15) of the NBA clubs ranked as either superior or average. Because nine clubs scored inferior when their performances were measured, in retrospect the NBA was moderately successful in choosing sites to relocate existing teams and in selecting markets for expansion franchises.

If ranked with respect to the three performance characteristics as those teams that were listed in Table 1.6, between 1995 and 2000 inclusive the expansion Toronto Raptors was an average franchise, and the expansion Vancouver Grizzlies rated as inferior. During spring 2001, the NBA approved the movement of the Grizzlies from Vancouver, Canada, to Memphis, Tennessee. The team had a deplorable attendance record, as well as apathetic media relationships and corporate support in Vancouver. Memphis, a medium-sized southern city, was chosen as the optimal site for the franchise rather than cities such as Anaheim, Las Vegas, Louisville, Norfolk, New Orleans or St. Louis. After the league's relocation announcement, in June 2001 the Shelby County Commission in Tennessee

Table 1.6
NBA Team Relocation and Expansion, 1950 to 2000

Year	Team	From	To	Expansion
1951–52	Blackhawks	Tri-Cities	Milwaukee	
1955–56	Hawks	Milwaukee	St. Louis	
1957–58	Pistons	Fort Wayne	Detroit	
1957–58	Royals	Rochester	Cincinnati	
1960–61	Lakers	Minneapolis	Los Angeles	
1961–62	Packers			Chicago
1962–63	Warriors	Philadelphia	San Francisco	
1963–64	Nationals	Syracuse	Philadelphia	
1963–64	Zephyrs	Chicago	Baltimore	
1966–67	Bulls			Chicago
1967–68	SuperSonics			Seattle
1968–69	Hawks	St. Louis	Atlanta	
1968–69	Bucks			Milwaukee
1968–69	Suns			Phoenix
1970–71	Braves			Buffalo
1970–71	Cavaliers			Cleveland
1970–71	Trail Blazers			Portland
1971–72	Rockets	San Diego	Houston	
1972–73	Royals	Cincinnati	Kansas City	
1974–75	Jazz			New Orleans
1976–77	Nets (ABA)			New York
1976–77	Nuggets (ABA)			Denver
1976–77	Pacers (ABA)			Indianapolis
1976–77	Spurs (ABA)			San Antonio
1978–79	Braves	Buffalo	San Diego	
1979–80	Jazz	New Orleans	Utah	
1980–81	Mavericks			Dallas
1984–85	Clippers	San Diego	Los Angeles	
1985–86	Kings	Kansas City	Sacramento	
1988–89	Hornets			Charlotte
1988–89	Heat			Miami
1989–90	Timberwolves			Minnesota
1989–90	Magic			Orlando
1995–96	Raptors			Toronto
1995–96	Grizzlies			Vancouver

Note: Year is the club's first season at the relocated or expansion site. The team movements within the same Standard Metropolitan Statistical Area are not listed in Table 1.6. The relocation of the Warriors from San Francisco to Oakland in 1971 and the Bullets from Baltimore to Washington, D.C., in 1973 are, therefore, excluded. Table 1.6 does not contain the Grizzlies' move from Vancouver, Canada, to Memphis, Tennessee, that occurred in 2001. ABA is the American Basketball Association.

Source: James Quirk and Rodney D. Fort, *Pay Dirt,* 446–459; Frank P. Jozsa, Jr. and John J. Guthrie, Jr., *Relocating Teams and Expanding Leagues in Professional Sports,* 34, 60, 89, 123.

approved a proposal to subsidize and construct a $250 million arena for the Grizzlies. The facility is scheduled to open for the 2003–2004 season. In retrospect, the NBA's decisions to expand the number of franchises and relocate its low-performance teams were shrewd strategies that, in total, benefited the respective communities, fans, owners, players, teams and the sport.[22]

Beyond the ranks assigned by Jozsa and Guthrie, what other information is available about the progress and success achieved by teams in professional basketball? As developed before in this chapter for the AL and NL in MLB and later for the NFL and NHL, a table was created to measure the inequality in playing strengths between twenty-seven clubs that performed in the NBA for eleven consecutive seasons, or from 1990 to 2000 inclusive (Table 1.7). Furthermore, the table is useful to compare how much parity existed in the NBA relative to the competitive balances that prevailed in the other sports leagues. To that end,

Table 1.7
NBA Team Performance Characteristics, 1990 to 2000

Team	Wins	Win-Loss Percentage	Postseason
Utah Jazz	595	.683	11
Seattle SuperSonics	559	.642	9
Phoenix Suns	553	.635	11
San Antonio Spurs	551	.633	10
Portland Trail Blazers	550	.632	11
Los Angeles Lakers	545	.626	10
Chicago Bulls	535	.615	8
New York Knicks	534	.613	11
Houston Rockets	510	.587	8
Indiana Pacers	500	.574	10
Miami Heat	465	.534	8
Orlando Magic	463	.532	6
Atlanta Hawks	459	.528	8
Charlotte Hornets	459	.528	6
Cleveland Cavaliers	454	.522	6
Detroit Pistons	426	.489	6
Boston Celtics	395	.454	4
Milwaukee Bucks	377	.433	4
Sacramento Kings	372	.427	4
Philadelphia 76ers	358	.411	4
New Jersey Nets	356	.409	4
Golden State Warriors	351	.403	3
Minnesota Timberwolves	337	.387	4
Denver Nuggets	319	.366	3
Washington Wizards	313	.359	1
Los Angeles Clippers	298	.342	3
Dallas Mavericks	292	.335	1

Note: Wins and Win-Loss Percentage are self-explanatory. Postseason is the number of first round appearances in the playoffs per team for eleven seasons. The Toronto Raptors and Vancouver Grizzlies are excluded in Table 1.4 because these clubs entered the NBA after 1990.

Source: The World Almanac and Book of Facts, 1991–2001.

a mean and standard deviation were calculated for each of the three performance characteristics, which were Wins, Win-Loss Percentage and Postseason. Then, these statistics were applied to estimate the variations of each characteristic. In sum, what does the list of teams, as arranged by the total number of wins in Table 1.7 indicate about parity in the NBA? (For reference, each sports league's means and standard deviations for the performance characteristics are included in Table A.1 of the Appendix.)

According to the Win-Loss Percentage column in Table 1.7, on average 30 percent (8) of the teams played above .600 and 19 percent (5) below .400 for the eleven seasons. Surprisingly, historically successful clubs such as the Boston Celtics, Detroit Pistons and Philadelphia 76ers performed worse than the Charlotte Hornets, Orlando Magic and Miami Heat, which were expansion clubs in the late 1980s. Furthermore, based on the statistics reported in Table A.1 of the Appendix 56 percent (15) of the NBA teams in Table 1.7 placed within one standard deviation of 441, the average number of wins, and 6.4, which was the mean for Postseason appearances. Moreover, 60 percent (16) of the basketball clubs were within one standard deviation of .507, the average Win-Loss Percentage. The NBA, therefore, from 1990 to 2000 inclusive experienced less competitive balance or more inequality in playing strengths than the AL or NL did. Based on the analysis of NBA team performances in their sports book, Jozsa and Guthrie ranked the Bucks, Clippers, Hawks, Heat, Nuggets, Mavericks, Pacers, Timberwolves and 76ers as inferior clubs, while the remaining teams in Table 1.7 were rated either average or superior. Unless the inferior group of clubs plays better and improves in performance after 2000, the NBA should consider their characteristics when contraction, realignment, relocation and revenue sharing strategies are discussed.

The NBA's attendance increased by 130 percent in the 1970s, 76 percent in the 1980s and 16 percent in the 1990s. Besides the slowdown in attendance growth, the league's operating profit, which peaked at $195 million in the 1992–1993 season, then declined annually through the 2000–2001 season. Although the NBA's total revenues grew by 100 percent since 1993, the average player's salary increased by 117 percent. Because of the large percentage change in salaries and team payrolls, between 1992 and 1997 the league's average ticket price increased by 80 percent, which resulted in less attendance and more operating losses for several small-to-medium-market franchises.[23]

The attendance drop-off aside, the NBA's merchandise sales and television ratings plateaued in the mid-to-late 1990s. Many sports columnists and reporters contend that NBA Commissioner David Stern and the league owners failed to improvise and launch any innovative marketing campaigns to prepare the sport's fans for Michael Jordan's retirement in 1998. Other sports commentators and journalists suggest that the double-digit rise in ticket prices, the bad publicity about how players unremorsefully break the law, and the payment of multimillion-dollar salaries by owners to self-interested, underachieving talent have diminished the long-term image of the sport. In turn, these issues have discouraged even diehard fans from attending games and purchasing apparel and merchandise at the arenas. Consequently, rather than follow the performances of their hometown NBA players and the progress of their team(s), a growing portion of young and adult sports fans prefer to attend minor league and college baseball games, play eighteen holes of golf, join a soccer game at a local field, shoot basketball hoops on a neighborhood court, or watch the New York Yankees compete against the Boston Red Sox on ESPN. In short, for the league's brand name to be recognized and adulated, Commissioner Stern and the NBA need to create marketing programs and jointly establish a stronger base of core fans who do not abandon the hometown club or sport when controversies and mishaps occur that involve coaches, owners, players or teams.[24]

To reverse the negative trends in attendance, merchandise sales and television ratings, Commissioner Stern recently implemented several strategies to increase the public's awareness of the NBA brand and to boost the league's image. Stern, an energetic and entrepreneurial sports executive, since 1999 has opened an NBA store in New York and a league restaurant in Orlando, launched a twenty-four-hour basketball cable channel, and beamed games across the world from Afghanistan to Zimbabwe. Furthermore, as a long-term goal to expand the NBA's global presence, in 1999 Stern announced that a developmental league would be organized to begin its initial season before 2005 somewhere in Asia, Europe or Latin America. The foreign-based league would be structured similar to the Women's National Basketball Association (WNBA), an organization whose business operations, member franchises and team payrolls are controlled and financed by the NBA. Because the women's league is televised in more than 125 countries, after six seasons it has become exceedingly popular overseas.[25]

Besides the programs and strategies discussed thus far, there are other international opportunities that have been aggressively pursued by the NBA. These include the employment of American players on Asian teams and the expanded television coverage of regular season and playoff games in large European cities. Without modern, U.S.-style arenas available in foreign countries, however, the NBA's ambition for international development of the sport is restricted. In a press interview held in September 1999, Commissioner Stern said his major objective is " ... to harness the power of his player's popularity to affect positive changes in society." The creation of advertising campaigns that feature anti-drug themes and the formation of a minor basketball league to replace the bankrupt Continental Basketball Association are steps to achieve Stern's goals.[26]

NATIONAL BASKETBALL DEVELOPMENT LEAGUE

In November 2001, a U.S.-based NBA minor league titled the National Basketball Development League (NBDL) began its inaugural season. The NBDL, which consists of eight teams located within medium-sized metropolitan areas in the Southeast, adopted a fifty-six-game season schedule that extends from November to March. Walt Disney Company's ESPN and News Corporation's

Fox Sports Net have contracted with the NBDL to televise its regular season and playoff games. To discourage teenage athletes from dropping out of high school to play professional basketball, the new league's players must be at least twenty years old. Classified as free agents, the active NBDL players are eligible to sign with any NBA team before, during or after a season. To control payrolls, player salaries are capped at $30,000, which is 10 percent less than what U.S. players would earn on professional teams based in Europe. Amy Privette Perko, president of Fayetteville, North Carolina's entry in the NBDL, expects that the league's teams will be competitive, generate entertainment for fans, get involved in local community activities, and be authorized to request ample resources for player development and promotional programs from the NBA. In brief, at least in the short term the NBDL has the money and support of the NBA to make the league viable and a worthy replacement for the defunct Continental Basketball Association.

After discussing the problems, strategies and successes of the AL, NL, minor league baseball, and the NBA and NBDL, the chapter focuses on sports leagues in professional football. After that, the business and operations of the eminent professional and minor ice hockey leagues and their member teams will be explored.[27]

NFL

In 1920, George Halas and the other owners of Midwest professional football franchises met in Canton, Ohio, and organized the American Professional Football Conference whose name, for unknown reasons, was changed to the American Professional Football Association (APFA). The organization hired professional athlete and former Olympian Jim Thorpe to be its president. Because of low attendance, many of the teams disbanded, and the APFA folded after its initial season. Reinvigorated by new leadership, the twenty-two-team league was revived in 1921. During the season, player-coach Thorpe transferred from the Canton, Ohio, team to the Cleveland Indians where he rarely played because of injuries. The Chicago Staleys, who were coached by George Halas and are now called the Chicago Bears, in 1921 won the league championship with a 9–1–1 record. Then, the APFA renamed itself the National Football League in 1922. That year, eighteen clubs were admitted to the league including the Oorang Indians, a native Indian team from Marion, Ohio. At 10–0–2, the Canton Bulldogs won the league title and the Indians finished in twelfth place at 3–6–0. To expand operations, the NFL membership increased to twenty-two teams in 1926. However, due to financial problems and internal disputes, in 1932 only eight clubs remained, which was the lowest number of franchises in the league's history.[28]

As factors in the development and growth of the NFL, there were many memorable events and incidents that involved the sport's fans, owners, players and teams, and the media industry. By decade, a few examples of those activities are

highlighted here. In the 1930s, the NFL held its first annual draft of college players, and a game played at Ebbets Field between the Brooklyn Dodgers and
Philadelphia Eagles was the first NFL contest to be televised nationally by the
National Broadcasting Corporation (NBC). In the 1940s, Red Barber announced
the first NFL championship game that was carried on network radio to 120 stations of the Mutual Broadcasting System, which had paid $2,500 for the broad-
cast rights. Furthermore, three competitive clubs—Baltimore Colts, Cleveland
Browns and San Francisco 49ers—from the All-American Football Conference
agreed to join the NFL after the conference and league merged in 1949. In the
1950s, the NFL Players Association was founded, and the Columbia Broadcasting System (CBS) became the first network to broadcast NFL regular season
games. After a dismal 1952 season, the Dallas Texans became the last league franchise to fail. In the 1960s, the American Football League and NFL merged and
formed the American and National Conferences, which each consisted of thirteen teams. Also, Judge Edward Weinfeld of the U.S. District Court in New York
City upheld the legality of the NFL's television blackout within a seventy-five-
mile radius of the clubs' home games. In the 1970s, a Monday Night Football
television program was introduced when ABC acquired the rights to broadcast
thirteen NFL regular season games. Furthermore, the NFL adopted sweeping rule
changes such as a sudden death overtime period, movement of the goal posts to
the end lines, and a scheduled four-game preseason and sixteen-game regular season. In the 1980s, the Oakland Raiders moved to Los Angeles after winning an
antitrust suit against the NFL, and player strikes occurred for fifty-seven days in
1982 and twenty-four days in 1987. Two years later, Paul Tagliabue replaced Commissioner Pete Rozelle to become the seventh chief executive of the league. In
the 1990s, the NFL launched the World League of American Football, and the expansion Carolina Panthers and Jacksonville Jaguars became the twenty-ninth and
thirtieth NFL franchises. Grouped, these historical events and incidents from the
1930s through 1990s influenced the NFL in its quest to be a prodigious and
wealthy sports league at the end of the twentieth century.[29]

Since 1920, there have been three NFL presidents, four commissioners and
one treasurer who served as president in the office of the commissioner. After
Jim Thorpe's brief tenure as president in 1920, Joe Carr was appointed president
in 1921 when the APFA reorganized. Carr moved the association's headquarters
to Columbus, Ohio, drafted a league constitution and by-laws, assigned teams
territorial rights and mandated season and playoff standards for the first time.
When Carr died in 1939, Carl Storck was named acting president. Two years
later, Storck resigned, and Elmer Layden became the first full-time commissioner
of the NFL. Because of the team owner's dissatisfaction with his policies, Layden's contract was not renewed in 1946, and Bert Bell, the co-owner of the Pittsburgh Steelers, replaced him. Enshrined in the Professional Football Hall of Fame
in Canton, Ohio, Bell built the NFL image and established long-term television
contracts with the DuMont Network and NBC. Unfortunately, the commissioner
died of a heart attack in 1959 during a game between the Philadelphia Eagles

and Pittsburgh Steelers. As a temporary measure, NFL Treasurer Austin Gunsel served as interim president in the commissioner's office during the last three months of 1959. After several ballots, in January 1960 Pete Rozelle was elected NFL commissioner and immediately moved the league offices to New York City. Later, Rozelle negotiated the first league-wide television contract and gained recognition as one of the best commissioners in sports history because of his thirty-year tenure. After Rozelle retired in 1989, on the sixth ballot of a three-day meeting in Cleveland, Paul Tagliabue became the commissioner. During Tagliabue's reign, the NFL has surged in attendance, revenues and wealth to become the premier league in professional sports.[30]

How successful is the NFL? One year after merging with the All-American Football Conference, the thirteen-team league played 142 regular season games before 2 million spectators. In 1970, 10 million fans watched twenty-six teams who participated in 182 games. Thirty years later, thirty-one NFL teams drew 20 million spectators to 248 games. With per game attendance of approximately 66,000 in 2000 and the cash inflows from a multibillion-dollar national television contract, the NFL has become an immensely profitable organization.[31]

Between 1950 and 2000 inclusive, there were fewer team movements and expansions in the NFL than in MLB, the NBA or NHL. As reflected in Table 1.8, one NFL team relocated in the 1960s and three each in the 1980s and 1990s. Meanwhile, four expansions occurred in the 1960s and two each in the 1970s and 1990s. In general, several factors including franchise ownership

Table 1.8
NFL Team Relocation and Expansion, 1950 to 2000

Year	Team	From	To	Expansion
1960–61	Cardinals	Chicago	St. Louis	
1960–61	Cowboys			Dallas
1961–62	Vikings			Minnesota
1966–67	Falcons			Atlanta
1967–68	Saints			New Orleans
1976–77	Seahawks			Seattle
1976–77	Buccaneers			Tampa Bay
1981–82	Raiders	Oakland	Los Angeles	
1983–84	Colts	Baltimore	Indianapolis	
1988–89	Cardinals	St. Louis	Phoenix	
1994–95	Rams	Los Angeles	St. Louis	
1994–95	Raiders	Los Angeles	Oakland	
1995–96	Panthers			Carolina
1995–96	Jaguars			Jacksonville
1998–99	Oilers	Houston	Memphis	

Note: Year is the team's first season at the relocated or expansion site. The ten American Football League clubs that joined the NFL in 1970 are excluded from Table 1.8.

Source: The World Almanac and Book of Facts, 1961 to 2001 inclusive; Jozsa and Guthrie, *Relocating Teams and Expanding Leagues in Professional Sports,* 53, 82, 112.

sales, low-to-mediocre win-loss percentages, excessive team debts and operating losses, inferior home attendance, deficient local radio and television contracts, and outdated stadiums explain why clubs relocated from Baltimore, Chicago, Houston, Los Angeles (twice), Oakland and St. Louis. Interestingly, a total of four moves were completed when the Cardinals relocated from Chicago and St. Louis and the Raiders from Oakland and Los Angeles.

After four clubs joined the league between 1960 and 1968, and two in 1976, no expansions occurred for nineteen years. Except for the Vikings in Minnesota and the Seahawks in Seattle, the NFL expansion sites were in southeastern and southwestern cities that had experienced above average population growth and contained strong local economies. In 2002, the Houston Texans began their first season as the thirty-second NFL team. Businessman Bob McNair outbid other groups of investors from Los Angeles and paid $700 million for the franchise. For the Texans' home-site games, a 69,500-seat retractable roof stadium valued at $367 million was constructed with funds from rental car and hotel taxes in the Houston area. Former Carolina Panthers head coach Dom Capers, who in his second season guided the club to the Western Division title and the National Football Conference Championship game against the Green Bay Packers, will lead the Texans.[32]

Based on their 1990 to 1996 average win-loss percentage and home attendance, and a 1997 estimated market value, four relocated and fifteen expansion teams in the NFL were graded by Frank P. Jozsa, Jr. and John J. Guthrie, Jr. in Chapter 5 of *Relocating Teams and Expanding Leagues in Professional Sports*. Four teams each were rated either superior or average, and eleven inferior. (If ranked according to their mean win-loss percentage and home attendance, and a 2000 estimated market value, between 1995 and 2000 the expansion Carolina Panthers and Jacksonville Jaguars were average franchises.) In sum, since 58 percent (11) of the NFL clubs were rated inferior, the league's decisions to approve expansions and team movements have been counterproductive and a disappointment to the sport's commissioner and the respective communities, fans and team owners. This suggests that, for several seasons beyond 2002 the expansion Houston Texans will struggle to play above .500 per season and to compete for division titles or qualify for wild-card games.[33]

To determine whether parity existed in the NFL, and how playing strengths compared to the other sports, Table 1.9 lists twenty-eight clubs that played in the league from the 1990 to 2000 seasons inclusive. For each team, three performance characteristics were recorded. They are the cumulative number of wins, the average win-loss percentage, and the number of appearances in postseason games. Then, a mean and standard deviation for each performance characteristic was calculated, and the results reported in Table A.1 of the Appendix. In turn, these statistics were used to measure the distribution of playing strengths among teams in the NFL for the eleven seasons. What does Table 1.9 reveal about parity in the NFL?

Table 1.9
NFL Team Performance Characteristics, 1990 to 2000

Team	Wins	Win-Loss Percentage	Postseason
San Francisco 49ers	119	.676	8
Buffalo Bills	111	.631	8
Kansas City Chiefs	109	.620	7
Dallas Cowboys	106	.602	8
Miami Dolphins	106	.602	8
Minnesota Vikings	106	.602	8
Denver Broncos	105	.597	6
Green Bay Packers	102	.580	6
Pittsburgh Steelers	102	.580	6
Tennessee Titans	101	.574	6
New York Giants	95	.543	4
Oakland Raiders	94	.534	4
Philadelphia Eagles	91	.520	5
Detroit Lions	88	.500	4
Washington Redskins	87	.497	4
New Orleans Saints	81	.460	4
Chicago Bears	78	.443	3
Tampa Bay Buccaneers	77	.438	3
Atlanta Falcons	76	.432	3
Indianapolis Colts	76	.432	4
Seattle Seahawks	76	.432	1
Baltimore Ravens	75	.426	2
San Diego Chargers	75	.426	3
New York Jets	74	.421	2
New England Patriots	73	.415	4
St. Louis Rams	68	.387	2
Arizona Cardinals	61	.347	1
Cincinnati Bengals	56	.319	1

Note: Wins and Win-Loss Percentage were calculated as in Table 1.7. Postseason is the sum of division titles and wild-card game appearances per team for eleven seasons. The Carolina Panthers, Cleveland Browns and Jacksonville Jaguars became expansion clubs after 1990. They are excluded from Table 1.9. Since the owner and players remained with the Ravens after relocation, the results for the Baltimore Ravens include the performance characteristics of the former Cleveland Browns. The results for the Oakland Raiders, Tennessee Titans and St. Louis Rams contain those of, respectively, the former Los Angeles Raiders, Houston Oilers and Los Angeles Rams.

Source: The World Almanac and Book of Facts, 1991 to 2001.

In Wins and Win-Loss Percentage, 65 percent (18) of the teams placed within one standard deviation of 88, the average Wins, and .500, the average Win-Loss Percentage. As listed from the upper to lower half of Table 1.9, the eighteen clubs extended from the Green Bay Packers with 102 wins, a .580 winning percentage and six postseason appearances to the New England Patriots with 73 wins, a .415 win-loss percentage and four postseason appearances. In qualifying for postseason games, 68 percent (19) of the teams placed within one standard deviation of 4.4, the mean number of postseason appearances. Based on the characteristics, statistics and three distributions, for the eleven seasons the NFL was slightly less equal in the distribution of playing strengths than the AL and NL as represented in Table 1.5, but had achieved greater parity than what existed in the NBA as portrayed in Table 1.7.

During the period, there was a distinct cluster of seven NFL teams who won from 101 to 106 games and nine clubs who earned 73 to 78 wins. The small difference of .028 (.602-.574) in average win-loss percentage for the first group, and .028 (.443-.415) for the second group partially explains why a moderate degree of parity existed in the NFL relative to the other leagues. Although considered by most sports analysts and economists as the organization that has the most equitable league-wide revenue sharing policies, between 1990 and 2000 the NFL's small-to-medium-market teams located in Arizona, Cincinnati, Indianapolis, San Diego, Seattle and Tampa Bay were not nearly as successful as the other small-to-medium-market clubs in Buffalo, Denver, Green Bay, Kansas City, Minnesota and Pittsburgh. Furthermore, the large-market franchises in Miami, Philadelphia and San Francisco played measurably better than those in Atlanta, Chicago and Washington. In sum, Table 1.9 depicts the average, marginal and total ranges for three performance variables between twenty-eight of the NFL's small-to-medium and large-market teams from the 1990 through 2000 season.

Since their early history, each of the American professional sport leagues has encountered recurring business problems and team-specific issues. At one time or another, for example, arena or stadium obsolescence, fan apathy, competitive imbalance within divisions and conferences, entry of rival leagues, free agency, inflated ticket prices and revenue disparities between high and low payroll clubs have exasperated the MLB, NBA, NFL and NHL commissioners and the majority of team owners. Currently, an internal, sensitive matter that NFL Commissioner Paul Tagliabue and the team owners must contend with and resolve is how and when to apply and enforce the league's personal conduct policy to minimize rule violations and rehabilitate players.

In May 2000, the NFL, with the cooperation, participation and support of the players union, shrewdly adopted several measures to police the crimes and other violent acts that players may commit while not in uniform. Designed to be a persuasive rather than a punitive policy, the major initiatives implemented by the league are: a screening process to identify at-risk players; a set of guidelines to clarify the duties of the club's career counselor and security director; a mandate that requires players to attend Life Skills presentations; and a list of fair standards that specify the penalties for car theft rings, drug trafficking, money laundering and other criminal infractions. Furthermore, each team's personal conduct program coordinator must periodically remind players to select and socialize with mature and reputable sports agents, and associates and friends. These issues aside, the league then adopted stringent requirements that involve performance enhancement drugs. To remove any suspicion about substance abuse by team players and to protect the athletes' health, in September 2001 the NFL added ephedrine and related "high-risk stimulants" to a list of banned substances classified as anabolic steroids. Furthermore, the league barred players from endorsing business firms who manufacture pills that contain the prohibited substances. Because of random tests and suspensions, the NFL's drug policies appear to be effective as players knowingly forgo income when they refrain from the endorsements of these products. Given the player controversies and substance abuse problems that have plagued the other sports leagues, and especially the NBA, the expectations are that Commissioner Tagliabue and the team owners will allocate sufficient money and resources to fully implement the rules and standards contained in the players' personal conduct policy.[34]

Other than the ever-present economic problems such as the escalation of player salaries, the plunge in television ratings, and the accounting losses suffered by the league's noncompetitive teams, there are two intermediate-to-long-term issues that Commissioner Tagliabue and the franchise owners must evaluate. The first issue is whether and when the league will select the Los Angeles area, which contains the second largest media market in the United States, as a site for an existing NFL team or an expansion club. The second issue is how will realignment in the 2002 season affect competitive balances and impact divisional rivalries within the American and National Football Conferences. If the league has discussed these matters, there has been no information leaked by the owners to the sport's fans or reported in the media.

Because of more sponsors and NFL inputs, the forty-three-year-old Arena Football League (AFL) is an expanding organization. Since 1995, the league's total attendance has doubled to 2.5 million, and by 2005 there are plans to place franchises in one hundred cities such as Denver, Detroit, Philadelphia and Washington, D.C. Besides the progress made by the AFL, another asset the NFL cherishes and invests in is the relatively less experienced group of teams that compete in Western Europe. The background, strategy and success of this organization are interesting topics to examine.[35]

NFL EUROPE LEAGUE

In February 2001, the NFL Europe League—formerly called the World League of American Football—celebrated its tenth anniversary. Founded in 1991 by the NFL and largely supported by the U.S. television networks, the league was organized in seventeen days when meetings, player trials and a common draft were jointly held in Orlando, Florida. The first season of play began with seven franchises located in the United States and one each in England, Germany and Spain. To market the brand in Europe, teams were allowed to list forty players on their rosters including four non-Americans. Strategically, the NFL Europe League differentiated itself from other European sports organizations by restructuring games to appear as family-oriented events. Besides the placement of cheerleader squads and marching bands on the sidelines, during games the action was reconfigured to continuously flow with an emphasis on offense and not defense. Instant replay reviews by referees, which are events that slow NFL games and bore spectators in the United States, are disallowed. To conclude each season, a World Bowl game is played to decide the league champion.[36]

At a press conference with the European media in July 2001, Commissioner Tagliabue praised the progress of the NFL Europe League. He singled out the 2001 attendance growth realized by each club in the six-city league, and the competitive play whereby 47 percent of regular season games were decided by less than eight points. Regarding the league's future, the commissioner has stated with pride: "I came over myself last year and visited Madrid and Paris but we don't have a timetable for expansion. We want to be deliberate and to continue to grow where we are." Because of the economic uncertainties and risks that occurred during the formation and development of the European Union, and the introduction and phase-in of the Union's new Eurocurrency, Tagliabue's vision for the NFL Europe League in its marketplace was insightful.[37]

The final league to be discussed is the sport least identified as American. Despite its origins in Canada, however, professional ice hockey has become more recognizable and popular as a number of franchises have been relocated to or expanded within U.S. metropolitan areas.[38]

NHL

The first amateur ice hockey leagues in North America and in the United States were, respectively, in 1885 when a four-team unnamed organization was established in Kingston, Ontario, and in 1896 when the four-team Amateur Hockey League was founded in New York State. In 1904, the first professional hockey league, named the International Pro Hockey League (IPHL), was formed in Michigan's Upper Peninsula. After the IPHL folded in 1907 because of poor attendance, the National Hockey Association (NHA) emerged in 1910, which was closely followed by the Pacific Coast League (PCL) in 1911. Due to internal squabbling, in 1917 the NHA disbanded and in November of that year, the five-team National Hockey League (NHL) was organized in Montreal, Canada. When the PCL terminated operations in the mid-1920s, the Stanley Cup became the exclusive possession of the NHL. In 1926, the ten-club NHL was reorganized into the Canadian and American Divisions, and each team played a forty-four-game schedule per season.[39]

The NHL and its member clubs adopted some necessary internal rule changes between the mid-1920s and mid-1970s. Discussed in decades, within these fifty years a number of significant reforms occurred as a few league teams developed into champions and formed dynasties. In the 1930s, franchises in Detroit, Montreal, Ottawa, Philadelphia, Pittsburgh and St. Louis changed nicknames, disbanded, relocated or temporarily retired from the league. The best clubs were the Montreal Canadiens who won Stanley Cups in 1930, 1931 and 1935, and the Toronto Maple Leafs who finished as the final opponent for the championship in 1933, 1935, 1936, 1938 and 1939. In the 1940s, six teams remained in the NHL after the dislocations of the 1930s, and the season schedule expanded to fifty and then to sixty games per team. Because of Stanley Cup victories in 1942, 1945 and 1947 through 1949, the Maple Leafs replaced the Canadiens to become the dominant NHL franchise. In the 1950s, the interleague draft was modified to ensure the availability of players, and each club chose twenty players to be protected from the draft. The Montreal Canadiens excelled to win five Stanley Cups, the Detroit Red Wings four and the Toronto Maple Leafs one. During this era, Bernie Geoffrion and Jean Beliveau starred for Montreal, Gordie Howe and Terry Sawchuk for Detroit, and Harry Lumley and Ted Kennedy for the Maple Leafs. Excluding goalkeepers, in the 1960s clubs were permitted to dress sixteen players for regular season games, and the league agreed on an unrestricted draft of players aged seventeen or younger. Competitively, the Canadiens and Maple Leafs fielded the best teams, and the Chicago Black Hawks' Bobby Hull and Stan Mikita tended to be the two leaders in points scored. In the 1970s, the newly organized twelve-member World Hockey Association competed against the NHL in the 1972–1973 season, and a helmet became a required piece of the player's uniform. Moreover, the Montreal Canadiens won six championships and the Boston Bruins and Philadelphia Flyers two each, while the Bruins' Phil Esposito and Canadiens' Guy Lafleur led the league in scoring during seven of the ten seasons. In total, these events, incidences, players and teams influenced the competitiveness, organizational structure and stature of the NHL, as well as the league's business potential and stability in Canada and the United States.[40]

Between 1943 and 1966, the NHL remained intact with clubs in Boston, Chicago, Detroit, Montreal, New York and Toronto. Before sparse but enthusiastic crowds, these teams played 210 games in 1950. Ten years later, in 210 games the NHL's attendance totaled 2.3 million, which converted to 11,000 spectators per game. Due to this momentum and progress, the various NHL commissioners and team owners recognized the demand for the sport and its long-term international popularity, particularly from dormant but potentially diehard hockey fans in the United States. Therefore, as depicted in Table 1.10 six expansions occurred in the 1960s, ten in the 1970s, seven in the 1990s and one in 2000. Meanwhile, between 1976 and 1998 six teams based in the United States and two in Canada relocated. Seven of these clubs moved to cities in the United States and one to Calgary in Canada.[41]

To compare the extent of competitive balance in the NHL with the parity that existed in the other sports leagues for eleven consecutive seasons, see Table 1.11. It lists the cumulative Points Earned per club and the number of seasons that each of the twenty-one teams qualified for the playoffs in order to compete for the Stanley Cup trophy. The means and standard deviations for Points Earned and Postseason are contained in Table A.1 of the Appendix. These statistics were used to determine the distributions for the franchises in Table 1.11. That is, the two tables and statistics are provided to analyze the variation of the two performance characteristics—Points Earned and Postseason—for twenty-one teams in the NHL from the 1990–1991 through the 2000–2001 seasons. However, because Points Earned and Postseason replaced Wins and Win-Loss Percentage as the two

Table 1.10
NHL Team Relocation and Expansion, 1950 to 2000

Year	Team	From	To	Expansion
1967–68	Blues			St. Louis
1967–68	Flyers			Philadelphia
1967–68	Kings			Los Angeles
1967–68	North Stars			Minnesota
1967–68	Penguins			Pittsburgh
1967–68	Seals			Oakland
1970–71	Canucks			Vancouver
1970–71	Sabres			Buffalo
1972–73	Flames			Atlanta
1972–73	Islanders			New York
1974–75	Scouts			Kansas City
1975–76	Capitals			Washington
1976–77	Golden Seals	Oakland	Cleveland	
1976–77	Scouts	Kansas City	Colorado	
1979–80	Jets			Winnipeg
1979–80	Nordiques			Quebec
1979–80	Oilers			Edmonton
1979–80	Whalers			Hartford
1980–81	Flames	Atlanta	Calgary	
1982–83	Rockies	Colorado	New Jersey	
1991–92	Sharks			San Jose
1992–93	Lightning			Tampa Bay
1992–93	Senators			Ottawa
1993–94	Mighty Ducks			Anaheim
1993–94	North Stars	Minnesota	Dallas	
1993–94	Panthers			Florida
1995–96	Nordiques	Quebec	Colorado	
1996–97	Jets	Winnipeg	Phoenix	
1997–98	Whalers	Hartford	Carolina	
1998–99	Predators			Nashville
1999–00	Thrashers			Atlanta
2000–01	Blue Jackets			Columbus

Note: Year is the team's first season at the relocation or expansion site.

Source: *The World Almanac and Book of Facts*, 1968–2001.

measures of team performances in ice hockey, any interpretation of the distributions in the NHL relative to the AL, NL, NBA and NFL is imprecise and inexact. In short, the characteristics and statistics that pertain to the NHL basically reflect how well the clubs performed on average during the seasons studied.

In Points Earned, 72 percent (15) of the NHL teams—listed from the St. Louis Blues to the Phoenix Coyotes—were within one standard deviation of 907, the average Points Earned (Table 1.11). Thus, in the NHL the spread of Points Earned contained approximately the same proportion of clubs with Wins as in the AL and NL, and a greater proportion of teams with Wins than in the NBA and NFL. Relative to the second performance characteristic, Postseason, 62 percent (13) of the NHL clubs were within one standard deviation of 7.5, which was the mean

Table 1.11
NHL Team Performance Characteristics, 1990 to 2000

Team	Points Earned	Postseason
Detroit Red Wings	1087	11
New Jersey Devils	1027	10
Pittsburgh Penguins	1014	11
St. Louis Blues	990	11
Philadelphia Flyers	973	7
Colorado Avalanche	961	8
Boston Bruins	942	8
Washington Capitals	934	9
Dallas Stars	922	8
Buffalo Sabres	915	10
Chicago Blackhawks	906	7
Montreal Canadiens	905	7
New York Rangers	900	6
Toronto Maple Leafs	865	7
Calgary Flames	864	5
Los Angeles Kings	856	6
Vancouver Canucks	846	7
Phoenix Coyotes	840	7
Edmonton Oilers	812	7
Carolina Hurricanes	786	4
New York Islanders	708	2

Note: Points Earned replaces Wins and Win-Loss Percentage to determine team standings. The performance characteristics of the Carolina Hurricanes, Colorado Avalanche, Dallas Stars and Phoenix Coyotes include those of, respectively, the former Hartford Whalers, Quebec Nordiques, Minnesota North Stars and Winnipeg Jets. Table 1.11 excludes the eight expansion clubs that entered the NHL after the 1990–1991 season.

Source: The World Almanac and Book of Facts, 1991–2001; John Davidson and John Steinbreder, *Hockey For Dummies,* 2nd ed. (Foster City, CA: IDG Books Worldwide, Inc., 2000), 48–50.

number of seasons that teams qualified for the league playoffs. As such, the distribution of Postseason in the NHL contained a higher proportion of teams than in the NBA, the same as in the AL, and less than in the NL and NFL. Consequently, from the 1990 to 2000 season-inclusive on average the competitive balance within the NHL fell below the parity achieved in the NL, was approximately the same as in the AL and NFL, and above the interteam playing strengths in the NBA. In sum, during the 1990s the NHL had a relatively large proportion of franchises that performed well enough to earn playoff spots and the opportunity to become the league champion. Furthermore, the Detroit Red Wings, New Jersey Devils and Pittsburgh Penguins excelled in performances and the Edmonton Oilers, Carolina Hurricanes/Hartford Whalers and New York Islanders played poorly.

In "Big League Troubles," Dan McGraw presents three line graphs about the economics of professional ice hockey. The graphs indicate that in the NHL average ticket prices rose 24 percent from 1994 to 1997, average player salaries accelerated by 795 percent from 1983 to 1997, and average per game attendance expanded by 27 percent from 1980 to 1997. Given these dismal percentage changes from a franchise owner's perspective, McGraw poses a question: "Can the NHL survive with ratings that are lower than late night television?" Since July 1998, when McGraw's article appeared in the *U.S. News & World Report*, the NHL has placed expansion franchises in three U.S. cities. They are the Thrashers in Atlanta, Georgia, the Blue Jackets in Columbus, Ohio, and the Predators in Nashville, Tennessee. Nevertheless, even though the league added teams and total attendance rose after 1998, the NHL Commissioner Gary Bettman and some club owners are confronted with severe financial problems that reflect how vulnerable the sport is and perhaps signal the demise of the league's weakest franchises. For example, in 1999 three transactions occurred that illustrate the financial dilemmas within the NHL.[42]

First, based on its estimated market value the bankrupt Pittsburgh Penguins was sold at a 40 percent discount to an ownership group headed by Hall of Fame player Mario Lemieux. Second, Wal-Mart heirs Bill and Nancy Laurie purchased the St. Louis Blues and the Kiel Center—now named the Savvis Center—for a bargain price of $100 million, which was $135 million less than the estimated market value of the arena and team combined. Third, NBA Detroit Pistons owner William Davidson bid $110 million for the Tampa Bay Lightning and its home arena, the Ice Palace. This amount was $7 million below the price Lightning owner Art Williams paid for the team and arena nine months prior to Davidson's offer. In general, these business deals indicate how the sports market had devalued three inferior NHL teams that did not entertain fans or appeal to corporate sponsors and the television networks in their respective market areas.[43]

Even more of a threat to the NHL is Canada where extreme financial hardships exist for ice hockey franchises. Because of high tax rates, substantial government and taxpayer resistance to subsidize sports teams and a weak currency, the majority of NHL teams struggle each season to compete against their stronger and richer division and conference rivals located in America. To worsen their economic predicament, the troubled franchises receive cash inflows in Canadian dollars and compensate their players in U.S. dollars. Thus, for these reasons the teams in Edmonton, Calgary, Ottawa and Vancouver have experienced a barrage of financial crises. Without public funds from government or subsidies from the league, the four Canadian clubs will likely fold or be forced to relocate to a U.S. metropolitan area. Perhaps, Canadian government officials and taxpayers will provide financial assistance after a reevaluation of each franchise's conditions and after realizing how fans and other citizens are committed to professional hockey. Otherwise, Commissioner Bettman, who previously had served as a senior vice president and general counsel for the NBA, must convince the league to either continue its support of the financially strapped franchises or to pursue other alternatives such as to merge or terminate one or more of the teams. Do the same business conditions and environments exist in the professional ice hockey minor leagues?[44]

MINOR LEAGUE HOCKEY

Currently, the NHL minor league system is based in the United States and organized like the hierarchical structure in professional baseball. In June 2000, there were 110 hockey teams in seven professional minor leagues. Similar to the skill levels of players in the AAA minor baseball leagues, the teams in the American Hockey League (AHL) compete at the highest level of play. As the premier player development organization for the NHL, in 2000 the twenty-seven-team AHL entered its sixty-fifth season, and 4.4 million spectators in twenty cities enjoyed the league's regular season. When the fifty-six-year-old International Hockey League folded in June 2001 for financial reasons, six of its teams joined the AHL. At the lowest tier of the sport is the West Coast and Western Professional Hockey Leagues, which employ the least experienced athletes who play at a basic level similar to a professional rookie baseball league in the United States.[45]

Ranked below the AHL in competitiveness and skill level are the East Coast Hockey League (ECHL) and Central Hockey League (CHL). They are comparable, respectively, to baseball's AA and A minor leagues. Organized in the early 1990s with fifteen teams in two divisions, the total attendance of the ECHL rose from 2.2 million in 1992 to 3.9 million in 2000 when twenty-five clubs participated in the Northern and Southern Conferences. Alternatively, a single owner formed the five-team CHL in 1992. When five teams who were individually owned entered the CHL in 1996, the existing centrally owned club operators were chafed at their inability to invest in players since one of the owners controls the league's operations. As these organizational problems occur, the CHL and other leagues must revise their ownership structures to attract wealthy investors who would furnish sufficient capital for the franchises to independently exist in the long term.[46]

A portion of minor league hockey teams has a direct affiliation with one NHL club. Also, there are hockey teams that supply players to and receive players from more than one parent club. Then there are independent minor league teams that have no agreements with NHL franchises. The fourteen-member United Hockey League, for example, is a serious "bus" league that stretches from Michigan to New York to North Carolina. It has less widespread talent than the ECHL and no NHL affiliations. In sum, because of the different owner relationships the operations in minor league hockey are more tenuous and unstable than in minor league baseball.[47]

SUMMARY

This chapter examined the origin and development of the AL and NL in MLB, and the NBA, NFL and NHL. Subsequent to the discussion of each major sports league, there were brief overviews of the organizational structures within the minor leagues in baseball and hockey, the NBDL in basketball, and the Arena Football League and NFL Europe League in football. By decade, a selection of key historical events, incidences and reforms were discussed to denote how each sports league organized and matured, especially before the 1990s. Then, the expansions and team movements in each sport were tabled to indicate the circumstances and time periods during which each league's growth and progress occurred.

For selected teams in each league, the values of three quantitative performance characteristics were calculated and placed in tables. Then, for each characteristic the mean and standard deviation statistics were applied to determine whether competitive balance or parity prevailed within each league from the 1990 to 2000 seasons inclusive. Essentially, the characteristics and statistics reveal the short- and long-term business conditions, issues and problems within each organization that will require leadership and innovative solutions from the various sports commissioners and league owners.

In MLB, the primary business issues that plague the sport are the operations of several inferior franchises, revenue differences between small-to-medium and large-market teams, exorbitant club payrolls, and inflated ticket prices. To resolve these hardships, the league might agree to liberate teams and allow their owners to relocate the respective franchises from small- to large-market areas, to revoke the charter of selected franchises, and to tilt the revenue sharing formula in favor of the lowest payroll clubs. In the NBA, the problems are stagnant attendance, deficient television ratings, inflated player salaries especially for the superstars, and the high cost for families to attend games. Commissioner David Stern has initiated marketing campaigns to entice spectators and increase the attendance at games. Furthermore, Stern has expanded the sport's broadcasts on the radio, television and Internet to international markets.

In the NFL, which is currently the most popular and prosperous league, there needs to be strict vigilance and enforcement of the personal conduct program for players, ample resources for the operations of the Arena Football League and the NFL Europe League, and the placement of one or more teams in the Los Angeles area. In the NHL, the weakest franchises should be eliminated, merged or relocated. Furthermore, Commissioner Gary Bettman needs to aggressively negotiate a moneymaking national broadcasting agreement and expand the exposure of professional ice hockey within the United States and elsewhere on cable, satellite and network television stations.

Chapter 2 focuses on the role of selected professional sports teams as members of the AL, NL, NBA, NFL and NHL. The chapter examines how particular clubs performed within their respective leagues during various seasons, what business, demographic and sports-specific factors influenced the franchises' financial performances, and how the teams excelled relative to those in the other sports leagues. In Chapter 2, there are tabled qualitative and quantitative data and statistics, and franchise-specific information that was applied to measure teams' performances and progress. After reading Chapter 2, the reader will appreciate and understand the unique relationships that exist between the leagues and their member clubs in America's professional team sports.

NOTES

1. The rival leagues in professional baseball, basketball and hockey are thoroughly discussed on pages 294–332, and in football on pages 333–361 of James Quirk and Rodney D. Fort, *Pay Dirt: The Business of Professional Sports* (Princeton, NJ: Princeton University Press, 1992).

2. See Stefan Fatsis, "NBA's Problems Mounting," *Wall Street Journal* (24 February 1998), W9; Mark Hyman, "How Bad Is the NBA Hurting?" *Business Week* (7 May 2001), 123.

3. The events and other incidents in "Organized Baseball" are documented in Frank G. Menke, *The Encyclopedia of Sports*, 5th ed. (Cranbury, NJ: A.S. Barnes, 1975), 71–77. For two classic titles on the history of professional baseball, see Harold Seymour, *Baseball: The Golden Age*, 2nd ed. (New York: Oxford University Press, 1989); Benjamin G. Radar, *American Sports: From the Age of Folk Games to the Age of Spectators* (Englewood Cliffs, NJ: Prentice-Hall, 1983).

4. See Lance E. Davis, "Self-Regulation in Baseball, 1909–71," in Roger G. Noll, ed., *Government and the Sports Business* (Washington, DC: The Brookings Institution, 1974), 349–386.

5. Frank G. Menke, *The Encyclopedia of Sports*, 74–76.

6. See Davis, "Self-Regulation in Baseball, 1909–71," in Roger G. Noll, ed., *Government and the Sports Business*, 377–382. For the tenures of MLB Commissioners, see "Major League Baseball," at http://www.mlb.com cited 1 August 2001.

7. For the history of team movements and league expansions in professional baseball, basketball and football since 1950, see Frank P. Jozsa, Jr. and John J. Guthrie, Jr., *Relocating Teams and Expanding Leagues in Professional Sports: How the Major Leagues Respond to Market Conditions* (Westport, CT: Quorum Books, 1999). The Data Supplement on pages 377– 511 in *Pay Dirt* is an excellent reference for the ownership histories, attendance records, and the radio and television income of franchises in the professional sports leagues.

8. At least four studies analyzed the competitive balance or parity that existed within the major sports leagues for various regular seasons. Each study applied data and statistics to unique quantitative models and reported different results. See Allan Barra, "Fair Ball?" *Wall Street Journal* (13 April 2001), W12; Thomas J. Kruckemeyer, *For Whom the Ball Tolls: A Fan's Guide to Economic Issues in Professional and College Sports* (Jefferson City, MO: Kruckemeyer Publishing, 1995); James Quirk and Rodney D. Fort, *Pay Dirt*, 240–293; Roberto Vincent-Mayoral, "Competitive Balance in Professional Sports Leagues: Determinants and Impact," Honors Thesis, Coe College, 2000.

9. In total, MLB had accumulated $1.4 billion in operating losses since the 1994–1995 strike and, in 2000 the league was $2.1 billion in debt. For the operating profits and losses of specific baseball franchises, see Ronald Blum, "Cash Flow: Baseball Wants Some," *The Daily News* (Jacksonville, NC: 15 July 2000), 1C, 3C; Michael K. Ozanian, "Selective Accounting," *Forbes* (14 December 1998), 124–134.

10. Either unable or unwilling to save themselves, the majority of baseball owners expect Commissioner Bud Selig to restore competitive balance between the clubs in MLB. For the Commissioner's reforms, see "More Power to Selig," at http://www.cnnsi.com cited 20 January 2001; "Bud Means Business," at http://www.cnnsi.com cited 22 November 2000; Sam Walker, "Poor, Poor Baseball," *Wall Street Journal* (7 December 2001), W8; "Selig Hopes to Avoid Repeat of '94," Charlotte *Observer* (30 August 2001), 4C.

11. The committee also recommended a salary cap in MLB and opposed the elimination of teams, which is a strategy that has been proposed by Commissioner Bud Selig and approved by the league owners. See "Economic Block: Baseball Panel Urges Increase in Revenue Sharing," at http://www.cnnsi.com cited 1 December 2000; Stefan Fatsis, "121 Teams? Not for Long," *Wall Street Journal* (16 November 2001), W10.

12. After he evaluated realignment in MLB, Frederick C. Klein remarked, "This isn't football or basketball, and distinctions between the baseball leagues help make this so. The game's history is a strength. Throwing out one of its foundations makes little sense." See Frederick C. Klein, "Baseball Makes a Move, Sort of, to Realignment," *Wall Street Journal* (17 October 1997), B13.

13. President George W. Bush, who was a former co-owner of the Texas Rangers, hopes to expose foreign dignitaries to big league baseball in Washington, D.C. The efforts of the Washington Baseball Club to fulfill President Bush's wishes are discussed in Mark Hyman and Paula Dwyer, "What Does This Town Need? New Senators," *Business Week* (14 May 2001), 54; Lorraine Woellert, "Baseball Owners Could Bobble This Ball," *Business Week* (3 December 2001), 59.

14. For how a sports economist views the contraction of MLB teams, see Andrew Zimbalist, "Why 'Yer Out!' Is a Bad Call for Baseball," *Business Week* (12 November 2001), 120.

15. See Mark Hyman, "And Then There Were 28 … " *Business Week* (11 October 1999), 98–100; Sean McAdam, "Baseball OKs Contraction," *Charlotte Observer* (7 November 2001), 1C, 5C; Stefan Fatsis, "121 Teams? Not for Long," 16 November 2001, W10.

16. Five articles provided the facts and history on minor league baseball. See Charles Gerena and Betty Joyce Nash, "Playing to Win," *Region Focus*, Vol. 4, No. 2, Fifth Federal Reserve District Economy (Richmond, VA: Spring 2000), 13–19; Roy Rowan, "Play Ball!" *Fortune* (4 September 2000), 310–326; Landon Hall, "Building Boom Brings Millions of Fans Back to Minor Leagues," at http://sports.yahoo.com cited 16 June 2001; Bill Kauffman, "A Diamond in the Rough," *Wall Street Journal* (1 September 2000), W13; Ron Green, Sr., "Drawing Crowds to Parks Now Major Fun for Minors," *Charlotte Observer* (4 September 2001), 5C.

17. See Matt Bai, "A League of Their Own," *Newsweek* (11 May 1998), 68; Tom Lowry, Ronald Grover, Lori Hawkins, and David Polek, "For the Love of the Game–And Cheap Seats," *Business Week* (28 May 2001), 46–47.

18. For the development and origins of professional basketball, which was formed in the eastern United States during the late 1800s, see Zander Hollander, ed., *The Modern Encyclopedia of Basketball* (Old Tappan, NJ: Four Winds Press, 1969), 211–220; Roger G. Noll, "Professional Basketball: Economic and Business Perspectives," in Paul D. Staudohar and James A. Mangan, eds., *The Business of Professional Sports* (Champaign: University of Illinois Press, 1991), 18–47; "National Basketball Association," at http://www.forbes.com cited 30 November 1999.

19. Zander Hollander, *The Modern Encyclopedia of Basketball*, 218–220.

20. Besides *The Modern Encyclopedia of Basketball* and "Professional Basketball: Economic and Business Perspectives," the emergence of the early leagues in professional basketball are discussed in Frank G. Menke, *The Encyclopedia of Sports*, 174–176.

21. See Frank P. Jozsa, Jr. and John J. Guthrie, Jr., *Relocating Teams and Expanding Leagues in Professional Sports*, 147, 149.

22. To ensure private-sector support, a Memphis business group planned to invest approximately $100 million in exchange for 50 percent of the franchise. As of early 2002,

the Grizzlies' agreement with the city specified that the club must remain in Memphis for ten to twenty-five years, and retains all income from the arena but is committed to pay off any financial deficits that may occur from the arena's operations. See Woody Baird, "Shelby County Commission OKs New Arena for NBA," at http://sports.yahoo.com cited 12 June 2001; "Memphis Arena on Hold," at http://www.cnnsi.com cited 11 July 2001.

23. Since the mid-1980s, the escalation in average ticket prices, player salaries and team payrolls in professional baseball, basketball, football and hockey suggests that financial problems and competitive imbalances exist within each sports league. For graphs that depict the economic environment of the professional sports markets, see Dan McGraw, "Big League Troubles," *U.S. News & World Report* (13 July 1998), 40–46.

24. See Mark Hyman, "How Bad Is the NBA Hurting?" 123; Stefan Fatsis, "NBA's Problems Mounting," W9; Ronald Grover, "Why the NBA Can't Find the Hoop," *Business Week* (10 April 2000), 132; Kyle Pope and Stefan Fatsis, "NBC, Turner Sports May See Less Profit Showing More Games in New NBA Pact," *Wall Street Journal* (12 November 1997), B9.

25. According to some industry experts, David Stern is the best commissioner in professional sports, the best in NBA history and perhaps the best ever in any sport. For Stern's views on the future of the NBA, see Joseph Coleman, "NBA Commissioner Sees More Globalization for Basketball," at http://www.yahoo.com cited 11 November 1999; "David Stern: This Time, It's Personal," *Business Week* (13 July 1998), 114–118.

26. For the international plans and strategies of NBA Commissioner David Stern, see "Expanding Their Borders," at http://www.cnnsi.com cited 28 September 1999; "TV Azteca and the NBA Extend Broadcast Partnership," at http://www.nba.com cited 29 August 1998.

27. See Marjo Rankin Bliss, "Perko to Build Team in NBDL," *Charlotte Observer* (24 June 2001), 9H; "NBDL Fact Sheet," at http://www.nba.com cited 31 July 2001; "NBDL Background Information," at http://www.nba.com cited 31 July 2001; "New League Has NBA Backing, Player Interest," *Charlotte Observer* (15 November 2001), 4C.

28. A complete and detailed chronology of professional football and especially the NFL is contained in the official *NFL 2001Record & Fact Book* (New York: National Football League, 2001), 269–405. For an abbreviated version of the NFL's history, see "History 101: Chronology of How the Modern-Day NFL Came to Pass," at http://www.cnnsi.com cited 1 July 2001. Other facts about professional football and the history of the NFL are discussed in James Quirk and Rodney D. Fort, *Pay Dirt*, 333–334.

29. For important historical events and incidents in the NFL, as reported by George Strickler, see Frank G. Menke, *The Encyclopedia of Sports*, 464–468. The latest general and specific information about the league's owners, players and teams is posted at a worldwide web site. See the "National Football League," at http://www.nfl.com cited 1 August 2001.

30. *NFL 2001 Record & Fact Book*, 278–289.

31. See various editions of *The World Almanac and Book of Facts* (Mahwah, NJ: World Almanac Books, 1950–2001) for players' performances and teams' seasons and sites. The Carolina Panthers provided game and attendance data on the Internet. See "Carolina Panthers," at http://www.nfl.com cited 1 July 2001. The NFL's total and per year team attendance are reported in James Quirk and Rodney D. Fort, *Pay Dirt*, 488–494.

32. To understand how the Houston Texans became the NFL's 32nd franchise, see "Finally an Identity," at http://www.cnnsi.com cited 7 September 2000.

33. See Jozsa and Guthrie, *Relocating Teams and Expanding Leagues in Professional Sports*, 142–146.

34. For specific provisions of the NFL's personal conduct policy, see Don Banks, "Taking a Stand Against Violence," at http://www.cnnsi.com cited 1 June 2000; Stefan Fatsis, "Muscling Out Supplemental Income," *Wall Street Journal* (30 November 2001), W14.

35. In the Arena Football League (AFL), players use a regulation-size football. The field is fifty yards long and teams emphasize offense. As its strategy, the NFL views the AFL as a brand-builder and not a minor league. For the business relationships between the NFL and AFL, see Tom Lowry, "Small-Time Football, Big-Time Buzz," *Business Week* (22 October 2001), 128.

36. See John Helyar, "NFL Hopes Offshoot Scores in Europe," *Wall Street Journal* (12 March 1991), B1, B6; "NFL Europe: The Adventure Begins," at http://www.nfleurope.com cited 31 July 2001.

37. In 1998, the World League of American Football became the NFL Europe League. For the league's progress, see "NFL Europe: Commissioner Praises NFL Europe League," at http://www.nfleurope.com cited 3 July 2001; "National Football League," at http://www.nfl.com cited 1 August 2001; "World League Renamed NFL Europe," at http://www.nfl.com cited 11 March 1998.

38. "Was this pond the birthplace of hockey?" In Windsor, Nova Scotia, a dispute exists between residents about where ice hockey originated. Some people claim the first game played occurred in the early 1840s on a pond owned by Howard Dill. New evidence suggests the game began on another body of water a thousand yards from Dill's pond, which is located on his seventy-five-acre pumpkin farm. The body of water is the property of the Atlantic Baptist Senior Citizen's Homes. Three local historians uncovered a passage in a novel that " . . . boys from Kings Edgehill School . . . could often be heard hollerin' and whoopin' like mad with pleasure while playing hurley on the long pond behind the school." For a report on this dispute, see Susanne Craig, "A Great Hockey Fight Rivets Nova Scotia and Two Old Gents," *Wall Street Journal* (23 January 2002), A1, A8.

39. The origin and history of the NHL is described in several sources. See James Quirk and Rodney D. Fort, *Pay Dirt*, 327–332; Frank G. Menke, *The Encyclopedia of Sports*, 666–668; John Davidson and John Steinbreder, *Hockey For Dummies*, 2nd ed. (Foster City, CA: IDG Books Worldwide, Inc., 2000); "National Hockey League," at http://www.nhl.com cited 1 August 2001; "NHL History," at http://www.nhl.com cited 30 March 2000.

40. Frank G. Menke, *The Encyclopedia of Sports*, 665–667; "Stanley Cup Dynasties," at http://www.nhl.com cited 29 November 2001; "The Stanley Cup," at http://www.nhl.com cited 29 November 2001.

41. In a 31 May 2001 memorandum, the NHL provided the total games and attendance for the 1960–1961 through 1999–2000 regular seasons and playoffs. For the NHL team locations and performances, see *The World Almanac and Book of Facts*, 1951–2001.

42. See Dan McGraw, "Big League Troubles," 45–46.

43. Besides the sale of these clubs, in June 1999 the NHL's Board of Governors approved the disposition of the Washington Capitals by the original owner Abe Pollin to a group headed by American Online Inc. executive Ted Leonsis. For more details about these transactions, see "NHL Hockey," at http://www.infoplease.com cited 12 April 2000; Stefan Fatsis and Kara Swisher, "Group Led by AOL's Leonsis to Acquire NHL's Capitals and Other Sports Stakes," *Wall Street Journal* (13 May 1999), A8.

44. Petti Fong, "Canada: Penny-Wise, Franchise-Foolish," *Business Week* (27 March 2000), 70; "Alberta Approves Lottery to Help Struggling NHL Teams," at http://www.

yahoo.com cited 19 June 2001; Cliff Mehrtens, "Player Promotions a Fact of Life in Leagues Such as ECHL," *Charlotte Observer* (27 January 2002), 10F.

45. See John Davidson and John Steinbreder, *Hockey for Dummies,* 59–66; "About the American Hockey League," at http://www.monarchshockey.com cited 29 November 2001.

46. Some leagues have adopted an alternative business model of professional sports team ownership. See Stefan Fatsis, "New Leagues Go for Central Ownership," *Charlotte Observer* (27 July 1997), B1, B2; John Davidson and John Steinbreder, *Hockey for Dummies,* 58; "Media Ownership of Teams," at http://www.resonator.com cited 20 November 2001; "2000 Inside the Ownership of Professional Sports Teams," at http://www.teammarketing.com cited 20 November 2001.

47. See Davidson and Steinbreder, *Hockey for Dummies,* 59; Cliff Mehrtens, "Checkers Not Lone Choice," *Charlotte Observer* (13 March 2002), 2C.

Chapter 2

Teams

The business success, fan base and economic outlook of the AL, NL, NBA, NFL and NHL primarily depend on the competitiveness, entertainment value and ownership quality of the member teams that coexist within each league. As discussed in Chapter 1, when a sports league agrees to amend any of its current bylaws and policies the decision will inevitably influence the performances of coaches, managers, players and teams, and the short- and long-term strategies of the respective franchise owners. For example, at league meetings to consider the adoption of a luxury tax, realignment of divisions, revisions to playoff system, sale of a franchise, and requests for team relocation, there are generally disputes and perhaps heated debates among the various owners because of the uncertainty and outcome if a proposal is approved, discarded or postponed. In short, as a league member each owner evaluates how a decision will impact his or her team and the performance of the opponents' club when a law, rule or standard is adopted, revised or tabled. Given this organizational process and to determine how sports teams were formed, the early history of clubs in professional baseball, basketball, football and hockey are initially discussed in the chapter. Then, a review of each league's most successful franchises from the 1950s through the 1990s is presented.

TEAM HISTORY

Prior to the late 1800s, the games in amateur and professional sports were frequently established on an ad hoc basis. That is, local players met and organized into groups to compete against each other for fun and then, to determine a winner. Eventually, formal team organizations emerged in each professional sport. For instance, some historians assert that ice hockey clubs first gathered in England during the 1820s and then fifty years later in Canada. Originally, a Canadian hockey team included nine players. In the 1880s, however, the preference for a smaller squad emerged when a team showed up with two men short at the Montreal Winter Carnival. Because of the team's obligation to participate at the Carnival, the standard size of a hockey club declined from nine to seven players. On a team, the number and position of these athletes consisted of three forwards, two defensemen, one goaltender and one rover. The rover had the option of skating ahead to attack the opponent or falling behind to defend his team's goal. Thus, the composition and development of teams evolved in professional ice hockey before those that formed in professional baseball, basketball and football.[1]

Before the 1840s, baseball games were played under haphazard rules, and teams arbitrarily ranged from eleven to twenty players. Then, in 1842 each club agreed to field twelve players who were called "scouts." These athletes consisted of one thrower, catcher, assistant catcher, infield rover and outfield rover, and four infielders and three outfielders. In 1845, the Knickerbockers Baseball Club in New York became the sport's first organized team. That year, a draftsman and surveyor named Alexander Cartwright designed a square playing field that now is shaped as a diamond. Following Cartwright's design and the adoption of standard rules recommended by a committee of experienced players, several teams organized and played the first baseball game on a diamond-shaped field in 1846. Three years later, the New York Knickerbockers Baseball Club became the first team to wear uniforms during practice. Between the late 1850s and early 1880s, various non-amateur teams joined the National Association of Professional Baseball Players and later the American Association and National League, which had each organized and played a season schedule. During that era, the popular baseball teams in the United States included the Brooklyn Atlantics, Chicago Unions, Cincinnati Red Stockings, New York Mutuals, Philadelphia Athletics and the Haymakers of Troy, New York. In short, by the late 1880s to the early 1890s the structure of the professional baseball leagues and their member teams had been established.[2]

During an intercollegiate football game between Princeton and Rutgers in November 1869, the teams played according to modified London Football Association regulations, which were soccer rules. By 1876, when the team sport of rugby had become more prominent than soccer, some primitive football regulations were first adopted. These rules related to games and team strategies such as blocking, downs, points, signals, tackling and touchdowns. In the early-to-mid-1890s, the Pittsburgh Athletic Club and Allegheny Athletic Association began to schedule football games, which were intensely competitive. Then, in 1897 a team called the Latrobe Athletic Association became the first football organization to play an entire season with only professional athletes. In 1899, an independent professional football team named the Morgan Athletic Club was founded on the south side of Chicago. Later, this club became known as the Normals, and renamed the Racine Cardinals, and eventually the Chicago Cardinals, St. Louis Cardinals and Phoenix Cardinals. This organization, currently nicknamed the Arizona Cardinals, is the oldest uninterrupted operation in professional football.[3]

Sports historians are uncertain about the precise date and location of the first professional basketball game and the respective teams that competed. Five years after James Naismith invented basketball in 1891, some researchers believe that the first professional game was played in Trenton, New Jersey. A second but less substantiated claim placed the first game at Herkimer, New York, in 1893. According to historians who speculate, in both games the teams were undisciplined and unorganized, and the players received only a small amount of expense money. After the mid-1890s, when the number of professional basketball leagues rapidly organized in the Midwest and Eastern United States, the more popular teams developed an identity and established a fan base. In various leagues, for several seasons the Cleveland Rosenblums, New York Celtics, New York Whirlwinds, Renaissance Big Five and Troy Trojans were recognized as the outstanding basketball teams in the nation. Interestingly, the Celtics gained stature because it won 90 percent of its 150 regular season games and attracted large crowds especially in Cleveland, Ohio, and New York City.[4]

Besides the aforementioned professional basketball clubs, in 1927 Abe Saperstein, a stout, short man with foresight and keen marketing talents, founded the Harlem Globetrotters. Although not affiliated with any established league, the Globetrotters had become an international basketball attraction by the early 1930s. Formed from a humble background by Saperstein, the team consists of African-American players who apply their unique athletic skills, court antics and humor in games to entertain fans throughout the world. The late Wilt Chamberlain, a two-time All-American at Kansas University and a superstar for the NBA's Los Angeles Lakers and Philadelphia/San Francisco Warriors, played for the Globetrotters and promoted the team with his ability to rebound errant shots and score points seemingly without effort. Because of its history and tradition, the club and its extraordinary players continue to barnstorm and perform for audiences on every continent.[5]

This concludes the early history of how professional teams in each sports league were formed and developed. After a brief update of pre-1950 teams and the league reorganizations that occurred after 1950, the most successful clubs in selected seasons are identified and ranked against their peers.

During one or more seasons in the 1940s, within each of the five professional leagues there were well-known franchises. The teams included the Boston Red Sox, Cleveland Indians and Detroit Tigers in the AL; Brooklyn Dodgers, Cincinnati Reds and St. Louis Cardinals in the NL; Philadelphia Warriors, Rochester Royals and Syracuse Nationals in the NBA; Chicago Bears, Green Bay Packers and New York Giants in the NFL; and the Detroit Red Wings, Montreal Canadiens and New York Rangers in the NHL. These and other celebrated clubs were among the sports enterprises that represented their respective leagues when the season began in 1950. That season there were eight teams each in the AL and NL, seventeen in the NBA, thirteen in the NFL and six in the NHL. Combined, a total of fifty-two clubs existed in the five leagues. Then, the championship teams were the AL New York Yankees, NL Philadelphia Phillies, NBA

Minneapolis Lakers, NFL Cleveland Browns and NHL Toronto Maple Leafs. Fifty years later, the proportions of the fifty-two teams that had remained at their home sites were 63 percent (10) of the original franchises in baseball, 12 percent (2) in basketball, 62 percent (8) in football and 100 percent (6) in ice hockey. Despite successful and unsuccessful seasons, and ownership sales, by 2000 this group of twenty-six, 1950-based teams had gradually established a relationship with their hometown fans. While playing their home games in new or renovated arenas or stadiums, the teams have gradually emerged as mainstream businesses and well-recognized sports organizations in their respective communities.[6]

As members of professional leagues, which of the numerous clubs in each sport competed at the highest level and dominated their rivals between 1950 and 2000? To answer that question, in ten-year increments the performances of the best teams in each league will be illustrated, showcased and ranked. Besides being informative and interesting to highlight, a historical examination of team performances exposes how the successful franchises have endured despite changes in coaches, managers, players and owners, division or conference realignments, and revisions in game and league rules and standards. However, before an analysis of team performances is undertaken, a brief review of how each sports league has been realigned is presented.

From 1903 through 1968, a baseball club won its league pennant, then played in the World Series. Beginning in 1969, the AL and NL were each divided into two six-team divisions. In MLB, therefore, for the first time an opportunity was created for clubs to win division and league titles and the World Series in a single season. Organized as the Eastern, Western and/or Central Divisions since 1950, the NBA was subdivided into four divisions and two conferences to begin the 1970–1971 season. Thus, after the regular season ended the basketball teams that were division winners qualified for the playoffs in order to compete for a conference title and then for the league championship. In the NFL, the American and National Football Conferences were established for the 1950 season. Three seasons later, the Eastern and Western Conferences replaced the American and National Football Conferences, respectively. Then, beginning in the 1967 season teams were placed in either the Capitol or Century Division of the Eastern Conference, or the Coastal or Central Division of the Western Conference. (The American Football League, meanwhile, reorganized from two four-team conferences in the 1960 season to two five-team divisions in the 1968 season, which was its next-to-last season as an independent league.) After the merger in 1970, the NFL established an Eastern, Central and Western Division each in the American and National Football Conferences (AFC and NFC). The NFL's realignment meant that in the postseason each division champion had to win a conference title to qualify for and compete in the Super Bowl, which initially became the league's championship game in 1967. In professional hockey, the twelve NHL teams were placed in either the East or West Division as of the 1967–1968 season. Then, for the 1974–1975 season the eighteen NHL clubs entered into either the Lester Patrick or Conn Smythe Division of the Clarence Campbell Conference, or the Charles F. Adams or James Norris Division of the Prince of Wales Conference. Thereafter, each season the hockey teams that won division titles qualified for the playoffs to compete for a conference championship and if successful, to play for the Stanley Cup, which has been awarded to the league champion since 1927. In general, from 1967 to 1975 inclusive, the teams in each sports league were reassigned to divisions and conferences because of expansion, organizational redevelopment, and to stimulate interteam rivalries between franchises located in the same or nearby geographic region.[7]

In the chronology of seasons that follows, from the 1950s to 1990s inclusive, the achievements of the best performing teams in each sports league are identified, ranked and described. During some ten-season periods, two teams from one league tied in rank if their performances were similar and clearly superior to the other clubs in winning division and/or conference titles, and league championships. Certainly, there were major and minor differences in the number of league teams and playoff games and in the regular season schedules and structures of divisions and conferences during various years and decades. Furthermore, no formula or method has been perfected to measure and compare the relative performances of the outstanding teams in MLB with those in the NBA, NFL and NHL. Nevertheless, a discussion of how the superior clubs performed in a given sport, compared with the outstanding teams in the other sports will reveal the successful tenure and league power of individual franchises. In sum, this analysis exposes the short- and long-term competitive imbalances that existed in each league during each of the five decades of competition. For some teams, the total period amounted to fifty years of playing in a league that originated with the 1950 season.

SEASONS

1950–1959

Ranked and ordered by league from first to fifth place, in the 1950s the top-performing teams were the NHL Montreal Canadiens, AL New York Yankees, NFL Cleveland Browns, NBA Boston Celtics and Minneapolis Lakers (tie), and the NL Brooklyn/Los Angeles Dodgers. Located in a mid-sized market, the Canadiens, coached by Dick Irvin and Hector "Toe" Blake, and led by Bernie Geoffrion, Jean Beliveau, Henri Richard and Maurice "Rocket" Richard, qualified for each playoff in the ten seasons and won five Stanley Cups with the first championship in 1953 and the second in 1956. One year later, for $5 million brewery owners Hartland and Thomas Molson acquired 60 percent of the Canadian Arena Company, the firm that controlled the team and Montreal Forum. Apparently undeterred by this ownership transaction, the club won Stanley Cups in 1957, 1958 and 1959. Besides the high caliber performances of the Canadiens, the Detroit Red Wings finished first in the regular seasons from 1950 to 1954, and proceeded to win Stanley Cups in 1950, 1952, 1954 and 1955.

Following the Canadiens and Red Wings in performances were the Toronto Maple Leafs who claimed one Stanley Cup, while the Boston Bruins appeared in eight playoffs, and the Chicago Blackhawks and New York Rangers in three.[8]

Nearly as successful as the Canadiens, during the 1950s the large-market New York Yankees won eight AL pennants and six World Series championships. Managed by a strategist, Casey Stengel, the club's star players were pitchers Allie Reynolds, Bob Turley, Don Larsen, Bobby Shantz and Whitey Ford, and sluggers Mickey Mantle, Tony Kubek and Yogi Berra. The Cleveland Indians in 1954 and the Chicago White Sox in 1959 challenged the Yankees, when in those years each club won the AL pennant but was defeated in the World Series by a superior NL team. Since the teams failed to win a title in the 1950s, and because of low win-loss percentages, the Boston Red Sox, Detroit Tigers, Philadelphia/Kansas City Athletics, St. Louis Browns/Baltimore Orioles and the Washington Senators were the least competitive clubs in the AL.

Although the team's accomplishments were slightly inferior to those of the Canadiens and Yankees, during the 1950s Paul Brown coached the small-market Cleveland Browns to seven division titles and three league championships, which were attained in 1950, 1954 and 1955. Even though the Browns' franchise was sold to a syndicate for $600,000 three years after entering the NFL in 1950, players such as place kicker Lou Groza, quarterback Otto Graham, running back Jim Brown and pass receivers Dante Levelli and Mac Speedie excelled. Other league champions who competed against the Browns in various seasons were the Detroit Lions, Los Angeles Rams and New York Giants. Because of inept coaches, owners and/or players, during the 1950s the Chicago Cardinals, Green Bay Packers, Philadelphia Eagles, Pittsburgh Steelers, San Francisco 49ers and Washington Redskins failed to win a conference title. These clubs won few games in the regular seasons, and several of the franchises incurred significant operating losses such as the Cardinals and Packers.[9]

Ranked after the Canadiens, Yankees and Browns in performances, and tied for fourth place were two NBA teams, the large-market Boston Celtics and the small-market Minneapolis Lakers. In total, these well-coached basketball clubs each won seven conference titles and six league championships. After the Boston Garden Corporation sold the Celtics in 1951 to the franchise's president, Walter Brown, Coach Red Auerbach formed a basketball dynasty with Bill Russell at center, Ed Macauley and Tom Heinson at the forwards, and Bill Sharman and Bob Cousy at the guard positions. In the early 1950s, the Lakers dominated the NBA standings and won three championships with Coach John Kundla and All-Pro players such as George Mikan, Slater Martin and Vern Mikkelson. However, because of its market size and mismanagement the team experienced financial problems in Minneapolis that resulted in ownership transfers in 1954, 1956, 1957 and 1958. After two years on financial probation with the league, in 1960 the club relocated to Los Angeles. In addition to the Celtics and Lakers, the Philadelphia Warriors, Rochester Royals, St. Louis Hawks and Syracuse Nationals also won conference titles and NBA championships in the 1950s. Meanwhile, the inferior basketball franchises in several cities such as Anderson, Baltimore, Chicago, Denver, Indianapolis, Sheybogan, Washington, D.C., and Waterloo terminated operations.[10]

The NL Brooklyn/Los Angeles Dodgers were less successful at winning titles than the Canadiens, Yankees, Browns, Celtics and Lakers. Between 1950 and 1957, the Dodgers claimed four league championships while in Brooklyn and won the 1955 World Series by beating the New York Yankees in seven games. One year after moving to Los Angeles, in 1959 the club won the NL pennant and in six games defeated the Chicago White Sox in the World Series. Managed by Chuck Dressen and Walt Alston, the Dodgers' key players were batting champion and outfielder Carl Furillo, pitchers Carl Erskine, Don Newcombe, Joe Black and Sal Maglie, Most Valuable Player (MVP) catcher Roy Campanella, and home run champion Duke Snider who also was an excellent outfielder. In the 1950s, the Dodgers' most fierce competitors, and the NL champions were the Braves who had relocated from Boston to Milwaukee in 1953, the Giants who had moved from New York to San Francisco in 1958, and the Philadelphia Phillies. Conversely, the Chicago Cubs, Cincinnati Reds, Pittsburgh Pirates and St. Louis Cardinals disappointed their fans by not winning an NL pennant in the 1950s. And, the Braves, Dodgers, Giants and Phillies outplayed these clubs. The next period for which team performances in each sports league are measured is from the 1960 to 1969 season inclusive.

1960–1969

Based on performances, seven elite teams rated from first to fifth among all franchises in the professional sports leagues during the 1960s. The teams consisted of the NBA Boston Celtics, NFL Green Bay Packers, NHL Montreal Canadiens and Toronto Maple Leafs (tie), AL New York Yankees and the NL St. Louis Cardinals and Los Angeles Dodgers (tie). Extending their outstanding seasons from the late 1950s, the Celtics, led by four-time MVP center Bill Russell, guards K.C. and Sam Jones, and small forward John Havelicek, won six NBA Eastern Conference titles and nine league championships. When the best players aged or retired in the late 1960s, the performances of the Celtics moderately diminished. Two seasons before Celtics Coach Red Auerback resigned to become the franchise's general manager, the Philadelphia 76ers won Eastern Conference titles in 1966 and 1967 as did the Baltimore Bullets in 1969. One year later, the New York Knickerbockers, led by Coach Red Holzman defeated the Los Angeles Lakers to win the league championship. Despite the Celtics' success, after Walter Brown died in 1964 the franchise was resold in 1965 for $3 million to Ruppert Knickerbocker, in 1968 to the Ballantine Brewing Company for $6 million and in 1969 to the Investors Funding Company for an unknown amount. If the six NBA expansion teams of the 1960s are excluded, because of inferior coaches and players, the well-established Cincinnati Royals and Detroit Pistons failed to win division titles in the 1960s.

In the NFL, between 1960 and 1969 Hall of Fame Coach Vince Lombardi and All-Pro players Bart Starr, Jim Taylor and Paul Hornung elevated the small-market Green Bay Packers to one Central Division title, six Western Conference crowns and five league championships, which included Super Bowl I in 1967 and II in 1968. To become champions, the Packers had to compete against other outstanding NFL clubs such as the Baltimore Colts, Cleveland Browns, Dallas Cowboys, Minnesota Vikings, New York Giants and Philadelphia Eagles. Otherwise, in the 1960s the Cardinals, who had relocated from Chicago to St. Louis in 1960, claimed no NFL titles nor did the league's two expansion teams, which were the Atlanta Falcons and New Orleans Saints.

The excellent achievements of the Celtics and Packers aside, during the 1960s the premier teams in the NHL were unanimously the Montreal Canadiens and Toronto Maple Leafs. Each club appeared in at least eight playoffs and won four Stanley Cups. Four outstanding players of the Canadiens were Claude Provost, Jacques Laperriere, Yvan Cournoyer and Serge Savard who each played one or more seasons for coaches "Toe" Blake and Claude Ruel. Likewise, the Maple Leafs became champions because of the memorable play of Johnny Bower, Marcel Pronovost, Andy Bathgate and Terry Sawchuk, and due to the coach and general manager, Punch Imlach. Because of improved performances, the Chicago Blackhawks finally won a Stanley Cup in 1961 after not winning a division title in the 1950s and a league championship since 1938. Meanwhile, between 1967 and 1969 the Detroit Red Wings, New York Rangers and the six NHL expansion teams won zero division titles in league competition.

In addition to the Celtics, Packers, Canadiens and Maple Leafs, the AL New York Yankees and the NL St. Louis Cardinals and Los Angeles Dodgers also performed superbly throughout the 1960s. Because of five consecutive league pennants from 1960 through 1964, and back-to-back World Series victories in 1961 and 1962, the Yankees were marginally more successful than the Cardinals and Dodgers, who each won two World Series but two fewer league championships than the Yankees. The Yankees' all-star players such as Elston Howard, Mickey Mantle, Roger Maris and Tom Tresh were expertly coached by Casey Stengel and Ralph Houk, and then by Yogi Berra in 1964. The other major contenders in the AL during this era included the Baltimore Orioles and Detroit Tigers, which each won one World Series championship game.

In the NL, the Cardinals excelled primarily because of Cy Young Award pitcher Bob Gibson and sluggers Ken Boyer and Orlando Cepeda. Meanwhile, the Dodgers successfully competed against the other NL clubs with strikeout pitchers Don Drysdale and Sandy Koufax, and with sluggers Frank Howard, Jim Lefebvre and Tommy Davis. During various seasons in the 1960s, the World Series champion New York Mets and Pittsburgh Pirates also played competitively, while the Chicago Cubs and Philadelphia Phillies, and an expansion team, the Houston Astros, played poorly. In sum, from 1950 through 1969 several teams were dominant in their respective sports. To determine whether the trend in team performances would continue after the 1960s, the outstanding clubs in the 1970s are featured next followed by the excellent teams in the 1980s and 1990s.

1970–1979

Based on the titles and championships won in their respective sports leagues, the seven top-ranked teams during these ten seasons were the NHL Montreal Canadiens, NFL Pittsburgh Steelers, AL Oakland Athletics, NL Cincinnati Reds and Pittsburgh Pirates (tie), and the NBA Los Angeles Lakers and Boston Celtics (tie). Similar to the dynasties established in the 1956–1960 and 1965–1969 seasons inclusive, the Canadiens played exceptional hockey and won seven divisions and four conference titles, and six Stanley Cups. Even though the franchise and Montreal Forum were sold by the Canadian Arena Company in 1971 for $15 million to Placements Rondelle Ltd. and Baton Broadcasting Ltd., and then resold seven years later to Molson Breweries, Coach Scotty Bowman and team leaders Guy Lafleur, Ken Dryden, Mario Tremblay and Yvan Cournoyer had formed a dynasty in the league. Remarkably, the club won four consecutive Stanley Cups in fifty-eight games from 1976 through 1979. Besides the Canadiens, the Boston Bruins and Philadelphia Flyers also had played competitive ice hockey when each team won two league championships. During the 1970s, the New York Islanders, one of ten expansion teams, won its first of four consecutive Stanley Cups in the 1979–1980 season.[11]

Ranked behind the Canadiens, the second best sports team in the 1970s was the NFL Pittsburgh Steelers. After 1973, the club won six Central Divisions and four each American Football Conference (AFC) titles and Super Bowls. With a strong defense anchored by Jack Ham, Jack Lambert, "Mean" Joe Greene and Mel Blount, and an offense that featured Super Bowl MVPs quarterback Terry Bradshaw, running back Franco Harris and wide receiver Lynn Swann, on average the Steelers outplayed their talented opponents. These clubs included the AFC Denver Broncos, Houston Oilers, Miami Dolphins and Oakland Raiders, and the National Football Conference (NFC) Dallas Cowboys, Los Angeles Rams and Minnesota Vikings. Meanwhile, crafty Tom Landry coached the Dallas Cowboys to seven Eastern Divisions and five NFC titles, and victories in Super Bowls VI in 1972 at Tulane Stadium and XII in 1978 at the Louisiana Superdome. The Steelers and Cowboys aside, the other Super Bowl champions in the 1970s were the AFC's Baltimore Colts, Kansas City Chiefs, Miami Dolphins and Oakland Raiders.

In MLB, besides five consecutive Western Division titles and three league pennants the AL Oakland Athletics won three back-to-back World Series in the 1970s. Coaches Dick Williams and Al Dark inspired pitchers Catfish Hunter, Dennis Eckersley and Vida Blue, and home run leader Reggie Jackson to excel and defeat Eastern Division champions such as the Baltimore Orioles, Boston Red Sox and Detroit Tigers. When the Athletics' championship reign ended in 1975, the New York Yankees proceeded to win three consecutive division titles and AL championships and the World Series in 1977 and 1978. In the NL, during the 1970s the Pittsburgh Pirates in the Eastern Division and the Cincinnati Reds in the Western Division played excellent baseball. Each club won six division titles and two World Series. The Pirates offense depended on MVPs Willie Stargell and Dave Parker, and the Reds on MVPs George Foster, Joe Morgan, Johnny Bench and Pete Rose.

After the Canadiens, Steelers, Athletics, Pirates and Reds, tied for fifth place as the outstanding teams of the 1970s were the NBA Los Angeles Lakers and Boston Celtics. In winning five divisions and four conference titles, and two league championships, the Lakers' well-renowned players included guard Jerry West, forward Elgin Baylor, and centers Wilt Chamberlain and Kareem Abdul-Jabbar. Likewise, the Celtics relied on shooting guard Charlie Scott, small forward John Havlicek, center Dave Cowens and power forward Paul Silas to win five division and two conference titles, and two league championships. Besides the Lakers and Celtics, during the 1970s six other NBA teams—Golden State Warriors, Milwaukee Bucks, New York Knickerbockers, Portland Trail Blazers, Seattle SuperSonics, and Washington Bullets—won league championships, which indicates that greater competitive balance existed in the NBA in the 1970s than in the 1950s and 1960s.

1980–1989

Subsequent to the performances of the top-ranked NHL Montreal Canadiens in the 1950s and 1970s, and based on division and conference titles and league championships won, the dominant sports team in the 1980s was the NHL Edmonton Oilers. Besides first-place finishes to win six divisions and six conference titles, the Oilers ended the decade with five Stanley Cup championships. Coaches Glen Sather and John Muckler and players such as Paul Coffey, Jari Kurri, Mark Messier and Wayne Gretzky led the club to its world championships, especially from 1984 to 1989. The Oilers' success was impressive given that the franchise had joined the NHL in 1979 when the World Hockey League disbanded. Besides the Oilers, from the 1980–1981 to 1989–1990 seasons the other Stanley Cup champions included the Calgary Flames, Montreal Canadiens and New York Islanders. The Islanders won Stanley Cups in 1980 through 1983 when the club lost only eighty-eight regular season games and participated in merely seventy-eight playoff games during the four seasons. Mike Bossy, Bryan Trottier and Ken Morrow were excellent Islanders' players, and Al Arbour coached each championship team. Because of the ten expansion teams that joined the NHL in the 1970s, more hockey clubs shared division titles, and parity slightly improved in the 1980s, relative to the 1950s, 1960s and 1970s when either the Detroit Red Wings, Montreal Canadiens or Toronto Maple Leafs dominated the league.[12]

When the NBA Los Angeles Lakers won nine divisions, seven conference titles and four league championships, it ranked behind the Edmonton Oilers as the second most impressive professional sports team of the 1980s. To prevent the all-time points NBA leader and Lakers' center Abdul-Jabbar from being double-teamed on offense, guards Ervin "Magic" Johnson and Bryon Scott, and forwards James Worthy and Michael Cooper cleverly passed the basketball and allowed their teammates to score. When Abdul-Jabbar, Johnson and Cooper played team defense, the Lakers dominated other top-notch NBA teams of the decade such as the Boston Celtics, Detroit Pistons, Milwaukee Bucks and Philadelphia 76ers.

Because the club won fewer division titles and league championships than the Edmonton Oilers and Los Angeles Lakers, the NFL San Francisco 49ers were rated as the third best sports team of the 1980s. Coached by Bill Walsh, 49ers' quarterback Joe Montana, wide receiver Jerry Rice and cornerback Ronnie Lott kept the team in contention for a division title each season. The 49ers won NFC championships and Super Bowls in the 1981, 1984, 1988 and 1989 seasons. During this era, other Super Bowl champions included the Chicago Bears, New York Giants, Oakland/Los Angeles Raiders (twice), Pittsburgh Steelers and Washington Redskins (twice). Thus, during the 1980s the San Francisco 49ers replaced the Pittsburgh Steelers as the best club in professional football.

Similar to the 1960s, the large-market Los Angeles Dodgers and the small-market St. Louis Cardinals dominated the NL in the 1980s. These teams won a combined seven division titles, five league championships and three World Series. Besides the NL Dodgers and Cardinals, the AL's small-market clubs in Baltimore, Oakland, Kansas City and Minnesota each won a World Series championship. In short, from the 1960s to 1980s inclusive four small-market teams—Cincinnati Reds, Oakland Athletics, Pittsburgh Pirates and St. Louis Cardinals—and one large-market team—Los Angeles Dodgers—were the outstanding clubs in MLB. In the AL, because the team won more division titles and league championships than any other club, the Oakland Athletics was the top-performing franchise in the 1980s. The best players on the Athletics' rosters were sluggers Mark McGwire and Jose Canseco, and pitchers Bob Welch and Dave Stewart. If the Athletics' performances are included, nine different AL teams won a league pennant and five succeeded in the World Series. Because of the diversity of teams in the distribution of league championships, during the 1980s the balance in playing strengths and parity improved in the AL.

1990–1999

The outstanding teams of this period, ranked by sport from first to fifth place, were the NBA Chicago Bulls, NFL Dallas Cowboys, NL Atlanta Braves, NHL Detroit Red Wings and Pittsburgh Penguins (tie), and the AL New York Yankees. The large-market Chicago Bulls won six NBA division and conference titles, and league championships. Coach Phil Jackson motivated superstar guard Michael Jordan and forwards Scottie Pippen and Dennis Rodman to win championships by playing superior defense. The NBA teams with high-powered offenses such as the Los Angeles Lakers, Phoenix Suns, Portland Trail Blazers and Utah Jazz struggled to score points when the Bulls played team defense. The Detroit Pistons, Houston Rockets and San Antonio Spurs also won the NBA Playoffs. In contrast, because of inferior coaches and players and owner mismanagement, twelve NBA clubs failed to win a division or conference title in the 1990s.

Based on winning five divisions and three conference titles, and Super Bowls XXVII in 1993 at the Rose Bowl, XXVIII in 1994 at the Georgia Dome, and XXX in 1996 at the Sun Devil Stadium, the second most impressive professional team of the 1990s was the Dallas Cowboys. To complement a brilliant defense, an alliance that consisted of quarterback Troy Aikman, running back Emmitt Smith and wide receiver Michael Irvin starred on offense. Coaches Jimmy Johnson and Barry Switzer challenged the great Cowboy athletes and teams to become world champions. Other football teams besides the Cowboys also excelled. Led by All-Pro quarterback John Elway and running back Terrell Davis, the NFL Denver Broncos ranked second in performance to the Cowboys. In the 1990s, the Broncos proceeded to win three divisions, four conference titles and consecutive Super Bowls in 1998 and 1999. In contrast to the Cowboys and Broncos, the Philadelphia Eagles and Phoenix/Arizona Cardinals performed poorly and did not win a division or conference title during the period.

In the NL, the Atlanta Braves won eight Eastern Division titles, five league pennants and one World Series in the 1990s. The Braves' Cy Young Award recipients Greg Maddux, John Smoltz and Tom Glavine were outstanding pitchers who, on average, each held his opponents to less than four runs per game. Because of excellent pitching and timely hitting, the Braves won the division title each season except in 1990 when the Cincinnati Reds were league champions and in 1994 when a player's strike prematurely ended the season. During the period, the NL New York Mets, Chicago Cubs, former AL Milwaukee Brewers, and the expansion Colorado Rockies and Florida Marlins failed to win a division title.

Ranked after the Bulls, Cowboys and Braves, and tied for fourth place in performance among all sports franchises were the NHL Detroit Red Wings and Pittsburgh Penguins. In the 1990s, each team won five division titles and two Stanley Cups. The outstanding players for each team consisted of defenseman Paul Coffey and defensive forward Sergei Federov for the Red Wings and points leaders Jaromir Jagr and Mario Lemieux for the Penguins. The Red Wings and Penguins aside, the other hockey clubs that played well and frequently won games included the Colorado Avalanche, Dallas Stars, New Jersey Devils and New York Rangers. Meanwhile, the Edmonton Oilers, New York Islanders and six expansion teams— Anaheim Mighty Ducks, Atlanta Thrashers, Florida Panthers, Nashville Predators, San Jose Sharks and Tampa Bay Lightning—failed to win division titles during the period. Due to competition, however, parity in the NHL improved in the 1990s because proportionately more teams shared the division and conference titles, and the Stanley Cup Championships than in each of the previous four decades.

Ranked in fifth place among the sports teams of the 1990s, the New York Yankees excelled by winning three division titles and AL pennants, and the World Series in 1996, 1998 and 1999. Manager Joe Torre inspired shortstop Derek Jeter, outfielders Bernie Williams and Paul O'Neill, pitchers Andy Pettitte, Jimmy Key and Mariano Rivera, and their Yankee teammates to outperform the other AL teams. Following the Yankees in performances were the Toronto Blue Jays who, from 1991 to 1993 won three division titles, two AL championships and two consecutive World Series. The Blue Jays' manager, Cito Gaston, cleverly used several skilled players such as twenty-game winner Jack Morris, batting champion John Olerud and World Series MVPs Pat Borders and Paul Molitor. Except for the Anaheim Angels, Detroit Tigers and Kansas City Athletics, and an expansion team, the Tampa Bay Devil Rays, during the 1990s eight AL teams won at least one division title, and five clubs claimed a league championship. These results indicate that a moderate distribution of playing strengths existed in the AL since several teams shared titles and became league champions.

Between 1950 and 2000, within the five sports leagues there were three hockey and two NBA teams that ranked the highest in performances by placing first among all teams for a decade of seasons. Alternatively, there were two AL, and two NL clubs and one NBA team that ranked in fifth place per decade. In sum, during fifty years of professional sports the most dominant teams on average played in the NHL, and then in the NFL, NBA, AL and NL. As such, based on the titles won and championship seasons in each league the outstanding teams included the Montreal Canadiens in the NHL, the Dallas Cowboys in the NFL, a tie between the Boston Celtics and Los Angeles Lakers in the NBA, the New York Yankees in the AL, and a tie between the Los Angeles Dodgers and St. Louis Cardinals in the NL. In short, during the majority of seasons the owners of these franchises blended an optimal combination of coaches or managers and players to compete and succeed in their respective sport.

In contrast to the aforementioned superior sports organizations, between 1950 and 1990 there were several teams in each sports league that ranked inferior in performance. During most decades, these clubs finished several seasons with win-loss percentages below .500, qualified for few playoffs and generally did not place in the upper half of their respective division or conference. To improve in performance, some inferior clubs were sold while others relocated to another metropolitan area. As a last resort, a few teams disbanded. Therefore, each decade there were various franchises in each sport that failed to win a division or conference title or a league championship. As depicted in Table A.2 of the Appendix, excluding the 1990s there were nine inferior teams in the AL, thirteen in the NL, ten in the NBA, twenty-one in the NFL and seventeen in the NHL.

Before 1990, the majority of member teams in each league somehow rebounded after a decade of below-average seasons. Then, for one or more seasons these clubs became competitive and won a division or conference title. For example, after ten consecutive seasons without winning a title, the Boston Red Sox in the AL, the St. Louis Cardinals in the NL, the Washington Redskins in the

NFL and the Boston Bruins in the NHL regrouped to win division or conference championships in succeeding years. A small group of teams, however, failed to win a division or conference title during two decades. They were the Detroit Tigers, Philadelphia Athletics/Kansas City Athletics/Kansas City Royals and Washington Senators/Texas Rangers in the AL; the Chicago Cubs, Cincinnati Reds, Montreal Expos and Pittsburgh Pirates in the NL; the Cincinnati Royals/Kansas City-Omaha Kings/Sacramento Kings and Detroit Pistons in the NBA; the Racine/Chicago/St. Louis/Phoenix/Arizona Cardinals, Green Bay Packers, Houston Oilers, New Orleans Saints, New York Jets and Philadelphia Eagles in the NFL; and the Detroit Red Wings, Los Angeles Kings, New York Rangers and the Toronto Maple Leafs in the NHL. Beyond two decades, the NFL Cardinals failed to win titles in the 1950s, 1960s, 1980s and the 1990s. Finally, no club in existence for fifty years, or from 1950 to 1999 inclusive, failed to win at least one division or conference title. (At 10–4, the NFL St. Louis Cardinals won the NFC's Central Division in the 1974 season because the club finished ahead of the Washington Redskins based on a 2–0 head-to-head sweep.)

If the expansion franchises and the former AL and now NL Milwaukee Brewers are excluded, in the 1990s there were twenty-three teams that were unsuccessful at winning their division or conference title in the five sports leagues (Table 2.1). Unless these clubs improve in performance after 2000, their attendance, gate receipts, merchandise sales and local broadcast revenues will lag behind the other league teams. Furthermore, if during the 1990s the inferior teams' morale declined and operating losses accumulated, then beyond 2000 the competitiveness and market value of these franchises will be jeopardized. Therefore, to avoid another decade of poor performances and financial losses, selected franchise owners have tried to upgrade their team's image, status and value. Beginning with the AL, a discussion of each team's strategy and progress follows.

TEAMS

AL

Between 1995 and 1999, the Anaheim—formerly California—Angels accumulated $83 million in operating losses. While struggling to be competitive in the Western Division, the club plays its home games in 45,000-seat Edison International Field of Anaheim, the third eldest stadium in the AL at thirty-six years old. Since installing premium seats and renovating the ballpark in the mid-1990s, the franchise's owner, Walt Disney Company, has increased the players' payroll and marketed the team as a permanent entity of the entertainment scene in Anaheim. These strategies have partially succeeded. In 1997, 1998 and 2000 the Angels' win-loss percentages exceeded .500, and the club's home attendance improved. Indeed, in Chapter 5 of their book, Frank P. Jozsa, Jr. and John J. Guthrie, Jr. rated the team as average based on its performance, attendance and estimated market value.[13]

Despite the burden of $45 million in total operating losses since 1995, Detroit Tigers owner Michael Ilitch reportedly provided $35 million to fund the con-

Table 2.1
Characteristics of Sports Teams Without Titles, by League, 1990 to 1999

League	Team	W-L	WC/P	VA98
AL	California/Anaheim Angels	.445	0	157
	Detroit Tigers	.451	0	137
	Kansas City Royals	.460	0	108
NL	Chicago Cubs	.479	1	204
	Montreal Expos	.487	0	87
	New York Mets	.493	1	193
NBA	Dallas Mavericks	.306	0	119
	Los Angeles Clippers	.332	3	102
	Denver Nuggets	.351	3	110
	Washington Wizards	.372	1	207
	Minnesota Timberwolves	.373	3	119
	Philadelphia 76ers	.390	3	196
	New Jersey Nets	.415	4	157
	Milwaukee Bucks	.418	3	94
	Golden State Warriors	.423	3	130
	Sacramento Kings	.428	3	119
	Detroit Pistons	.502	6	206
	Cleveland Cavaliers	.533	6	161
NFL	Phoenix/Arizona Cardinals	.313	0	231
	Philadelphia Eagles	.521	2	249
NHL	Edmonton Oilers	n.a.	6	67
	New York Islanders	n.a.	2	111
	Winnipeg/Phoenix Coyotes	n.a.	7	87

Notes: The W-L is the club's average win-loss percentage, and the WC/P is the number of seasons each team qualified for a wild-card or playoff game during the 1990s. The VA98 is the franchise's estimated market value in 1998 and the n.a. means not applicable. The Edmonton Oilers earned 72, New York Islanders 66 and the Winnipeg/Phoenix Coyotes 75 points per season during the 1990s. The NHL' ten-season average was 84 points earned.

Source: The World Almanac and Book of Facts (Mahwah, NJ: World Almanac Books, 1991 to 2001); Michael K. Ozanian, "Selective Accounting," *Forbes* (14 December 1998), 124–134.

struction of 40,000-seat, open-air grass Comerica Park, which replaced Tiger Stadium in 2000. Although the club won ten more games in 2000 than in 1999, the Chicago White Sox, Cleveland Indians and Minnesota Twins are tough competitors for the Tigers in the league's Central Division. The Angels and Tigers aside, in the 1990s the Kansas City Royals did not qualify for the AL playoffs. After the completion of renovations to twenty-nine-year-old, 40,000-seat Kauffman Stadium, in 2000 former Wal-Mart Chief Executive Officer David Glass purchased the Royals for $95 million. The team's winning percentage increased from .398 in 1999 to .475 in 2000. Yet, in 2001 the club finished last in the Central Division with a .401 win-loss percentage and twenty-six games behind the Cleveland Indians who won the title. In sum, since 1990 the Angels, Tigers and

Royals have lagged behind their competitors in average win-loss percentages and in winning division titles.[14]

NL

The Wrigley Company, owner of the Chicago Cubs, in July 2001 proposed a $11 million upgrade to 38,000-seat Wrigley Field, which was built in 1914. The upgrade includes expenditures for advertising signs and 2,300 new seats. The team, also, agreed to schedule twelve more night games. In 2001, the club's win-loss percentage improved to .543 because of the low earned run averages of its outstanding pitching staff and the number of home runs and runs batted in achieved by slugger Sammy Sosa. Because of the franchise's popularity and tradition in Chicago, the Cubs' operating losses decreased from $6 million per year in the mid-1990s to $1 million in 2000. Without winning a title since 1989 and a World Series championship since 1908, the team is overdue to top the Central Division soon.[15]

Unless twenty-six-year-old, 46,000-seat Olympic Stadium in Montreal is replaced with a new ballpark that contains an abundance of luxury boxes and club seats, the Expos will lack sufficient revenues to play above .500 and compete for the league's Eastern Division title. During the mid-1990s, the club minimized payroll costs and held operating losses below $2 million per year. After owner Jeffrey Loria boosted payroll from $16 million to $22 million in 2000, the Expos won 42 percent of its games. Nevertheless, in 2001 the team finished twenty games behind the champion Atlanta Braves in the Eastern Division. In the long term, a move from Montreal to Las Vegas in Nevada, Portland in Oregon or Washington, D.C., may be the best option for the franchise. Otherwise, before 2005 the league will disband the club and revoke its charter.[16]

The New York Mets, a large-market franchise, was a wild-card team in 1999 and 2000. That year, the club won the NL pennant but was defeated in the World Series by the New York Yankees in six fan-frenzied games. In 2001, the Mets played well enough to earn a .506 win-loss percentage yet faded to third place in the Eastern Division behind the Atlanta Braves and Philadelphia Phillies. After 2002, the Mets expect to win division and conference titles and increase its market value if the club moves from thirty-eight-year-old, 55,800-seat Shea Stadium into a modern ballpark in the New York City area.[17]

NBA

A Continental Airlines' Arena lease agreement, which the franchise owner signed in 1998 with the New Jersey Sports and Exposition Authority, provides incremental revenues for the New Jersey Nets. The agreement is worth an additional $10 million to $20 million a year to the club because its owner receives 100 percent of the concession receipts and on-site parking fees, 40 percent of the gross revenue from the sale of luxury suites, and at least 30 percent of the revenues from advertising in the new Arena. However, since a .549 winning percentage and playoff appearance in the 1997–1998 season, on average the Nets have won less than 42 percent of their games. In 2000, the club's operating losses totaled $9 million, which valued the franchise at $166 million and ranked it sixteenth in the NBA. Beyond 2000, the Nets will likely remain a mediocre franchise unless majority owner Lewis Katz spends his wealth on veteran players who are underappreciated and on free agents. Led by point guard Jason Kidd, power forward Kenyon Martin and small forward Keith Van Horn in the 2001–2002 season, it appears that the Nets have developed into a competitive team in the Atlantic Division of the Eastern Conference.[18]

In 2001, the Sacramento Kings signed Chris Webber to a seven-year, $122 million contract. Webber, a former University of Michigan All-American, is an NBA star. Because the team appeared in three consecutive playoffs, since 1998 the Kings' estimated market value has increased above $150 million despite annual operating losses that exceeded $5 million per year. The Maloof family gained control of the team in 1999. Brothers Joe and Gavin Maloof are energetic, hardworking and loyal owners, who seek to transform the Kings into a successful and well-respected franchise. If the key players remain injury-free, the club will be competitive in the Pacific Division with a front line of Chris Webber, Peja Stojakovic and Vlade Divac. Indeed, in the 2001–2002 season the Kings were one of the best teams in the league.[19]

Because of excellent coaching and the gradual maturity of each team's star players, in the 2000–2001 season the Dallas Mavericks, Milwaukee Bucks, Orlando Magic and Philadelphia 76ers qualified for the NBA playoffs. That season, the Mavericks won fifty-three games due to the hustle and offensive skills of Steve Nash, Dirk Nowitzki, Michael Finley, and a former Washington Wizards all-star from the University of Michigan, small forward Juwan Howard. Billionaire Mark Cuban, who founded and sold broadcast.com, in 2000 purchased the Mavericks from Ross Perot Jr. Cuban inspires the club with his enthusiasm, especially at home games. Since the team moved from the obsolete Reunion Arena to the state-of-the-art American Airlines Center, the Mavericks have significantly improved its performances to compete for the Western Conference title. For these reasons, the team can challenge its chief Midwest Division rivals who are the Minnesota Timberwolves, San Antonio Spurs and Utah Jazz.[20]

The Bucks' Sam Cassell and Ray Allen, the Magic's Mike Miller and Tracy McGrady, and the 76ers' Allen Iverson and Aaron McKie each propelled his team to a successful 2000–2001 season. If the former Duke University All-American Grant Hill remains healthy for the Magic, he and the other players highlighted will improve their clubs' winning percentage and attendance at, respectively, the fourteen-year-old, 18,000-seat Bradley Center in Milwaukee, the thirteen-year-old, 17,000-seat TD Warehouse Center in Orlando, and the six-year-old, 20,000-seat First Union Center in Philadelphia. Because of a bank merger in fall 2001, the First Union Center will be renamed the Wachovia Center in 2003.

For several seasons, the Denver Nuggets, Golden State Warriors, Los Angeles Clippers, Minnesota Timberwolves and Washington Wizards have been marginal franchises. Since 1990, on average these clubs won less than 40 percent of their games. Moreover, in the majority of years, the teams operated at a loss. However, rather than remain mediocre in performances after 1999, the owners of the Nuggets, Clippers, Timberwolves and Wizards implemented new strategies. For example, in 2000 the Ascent Entertainment Group sold the Nuggets and the 19,000-seat American West Arena for $450 million to E. Stanley Kroenke, the vice-chairman of the NFL St. Louis Rams. Furthermore, Dan Issel, former president of the club, hired former Nuggets' player Kiki Vandeweghe to be general manager in 2001. Furthermore, in 2002 the club signed 6-foot, 11-inch Mengke Bateer who averaged twenty-two points and twelve rebounds for the Beijing Ducks in China. Bateer is the second Chinese player in the NBA. These actions instilled new leadership in the Denver organization and probably will propel the team to compete for a playoff spot in the Midwest Division of the Western Conference.[21]

Former Los Angeles Lakers center Kareem Abdul-Jabbar and retired Boston Celtics guard Dennis Johnson were recently hired as assistant coaches for the Los Angeles Clippers. The team has a nucleus of young players, which includes Elton Brand, Lamar Odom and Michael Olowokandi. In the 1999–2000 season, the Clippers drew 500,000 fans and set a home attendance record at the 19,200-seat Staples Center in Los Angeles. Because of Coaches Abdul-Jabbar and Johnson, and a talented group of inexperienced but athletic players, beyond 2000 perhaps the club will improve its performances and qualify for the playoffs in the Pacific Division of the Western Conference.

The Minnesota Timberwolves and Washington Wizards should also win more games and become above-average clubs. Since 1997, the Timberwolves have played above .500 and qualified for the playoffs. In the 2000–2001 season, the team established a home court record of 30–11 because of players such as Kevin Garnett, Terrell Brandon and Wally Szczerbiak. In 1999, Michael Jordan invested a portion of his wealth in the Wizards' franchise and became the president of basketball operations. Immediately, he reinvigorated the club. When Juwan Howard was traded to the Dallas Mavericks, Jordan revamped the Wizards' offensive and defensive formations. Then, he sold his ownership rights and joined the team in 2001 to play at small forward. In short, especially at the twelve-year-old, 19,000-seat Target Center in Minneapolis, and the five-year-old, 20,700-seat MCI Center in Washington, D.C., respectively, the Timberwolves and Wizards have prepared to improve in performance with their current coaches, ownership and roster of players.

Meanwhile, on average the Detroit Pistons and Cleveland Cavaliers played above .500 in the early to mid-1990s. However, because of coaching mistakes, player injuries and flawed ownership decisions, the performances of the Pistons and Cavaliers have declined since the mid-1990s. Apparently, each club lacked the appropriate personnel to win a division title in the 1990s. If the negative trends in performances continue, these franchises will flounder beyond 2000 without a strategic transformation of coaches and players.

NFL

Relative to the other NFL teams, in 1999 the Arizona Cardinals ranked last in local television and radio revenues. Furthermore, since 1996 the Cardinals' annual profit averaged $3.6 million, an amount far below the $11.6 million that other NFL franchises had earned per year. To escape from Arizona State University's Sun Devil Stadium, and to substantially increase the club's revenues, in November 2000 Maricopa County voters approved Proposition 302, which raises hotel and car rental taxes for thirty years to partially fund the construction of a $334 million, 68,000-seat football stadium. Scheduled to open in Tempe, Arizona, before 2005, the natural grass, retractable roof stadium will be climate controlled and earn for the franchise an estimated $11 million to $15 million a year from advertising, naming rights fees and 88 luxury boxes and 7,000 club seats. The Cardinals pledged $85 million and the Fiesta Bowl $10 million for the construction of the new facility. A team official remarked that the cash flows from the new stadium and the promotion of Dave McGinnis to head coach will make the team more competitive and a contender for a division title before 2006. However, one threat to the project is a Phoenix airport conflict that may scuttle the deal or delay the plan to build a modern stadium for the Cardinals.[22]

The Philadelphia Eagles won Eastern Division titles in the 1980–1981, 1988–1989 and 2001–2002 seasons and an NFC Championship in the 1980–1981 season. In the 1990s, the Eagles had qualified for two playoffs and two wild-card games, and in 2000, earned a playoff berth after finishing 11–5 and second in the Eastern Division behind the NFC champion New York Giants. The team plays its home games in 65,000-seat Veterans Stadium, which was built in 1971. With operating profits of $11 million, in 1999 the team ranked eleventh in the NFL. In 2001, the club opened the NovaCare Complex, which is the franchise's new headquarters and training facility. Furthermore, team owner Jeff Laurie announced that the construction of a new stadium, which contains 117 luxury suites and 9,000 club seats, had begun. Given its large-market location, annual profits and football tradition, the Eagles are an above-average franchise that is capable of winning another conference title by the mid-2000s.[23]

NHL

According to Table 2.1, in the 1990s the Edmonton Oilers, New York Islanders and Winnipeg/Phoenix Coyotes failed to win an NHL title or championship. Why did these performances occur? In 1998, twenty-six NHL franchises were ranked by estimated market value. The Islanders placed thirteenth at $111 million, the Phoenix Coyotes twenty-third at $87 million and the Edmonton Oilers twenty-sixth at $67 million. That year, each club earned operating profits.

Therefore, in part, income and wealth were minor factors in the franchises' performances.

Besides market value and operating income, the history and team records of the three franchises reveal the progress and success of the organizations. In 1972, Roy L. M. Boe paid $6 million to the NHL and a $5 million indemnity to the New York Rangers to place the expansion Islanders in New York. Seven years later, when Boe went bankrupt the team was sold to a syndicate for an unknown price. Since its expansion year, the Islanders won Stanley Cups in 1980 to 1983, finished second in the league to the Edmonton Oilers in 1984, and appeared in two playoffs in the 1990s. During the 1999–2000 season, the club finished last in the Atlantic Division of the Eastern Conference and twenty-sixth in points earned. In the 2001–2002 season, however, the Islanders improved to challenge its division rivals who were the New Jersey Devils, New York Rangers, Philadelphia Flyers and Pittsburgh Penguins.[24]

Ben Haskin and Saul Simken, the original owners of the Winnipeg Jets, in 1972 paid $25,000 for the club to join the World Hockey Association (WHA). After a $250,000 loss in its first season, the team was sold in 1976 to Hockey Ventures, Inc., who then resold it two years later to Bob Graham and Barry Shenkarow for an unknown price. After payments of $6 million to the NHL, and $1.5 million in compensation to the WHA teams that did not join the league, the Jets entered the NHL in 1979. While located in Winnipeg, the Jets failed to win a Stanley Cup or play for the league championship as a final opponent. After playoff defeats in 1992 and 1993, the franchise relocated to Phoenix in 1996. Renamed the Coyotes in Phoenix, as a member of the Pacific Division the team qualified for four consecutive playoff berths from 1996 to 1999 inclusive. Since 1996, the club has played its home games in the America West Arena. This facility is also the home of the NBA Phoenix Suns, AFL Arizona Rattlers, WNBA Phoenix Mercury and the Arizona Sandsharks, a major indoor soccer league franchise. In 1999, Arizona voters approved a referendum to fund an arena stadium district and build the Coyotes a new arena. When constructed, the arena will replace the Alltel Ice Den, which is the team's corporate headquarters and its official training center in the city of Scottsdale. When Steve Ellman's group completed the purchase of the Coyotes in early 2001, Wayne Gretzky became the club's managing partner and the head of hockey operations.[25]

Because it could not survive as an independent league, the WHA disbanded in 1979. For a $6 million entry fee and payments of $1.5 million each to the canceled WHA's Birmingham Bulls and Cincinnati Stingers, the Edmonton Oilers joined the NHL. Led by all-time points leader Wayne Gretzky, outstanding defenseman Paul Coffey and goalie Grant Fuhr, the Oilers became Stanley Cup champions in 1984, 1985, 1987, 1988 and 1990. Even after Gretzky's departure and a decline in attendance, the club appeared in six playoffs in the 1990s but failed to be a final opponent in the Stanley Cup game. In 2001, the provincial government in Alberta, Canada, approved a sports lottery whose proceeds will be shared, after prizes and expenses are distributed, between the Calgary Flames and Edmonton Oilers. Each team will receive approximately C$600,000 per year from the lottery. Nevertheless, despite improvements in the franchises' operations and finances, because of inflated player salaries, minimal growth in home attendance and high-ticket prices, after the 2001 season the Islanders, Coyotes and Oilers will continue to struggle to win an NHL conference title and Stanley Cup.[26]

SUMMARY

Chapter 2 pinpointed how professional team sports formed in each league, and tracked the development, growth and prosperity of selected franchises in the AL, NL, NBA, NFL and NHL. From the 1950s to the 1990s inclusive, the top-performing clubs in each sports league were ranked based on their ability to win division and conference titles, and also league championships as represented by winning a World Series, NBA Playoff, Super Bowl or Stanley Cup. The prominent coaches, managers and players who contributed to the success of these high-quality, productive teams were identified and their performances discussed. Then, the characteristics of each league's low-performing teams were tabled. Based on this data, the circumstances and factors that contributed to each club's dismal play were highlighted. Finally, this chapter concluded by summarizing the history of twenty-three inferior clubs and the significant strategies and tactics that will affect the future competitiveness and progress of these lackluster teams.

Partially based on the information about leagues in Chapter 1 and teams in Chapter 2, the roles and strategies of specific professional sports franchise owners are explored in Chapter 3. That chapter examines the background and conduct of selected owners, and how and why these individuals or groups have influenced their teams' future performances. As such, Chapter 3 provides the basis to predict which franchise owners will be leaders in their respective sports leagues and which clubs are destined to win titles and championships in the mid-2000s.

NOTES

1. You can learn about the formation and early history of the NHL and its teams by reading "NHL History," at http://www.nhl.com cited 30 March 2000. Other NHL and team information was excerpted from John Davidson and John Steinbreder, *Hockey For Dummies*, 2nd ed. (Foster City, CA: IDG Books Worldwide, Inc., 2000), 9–11, 45–47; "NHL Hockey," at http://www.infoplease.com cited 12 April 2000.

2. Frank G. Menke, *The Encyclopedia of Sports*, 5th ed. (Cranbury, NJ: A.S. Barnes, 1975), 52–77.

3. For a year-by-year chronology of how the NFL evolved into its present form, see "History 101: Chronology of How the Modern-Day NFL Came to Pass," at http://www.cnnsi.com cited 1 July 2001. There are detailed dates and facts about NFL games, players, seasons and teams from 1869 to 2001 inclusive in the *NFL 2001 Record & Fact Book* (New York: National Football League, 2001), 269–405.

4. See Frank G. Menke, *The Encyclopedia of Sports*, 174–175; Zander Hollander, ed., *The Modern Encyclopedia of Basketball* (Old Tappan, NJ: Four Winds Press, 1969), 211–220; Roger G. Noll, "Professional Basketball: Economic and Business Perspectives," in Paul D. Staudohar and James A. Mangan, eds., *The Business of Professional Sports* (Champaign: University of Illinois Press, 1991), 18–47.

5. Ibid.

6. The final regular season standings, geographic locations and nicknames for the clubs in each sports league were obtained from *The World Almanac and Book of Facts* (Mahwah, NJ: World Almanac Books, 1951–2001). Furthermore, the divisions, conferences and league champions, and the respective team coaches, managers and players are contained in various editions of *The World Almanac and Book of Facts*. The Web sites of each sports league are an excellent source of data and information about the operations and performances of former and current teams.

7. For the composition of leagues and the geographic placement of teams, see *The World Almanac and Book of Facts*, 1965–1977.

8. See James Quirk and Rodney D. Fort, *Pay Dirt: The Business of Professional Team Sports* (Princeton, NJ: Princeton University Press, 1992), 468–469; "Stanley Cup Dynasties," at http://www.nhl.com cited 29 November 2001.

9. *The World Almanac and Book of Facts*, 1951–1961; James Quirk and Rodney D. Fort, *Pay Dirt: The Business of Professional Team Sports*, 413; *NFL 2001 Record & Fact Book*, 281–282.

10. Roger G. Noll, "Professional Basketball: Economic and Business Perspectives," 18–47; James Quirk and Rodney D. Fort, *Pay Dirt*, 447–448, 453–454.

11. Besides the ownership histories of the AL, NL, NBA, NFL and NHL teams, on pages 479–511 in *Pay Dirt* James Quirk and Rodney D. Fort provide the franchises' attendance records and each club's radio and television income for selected seasons.

12. See Quirk and Fort, *Pay Dirt*, 466–467; "National Hockey League," at http://www.nhl.com cited 1 August 2001; *The World Almanac and Book of Facts*, 2001.

13. Besides various editions of *The World Almanac and Book of Facts*, the past, present and future capacity, location and name of sports teams' arenas and stadiums are provided in "Ballparks," at http://www.ballparks.com cited 1 November 2001. For the potential sale of the Anaheim Angels, see Bruce Orwall and Matthew Rose, "Disney Held Talks With Condé Nast, Hearst to Sell Fairchild Magazine Unit," *Wall Street Journal* (16 August 1999), B12.

14. See "Loan Closed Tuesday to Finance New Tiger Ballpark," at http://baseball. yahoo.com cited 26 August 1998; "Sale of Royals to Glass Approved," at http://www. cnnsi.com cited 18 April 2000.

15. The proposal to use private money to improve Wrigley Field for the NL Chicago Cubs is an unexpected deal since twelve years ago the AL Chicago White Sox spent $167 million, which was raised from hotel taxes, to build Comiskey Park. Furthermore, the Chicago Bears have requested taxpayer subsidies for a $600 million renovation of Soldier Field. For the planned makeover of Wrigley Field, see the Editorial, "Our Kind of Town," *Wall Street Journal* (20 July 2001), W15.

16. Was Jeffrey H. Loria, who purchased the Montreal Expos in late 1999 and the Florida Marlins in early 2002, ready to move the Expos to one of the U.S. cities clamoring for a professional baseball team? For a discussion of this question and why baseball owners approved the takeover of the Expos by the commissioner's office and the sale of

the Marlins to Loria, see Mark Hyman, "Bronx Cheers in Montreal," *Business Week* (26 June 2000), 181; "Sales of Marlins, Expos Imminent," *Charlotte Observer* (2 February 2002), 8C; Ronald Blum, "Expos, Marlins Switches Approved," *Charlotte Observer* (13 February 2002), 6C.

17. Before he left office in 2001, Mayor Rudy Giuliani signed contracts that committed New York City to build baseball stadiums for the NL Mets and AL Yankees. According to the contracts, the Mets are not required to pay the city a percentage of its advertising revenues, and the Yankees can abandon New York on sixty days' notice if a new stadium is not constructed. Furthermore, to cover planning costs each club will receive $25 million over five years. See "Foul," *Wall Street Journal* (16 January 2002), A14.

18. According to the arena lease, the NBA's New Jersey Nets will play at the Meadowlands sports complex through the 2007–2008 season. The lease agreement includes penalties if the team moves from New Jersey before 2004, but no penalties if the team relocates to Newark. See John Curran, "Nets Get Sweeter Lease," at http://sports.yahoo.com cited 2 December 1998.

19. The Maloof family includes four brothers. In the late 1990s, they owned the Fiesta Casino Hotel in Las Vegas, Nevada, a beer distributorship in Albuquerque, New Mexico, and several banks. The late George Maloof Sr. controlled the NBA Houston Rockets during the late 1970s and early 1980s. For the family's interest in the NBA's Sacramento Kings, the Women's National Basketball Association's Sacramento Monarchs, and the Major Indoor Soccer League's Sacramento Knights, see "Maloof Family Gains Control of Kings," at http://www.cnnsi.com cited 1 July 1999. Other ownership rights that the Maloofs have pursued are discussed in "Kings Co-Owners Buy Into Lakers," at http://www.cnnsi.com cited 4 November 1998.

20. For a detailed history of the Dallas Mavericks and the other current professional basketball teams in the NBA, see "National Basketball Association," at http://www.nba.com cited 1 August 2001; Idem., at http://www.forbes.com cited 30 November 1999.

21. See Nancy D. Holt, "Pepsi Center Scores in Financing Game," *Wall Street Journal* (3 March 1999), B12; "New Denver Center Is NBA's 2nd Chinese Player," *Charlotte Observer* (27 February 2002), 4C.

22. During the court trial, confidential documents were filed as evidence in the Oakland Raiders' lawsuit against the NFL. These documents contained the sources of revenues and profits for the NFL teams including the Arizona Cardinals. See "Owners Not Pleased With Davis After Lawsuit Against NFL," at http://www.cnnsi.com cited 24 May 2001. Furthermore, the financial status of the Arizona Cardinals was reported in "Follow the Leaders," at http://www.cnnsi.com cited 15 May 2001. For the proposal to construct a football stadium in the Phoenix area, see "Cardinals Agree to Deal for New Stadium," at http://www.yahoo.com cited 1 November 2001.

23. See Charles Chandler, "Panthers in NFL's Top 12 for Making a Profit," *Charlotte Observer* (16 April 2001), 1C. For the progress on the construction of new facilities, see "National Football League," at http://www.nfl.com cited 1 August 2001; "Ballparks," at http://www.ballparks.com cited 1 November 2001; Mark Hyman, "The Egghead in the Owner's Box," *Business Week* (28 January 2002), 88.

24. For the ownership history and attendance of selected NHL clubs, see James Quirk and Rodney D. Fort, *Pay Dirt*, 463–474, 501–504. The teams' franchise values and operating profits were reported in Michael K. Ozanian, "Selective Accounting," *Forbes* (14 December 1998), 124–134.

25. See "Phoenix Coyotes," at http://www.phoenixcoyotes.com cited 27 January 2002; "NHL Hockey," at http://www.infoplease.com cited 12 April 2000.

26. See "Alberta Approves Lottery to Help Struggling NHL Teams," at http://www.yahoo.com cited 19 June 2001; Jerry Colangelo, "Sports and the Media," at http://proquest.umi.com cited 24 September 2001; James Quirk and Rodney D. Fort, *Pay Dirt*, 463–478.

Chapter 3

Owners

The U.S. professional sports leagues are composed of franchises that are headed by an owner or ownership group. Periodically, the franchise owners meet and agree to cooperate in a communal business and legal relationship. According to a typical sports organization's constitution, after a contract is signed with the league an owner is granted a nonassignable franchise to operate his team within an exclusive geographic market area. Besides territorial restrictions, the contract also specifies the type of ownership arrangement. It may be a community foundation, corporation, general or limited partnership, joint stock company, private syndicate, sole proprietorship or trust. For their admission standards, sports leagues generally require that owners be sufficiently capitalized, be able to pay the players' compensation based on the team payroll, and be of good moral character. In turn, as a member of a sports organization each owner receives the right to discuss and vote on league-related matters as contained in a constitution's by-laws. These matters, for example, usually relate to broad and specific issues such as national broadcast agreements, expansion of teams, licensing trademarks, relocation of a club from one geographic area to another, and the allocation of teams' revenues derived from gate receipts, and from merchandise sales and contracts with local and regional radio and television networks.[1]

When the five dominant sports leagues—AL, NL, NBA, NFL and NHL—emerged in the United States between the late 1800s and 1940s, many well-to-do families and individuals, and prominent ex-players assumed the risks of entrepreneurship and invested in a professional sports enterprise to join a league. During the early-to-mid-1900s, when the formation, development and growth of the major sports organizations in America were unstable, individual franchise owners tended to establish sole proprietorships. Furthermore, to own and operate teams several families and other groups formed community foundations, general or limited partnerships, syndicates or trusts. Nevertheless, because of bank crises, the Great Depression of the 1930s, World Wars I and II, and managerial inexperience, individual and group bankruptcies frequently occurred in professional team sports. This forced many team owners to dissolve their franchises, relocate the teams to another site, resell the clubs, or suspend operations and wait until the economic environment had improved.

To illustrate, in the 1930s the owners of the AL Boston Red Sox, the NL Boston Braves, Cincinnati Reds and Los Angeles Dodgers, the NFL Green Bay Packers and Philadelphia Eagles, and the NHL Detroit Red Wings experienced threatening financial difficulties. (The NBA organized as a single entity in the late 1940s.) Yet, rather than immediately declare bankruptcy and terminate their contracts, some franchise owners simply decided to withdraw from their current affiliations and join a rival league in a nearby area, or to merely change the club's nickname and then move its operations to another city. For example, after the NFL Portsmouth Spartans went broke following the 1933 season, owner George A. Richardson shifted the team to Detroit and renamed it the Detroit Lions in 1934. Three years later, majority owner George Marshall relocated the Boston Redskins to Washington, D.C., and nicknamed it the Washington Redskins. When operating losses accumulated because of the owners' incompetence, the NFL cancelled several franchises such as the Akron Indians, Canton Bulldogs, Columbus Tigers, Los Angeles Buccaneers and St. Louis All Stars. Likewise, the NHL folded the Brooklyn Americans, Montreal Wanderers, Philadelphia Quakers and St. Louis Eagles. In short, prior to the early 1950s only a portion of sports team owners in each league had established a viable long-term business organization in their respective communities, and a franchise that could thrive during domestic economic depressions and destabilizing global military conflicts.[2]

Beginning in the 1950s, the benefits of television programming and its widespread appeal changed the mindset and strategy of sports league executives and team owners. Although home-game gate receipts remained the largest component of a club's total revenues, owners realized that the local, regional and national broadcast of games and other sports events presented them with an opportunity to increase the cash inflows and net earnings of their franchises. Consequently, to bid for high-quality coaches, managers and players and to compete for and win titles and championships, each franchise owner had to pursue the revenue sources that provided the most operating income for his team. As such, by the mid-to-late 1950s the majority of owners viewed their sports franchise as primarily a viable business investment that potentially could earn surplus profits and yield a competitive rate of return. As a league member, therefore, in the short term each owner's mission was to ensure that his club entertained spectators and won sufficient games to qualify for the league playoffs when the regular season ended. Based on the future growth of the local economy and the franchise's operations, in the long term each owner's overriding objective was to improve the team's quality and thereby maximize the market value of the club. Meanwhile, since the 1950s numerous franchises in each sports league have been sold and resold as the ownership types gradually shifted—except in the NFL—from general and limited partnerships, private syndicates, sole proprietorships and trusts to joint stock companies and corporations, and especially to large-scale entertainment, media and technology conglomerates.

When a club is sold, presumably to improve the team's future performances and to win division and conference titles and league championships the new owner(s) will screen and hire the most competent and effective coaching staff, general manager and administrative personnel, and employ skilled players at each position. Given these tasks, does a change in franchise owners make a noticeable difference in a specific team's future performances? To ascertain whether a selected group of new owners influenced their club's success, a directed sample was taken to pick five teams in each of five decades, that is, from the 1950s to the 1990s inclusive. Then, the average three-year pre-sale and post-sale winning percentages and the number of division and conference titles and leagues championships won were determined for the chosen twenty-five teams that had each experienced an ownership change. To illustrate, the AL Detroit Tigers were sold in 1956, the NL Cincinnati Reds in 1966, the NBA Chicago Bulls in 1972, the NFL Dallas Cowboys in 1988 and the NHL Pittsburgh Penguins in 1991. Thus, for the Detroit Tigers the data consisted of the average winning percentages and the number of titles won, including league championships from the 1953–1955 and 1957–1959 seasons inclusive. According to the statistics collected, the Detroit Tigers won 44.8 percent of their games and zero titles and championships during the three pre-sale seasons, and 50 percent of their games and zero titles and championships in the three post-sale seasons. The results for the other twenty-four teams appear in Table 3.1, which is interpreted for each league as follows.[3]

OWNERSHIP PERFORMANCES

In the AL, 80 percent (4) of the teams improved their performances in the post-sale period, and particularly the Minnesota Twins. In 1984, Minnesota businessman Carl Pohlad organized a syndicate to acquire the Twins. He paid H. Gabriel Murphy and Calvin Griffith, who had inherited 50 percent of the team in 1955 when his father Clark Griffith died, an estimated $32 million to $38 million for the franchise. Before Pohlad's purchase, the team had lackluster seasons in 1981 to 1983. Then, clutch hitter Kirby Puckett joined the club in 1984, and Tom Kelly was appointed the Twins' manager in 1986. One year later, the club defeated the St. Louis Cardinals in seven games to win the World Series. Besides the special hits from Puckett, the club's stars were the World Series' Most Valuable Player (MVP) pitcher Frank Viola and sluggers Don Baylor, Gary Gaetti and Kent Hrbek. Similarly, during the post-sale periods the Baltimore Orioles and New York Yankees each won titles, respectively, after John Hoffberger purchased the Orioles from a group in 1965 for an unknown price and George Steinbrenner headed a syndicate that acquired the Yankees from the

Table 3.1
Team Pre-Sale and Post-Sale Performances, by League, for Selected Years

League	Team	Year Sold	W-L Pre-Sale	W-L Post-Sale	Titles Pre-Sale	Titles Post-Sale
AL	Detroit Tigers	1956	.448	.500	0	0
	Baltimore Orioles	1965	.535	.547	0	2
	New York Yankees	1973	.530	.559	0	2
	Minnesota Twins	1984	.368	.499	0	3
	Oakland Athletics	1995	.487	.446	1	0
NL	St. Louis Cardinals	1953	.536	.468	0	0
	Cincinnati Reds	1966	.549	.533	0	0
	Atlanta Braves	1976	.477	.405	0	0
	Philadelphia Phillies	1981	.544	.535	4	2
	San Diego Padres	1994	.467	.506	0	1
NBA	Syracuse Nationals	1956	.555	.552	2	0
	Los Angeles Lakers	1965	.592	.547	2	0
	Chicago Bulls	1972	.598	.508	0	1
	Seattle SuperSonics	1984	.577	.411	0	0
	Sacramento Kings	1992	.311	.447	0	0
NFL	San Francisco 49ers	1957	.475	.555	0	0
	Cleveland Browns	1961	.692	.667	0	2
	New Eng. Patriots	1975	.357	.706	0	1
	Dallas Cowboys	1988	.510	.396	1	0
	Miami Dolphins	1990	.469	.584	0	1
NHL	Montreal Canadiens	1957	92	92	2	2
	Boston Bruins	1963	42	47	0	0
	Los Angeles Kings	1979	80	76	0	0
	Hartford Whalers	1988	85	74	1	0
	Pittsburgh Penguins	1991	82	93	0	2

Note: The W-L is each club's average three-year win-loss percentage during the pre-sale and post-sale seasons. Titles are the number of division, conference and league championships won by the team during the pre-sale and post-sale seasons. To measure performances, in the NHL the W-L entries in the pre-sale and post-sale periods are each team's three-year average points earned and not the mean win-loss percentages.

Source: The World Almanac and Book of Facts (Mahwah, NJ: World Almanac Books, 1950–1998); James Quirk and Rodney D. Fort, *Pay Dirt: The Business of Professional Team Sports* (Princeton, NJ: Princeton University Press, 1992), 377–478.

Columbia Broadcasting System (CBS) in 1973 for $10 million. The Oakland Athletics, meanwhile, moderately slumped during the post-sale period after winning the AL pennant in 1992.

Contrary to the performances of four AL clubs, in the NL 80 percent (4) of the teams declined in average winning percentage during the post-sale seasons, especially the Atlanta Braves. Ted Turner acquired the franchise in 1976 for $11 million from a syndicate headed by William Bartholomay and Donald Reynolds who had owned the club since 1962. Although the Braves won only 47.7 percent of its games between 1973 and 1975, home run sluggers Dave Johnson, Darrell Evans and Hank Aaron, and batting champion Ralph Garr played well. After Aaron broke Babe Ruth's career home run record of 714 in 1974, he was traded to the Milwaukee Brewers, and the Braves floundered. During a seventeen-game losing streak in 1977, owner Turner violated league rules and managed the team for one game. For his infraction, MLB Commissioner Bowie Kuhn banned Turner from the dugout. Likewise, after a subsidiary of Anheuser Busch Inc. obtained the St. Louis Cardinals from Fred Saigh in 1953 for $3.8 million, and Francis Dale purchased the Cincinnati Reds from Bill DeWitt in 1966 for an unknown price, and Bill Giles bought the Philadelphia Phillies from Rudy Carpenter in 1981 for $31 million, each team's average winning percentage fell. Conversely, after a syndicate headed by Tom Warner sold the club to John Moores and Larry Lucchino in 1994 for an unknown price, the San Diego Padres won the Western Division title in 1996 and two years later the NL pennant. After taking control, apparently owners Anheuser Busch, Dale and Giles were unable to inspire their teams to titles as Moores did.

In the NBA, during the post-sale seasons the average winning percentage increased for the Sacramento Kings, but noticeably decreased for the Los Angeles Lakers and Chicago Bulls, particularly for the Seattle SuperSonics. In 1967, which was the expansion year for the SuperSonics, owners Gene Klein and Sam Schulman headed a syndicate that paid a fee of $1.8 million to enter the NBA. Then, after Schulman had acquired Klein's interest in 1984, he sold the club for $21 million to Ackerly Communications after reporting operating losses that amounted to $2 million in the 1981–1982 season and $1 million in the 1982–1983 season. Before Schulman's sale, the SuperSonics had some excellent teams in the late 1970s. The club finished runner-up to the champion Washington Bullets in 1978, and led by Coach Len Wilkens it won the Pacific Division and NBA Championship in 1979. Within five years, however, the franchise's performances diminished. In 1984, All-Star guard Fred Brown retired and Len Wilkens was replaced as head coach. By 1986, the SuperSonics had lost other skilled players besides Brown, such as Jack Sikma, Gus Williams and David Thompson. Thus, in 1984 Ackerly Communications had purchased a deteriorated franchise that was in disarray. Similarly, after Jack Kent Cooke bought the Los Angeles Lakers from Bob Short for $5 million in 1965, and Arthur Wirtz purchased the Chicago Bulls from a syndicate for $5.1 million in 1972, the teams' average win-loss percentages fell although the Bulls won the Midwest Division title in the 1974–1975 season. In sum, because of personnel changes and lack of team leadership the Lakers, Bulls and SuperSonics experienced their worst performances in the seasons after the teams were sold. Finally, two years after the club was defeated by the Minneapolis Lakers for the NBA Championship, Leo Ferris sold the Syracuse Nationals to Jack Egan for an unknown price. As a member of the Eastern Division, the team finished last in the 1956 season, was defeated in the playoffs by the Boston Celtics in the 1957 season, and failed to qualify for the playoffs in the 1958 season.

During the post-sale seasons in the NFL, the average winning percentage and number of titles won significantly improved for the New England Patriots but not for the Dallas Cowboys. After Billy Sullivan bought out three minority owners for $7 million in 1975, the Patriots became significantly competitive. The club's average winning percentage nearly doubled from the 1972–1974 to 1976–1978 seasons inclusive, and the team qualified for a wild card in 1976. Two years later, the Patriots won the Eastern Division title of the American Football Conference (AFC) but were defeated by the Houston Oilers 31–14 in the divisional playoffs. For their outstanding play, owner Sullivan rewarded his best players such as NFL Hall of Fame offensive guard John Hannah and cornerback Mike Haynes, and All-Pro tight end Russ Francis.

In contrast to the Patriots, a group led by majority owner Jerry Jones purchased the Cowboys and the Texas Stadium lease from a syndicate for $140 million in 1988. After the retirement of running back Tony Dorsett in 1987 and defensive tackle Randy White in 1988, Jones decided to rebuild the team with free agents and rookies. He fired Tom Landry who had coached the team since 1960. Although the club finished its regular seasons at 3–13 in 1988, 1–15 in 1989 and 7–9 in 1990, Jones' strategy eventually succeeded. The Cowboys won the Eastern Division titles of the National Football Conference (NFC) from 1992 through 1996 and the Super Bowls that were played in 1993, 1994 and 1996.

The Patriots and Cowboys aside, the Miami Dolphins performed better after billionaire H. Wayne Huizenga joined the Robbie family to become the team's minority owner in 1990. Two years later, the Dolphins won the Eastern Division title but lost to the Buffalo Bills 29–10 in the AFC championship game. Since 1992, the franchise has continued to excel. The club won AFC titles in 1994, 1999 and 2000, and earned wild cards in 1995, 1997–1999 and 2002.

Relative to the pre-sale periods in the NHL, during the three-year post-sale seasons the average points earned decreased for the Los Angeles Kings in 1980–1982 and for the Hartford Whalers in 1989–1991, increased for the Boston Bruins in 1964–1966 and for the Pittsburgh Penguins in 1992–1994, and remained equal for the Montreal Canadiens in 1958–1960. Except for the Whalers in the Adams Division and the Penguins in the Patrick Division, the changes in average points earned in the post-sale period were marginal for the nondivisional Bruins and for the Kings in the Norris Division. For $31 million, a consortium sold the Whalers to Donald Conrad and Richard Gordon in 1988 when the Colonial Realty Company owned 37 percent of the franchise. Four years later, the club filed for bankruptcy as the team struggled to earn points in its division. Meanwhile, thirteen years after acquiring the franchise from Al Savill and his group, Penguins owner Edward DeBartolo Sr. sold the team for an unknown price to a syndicate in 1991. The club excelled after DeBartolo's sale. All-NHL players Mario Lemieux and Jaromir Jagr made significant contributions to the team's Prince of Wales Conference titles in the 1991, 1993 and 1994 seasons, and to the Stanley Cup championships in 1991 and 1992. Interestingly, the Montreal Canadiens won five consecutive Stanley Cups even though the franchise changed owners in 1957 when the Molsons bought a majority share for $4 million to $5 million.

In sum, Table 3.1 indicates that compared with the pre-sale seasons 55 percent (11) of the non-NHL teams declined in average winning percentage from .556 to .493, and netted three less titles during the post-sale periods. Furthermore, for the nine non-NHL clubs whose winning percentages increased, ten additional titles were won after the replacement of the pre-sale owners. Finally, in the NHL the average points earned rose from 76.2 to 76.4, and the titles won increased from three to four as a result of the five team ownership transfers listed in Table 3.1.

Because hard core and casual fans demand sports information to read, for decades the various media such as daily newspapers, weekly magazines and monthly sports journals have printed historical and current statistics about player and team performances, and they have published memorable articles about coaches, games, managers and seasons. In local newspapers, the box scores and final standings typically provide recent information on how players and teams have performed within their respective division, conference and league. In post-game interviews with the media, coaches and managers comment on the outcome of a play or game and brag about the unique talents of selected players such as AL catchers, NL shortstops, NBA centers, NFL quarterbacks or NHL goalies. Likewise, in statements to reporters a football wide receiver may describe a complex pass pattern that led to a first down, or a baseball pitcher may display the grip on his overhand curveball that is used to strike out batters. Inevitably, fans read and discuss these and other facts obtained from interviews and press releases to expand their knowledge about professional teams and players and to be informed about how sports personalities excel on the court, field or ice.

Besides the insightful stories about coaches, games, players, seasons and teams, since the early 1990s sports analysts, editors and journalists have increasingly reported detailed business and personal information and statistics about the corporations, families and individuals that operate and own sports franchises. To illustrate, in 1993 an article appeared in *Sports Illustrated* in which the author ranked, according to net worth, the wealthiest ninety-three individuals and partners who were franchise owners. The article's list of owners ranged from multibillionaire Paul Allen, who was the co-founder of Microsoft Corporation and is now the boss of the NBA Portland Trail Blazers, to multimillionaire George W. Bush, who was the managing general partner of the AL Texas Rangers and is now the president of the United States. Based on the expert appraisal of asset values and debts, *Sports Illustrated* reported that in 1993 the ninety-three owners' net worth totaled $32 billion, which equaled $344 million per owner. Those proprietors aside, the article also included the various sports franchises that were operated by consortiums, corporations and noncorporate business groups. Within the latter classification, there were thirteen teams listed such as the Kansas City Royals and Toronto Blue Jays in the AL, Chicago Cubs and St. Louis

Cardinals in the NL, Boston Celtics and New York Knickerbockers in the NBA, Green Bay Packers in the NFL, and the Montreal Canadiens and New York Rangers in the NHL. Based on the information contained in the article, Table A.3 was constructed and placed in the Appendix. It shows the five richest owners in each league and the value of their franchise(s) in 1993. Table A.3 reveals that, on average, the net worth of NBA owners was the highest at $2.4 billion each, and NL owners the lowest at $660 million per person. In estimated market value, the NFL franchises ranked first at $123 million per team and the NHL fifth at $63 million per team. Three individuals owned two professional clubs. They were Michael Ilitch who headed the AL Detroit Tigers and NHL Detroit Red Wings, Ted Turner who controlled the NL Atlanta Braves and NBA Atlanta Hawks, and H. Wayne Huizenga who owned the NL Florida Marlins and NHL Florida Panthers. Collectively, in 1993 the three owners' net worth totaled $3.3 billion or $1.1 billion each.[4]

Besides wealth, there are other pertinent details and facts about franchise owners and the business aspects of team ownership that intrigue the general public, media and sports fans. To expose, for example, how frequently teams were bought and sold in the mid-1990s, the majority owners of professional sports franchises, as reported in *Forbes* in 1999 were compared with the owners included in the aforementioned 1993 article published in *Sports Illustrated*. Given the individuals and groups of majority owners presented in *Forbes* and *Sports Illustrated*, from 1993 to 1999 inclusive there were ownership changes and principal owner replacements for forty-seven franchises. By league, this occurred for five teams in the AL, eight in the NL, nine in the NBA, eleven in the NFL and fourteen in the NHL. Several of these transactions were newsworthy events.[5]

To illustrate, in the AL the Walt Disney Company, which owns sports-related assets such as the ESPN Zone and the NHL Mighty Ducks, exercised its option to purchase the Anaheim Angels for $110 million when Gene Autry died in 1999. One year later, Rogers Communication acquired 80 percent of the Toronto Blue Jays from principal owner John Labatt Ltd., a brewing, dairy and entertainment company that had purchased 90 percent of the team in 1991. (The Canadian Imperial Bank of Commerce owned the remaining share of the franchise.) In the NL, Kevin McClatchy and his financial partners replaced seven public-private Pittsburgh-area organizations and three of its businessmen to become the principal owners of the Pittsburgh Pirates in 1996. One year earlier, Anheuser Busch Inc. relinquished control of the St. Louis Cardinals to Fred Hansen, Andrew Baur and William DeWitt Jr. Besides Time Warner's purchase of the Atlanta Braves from Ted Turner, another corporate acquisition of a sports enterprise occurred when Ruppert Murdoch's Fox Group, a unit of his News Corporation, acquired the Los Angeles Dodgers from the O'Malley family in 1998.

There were other sales of MLB teams that aroused the media and the attention of sport fans. The controversial owner Marge Schott sold the NL Cincinnati Reds to financier and insurance executive Carl Lindner, and baseball's

Commissioner Bud Selig relinquished control of the NL Milwaukee Brewers to his daughter, Wendy Selig-Prieb. In 1995, Vince Naimoli and an investment partnership were awarded the ownership of the expansion AL Tampa Bay Devil Rays after the league had blocked their attempt to purchase the San Francisco Giants in 1992. Three years later, Jerry Colangelo headed a syndicate that included the St. Louis Post Dispatch to establish control of the expansion NL Arizona Diamondbacks.[6]

Nine years after H. Wayne Huizenga had replaced Tim Robbie as the principal owner of the NFL Miami Dolphins in 1990, he sold the 1997 World Series Champion Florida Marlins to John Henry for $150 million. To reduce expenses, before the sale Huizenga had traded most of his highest-salaried ballplayers and also fired manager Jim Leyland. In 1999, Marlin fans were furious at Huizenga when the team finished last in the NL Eastern Division. Then, in 2002 John Henry sold the Florida Marlins to Jeffrey Loria for $158 million after Loria sold the Montreal Expos for $120 million to Baseball Expos LP, which is a Delaware limited partnership controlled by the other twenty-nine MLB teams. According to *Forbes* magazine in November 2001, Henry's price was $28 million above the Marlins' estimated market value. Based on the league bylaws, the sale required the approval of at least twenty-three NL owners.[7]

As well as the sale of baseball franchises, since the early 1990s selected ownership transfers were unanticipated but observed also for several clubs in the NBA, NFL and NHL. First, in 1996 Pat Croce and media conglomerate Comcast Inc.—later renamed Comcast-Spectator Inc.—purchased the NBA Philadelphia 76ers from Harold Katz who had acquired the team for $12 million in 1981 from F. Eugene Dixon. Second, AOL Time Warner Inc.—formerly Time Warner Inc.—established ownership of the NL Atlanta Braves, NBA Atlanta Hawks and NHL Atlanta Thrashers in 2000. Third, the Dallas Mavericks were sold twice. Donald Carter and his syndicate, who paid an expansion fee of $12 million in 1980, dealt the club for an unknown price to Ross Perot Jr. who then resold the Mavericks to dot.com billionaire Mark Cuban. Fourth, Cablevision Systems, which was previously named Paramount Communications, became the principal owner of the New York Knickerbockers, a club estimated to be the highest-valued NBA franchise at $334 million in 1999. Fifth, three different heirs, who were the relatives of family owners, assumed majority control of NFL teams. The new principal owners and their predecessors included the Atlanta Falcons' Taylor Smith and his dad, Rankin; the Chicago Bears' Virginia McCaskey and her mother, Virginia; and the Indianapolis Colts' James Irsay and his father, Robert. Sixth, in December 2001 Home Depot co-founder Arthur Blank offered to purchase the Atlanta Falcons from majority owner Taylor Smith for $545 million. Although the team placed runner-up to the Denver Broncos in Super Bowl XXXIII, the Falcons had played above .500 in only eight seasons since its expansion in 1965. The league approved Blank's acquisition of the Falcons in 2002.[8]

In contrast to the ownership rules in MLB and in the NBA and NHL, corporations are prohibited from controlling NFL franchises. As such, during the mid-1990s four cross-ownership deals occurred that involved teams in the NHL, NBA and AL. First, the principal owner of the NHL Philadelphia Flyers, Ed Snider's Spectator Corporation, merged with Comcast Inc. in 1996 to create Comcast-Spectator Inc. that owns the Philadelphia 76ers, when Pat Croce relinquished his share of the club. Second, the Ascent Entertainment Group, which was the principal owner of the NBA Denver Nuggets, purchased the NHL Colorado Avalanche from Marcel Aubut. (In 1988, Aubut and his syndicate had acquired the Quebec Nordiques for approximately $18 million from the Carling O'Keefe Brewery.) Then, in the late 1990s Wal-Mart heir and real estate tycoon Stan Kroenke purchased the Nuggets and Avalanche from the Ascent Entertainment Group for an unknown price. Third, the AL Texas Rangers' leveraged buyout specialist and owner Thomas Hicks bought the NHL Dallas Stars from Norm Green, who had acquired the Minnesota North Stars in 1990 from Howard Baldwin and Morris Belzberg for $40 million. Fourth, the NBA Vancouver Grizzlies' cell phone entrepreneur and proprietor John McCaw Jr. acquired the NHL Vancouver Canucks from principal shareholder Frank Griffiths Sr. Griffiths became the majority owner of the ice hockey franchise in 1974 when co-owner Tom Scallen was sent to prison.

Other NHL teams besides the Flyers, Avalanche, Stars and Canucks were sold outright or experienced principal ownership changes. These clubs were the Buffalo Sabres, Carolina Hurricanes, Edmonton Oilers, Los Angeles Kings, New York Islanders, New York Rangers, Phoenix Coyotes, St. Louis Blues, Tampa Bay Lightning and Toronto Maple Leafs. In short, throughout the 1990s proportionately more NHL teams were sold or had replaced their principal owners than the ownership deals that occurred in MLB and in the NBA and NFL. This high turnover rate of franchises is not unique in professional ice hockey. As reflected in Table A.3 of the Appendix, the average value of the top five NHL franchises was $63 million in 1993. This amount was considerably below the averages of the five highest-valued teams in the AL at $112 million, NL at $132 million, NBA at $78 million and the NFL at $123 million. Indeed, because of lower sales prices economic theory predicts that the turnover of hockey team owners will occur more frequently than the ownership transfers in the other sports leagues.[9]

For this chapter's theme, a financial study was performed to reveal whether, which and by what amount various owners benefited from their investments in sports teams. To accomplish this task, the most relevant accounting values available from balance sheets and earnings statements should be collected and interpreted. However, rather than attempt to estimate a franchise's annual net earnings or after-tax profit, which is confidential information and not reported to the public, the next best data to use is each team's yearly operating income, or total revenues less operating costs. In finance, operating income includes the total interest payments on long-term debt and a noncash expense for the depreciation of player contracts. In sum, to measure the financial performances of sports franchises and to evaluate which owners benefited from their investments, each team's operating income is examined and not its pre- or after-tax earnings or profit.

Before the study is discussed, in Tables 5–1 through 5–4 of *Hard Ball: The Abuse of Power in Pro Team Sports,* James Quirk and Rodney D. Fort determined that the sports teams' 1990 to 1996 estimated operating income averaged $3.6 million in MLB—$3.9 million in the AL and $3.3 million in the NL, $8.6 million in the NBA, $5.1 million in the NFL and $3.7 million in the NHL. During those seven seasons, on average 39 percent (11) of the clubs had operating losses in MLB—50 percent (7) of the teams in the AL and 33 percent (4) in the NL, 3 percent (1) in the NBA, 9 percent (3) in the NFL and 20 percent (6) in the NHL. Based on the average growths in franchise market values and sales prices, Quirk and Fort concluded that, except for a few clubs, professional team sports is not an extremely profitable business, because owners typically earn average to below-average incomes and annual financial returns from their investments in team operations.[10]

Given those results, an updated financial analysis was completed to further examine the business of sports teams and the financial benefits of ownership. This study required that the aforementioned tables in *Hard Ball* be revised. The two specific changes made to Tables 5–1 through 5–4 were as follows. First, based on the availability and reliability of published values, the estimated annual operating incomes were derived from 1994 to 1998 inclusive for all teams in the AL, NL, NBA and the NFL, and from 1994 to 1997 inclusive for all teams in the NHL. Second, for those years the analysis included the expansion and relocated teams within each sports league. Nevertheless, even though the years were revised from 1990–1996 to respectively, 1994–1998 and 1994–1997, the average estimated operating incomes of the teams, which appear in Tables 3.2 to 3.6 of this chapter, generally reaffirm the conclusions stated by Quirk and Fort in *Hard Ball.* An interpretation of the tabled values, for each league, reveals why sports franchises are risky businesses to own and operate even for wealthy businessmen.

In MLB, from 1994 through 1998 the annual operating income per team averaged $2.8 million and 42 percent (13) of the franchises realized losses (Tables 3.2 and 3.3). By league, 53 percent (8) of the teams incurred losses in the AL and 31 percent (5) in the NL. One year after the players' strike ended in 1995, the gross revenues received from the clubs' gate receipts, home ballparks and local broadcasts soared for the AL Baltimore Orioles, Cleveland Indians, Texas Rangers and Toronto Blue Jays, and for the NL Chicago Cubs, Colorado Rockies and Houston Astros. Likewise, in the expansion year of 1998 the owners of the AL Tampa Bay Devil Rays and NL Arizona Diamondbacks earned excess revenues from their operations. In contrast, since their debt to value or leverage ratios exceeded 60 percent, from 1994 through 1998 the average pre-tax profits and net earnings were likely negatives for the small-market AL Oakland Athletics and large-market Texas Rangers, and for the small-market NL Pittsburgh Pirates and San Diego Padres. Furthermore, because of high leverage ratios the net profits were extremely negative for the large-market AL Detroit Tigers and the NL Houston Astros and San Francisco Giants. Meanwhile, the average pre-tax profits and net earnings were probably positive for low leverage teams such

Table 3.2

Estimated Operating Income for AL Teams, 1994 to 1998

Teams	1994	1995	1996	1997	1998	Average
New York Yankees	8.7	24.0	38.3	21.4	23.0	23.1
Tampa Bay Devil Rays					20.6	20.6
Baltimore Orioles	5.5	6.0	19.0	18.7	8.5	11.5
Cleveland Indians	−4.5	1.4	15.6	15.4	19.0	9.4
Texas Rangers	5.2	7.6	18.9	9.1	0.5	8.3
Boston Red Sox	0.2	15.4	16.3	7.7	−7.6	6.4
Oakland Athletics	−10.6	−4.8	11.3	7.5	3.3	1.3
Milwaukee Brewers	−12.0	1.0	6.6	−4.8		−2.3
Toronto Blue Jays	1.4	−1.6	14.5	−20.5	−9.5	−3.1
Seattle Mariners	12.1	−9.8	−1.7	11.4	−8.6	−4.2
Detroit Tigers	−15.7	−5.3	3.8	− 0.4	−4.5	−4.4
Chicago White Sox	−5.8	−8.0	−5.2	−4.2	0.2	−4.6
Anaheim Angels	−8.7	−3.0	−2.4	−9.6	−0.2	−4.8
Minnesota Twins	−9.6	2.5	−1.3	−16.5	−7.1	−6.4
Kansas City Royals	−17.4	−6.9	4.7	−11.8	−10.9	−8.5

Note: The teams' estimated operating income, represented in millions of dollars, reflects the players' strike in 1994 and 1995. The Milwaukee Brewers switched from the American to National League in 1998. The Tampa Bay Devil Rays were an expansion team in 1998.

Source: James Quirk and Rodney D. Fort, *Hard Ball: The Abuse of Power in Pro Team Sports* (Princeton, NJ: Princeton University Press, 1999), 206; Michael K. Ozanian, "Selective Accounting," *Forbes* (14 December 1998), 126; Kurt Badenhausen and William Sicheri, "Baseball Games," *Forbes* (31 May 1999), 114.

Table 3.3

Estimated Operating Income for NL Teams, 1994 to 1998

Team	1994	1995	1996	1997	1998	Average
Arizona Diamondbacks					22.5	22.5
Colorado Rockies	4.6	11.5	23.0	38.3	19.5	19.4
New York Mets	−2.2	20.8	11.0	8.1	−5.2	6.5
Chicago Cubs	3.7	4.8	18.3	8.1	−7.9	5.4
Atlanta Braves	−5.3	−2.9	−0.4	18.2	16.4	5.2
Florida Marlins	9.0	6.8	2.8	−5.5	8.6	4.3
San Diego Padres	−1.6	−5.1	2.5	−6.7	−8.0	3.8
Los Angeles Dodgers	−4.1	12.8	13.5	0.9	−11.7	2.3
Montreal Expos	−3.8	7.1	6.2	−3.7	5.6	2.3
St. Louis Cardinals	−4.0	0.9	3.2	2.4	1.6	0.8
Pittsburgh Pirates	−6.1	−1.7	1.4	7.5	2.6	0.7
Houston Astros	−8.4	−4.5	11.5	2.3	−3.7	−0.6
Philadelphia Phillies	−3.7	3.4	−6.5	−2.5	4.5	−1.0
San Francisco Giants	−10.3	−1.4	−6.0	0.2	−6.4	−4.8
Milwaukee Brewers					−8.8	−8.8
Cincinnati Reds	−16.8	−11.8	−14.0	−19.9	0.6	−12.4

Note: The teams' estimated operating income, valued in millions of dollars, reflects the players' strike in 1994 and 1995. The Milwaukee Brewers switched from the American to the National League in 1998. The Arizona Diamondbacks was an expansion team in 1998.

Source: See Table 3.2.

as the large-market AL Boston Red Sox, and NL Chicago Cubs, Los Angeles Dodgers and New York Mets, and for the small-market NL Florida Marlins and St. Louis Cardinals. In brief, only the AL Baltimore Orioles and New York Yankees and the NL Colorado Rockies earned double-digit operating income if the amounts were averaged for the five seasons listed in the tables.

In the NBA, from 1994 to 1998 inclusive the yearly estimated operating income was $7.1 million per franchise, and 24 percent (7) of the teams operated at a loss (Table 3.4). The lockout initiated by the owners in 1998, which reduced the regular season schedule to fifty games, and Michael Jordan's retirement, announced in January 1999, are two primary reasons for the unusually high

Table 3.4
Estimated Operating Income for NBA Teams, 1994 to 1998

Team	1994	1995	1996	1997	1998	Average
Detroit Pistons	31.8	28.5	25.7	30.0	−1.7	22.9
Chicago Bulls	22.8	26.2	33.2	8.6	20.4	22.2
New York Knicks	32.9	31.8	22.9	18.3	4.0	22.0
Phoenix Suns	22.6	30.4	15.3	15.3	5.8	17.9
Portland Trail Blazers	7.6	6.8	33.5	34.2	−13.5	13.7
Utah Jazz	16.2	17.4	14.8	20.7	−0.7	13.7
Los Angeles Lakers	15.8	6.2	19.9	24.8	−0.9	13.2
Houston Rockets	9.2	25.1	13.4	20.3	−3.6	12.9
Boston Celtics	10.8	16.7	16.4	10.5	2.3	11.3
Cleveland Cavaliers	9.9	21.5	11.9	13.5	−0.1	11.3
Charlotte Hornets	11.4	15.7	14.9	9.2	−2.2	9.8
San Antonio Spurs	15.5	17.2	15.2	0.7	−6.7	8.4
Minn.Timberwolves	4.5	18.0	6.7	5.8	4.2	7.8
Seattle SuperSonics	8.6	9.2	12.0	3.3	−2.3	6.2
Washington Wizards	4.9	10.9	4.6	8.2	−2.8	5.2
New Jersey Nets	6.7	10.8	7.3	8.4	−8.6	4.9
Philadelphia 76ers	1.6	6.9	2.1	8.6	1.8	4.2
Orlando Magic	8.3	14.5	8.5	−1.9	−9.1	4.1
Toronto Raptors			14.4	1.6	−8.0	2.7
Golden State Warriors	3.9	10.3	7.8	−2.5	−7.7	2.4
Denver Nuggets	8.7	9.9	4.4	−6.8	−9.8	1.3
Milwaukee Bucks	7.7	13.9	−3.5	−3.2	−14.9	0.0
Sacramento Kings	4.6	7.9	4.3	−5.2	−12.5	−0.2
Dallas Mavericks	6.2	9.3	4.6	−6.8	−14.7	−0.3
Indiana Pacers	0.8	8.9	9.1	−4.8	−19.4	−1.1
Vancouver Grizzlies			5.4	1.3	−12.4	−1.1
Miami Heat	4.7	10.3	4.8	−7.5	−20.7	−1.7
Los Angeles Clippers	2.8	7.7	−1.4	−4.9	−13.2	−1.8
Atlanta Hawks	2.1	4.2	−2.8	−9.1	−19.3	−5.0

Note: The teams' estimated operating income is stated in millions of dollars. The years extended from 1994, which is the 1994–1995 season through 1998, which is the 1998–1999 season. The Toronto Raptors and Vancouver Grizzlies were expansion teams in 1996.

Source: James Quirk and Rodney D. Fort, *Hard Ball,* 208; Michael K. Ozanian, "Selective Accounting," *Forbes* (14 December 1998), 130; Kurt Badenhausen, "NBA Owners Score Big," at http://www.forbes.com cited 30 November 1999.

volume of operating losses incurred by the majority of NBA teams in the 1998–1999 season. Because of debt to value ratios of 114 percent for the Miami Heat, 96 percent for the Toronto Raptors, 80 percent for the Golden State Warriors and 76 percent for the Dallas Mavericks, the owners of these overleveraged franchises presumably suffered disproportionate pre-tax losses and negative profits as a result of the teams' operations, the league lockout and Jordan's retirement. Alternatively, due to its low 10 percent leverage ratio Jerry Reinsdorf's Chicago Bulls was likely the only NBA team to record positive net profits in 1998, after earning nearly $21 million in operating income during Jordan's farewell season. In 1998, the Cleveland Cavaliers, Detroit Pistons and Los Angeles Clippers had zero long-term debt on their balance sheets, which is a rare financial feat for NBA and other league teams. In sum, 37 percent (10) of the teams in Table 3.4 averaged double-digit operating income from 1994 through 1998. Moreover, three of those clubs—Cleveland Cavaliers, Portland Trail Blazers and Utah Jazz—were located in small markets.

In contrast to team operations in MLB and the NBA, in the NFL the annual estimated operating income was $7.6 million a franchise, and 14 percent (5) of the clubs experienced losses (Table 3.5). After 1994, the relocation from Los Angeles of Georgia Frontiere's Rams to St. Louis and Allen Davis' Raiders to Oakland significantly improved the cash inflows of each franchise. The increase in operating incomes of these teams resulted from more stadium revenues and profitable broadcasting markets in the St. Louis and Oakland areas. With their plush stadiums and high-volume merchandise sales, owners Jerry Jones of the Dallas Cowboys, Malcolm Glazer of the Tampa Bay Buccaneers, and the Jack Kent Cooke trust of the Washington Redskins earned an immense amount of cash inflows in 1998. However, after the interest payments on outstanding long-term debt were deducted from operating income, in 1998 the pre-tax profits of H. Wayne Huizenga's Miami Dolphins and the Cooke trust's Washington Redskins were considerably diminished. Otherwise, because of minimal or no stadium debts and/or high estimated market values, nine NFL franchises including the wealthy Dallas Cowboys had leverage ratios below 10 percent. The other low-leverage teams were the Arizona Cardinals, Atlanta Falcons, Detroit Lions, Green Bay Packers, Kansas City Chiefs, New York Jets, Oakland Raiders and St. Louis Rams.

In the NHL, the annual estimated operating income per team was revised from $3.7 million in 1990–1996 as reported in *Hard Ball* to $2.6 million in 1994–1997 (Table 3.6). Furthermore, from 1994 through 1997 only 17 percent (4) of the NHL teams—Florida Panthers, Tampa Bay Lightning, Vancouver Canucks and Buffalo Sabres—operated at a loss, and four clubs—Edmonton Oilers, Dallas Stars, Los Angeles Kings and Ottawa Senators—averaged between $0 and $1 million in operating income. Because of high gross revenues and/or low operating expenses, in 1997 the owners of the New York Islanders, Montreal Canadiens, St. Louis Blues and Washington Capitals enjoyed a surge in operating income. Meanwhile, the owners of the Chicago Blackhawks, Detroit Red Wings,

Table 3.5
Estimated Operating Income for NFL Teams, 1994 to 1998

Team	1994	1995	1996	1997	1998	Average
Dallas Cowboys	32.2	16.4	30.2	41.3	56.7	35.4
Miami Dolphins	13.2	13.3	20.7	31.6	32.9	22.3
St. Louis Rams		12.2	16.4	17.1	33.2	19.7
Washington Redskins	−6.0	0.2	7.5	31.7	48.8	16.4
Tampa Bay Buccaneers	1.6	9.6	8.9	2.6	41.2	12.8
Philadelphia Eagles	8.4	15.1	6.7	13.0	19.1	12.5
Kansas City Chiefs	3.4	11.5	10.9	3.7	31.0	12.1
Baltimore Ravens		5.8	9.0	−1.0	33.2	11.8
Chicago Bears	9.1	14.1	2.9	2.7	19.7	9.7
New Orleans Saints	1.5	12.0	4.7	18.5	11.3	9.6
San Francisco 49ers	9.2	19.0	3.6	0.6	12.7	9.0
Oakland Raiders		10.2	3.6	2.5	17.3	8.4
Green Bay Packers	5.0	13.2	7.2	−1.2	16.4	8.1
Atlanta Falcons	2.1	16.3	5.4	−0.8	16.8	8.0
New York Giants	8.0	10.0	−5.7	0.4	25.2	7.6
Minnesota Vikings	1.8	10.3	8.9	6.7	5.1	6.6
Arizona Cardinals	−3.4	14.9	0.8	8.5	10.6	6.3
San Diego Chargers	1.1	8.2	6.7	6.1	8.2	6.1
Cleveland Browns	6.0					6.0
Pittsburgh Steelers	3.1	6.4	4.9	−1.6	15.5	5.7
Buffalo Bills	3.7	9.3	−2.5	6.6	10.7	5.6
Denver Broncos	7.8	11.1	0.7	2.5	5.0	5.4
Houston Oilers	2.8	6.9	5.2			5.0
Indianapolis Colts	−3.8	7.2	3.0	0.4	15.8	4.5
Cincinnati Bengals	1.1	1.3	10.1	1.7	3.4	3.5
New England Patriots	−5.4	1.6	0.1	8.1	13.5	3.6
Tennessee Oilers/Titans				−0.4	4.1	1.9
New York Jets	−1.8	3.6	−8.0	2.1	12.1	1.6
Carolina Panthers		−18.9	1.7	0.7	18.8	0.6
Seattle Seahawks	−6.6	12.1	3.3	−10.9	6.4	−0.9
Detroit Lions	−4.1	−0.1	3.3	−20.9	16.4	−1.1
Jacksonville Jaguars		−16.7	−4.8	14.1	29.3	−1.3
Los Angeles Raiders	−1.3					−1.3
Los Angeles Rams	−1.8					−1.8

Note: The teams' estimated operating income is in millions of dollars. Each year represents a season. For example, 1994 is the 1994–1995 season. The Los Angeles Raiders relocated to Oakland in 1995, Los Angeles Rams to St. Louis in 1995, Cleveland Browns to Baltimore in 1995 and the Houston Oilers to Tennessee in 1997. The Carolina Panthers and Jacksonville Jaguars were expansion teams in 1995.

Source: James Quirk and Rodney D. Fort, *Hard Ball*, 207; Michael K. Ozanian, "Selective Accounting," *Forbes* (14 December 1998), 132; "Team Values," at http://www.forbes.com cited 7 September 1999.

New York Rangers, San Jose Sharks and Vancouver Canucks realized a large reduction in operating income. Interestingly, in the NHL there were extreme differences in the teams' debt to value ratios. The Detroit Red Wings, Anaheim Mighty Ducks, New Jersey Devils and Tampa Bay Lightning had 0 percent long-term debt on their financial statements. Conversely, the leverage ratios of 229 percent for the Los Angeles Kings, 153 percent for the Pittsburgh Penguins and 134 percent for the Buffalo Sabres represented the other extreme. Desperate for cash while in a Chapter 11 bankruptcy proceeding, in the mid-to-late 1990s the Penguins had to borrow money from various creditors to pay their monthly

Table 3.6
Estimated Operating Income for NHL Teams, 1994 to 1997

Team	1994	1995	1996	1997	Average
Chicago Blackhawks	12.5	22.0	26.9	13.6	18.8
Boston Bruins	13.8	11.4	17.8	18.0	15.3
Anaheim Mighty Ducks	17.1	8.7	6.9	6.3	9.8
Detroit Red Wings	17.0	13.0	9.1	−1.9	9.3
New York Rangers	14.8	9.7	10.2	−3.9	7.7
New York Islanders	−0.8	13.1	3.9	12.9	7.3
Philadelphia Flyers	7.4	9.6	9.7	2.0	7.2
San Jose Sharks	12.5	7.1	8.1	−2.6	6.3
Pittsburgh Penguins	2.2	0.8	10.1	8.7	5.5
Toronto Maple Leafs	7.1	3.5	3.4	6.8	5.2
St. Louis Blues	−2.8	0.1	6.3	13.6	4.3
Washington Capitals	−2.8	3.4	0.5	14.1	3.8
New Jersey Devils	0.6	5.6	4.3	4.4	3.7
Montreal Canadiens	6.6	−2.3	−0.4	8.3	3.1
Calgary Flames	−0.3	2.7	7.8	0.6	2.7
Quebec Nordiques	1.1				1.1
Edmonton Oilers	−1.9	2.7	−0.1	2.3	0.7
Dallas Stars	3.1	2.2	−1.0	−2.6	0.4
Ottawa Senators	2.8	−2.8	0.1	1.2	0.3
Los Angeles Kings	3.6	0.0	−2.0	−1.0	0.2
Colorado Avalanche		2.6	−0.6	−6.9	−1.6
Florida Panthers	0.5	2.9	−0.9	−9.3	−1.7
Tampa Bay Lightning	0.7	−2.7	−4.2	−1.7	−1.9
Vancouver Canucks	1.4	0.9	−0.3	−10.4	−2.1
Buffalo Sabres	−6.5	−1.1	−3.3	−1.3	−3.1
Winnipeg Jets	−3.6	−3.2			−3.4
Phoenix Coyotes			−11.7	0.7	−5.5
Hartford Whalers	−6.8	−1.0	−9.2		−5.7
Carolina Hurricanes				−13.4	−13.4

Note: The teams' estimated operating income is reported in millions of dollars. Each year is a season such as 1994–1995 through 1997–1998. The Nordiques relocated from Quebec to Colorado in
1995 and was renamed the Avalanche, the Jets from Winnipeg to Phoenix in 1996 and was renamed
the Coyotes, and the Whalers from Hartford to Carolina in 1997 and was renamed the Hurricanes.
Source: James Quirk and Rodney D. Fort, *Hard Ball*, 209; Michael K. Ozanian, "Selective Accounting," 134.

payroll expenses. (Because of deficient cash inflows and excessive debts, in 1971
and 1975 the Penguins were broke and virtually bankrupt.)

In sum, Tables 5–1 through 5–4 in *Hard Ball* indicate that from 1990 to 1996
inclusive, on average the teams in the NBA ranked first, MLB second, NFL third
and NHL fourth in annual estimated operating income. Alternatively, because
of the disproportionate impact of the player strikes in the 1994 and 1995 seasons, and the owner lockout in the 1998 season, the league rankings changed
when the years appeared as in Tables 3.2 to 3.6. The readjustment of years
placed the NFL first, NBA second, MLB third and NHL fourth. Thus, based on
the values in the revised tables the NFL moved from third to first in estimated

annual operating income, NBA first to second, MLB second to third, and the NHL remained in fourth. Moreover, the players' strike, owners' lockout and other events adversely impacted the pre-tax profits and net earnings of clubs with high leverage ratios such as the Minnesota Twins in the AL, Pittsburgh Pirates in the NL, Miami Heat in the NBA, Washington Redskins in the NFL and Los Angeles Kings in the NHL.

Besides the general and specific run-of-the-mill facts and accounting information, the histories of team performances and financial data provide sports fans and others with insights about the behavior, belief, managerial skill, and the business philosophy and strategy of various sports franchise owners. Based on the research for this book, the following six italicized statements and/or assumptions are discussed next. The statements' topics relate to franchise owners and their incentives to control, operate and manage a business enterprise within one or more of the major professional sports leagues.

OWNERSHIP: FACT OR FICTION?

Because they operate their teams as monopolists, the majority of professional sports franchise owners earn excessively high profits and percentage returns on their investments. Based on the average estimated operating incomes that were reported in *Hard Ball,* between 1990 and 1996 18 percent (21) of the total professional sports teams experienced an operating loss. If deductions for interest expense on outstanding debt and player depreciation are considered, an estimated 35 percent (42) or more of the teams realized after-tax or net losses. As depicted in Tables 3.2 to 3.6 of this chapter, 75 percent (76) of the clubs had operating profits. However, because of high leverage ratios approximately one-half of those teams likely had incurred net losses. Nevertheless, because of the market power in their geographic areas the various sports franchises that were sold in the 1990s earned at least average rates of return during their existence. By league, these rates for the clubs sold were approximately 18 percent in the NBA, 13 percent in the NFL, 12 percent in MLB and 11 percent in the NHL. Therefore, based on those average long-term financial returns, the majority of professional sports firms are a moderately profitable investment for entrepreneurs who own these businesses.[11]

In addition to the positive yet albeit moderate investment returns, there are extenuating circumstances and prudent reasons why wealthy businessmen own risky professional sports franchises. As an employee of the organization, a fraction of owners reward themselves with a multimillion-dollar salary as compensation for funding the franchise. Other owners benefit from tax shelters and write-offs that are allowed by the federal government. Furthermore, some sports moguls earn high returns on other business ventures interrelated with their clubs. The strong demand from fans and the television networks for games and for other sports entertainment events are also an important factor that motivates a businessman to be a franchise owner. To illustrate, in MLB spectators paid $9 per seat and filled 50 percent of the teams' stadium capacity in 1988. Ten years later, fans spent $15 per seat and filled 59 percent of the available seats. These reasons, in part, explain why in 1999 the small-market Oakland Athletics attracted a bid of $122 million, which was a 44 percent markup above the $85 million that investors paid for the franchise in 1995 and 860 percent greater than what Walter Haas had purchased the team for in 1980. When teams play in a new or refurbished taxpayer-subsidized stadium, the respective franchise owners prosper from an increase in advertising revenues and in concession and merchandise sales within the facility, from higher gate receipts, and from the local and regional broadcasts of games. For proof, since 1999 the bosses of the NFL Baltimore Ravens, Denver Broncos, Cleveland Browns, Pittsburgh Steelers and Tennessee Titans have pocketed millions of dollars from the construction of their new stadiums.[12]

The owners of large-market clubs are reluctant to implement any reforms and to share even marginal amounts of their gate and local broadcast revenues and operating incomes with the owners of small-market clubs. This statement is false. For example, in January 2001 Commissioner Bud Selig and MLB owners initiated a deep-rooted overhaul of the sport's economic system. With the approval of the baseball players union, a draft to reallocate a portion of the leagues' athletes will be implemented. That is, the teams with the eight worst average win-loss records during the previous three seasons will be authorized to choose one player who was left unprotected by the teams with the eight best average winning percentages. Despite the reported opposition from the owners of high-revenue, large-market teams such as NL New York Mets' Nelson Doubleday and AL New York Yankees' George Steinbrenner, the draft is structured to reduce the player development and recruitment costs of the low-revenue, small-market clubs. These teams include the NL's Florida Marlins, Montreal Expos, Pittsburgh Pirates and San Diego Padres, and the AL's Kansas City Royals, Minnesota Twins, Oakland Athletics and Tampa Bay Devil Rays.[13]

Unlike the other leagues, in the NFL a spirit of compromise, cooperation and unity prevails between the team owners. For instance, all revenues from national television broadcasts and licensing contracts are shared equally by the league franchises, and there are limits for maximum and minimum team payrolls. Beginning in the 2002 season, 40 percent of gate receipts earned by each visiting team during preseason and regular season games will be consolidated by the commissioner's office and then distributed in equal proportions to all NFL clubs. Because of the reallocation of revenues from the successful large-market to struggling small-market franchises, these strategies will further reduce the imbalances in playing strengths that exist between the perennial winning teams and the also-rans.[14]

To create more opportunities for cash inflows and operating revenues within their market areas, some team owners are more aggressive, bold and competent than other owners. Within all United States manufacturing and service industries, including professional sports, there are small, medium and large business firms headed by executives who have exhibited dynamic leadership skills and applied a variety of managerial tactics to be innovative when marketing their products and services. As such, there are individuals who have succeeded as executives in nonsports businesses but failed to be shrewd owners of professional sports franchises. In the NFL, for example, during numerous seasons more stable and talented owners would have especially benefited the Arizona Cardinals, Atlanta Falcons, Cincinnati Bengals, New Orleans Saints, Oakland Raiders, Philadelphia Eagles, San Diego Chargers and Seattle Seahawks. Furthermore, for various reasons some sports team owners have been unable to assemble organizations that can cope with adversity and controversy that involved coaches, players and themselves. For instance, the owners of the NBA Hornets, George Shinn and Raymond Woolridge, were not well respected in the city of Charlotte and Mecklenburg County, North Carolina. In June 2001, a referendum to allocate public money for the construction of a $200 million arena in downtown Charlotte was overwhelmingly defeated by the voters. In part, this occurred because of Shinn's alleged sexual misconduct and Woolridge's inability or indifference to negotiate in good faith with the city and county governments about how the arena should be financed. For selected franchises, however, the owners are passionate about their league, sport and team, and they work to be role models in their communities. With revolutionary zeal, these proprietors have adopted managerial strategies to generate goodwill among the clubs' local and regional sports fans and perhaps to create wealth for their organizations. To illustrate this phenomenon, five owners are highlighted.[15]

Ray Chambers and Lewis Katz, who were key members of a group that paid $150 million to acquire the NBA New Jersey Nets, in July 2001 placed 35 percent of their ownership shares in a trust for the benefit of inner-city youth who reside in New Jersey. Their proportion of the trust's profits will be contributed to mentoring programs, scholarships and other educational and social services for at-risk teenagers who live in Camden, Jersey City, Newark, Paterson and Trenton.[16]

Since 1988, the NFL Dallas Cowboys' owner Jerry Jones has redefined stadium economics and exploited lucrative revenue sources such as corporate sponsorships and the television networks. In Dallas, Jones opened a Cowboys golf course in June 2001 and expanded the brands of football equipment and merchandise available for sale at twelve Cowboy retail stores. His grand vision is the construction of a 100,000-seat, retractable-domed, air-conditioned stadium that will operate as a theme park and home field for the team. Furthermore, in November 2001 Jones and his family launched the Dallas Desperados, which began its inaugural season as the twentieth team in the Arena Football League.[17]

Chambers, Katz and Jones aside, Mark Cuban, the animated and effervescent owner of the NBA Dallas Mavericks produced the NBA's first international Webcast, which features play-by-play games in English, Mandarin and Spanish. Known for his courtside antics, glib tongue and rapport with his coaches and players, Cuban is an astute businessman who quantifies the maturity and

financial implication of each player's contract as a short- and long-term strategy to make his team more efficient. Furthermore, he digitizes the tapes of
opponents' games and converts them to CD-ROMs for his coaching staff and
players to analyze. At either the former Reunion Arena or current American
Airlines Center in Dallas, Mark has run on court to protect his players during
a game brawl, has accumulated $1 million in league fines for harassing referees,
and has lifted weights and performed calisthenics with his players before and
after practices. Maverick fans appreciate and relish Cuban's enthusiasm and vi-
tality. In the 2000–2001 season, the club's revenues rose 70 percent from ticket
sales and 30 percent from corporate sponsorships. Because of Cuban's involvement, the Mavericks have become a competitive and high-performance team in
the Midwest Division of the Western Conference.[18]

Lastly, leveraged buyout specialist Tom Hicks, the owner of the AL Texas
Rangers and NHL Dallas Stars, intends to organize and develop a synergistic
conglomerate. Since 1998, his strategies have doubled the Rangers' broadcast
revenues and tripled the Stars' cash inflows from the radio and television networks. In 2001, the Rangers ranked seventh in revenue among the teams in
MLB, and the Stars placed sixth in payroll and revenues in the NHL. For the future, Hicks plans to commercialize 230 acres of real estate that surrounds The
Ballpark, which is the Rangers' home field located in the suburb of Arlington,
Texas. Then, he plans to join with real estate mogul Ross Perot Jr. on a similar
venture in a downtown complex, where a new $350 million stadium would be
the anchor investment for his sports teams. Basically, Hicks has parlayed two
professional teams into one huge television deal and turned two sports facilities
into real estate developments.[19]

*After 2000, fewer individuals and families and more corporations and joint
stock companies will acquire and operate professional sports teams.* Since franchise values have skyrocketed from less than $5 million in the 1950s to $20 million in the 1970s, and then above $600 million in the early 2000s, only a small
fraction of individuals and families are willing and can afford to successfully
own and operate sports teams as partnerships and sole proprietors. Beginning
with CBS's purchase of the New York Yankees from Dan Topping and Del Webb
for $11.2 million in 1964, team ownership has drifted to large and well-financed
conglomerates, entertainment and media corporations, and joint stock companies. Relative to their role as operators of a sports franchise, the executives of
these organizations have a competitive attitude and business expertise. They are
competent, profit-oriented and accountable to the corporation's board of directors and common stockholders. Furthermore, executives are unlikely to divert
funds from sports operations into other corporate businesses, and are unautho-
rized to pay themselves income for consulting fees. As they monitor the business operations of a professional sports franchise, corporation executives will
seek to establish a combination of potential strategic alliances. If successful, this
business maneuver will result in synergies from the live-event programming
in a multichannel network and from the cable and satellite broadcasts of games.

There are other strategies and tactics that corporate executives may pursue for their sports franchises. They could exploit and market the sports team as a brand, blend sports assets with the parent companies' entertainment properties, and develop an arena or stadium complex where a sports game is just one event. Despite these opportunities, however, corporate executives must avoid conflicts of interest. That is, they should be ethical and adhere to league rules that discourage owners from undermining salary-cap regulations by offering side deals such as stock options or movie roles to their best ballplayers. In retrospect, if winning is an essential goal of the team owner besides the maximization of net profits, then corporate executives and joint stock company managers may become more committed and loyal to their local fans and host communities than individual owners and families who had relocated their clubs for self-interest reasons. Those proprietors included Peter O'Malley and Horace Stoneham in MLB, Bob Short and Donald Sterling in the NBA, Art Modell and Robert Irsay in the NFL, and John McMullen and Jack Vickers in the NHL. With respect to recent seasons, a partial list of corporate owners consisted of the News Corporation and Tribune Company in MLB, Cablevision Systems and Comcast-Spectator Inc. in the NBA, and the YankeeNets system and Walt Disney Company in the NHL. (In the NFL, the corporate ownership of league franchises is prohibited. Furthermore, partnerships are limited to twenty-five individuals, and one person must own at least 30 percent of an NFL team.)[20]

Despite the benefits, costs and risks of corporate ownership, since the late 1990s several individuals and noncorporate groups have acquired franchises in each sports league. Businessmen such as David Glass purchased the AL Kansas City Royals, Carl Lindner the NL Cincinnati Reds, Gavin and Joseph Maloof the NBA Sacramento Kings and Daniel Snyder the NFL Washington Redskins. Furthermore, a partnership headed by coach/player Mario Lemeiux bought the NHL Pittsburgh Penguins. Nouveau riche entrepreneurs, who became prosperous from investments in computer technology and information systems, have also discovered the challenge and glamour inherent in sports team ownership. Previously, these investors earned fortunes when they created and expanded their Internet and software companies. Rather than earn more money in the technology sector, wealthy dot.com and media businessmen have purchased professional sports franchises to differentiate themselves from their peers and to satisfy their need for ego gratification and power. Besides the aforementioned franchise owners such as the NBA Dallas Mavericks' Mark Cuban and the NFL Seattle Seahawks' Paul Allen, former BMC Software Chairman John Moores operates the NL San Diego Padres. In the NHL, Computer Associates' Charles Wang and Sanjay Kumar control the New York Islanders, AOL Time Warner's Ted Leonsis the Washington Capitals, and Compuware's Peter Karmanos the Carolina Hurricanes.[21]

A group of active and former professional players are likewise potential investors in a sports team. There are numerous current and former players who are wealthy and eager to be proprietors. Indeed, large portions of them understand the business returns and risks associated with ownership. Some players are retired in a city or the suburb of a metropolitan area that hosts a professional team. Kansas City Royals legend George Brett, former Oakland Athletics slugger Reggie Jackson, and Cincinnati Reds infielder Joe Morgan have maneuvered to purchase professional baseball clubs. Also, retired Baltimore Orioles' Cal Ripken Jr., Minnesota Twins' Kirby Puckett and San Diego Padres' Tony Gwynn have expressed an interest in or are already a minority owner of a major or minor league franchise. Even former Denver Broncos quarterback John Elway and Los Angeles Lakers basketball star Ervin "Magic" Johnson are potential proprietors of NFL or AFL, and NBA or NBDL clubs. If more ex-players were owners, there would be less alienation and incrimination from fans because of league lockouts and player strikes. Moreover, with former players in control of team policies there would be more participation by Asian, African and Latin Americans in the executive offices of franchises, which is a development long overdue. One uncertainty in diversifying ownership, however, is whether ex-players would be fair and impartial in their decisions. That is, would ex-players choose to align themselves with the league or union during management-player disputes and contract negotiations?[22]

Other managerial and ownership strategies have been proposed in professional team sports. In 1999, three diehard football loyalists attempted to raise $500 million to acquire the NFL New York Jets. These fanatics established a worldwide web site named buythejets.com on behalf of Jets fans and other investors. Their goal was to solicit contributions of at least $5,000 in order to join an ownership consortium. If the plan succeeded, each contributor would be a part owner of the Jets and therefore eligible to vote for a team president and management board, and to decide whether the club should raise or reduce ticket prices. Furthermore, the ownership group would determine where the Jets would play their home games. In 2000, New York State Senator Nick Spano requested that Jets owner Robert Wood Johnson consider the relocation of the team from the Meadowlands to the Yonkers Raceway. The Rooney family, who controls the NFL Pittsburgh Steelers, owns the Raceway.[23]

If a team's operating and pre-tax losses accumulate, in the future leagues will relinquish their opposition and authorize franchise owners to move their small-market clubs to sites within or surrounding medium-sized and large metropolitan areas. In each professional sports league, there are franchises that are hopelessly unprofitable because of entrenched demographic and financial circumstances, and deplorable economic conditions. For instance, some clubs have a slim chance to play and win their division and conference titles because they are located in an inferior and/or small sports market. Other teams play in an obsolete facility or have an owner who fails to comprehend how the professional sports business operates. Therefore, these organizations are normally not capable or prepared to compete for a league championship. Given this dilemma, would a current owner unhesitatingly demand permission from the league to move his franchise if one or more of these conditions are endemic and unavoidable? One well-reasoned response to that question is as follows.

Despite the cumulative operating and pre-tax losses that occur for several seasons in a facility, historically franchise owners have been reluctant to move their operation from a metropolitan area unless they perceive that the long-term market value of the enterprise will decline at the current site. Yet, owners cannot tolerate this predicament forever. In Vancouver, Canada, because of weak attendance and the disparity in value between the Canadian and U.S. dollars, in 2001 the NBA approved the relocation of the Grizzlies to Memphis, which is a mid-sized city in western Tennessee. Because of the escalation in player salaries and the high province and federal government taxes, except for the NHL Toronto Maple Leafs who are stable, the Canadian-based hockey franchises are unprofitable, and the respective team owners demand public subsidies. If these business and economic conditions persist, before 2005 a few Canadian NHL teams will be forced to disband or relocate to the United States along with the NL Montreal Expos, AL Toronto Blue Jays and eventually the NBA Toronto Raptors. Very few owners in the professional sports business are willing to absorb millions of dollars in losses each year and to remain idle while their investments perpetually lose market value.[24]

Besides relocation, another option being considered by various sports authorities is to downsize the league and eliminate weak franchises and remove their respective owners. This option has been discussed, especially by MLB and perhaps by the NBA, NFL and NHL. Although it is a desperate action, the elimination of poorly operated franchises would motivate each league's existing owners to improve their teams' finances and performances, or otherwise confront the possibility of a future disenfranchisement.

In MLB, and the NBA and NHL the *cross-ownership of teams will continue and succeed because of operating externalities and other financial benefits.* With an increased emphasis on greater investment returns, higher market values and less risks, the future business model for successful franchise operations is for a well-financed corporate owner to establish a large presence in an area and control multiple teams, facilities and a regional sports broadcast network. This model creates synergy, which is an intangible asset that can be sold by franchise owners to investors as securities in the public equity markets. With their synergistic sports and non-sports holdings, current corporate owners of sports franchises such as the AOL Time Warner Inc., Ascent Entertainment Group, Cablevision Systems, CBS, Comcast-Spectator Inc., News Corporation, Tribune Company and the Walt Disney Company have adopted this model to attract investment capital and to maximize the organizations' long-term value for its shareholders.[25]

SUMMARY

This chapter discussed the motivation, role and significance of individuals and groups who own and operate franchises in one or more of the professional sports leagues. First, for each sport league the wherewithal and strategies of owners that operated clubs prior to 1950 were examined. Then, to measure the influence of new owners on twenty-five clubs that were sold between 1950 and 2000, the pre-sale and post-sale win-loss percentages and titles won were determined and tabled for each team. The differences in the pre-sale and post-sale average win-loss percentages and the number of titles won reflected how the clubs in each league performed under new ownership.

Based on the average annual estimated operating income per season, five tables were presented that depict the financial performances of all teams in the AL, NL, NBA, NFL and NHL during the mid-1990s. The strategies of various owners and the success of their clubs were highlighted. The traditional and new business models that owners have adopted, which consider host communities and local fans, were discussed. Finally, six introspective issues, which were framed as statements about owners and their contribution to professional sports leagues and teams, were listed and analyzed.

Chapter 4 explores how, when and why selected ballplayers have succeeded by playing for professional teams that exist within leagues and the sports industry. Besides possessing their athletic skills, charisma, leadership and prowess to compete and win titles and league championships for their respective teams, ballplayers also influence the culture and growth of professional sports in America. These and other matters are explored in Chapter 4.

NOTES

1. For background information and incidents about the business and legal aspects of professional sports leagues, franchises, owners, players and unions, see Michael E. Jones, *Sports Law* (Upper Saddle, NJ: Prentice-Hall, 1999), 115–127. To determine whether a sports team is a profitable investment, potential investors should consider several factors. These include the club's economic value, financial and legal obligations, and the organization's ownership structure and marketing expertise. For an analysis of the fundamental business elements of a team and the financial advantages and disadvantages of ownership, see Michael K. Ozanian, "How to Buy a Sports Team," *Financial World* (20 May 1996), 66; Jordan Rappaport and Chad Wilkerson, "What Are the Benefits of Hosting a Major League Sports Franchise?" *Economic Review* (First Quarter 2001), 55–86.

2. Team ownership and sales transactions in MLB, and in the NBA, NFL and NHL are described in James Quirk and Rodney D. Fort, *Pay Dirt: The Business of Professional Team Sports* (Princeton, NJ: Princeton University Press, 1992), 378–478.

3. See various editions of *The World Almanac and Book of Facts* (Mahwah, NJ: World Almanac Books, 1950–2001) to obtain the win-loss percentages, division and conference titles and league championships won, and the player performances and statistics for professional sports teams in MLB, and in the NBA, NFL and NHL. In a Data Supplement, *Pay Dirt* contains the ownership histories of franchises in each professional sport since the respective organizations were founded to the early 1990s.

4. See John Steinbreder, "The Owners," *Sports Illustrated* (13 September 1993), 64–87; "2000 Inside the Ownership of Professional Sports Teams," at http://www.teammarket ing.com cited 20 November 2001; "The Owners: Who Are These Guys?" at http://

www.resonator.com cited 20 November 2001; "Media Ownership of Teams," at http://www.resonator.com cited 20 November 2001.

5. Ibid.

6. Michael K. Ozanian, "Selective Accounting," *Forbes* (14 December 1998), 124–134; Kurt Badenhausen and William Sicheri, "Baseball Games," *Forbes* (31 May 1999), 112–117

7. The sale of the Florida Marlins was discussed in "Sources Say Marlins Owner Ready to Sell," *Charlotte Observer* (23 November 2001), 14C; "Sales of Marlins, Expos Imminent," *Charlotte Observer* (2 February 2002), 8C; Ronald Blum, "Expos, Marlins Switches Approved," *Charlotte Observer* (13 February 2002), 6C.

8. For specific information about NBA teams such as the majority owners, estimated market values, annual changes in values and the total revenues, operating incomes, and debt to value ratios, see the "National Basketball Association," at http://www.forbes.com cited 30 November 1999. For the NFL clubs, selected ownership data is available in "Team Values," at http://www.forbes.com cited 7 September 1999. The deal to sell the Falcons by majority owner Taylor Smith to Arthur M. Blanks is newsworthy. See Maria Saporta, "Home Depot Founder to Buy Falcons for $545 Million," *Charlotte Observer* (7 December 2001), 1C.

9. See James Quirk and Rodney D. Fort, *Pay Dirt,* 378–478; Michael K. Ozanian, "Selective Accounting," 130–134.

10. According to economists, the underlying cause of the problems in professional team sports is the monopoly power of sports leagues, and how the leagues exercise that power. For a thorough discussions of this viewpoint, see James Quirk and Rodney D. Fort, *Hard Ball: The Abuse of Power in Pro Team Sports* (Princeton, NJ: Princeton University Press, 1999).

11. Ibid., 206–213.

12. See "Mr. A's Owner?" at http://www.cnnsi.com cited 2 July 1999; "A's Settle Dispute With Authorities: Team Remains up for Sale," at http://www.yahoo.sports.com cited 2 December 1998; Ron Gloster, "A's to Stay in Oakland for at Least Two More Seasons," at http://www.yahoo.sports.com cited 2 December 1998; Idem., "Groups Looking Into Bid for Oakland Athletics," at http://baseball.yahoo.com cited 29 October 1998; "Price Check," at http://www.cnnsi.com cited 27 October 1998.

13. See Ronald Blum, "MLB Owners OK Rules to Share Wealth," at http://wire.ap.org cited 18 January 2001.

14. "Equal Portions: NFL Owners Approve New Revenue-Sharing Plan," at http://www.cnnsi.com cited 17 January 2001.

15. Several professional sports teams would benefit from a change in ownership. For a discussion of which franchises are operated at less than maximum efficiency, see Ira Miller, "Bad Teams Often Have Something in Common—Bad Owners—NFL Insider," at http://sports.yahoo.com cited 23 November 1999; Frank Deford, "Incompetent Owners Ruining Baseball," at http://www.cnnsi.com cited 26 July 2000; Ron Green Sr., "Once Man of the Hour, Shinn a Passing Thought," *Charlotte Observer* (24 September 2001), 2C. In 2001, owner Rich Devos announced the sale of the NBA Orlando Magic and the Sportsplex. Because of high costs, the franchise operates at a deficit. For an exclusive question-and-answer interview about the sale, see Lynn Hoppes, "Why Are You Selling the Magic?" *Orlando Sentinel* (13 January 2002), C1, C9.

16. See Richard O'Brien and Mark Mravic, "Owners You Can Trust," *Sports Illustrated* (21 December 1998), 32–33.

17. For Jerry Jones' strategy, see "Football," *Charlotte Observer* (14 November 2001), 6C.

18. John McFarland, "Cuban's Comments Draw Record Hit—$500,000," *Charlotte Observer* (9 January 2002), 4C.

19. See John Helyar, "A Team of Their Own," *Fortune* (14 May 2001), 190–197; Daniel Fisher and Michael K. Ozanian, "Cowboy Capitalism," *Forbes* (20 September 1999), 170–178.

20. Andrew Zimbalist, "Not Suitable For Families," *U.S. News & World Report* (20 January 1997), 9; Roy S. Johnson and Rajiv M. Rao, "Take Me Out to The Boardroom," *Fortune* (21 July 1997), 42–48.

21. See Ronald Grover, "Pro Basketball's Family Act," at http://proquest.umi.com cited 30 August 2001; Edward Cone, "Boys and Their Toys," *Interactive Week* (5 June 2000), 34–41.

22. Several wealthy current and former ballplayers are eyeing the owner's box. For the motivation and implication of this ownership model, see Ronald Grover, "Superstars Could Make Super Owners," at http://proquest.umi.com cited 30 August 2001; Mark Hyman, "Up From the Dugout," *Business Week* (24 March 1997), 211; "High Rollers," at http://www.cnnsi.com cited 24 July 1999; Hamil R. Harris, "ABA Returns With Black Ownership," at http://proquest.umi.com cited 30 August 2001.

23. See Rachel Emma Silverman, "How Much for Those Jets Tickets? That's It—Let's Just Buy the Team," *Wall Street Journal* (19 August 1999), B1; Mark Hyman, "The Jets: Worth a Gazillion?" *Business Week* (6 December 1999), 99–100; "Life in Yonkers?" at http://www.cnnsi.com cited 19 January 2000; "Good Luck Woody!" at http://www.buythejets.com cited 3 September 2001.

24. Since the 1950s, the NHL's decision to expand the league has entailed risks. The Canadian teams play hard but are losing fans and money. These trends are discussed in three articles. See Trent Frayne, "Too Many Teams, Too Few Players," *Maclean's* (4 January 1993), 64; Wayne M. Barrett, "Crying All the Way to the Bank," *USA Today Magazine* (January 1995), 59; D'Arcy Jenish, "The Troubled State of Sport," *Maclean's* (11 September 2000), 36–37.

25. See Brian Garrity, "Sports Owners Look to Maximize Equity Value in Synergies," *The Investment Dealer's Digest* (30 November 1998), 9–10; "Kings Co-Owners Buy Into Lakers," at http://www.cnnsi.com cited 4 November 1998; Stefan Fatsis and Kara Swisher, "Group Led by AOL's Leonsis to Acquire NHL's Capitals and Other Sports Stacks," *Wall Street Journal* (13 May 1999), A8.

Chapter 4

Players

Besides competitive team rivalries, local and national economic conditions, and the investment capital and leadership provided by franchise owners, there are other factors that affect the business success, entertainment value and future growth of the five American professional sports leagues—AL, NL, NBA, NFL and NHL, namely athleticism, image and popularity of the teams' players. These recognizable, talented and well-conditioned men have superior athletic skills that are developed to play professional baseball, basketball, and football or hockey games at a furious pace. During games, some players can hit and pitch 95-mile-per-hour fastballs, jump and shoot to score more than thirty points in less than forty minutes, block 300-pound linemen and tackle 250-pound running backs, or slap shot a one-inch thick vulcanized rubber puck to a teammate while rigorously skating on ice. Despite the unrealistic expectations of most sports fans and the media, and pressures from family and friends, and perhaps friction from contacts with coaches, owners and teammates, ultimately it is the individual efforts and collective performances of the players that determine whether a team excels during a season and wins a World Series, NBA Championship, Super Bowl or Stanley Cup.

Prior to the 1970s, the U.S. professional sports leagues adopted rules that discouraged franchise owners from bidding against each other for the services of players. The existence of two labor systems, one to draft rookies and the other to re-sign veterans essentially meant that the owners controlled each player's annual compensation, conditions of employment and to which team he would be assigned. As a result of these labor systems, free agents and all active players were forced to accept an owner's contract offer or else retire from the sport. Without group representation, therefore, the professional players had restricted freedoms, which limited their mobility, right to be traded and opportunity to earn more income. In response to economic cycles and market forces, and after many years of conflict, litigation and negotiation with the leagues, eventually the players in each professional sport organized and joined an association or

union as a forum to expand and protect their rights and to discuss their griev-
ances as employees of private sector organizations. To conclude these actions, a
Collective Bargaining Agreement (CBA) was signed by representatives of a players association or union and a league. Indeed, the CBA became the legal docu-
ment that contractually defined the employment relationship between franchise
owners and players on matters related to hours, wages and working conditions.
As it evolved in each sports league, the typical CBA highlighted specific employee and employer concerns, and especially those issues that involved free
agency, player compensation and seniority, and the team's commitments to its
athletes. For example, in the late 1990s MLB's CBA contained clauses that mandated a flat payroll tax on players' salaries, a luxury tax on team payrolls that
exceeded a specific dollar amount, a procedure to resolve salary disputes through
arbitration, a program for substance abuse, and a system to determine how players are classified and paid as free agents and veterans.[1]

In the NBA, a CBA generally has included elements such as the minimum
wages for rookies and experienced players, teams' salary cap levels, long-term
contract guarantees and incentives for players, participation requirements and
rules of the league's antidrug program, and compensation payments that pertain to restricted and unrestricted free agents. The NFL's CBA has normally encompassed minimum salary schedules for players based on league experience,
rookie and team salary caps, clauses that incorporate incentive payments and
signing bonuses, rules and salary levels for franchise and transition players, drug
violation policies, and the options and expiration period for players who qualify for restricted and unrestricted free agency. In the NHL, a typical CBA contains sections that outline a compensatory draft system for clubs, teams' roster
limitations, player performance and nonperformance bonus schemes, minimum
salary levels for rookies and veterans, arbitration eligibility and requirements,
and the player categories that relate to restricted and unrestricted free agency.[2]

In short, according to the traditional CBAs in professional sports, the league
officials and player representatives must collectively bargain in good faith on
mandatory compensation and employment topics such as arbitration and/or me-
diation, free agency, guaranteed player contracts, minimum salary and perhaps
maximum payroll levels, pension benefits, salary caps and seniority. If the league
and/or union knowingly decide to violate a CBA requirement, the filing of an
unfair labor practice and complaint may result in monetary damages to be levied
against the guilty party by a court. Nevertheless, despite clauses that incorporate player bonus payments, luxury taxes on high-revenue teams, specific rules
on free agency, and a cap on salaries or payrolls, since 1975 there have been six
work stoppages that interrupted MLB, one at the NBA, and two each at the NFL
and NHL. In sum, although their actions and strategies are partially regulated
by CBAs, leagues and player unions constantly challenge each other's business
and legal freedoms and rights.

For years, various economic, financial and social events and problems have
impacted the professional sports leagues and caused them to initiate reforms.

One issue frequently discussed in newspapers and magazines and by television commentators concerns the league commissioners, franchise owners, players and sports fans. That is the extravagant player salaries and extraordinary growth in team payrolls. To bid on talented free agents and to re-sign their veteran players, team owners reduce their nonoperating expenses and/or generate more cash inflows from their arena or stadium. If owners are able to attract corporate sponsorships, raise ticket prices, furnish and sell club seats and luxury suites at peak prices to local businesses and spectators, and contract with networks to broadcast home and away games on the local and regional radio and television stations, then more revenues are available to bid for top-notch players whose contracts are due to expire. In brief, during the 1990s the competition between team owners to employ skilled players resulted in higher payrolls and, for most clubs, less operating income and net earnings. In turn, this financial dilemma created imbalances and inequities within each league as superior players abandoned the struggling small-to-medium-market teams to join the wealthier large-market franchises.

Professional sports analysts and public policy economists have thoroughly researched the payroll disparities that exist between teams in various divisions and conferences. In one empirical study, the authors determined that from 1990 through 1996 the payroll differences between clubs explained approximately 25 percent of the average performances of teams in the AL, NL and NFL, and about 46 percent of the average win-loss records of clubs in the NBA and 50 percent in the NHL. The authors also concluded that the strong revenue potential of the large metropolitan market areas provides a financial incentive for the star players on small-market teams to migrate after one or more successful seasons to the big-city teams. Thus, because of potentially higher incomes the most talented players in each sports league will ultimately play for franchises located in the Chicago, Los Angeles and New York metropolitan areas.[3]

From 1990 to 1996 inclusive, for each sports league the respective ranks in average player costs per year of the dominant teams in Chicago, Los Angles and New York City were as follows. In the AL, the White Sox in Chicago placed fifth and the Yankees in New York first. In the NL, the Cubs in Chicago ranked sixth, the Dodgers in Los Angeles second and the Mets in New York fifth. In the NBA, the Bulls in Chicago were ninth, the Lakers in Los Angeles first and the Knickerbockers in New York third. In the NFL, the Bears in Chicago rated eighteenth and the Giants in New York third. In the NHL, the Black Hawks in Chicago finished seventh, the Kings in Los Angeles second and the Rangers in New York first. Furthermore, economic theory predicts that the least skilled athletes will be allocated to teams located in small-market areas such as the Cleveland Indians and Minnesota Twins in the AL, Montreal Expos and Pittsburgh Pirates in the NL, Denver Nuggets and Milwaukee Bucks in the NBA, Cincinnati Bengals and San Diego Chargers in the NFL, and the Edmonton Oilers and San Jose Sharks in the NHL. In fact, from 1990 through 1996 the average annual payroll of clubs in those cities reflected each area's population and wealth.

By league and team, the values were as follows. In the AL, the average payroll for the Indians in Cleveland was twelfth and for the Twins in Minnesota fourteenth. In the NL, the Expos in Montreal placed fourteenth in player costs and the Pirates in Pittsburgh twelfth. In the NBA, the payrolls of the Nuggets in Denver ranked nineteenth and the Bucks in Milwaukee twenty-third. In the NFL, the team payrolls for the Bengals in Cincinnati and for the Chargers in San Diego tied for twenty-second. In the NHL, the average salary for the Oilers in Edmonton was twenty-seventh and for the Sharks in San Jose twenty-fifth. Indeed, for the seven seasons the majority of low-payroll teams in each sport rarely won conference titles and league championships.[4]

To publish his sports book, *For Whom the Ball Tolls: A Fan's Guide to Economic Issues in Professional and College Sports,* Thomas J. Kruckemeyer studied two variables for clubs. That is, the total payroll and payroll per win. By variable, he ranked every team in MLB for the 1988 and 1994 seasons and in the NHL for the 1989–1990 and 1993–1994 seasons. (The variables for the NFL and NHL teams were not ranked.) Within MLB, in the 1988 season the high-payroll NL Los Angeles Dodgers and New York Mets and the AL Boston Red Sox placed in the top ten in payroll per victory and each club won division titles. The Dodgers, whose total payroll at $16.4 million placed second to the top-rated AL New York Yankees at $20.7 million, won the 1988 World Series by defeating the AL champion Oakland Athletics whose payroll at $10.7 million rated eighteenth in baseball. Six years later, the six division winners in MLB had payrolls that ranked: first—New York Yankees at $31.7 million; third—Chicago White Sox at $29.5 million; fourth—Cincinnati Reds at $29.4 million; sixth—Los Angeles Dodgers at $28.4 million; fifteenth—Texas Rangers at $21.2 million; and twenty-seventh—Montreal Expos at $13.5 million. On August 11, however, the 1994 season abruptly ended when the players initiated a work stoppage that eliminated the Playoffs and World Series.[5]

Within the NHL, in total team payroll the division leaders in the 1989–1990 season were ranked, respectively: second—New York Rangers at $7.8 million; third—Chicago Black Hawks at $7.1 million; sixth—Boston Bruins at $6.8 million, and twelfth—Calgary Flames at $5.8 million. In the 1990 Stanley Cup game, the Smythe Division runner-up Edmonton Oilers, who ranked eighth in total payroll and payroll per point, defeated in five games the Adams Division champion Boston Bruins, who were sixteenth in payroll per victory. The Oilers' MVP Mark Messier, and Bill Ranford who was the MVP in the Playoffs, dominated the Bruins' outstanding defenseman Ray Bourque and All-Star Cam Neely. Meanwhile, in the NHL's 1993–1994 season the total payrolls of the division leaders ranked them, respectively: first—Pittsburgh Penguins at $20.7 million; second—New York Rangers at $19.4 million; fifth—Detroit Red Wings at $16.6 million; and fifteenth—Calgary Flames at $12.7 million. In 1994, the Rangers won the Stanley Cup in seven games by beating the Vancouver Canucks, who were eighteenth in total payroll and payroll per point. Coached by Mike Keenan, the Rangers' MVP Brian Leetch and scoring ace Sergei Zubov outplayed the Canucks' Pavel Bure, who finished the regular season ranked first in goals and power-play goals and fifth in points. In sum, Kruckemeyer found that for the 1988 and 1994 seasons in MLB and for the 1989–1990 and 1993–1994 seasons in the NHL, the high-payroll teams tended to win division and/or conference titles and league championships more frequently than the low-payroll clubs did. Therefore, this research demonstrates how total payroll and payroll per point related to player and team performances during two se-lected seasons each in MLB and the NHL. The chapter's next section elaborates further about player salaries and discusses in detail how much money various franchise owners spent on payrolls and how the respective teams performed for particular seasons in MLB, and in the NBA, NFL and NHL.[6]

PLAYER SALARIES AND TEAM PAYROLLS BY SPORT

MLB

Between 1990 and 2000, the average payroll in baseball increased by 282 per-cent, or from $17 million each for twenty-six clubs to $65 million each for thirty teams. In 1990, the small-market low-payroll Pittsburgh Pirates and Cincinnati Reds won the NL Eastern and Western Divisions, respectively, and competed for the NL championship. The large-market high-payroll New York Mets finished the regular season in second place, four games behind the Pirates, and the large-market high-payroll Los Angeles Dodgers ended in second place, five games be-hind the Reds. The Pirates, who were fifth in team batting and third in pitching among the league teams featured Cy Young Award hurler Doug Drabek and MVP Barry Bonds, while the Reds placed first in batting and second in pitching in team performance. The payroll leaders in the AL, the large-market New York Yankees and California Angels, finished seventh and fourth in their respective Divisions in the 1990 season, and the small-market low-payroll Minnesota Twins finished seventh and the Seattle Mariners fifth in the Western Division. In the AL Championship Series, the small-to-medium-market, high-payroll Oakland Athletics beat the large-market, high-payroll Boston Red Sox in four consecu-tive games. For the Athletics, sluggers Mark McGwire and Jose Canseco com-bined to clout seventy-six home runs and account for 209 runs-batted-in, and Cy Young Award pitcher Bob Welch and his teammate Dave Stewert won forty-nine total games. When the AL and NL champions met, the Reds defeated the Athletics in four games to win the 1990 World Series. That year in MLB the small-market Kansas City Royals had the largest payroll at $23 million, and the small-market Baltimore Orioles squad received the lowest total salary at $8 mil-lion. The Royals ended the season at 75–86 and sixth in the AL Western Divi-sion and the Orioles at 76–85 and fifth in the AL Eastern Division.[7]

In 1990, the MLB players received an average salary of $579,000. If all players in the sport are included, the Oakland Athletics' Jose Canseco signed the most lu-crative contract whereby he earned a salary of $4.7 million a year for five seasons. Canseco aside, in 1990 the other high-priced baseball players were accomplished veterans. They included at a $3.8 million annual salary the New York Yankees' Don Mattingly who was the AL batting champion in 1984 and MVP in 1985; at a $3.7 million income the San Francisco Giants' infielder Will Clark; and at a $3.5 million wage the Oakland Athletics' pitching star Dave Stewart.[8]

Since the early-to-mid-1990s, baseball team payrolls have inflated because wealthy team owners, who were dedicated to win games, had aggressively bid to employ skilled free agents, rookies and seasoned players. A thorough search of sources revealed several references on various annual team payrolls, and the salaries and long-term contracts of professional baseball players. Based on published team payrolls, Tables 4.1 for the AL and 4.2 for the NL were developed to discover which clubs paid the *most* and *least* for each victory in 1998, and then two seasons later changed rank because of adjustments in their total payroll and/or the number of wins. To determine the ranks, Tables 4.1 and 4.2 contain the ratios of annual payroll per win for each team in the 1998 and 2000 seasons and how the teams ranked during those years. Thus, the column labeled Rank in 1998 lists in order, from top to bottom, the most inefficient or highest payroll per win club to the most efficient or lowest payroll per win club. For example, the AL team that paid the most money in salaries for a victory in 1998, the Baltimore Orioles, is ranked first while the club with the least expenditures per win, the Detroit Tigers, placed fourteenth.

The mean (average) payroll per victory in the AL increased by 56 percent, or from $523,000 in 1998 to $818,000 in 2000, and in the NL by 71 percent, or from $464,000 in 1998 to $795,000 in 2000. In the AL, the Baltimore Orioles had the highest payroll at $72 million and the Detroit Tigers the lowest at $19 million in 1998 (Table 4.1). That year, the Orioles ranked sixth in team batting and seventh in pitching among fourteen teams in the league. Veteran Orioles' players such as Cal Ripken, Harold Baines and Roberto Alomar were disappointments in hitting, and the club's only effective pitcher was Mike Mussina who finished the regular season at 13–10. The Orioles paid $71,811,000 in payroll for seventy-nine wins and finished the regular season behind the New York Yankees, Boston Red Sox and Toronto Blue Jays in the Eastern Division. The Detroit Tigers, which was the most efficient AL club in payroll per win at $295,000, spent $19,175,000 for sixty-five victories. In the 1998 season, the Tigers placed two games ahead of the Tampa Bay Devil Rays who paid $27,342,000 in payroll costs for sixty-three wins. Surprisingly, the payroll per win marginally declined from $494,000 in 1998 to $413,000 in 2000 for the Kansas City Royals and from $350,000 to $340,000 for the Minnesota Twins. Indeed, from 1998 to 2000 the Royals reduced its total payroll costs by $4 million and won five more games, and the Twins cut its payroll costs by $1 million and lost only one additional game.

Interestingly, Table 4.1 denotes that twelve AL clubs spent more per victory in 2000 than in 1998. Furthermore, relative to the league competitors eight teams fell in rank in 2000 and became more cost efficient such as the Anaheim Angels, Baltimore Orioles, Cleveland Indians, Seattle Mariners and Texas Rangers. Con-

Table 4.1
Team Payroll Per Win and Rank in the AL, 1998 and 2000

Team	1998 Payroll/Win	Rank	2000 Payroll/Win	Rank
Baltimore Orioles	909	1	1,087	3
Texas Rangers	687	2	1,023	4
Cleveland Indians	669	3	1,005	5
Boston Red Sox	646	4	1,141	2
New York Yankees	575	5	1,314	1
Seattle Mariners	574	6	767	9
Anaheim Angels	569	7	721	10
Kansas City Royals	494	8	413	13
Chicago White Sox	439	9	564	11
Tampa Bay Devil Rays	434	10	944	6
Toronto Blue Jays	388	11	804	8
Minnesota Twins	350	12	340	14
Oakland Athletics	303	13	472	12
Detroit Tigers	295	14	868	7

Note: The two Payroll/Win columns are each team's annual payrolls divided by the number of regular season wins. The values are presented in hundreds of thousands of dollars. Rank is self-explanatory.

Source: "Baseball: 1998 Team Payrolls," at http://www.usatoday.com cited 19 May 1999; "Baseball: Final 2000 Payroll Figures," at http://www.cnnsi.com cited 21 March 2001; *The World Almanac and Book of Facts* (Mahwah, NJ: World Almanac Books, 1999, 2001).

versely, six teams increased in rank as their total payrolls rose and/or wins declined such as the Boston Red Sox, Detroit Tigers, New York Yankees, Tampa Bay Devil Rays and Toronto Blue Jays.[9]

In contrast, the NL Los Angeles Dodgers spent $62,748,000 for eighty-three victories in the 1998 season and finished third in the Western Division behind the San Diego Padres and San Francisco Giants (Table 4.2). At $1.9 million per player, the Dodgers' total payroll was eightfold greater than the Montreal Expos who experienced the lowest-payroll per win at $127,000. In performance, the Dodgers finished thirteenth in team batting and fifth in pitching. Their best hitter, Gary Sheffield, batted .302 and only two Dodgers' pitchers recorded a win-loss percentage above .500. The Expos, meanwhile, placed fourth in the Eastern Division. In team statistics, the club finished the 1998 season fourteenth in batting and ninth in pitching. In sum, the performances of the Dodgers and Expos were inferior despite the wide differences in each club's total payroll and payroll per wins.

In the NL, two high-valued contracts were signed in late 1998 when the Dodgers agreed to pay Kevin Brown $105 million, or $15 million annually for seven seasons, and the Arizona Diamondbacks guaranteed Randy Johnson $52.4 million, or $13.1 million per year for four seasons. As a pitcher for the San Diego Padres in 1997, Brown's win-loss record was 16–9, and he achieved an earned run average (ERA) of 2.69. In 1998, for the Dodgers the ace pitcher finished at

Table 4.2
Team Payroll Per Win and Rank in the NL, 1998 and 2000

| | 1998 | | 2000 | |
Team	Payroll/Win	Rank	Payroll/Win	Rank
Los Angeles Dodgers	756	1	1,221	1
New York Mets	666	2	1,061	2
Colorado Rockies	619	3	789	10
Atlanta Braves	582	4	995	5
Chicago Cubs	553	5	1,004	4
San Francisco Giants	545	6	614	12
San Diego Padres	541	7	844	7
St. Louis Cardinals	531	8	847	6
Arizona Diamondbacks	486	9	1,023	3
Houston Astros	473	10	809	9
Milwaukee Brewers	431	11	568	14
Philadelphia Phillies	381	12	829	8
Florida Marlins	280	13	391	16
Cincinnati Reds	268	14	619	11
Pittsburgh Pirates	198	15	525	15
Montreal Expos	127	16	589	13

Note: See Table 4.1

Source: See Table 4.1

18–7 with an ERA of 2.38 and 257 strikeouts. Alternatively, as a pitcher for the Seattle Mariners Johnson was 20–4 with an ERA of 2.28 and 291 strikeouts in 1997. One year later, he fell to 9–10, recorded an ERA of 4.33, but struck out 213 hitters for the Diamondbacks. In the 1999 season, Kevin Brown pitched worse for the Dodgers who finished third in the Eastern Division. Meanwhile, Randy Johnson won the Cy Young Award for the Diamondbacks who finished first in the Western Division but were defeated in four games by the New York Mets in the Playoffs.[10]

In 2000, the payroll per team equaled $65 million in MLB. The payroll for the New York Yankees at $114 million and the Los Angeles Dodgers at $105 million meant that each team paid the highest salaries per player in their respective leagues. On the other hand, the Minnesota Twins at $24 million and the Florida Marlins at $31 million each spent the least in total payroll. In the NL, the Dodgers finished second to the San Francisco Giants in the Western Division and failed to qualify for the Playoffs. The Yankees won the AL Championship in six games by beating the Seattle Mariners, who ranked eleventh in payroll. Then, in the 2000 World Series the Yankees topped the New York Mets whose payroll at $99 million ranked second in the NL. In the regular season, Yankees' pitchers Andy Pettitte and Roger Clemens combined to win 32 games, and Bernie Williams and David Justice totaled 71 home runs and batted in 197 runs. Likewise, the World Series MVP shortstop Derek Jeter and catcher Jose Pasada played brilliantly for the Yankees.[11]

When the team ranks in the 1998 and 2000 seasons are compared, the AL Detroit Tigers—from fourteenth to seventh—and the NL Arizona Diamondbacks—from ninth to third—experienced the largest rise in ranks. Even though the clubs won more games in 2000 than in 1998, the Tigers and Diamondbacks each raised its payrolls by large amounts. Thus, their payroll per victory increased. Besides the Tigers and Diamondbacks, other clubs with significant increases in rank included the AL Tampa Bay Devil Rays who rose from tenth to sixth and the NL Philadelphia Phillies who increased from twelfth to eighth. In 2000, the Devil Rays increased their payroll by $38 million and won six more games than in 1998, and the Phillies expanded salaries by $25 million and won ten fewer games. Meanwhile, the AL Kansas City Royals—from eighth to thirteenth—and the NL Colorado Rockies—from third to tenth—recorded the greatest decrease in ranks. In part, because of payroll changes the Royals and Rockies each won five more games and their payroll per victory declined in 2000 relative to 1998. Other than the Royals and Rockies, the teams that experienced major decreases in rank were the NL San Francisco Giants who fell from sixth to twelfth, Milwaukee Brewers from eleventh to fourteenth, and the Florida Marlins from thirteenth to sixteenth. In sum, the AL Devil Rays, Royals and Tigers, and the NL Brewers, Diamondbacks, Giants, Marlins, Phillies and Rockies each implemented significant changes in payroll and/or incurred large deviations in victories to rise or fall in rank from 1998 to 2000.

Based on Tables 4.1 and 4.2, 57 percent (8) of the clubs in the AL and 31 percent (5) in the NL became more cost efficient because their payroll per win ratios declined from the 1998 to 2000 season. Furthermore, 85 percent (12) of the teams in the AL and 100 percent (16) in the NL spent more money to earn a win in 2000 than in 1998. Grouped, the AL owners were more effective than the NL owners in controlling payroll expenditures to achieve victories.

Because of the public demand for—and the entertainment value of—professional sports, baseball players monetarily prospered in the 1990s. The average salary in MLB rose 238 percent, or from $588,000 in 1990 to $1,988,034 in 2000. In December 2000, the former Seattle Mariners' free agent shortstop Alex Rodriguez signed a ten-year contract with the Texas Rangers for $25.2 million a year. Since he can voluntarily opt out of the contract's final three years, between 2001 and 2007 Rodriguez will be paid a total of $128 million. There is residual money in Rodriguez's contract. This amount includes a five-year, $10 million signing bonus and $33 million in deferred payments to be paid from 2011 to 2020. Due to the extended life of the contract, the discounted value of the deal was estimated to be $165 million in 2000. The Rangers'owner, financier Tom Hicks, hoped that Rodriguez would add at least $7 million in revenues to his club in 2001. That season, did the Rangers win more games? Although Rodriguez had an outstanding performance, the club finished fourth in the Western Division and forty-three games behind the Mariners.[12]

Besides the Rangers, in 2000 the Boston Red Sox signed Manny Ramirez to a $160 million, eight-year contract. Unexpectedly, his enormous salary created tension between the city of Boston and the team. At the Sox's new ballpark construction area, which is adjacent to historic Fenway Park, Boston's City Council planned to reevaluate the $140 million in taxpayer money for site preparation and the $72 million for a parking garage. Moreover, Sandy Alderson, an executive in the MLB commissioner's office said huge player contract commitments such as Rodriguez's and Ramirez's place baseball in a deepening crisis because of the growing revenue disparities between the big media market teams who sign extensive television deals and erect new stadiums, and the other clubs who have neither opportunity to create revenues. In brief, the wide differences in team payrolls are one reason that large-market baseball clubs win more titles and championships than teams located in small-to-medium markets. Given that this dilemma exists in MLB, what were the player salaries and team payrolls in the NBA relative to the other sports leagues?[13]

NBA

In professional basketball, the average payroll per win rose by 27 percent or from $941,000 in the 1997–1998 season to $1,200,000 in the 1999–2000 season (Table 4.3). The highest and lowest team payrolls were, respectively, in 1997–1998 the Chicago Bulls at $62 million and the Los Angeles Clippers at $24 million, and in 1999–2000 the Portland Trail Blazers at $74 million and the Los Angeles Clippers at $23 million. In 1997–1998, for each victory 31 percent (9) of the NBA clubs paid in excess of $1 million, and 41 percent (12) expensed less than $700,000 per win. The cost inefficient Denver Nuggets spent approximately $26 million in payroll for eleven wins, and the Golden State Warriors spent about $51 million for twenty-eight victories. Yet, in the 1997–1998 season neither the Nuggets nor the Warriors had a player finish in a top-ten performance category in the league.

When the regular season concluded, the Utah Jazz had tied the Bulls by winning sixty-two games despite ranking sixteenth in total payroll at $28 million and twenty-ninth in payroll per victory. The Jazz's power forward, rugged Karl Malone, had an outstanding season. He scored twenty-seven points-per-game (ppg) and was the sixth best NBA performer in rebounds-per-game (rpg). For his accomplishments, Malone was voted the league's MVP and made the All-League and All- Defensive teams. Besides the Jazz, two other cost-effective clubs were the Charlotte Hornets at $544,000 per win and the Cleveland Cavaliers at $591,000. In the regular season, the Hornets finished third at 51–31 in the Central Division of the Eastern Conference. Head Coach Dave Cowens organized a well-balanced team, and six of the Hornets scored ten or more ppg. Because of his accurate long-range jump shot, small forward Glen Rice scored 22.3 ppg. At 47–35, the Cavaliers' best players were their assists and steals play maker, Brevin Knight, and their offensive leaders such as Larry Kemp at 18 ppg and Chuck Person at 15 ppg. Interestingly, in 1997–1998 the Cavaliers and Houston Rockets each paid $28 million in player salaries, but the Rockets won six fewer games than the Cavaliers and placed nineteenth in payroll per win. Apparently, Houston's Clyde Drexler, Charles Barkley, Kevin Willis and Hakeem Olajuwon were overpaid given their contributions to the Rockets' performances.[14]

Table 4.3

Team Payroll Per Win and Rank in the NBA, 1997–1998 and 1999–2000

Team	1997–1998 Payroll/Win	1997–1998 Rank	1999–2000 Payroll/Win	1999–2000 Rank
Denver Nuggets	2,350	1	1,230	13
Golden State Warriors	1,800	2	1,900	1
Toronto Raptors	1,579	3	771	29
Los Angeles Clippers	1,415	4	1,493	8
Dallas Mavericks	1,352	5	985	17
Vancouver Grizzlies	1,340	6	1,713	3
New York Knicks	1,314	7	1,420	10
Orlando Magic	1,116	8	1,010	15
Sacramento Kings	1,003	9	910	20
Chicago Bulls	995	10	1,580	5
Washington Wizards	973	11	1,810	2
Philadelphia 76ers	917	12	860	23
New Jersey Nets	791	13	1,700	4
San Antonio Spurs	765	14	800	27
Boston Celtics	760	15	1,320	11
Phoenix Suns	752	16	870	22
Detroit Pistons	733	17	1,000	16
Milwaukee Bucks	692	18	1,088	14
Houston Rockets	682	19	1,530	7
Indiana Pacers	669	20	970	18
Atlanta Hawks	642	21	1,540	6
Miami Heat	628	22	980	19
Portland Trail Blazers	619	23	1,250	12
Minnesota Timberwolves	606	24	840	25
Seattle SuperSonics	601	25	850	24
Los Angeles Lakers	599	26	810	26
Cleveland Cavaliers	591	27	1,450	9
Charlotte Hornets	544	28	780	28
Utah Jazz	459	29	890	21

Note: See Table 4.1. The values in the two Payroll/Win columns are in millions of dollars for each year. Rank is self-explanatory.

Source: "NBA: Team Payrolls," at http://www.usatoday.com cited 19 May 1999; *The World Almanac and Book of Facts,* 1999, 2001.

In the 1999–2000 NBA season, 55 percent (16) of the teams paid $1 million or more per win, and no club spent less than $771,000 for each victory. Ranked sixth in total payroll at $53 million, the cost-inefficient Washington Wizards won merely twenty-nine games to place second in payroll per win at $1.81 million, which was slightly less than the Golden State Warriors at $1.9 million. Even Mitch Richmond's 17.4 ppg and Juan Howard's 14.9 ppg did not elevate the 29–53 Wizards above a seventh-place finish in the Atlantic Division of the Eastern Conference. Meanwhile, the Warriors at 19–63 disappointed their hometown fans despite the efforts of former University of North Carolina forward Antawn Jamison who averaged 19.6 ppg. Alternatively, the Toronto Raptors experienced the largest drop in payroll per win when the club declined in rank from third in 1997–1998 to twenty-ninth in 1999–2000. When the team payroll increased from $25 million in 1997 to $35 million in 1999, that season the Raptors won twenty-nine more games and finished third in the Central Division at 45–37. Butch Carter coached shooting guard Vince Carter, who averaged 25.7 ppg, and Carter's teammates Tracy McGrady and Doug Christie to qualify the club for the NBA Playoffs against the New York Knicks. In the Playoffs, the Knicks featured an offense led by Allen Houston and Latrell Sprewell, and rebound leader Patrick Ewing that defeated Coach Carter and his Raptors in three games.

Besides the Raptors, the Denver Nuggets, who had dropped in rank from first in 1997–1998 to thirteenth in 1999–2000 after winning twenty-four more games, and the Dallas Mavericks who fell in rank from fifth to seventeenth after winning twenty more games, each decreased its payroll per victory ratio and became more efficient in the 1999–2000 season. The best players on offense for the Nuggets were Antonio McDyess at 19.2 ppg and Nick Van Exel at 16.1 ppg. The Mavericks, in the 1999 season, depended on the productivity of Chuck Finley and Dirk Nowitzki. Finley hit approximately 46 percent of his shots, 82 percent of his free throws and averaged 22.6 ppg, while German-born Nowitzki scored 17.5 ppg. In contrast, a $19 million increase in payroll and fifteen fewer wins propelled the Cleveland Cavaliers from twenty-seventh to ninth place in payroll per win. The Cavaliers aside, the other rank changes of cost-inefficient clubs, that is, whose payroll per victory significantly rose in 1999–2000 relative to 1997–1998, included the Houston Rockets' nineteenth to seventh, New Jersey Nets' thirteenth to fourth, Atlanta Hawks' twenty-first to sixth and the Portland Trail Blazers' twenty-third to twelfth. Thus, each club's payroll per win exceeded $1 million in 1999–2000.[15]

In the late 1990s, the NBA's salaries were highly skewed because a small proportion of player salaries was located in the middle one-third of the income distribution. In 1997, the average player's salary was $2.6 million. Nevertheless, 24 percent of the NBA players either collected a minimum salary of $242,000 as a rookie or $326,000 as a veteran. Meanwhile, the five highest salaries were earned by the Chicago Bulls' Michael Jordan at $33.1 million, New York Knicks' Patrick Ewing at $20.5 million, Orlando Magic's Horace Grant at $14.2 million, Los Angeles Lakers' Shaquille O'Neal at $12.8 million and San Antonio Spurs' David Robinson at $12.3 million. Jordan, O'Neal and Robinson each scored more than 20 ppg and made the All-League first team. However, even though the Knicks made the playoffs, Ewing did not rank as a top-ten performer on offense or defense, and Grant scored a meager 12.1 ppg for the Magic. Thus, during the late 1990s, Ewing and Grant were overpaid based on their ppg and rpg performances.[16]

In 1998, there were six small-market teams below the salary cap. And, these teams did not qualify for the NBA Playoffs. This result indicates that the large-market clubs dominated postseason play, which contributed to the team owners' lockout of the players in late 1998 and early 1999. Nonetheless, a year later the average NBA salary increased to $3.6 million. When Jordan retired in January 1999, the Lakers' Shaquille O'Neal earned the league's highest salary at $17.1 million, followed by the Minnesota Timberwolves' Kevin Garnett at $16.8 million, and then the Miami Heats' Alonzo Mourning, the Knicks' Patrick Ewing and the Washington Wizards' Juan Howard at $15 million.

After the winning percentage of the Sacramento Kings stabilized in the 1998–1999 season, and improved in the 1999–2000 and 2000–2001 seasons, the team's vice president of basketball operations, Geoff Petrie, announced that veteran Chris Webber had signed a seven-year, $122.7 million contract. After he was selected as the Orlando Magic's first-round draft pick in 1993, Webber was traded to the Golden State Warriors where he earned Rookie of the Year in 1994. In 1997–1998, Webber scored 22 ppg for the Washington Wizards, then averaged 20 ppg and led the NBA with 13 rpg in 1998–1999. One year later, he scored 24.5 ppg, rebounded 10.5 basketballs per contest, and elevated the Kings to challenge the Los Angeles Lakers in the Western Conference Playoffs. Therefore, superstar Webber will be a key player in the future seasons of the Kings' franchise, and for their teams so will the Raptors' Vince Carter, Mavericks' Dirk Nowitzki and the Warriors' Antawn Jamison. These energetic players will keep their clubs in contention each season for a division title and a conference championship.

In short, for the two seasons studied, 55 percent (16) of the NBA clubs rose in rank, 38 percent (11) fell and 7 percent (2) retained their rank. Furthermore, 79 percent (23) of the teams experienced an increase and 21 percent (6) a decrease in payroll per win. Thus, the NBA's percentage changes in payroll per win were less than what occurred in MLB where 93 percent (28) of the teams experienced an increase in payroll per victory. In the next section, the payroll data and ranks for the NFL teams are examined.[17]

NFL

From 1989 to 1990, the average payroll of the twenty-eight NFL teams increased by 23 percent, or from $15.6 million to $19.2 million. In 1990, the 14–2 San Francisco 49ers at $29.7 million and the 9–7 Pittsburgh Steelers at $13.1 million had, respectively, the highest and lowest payrolls in the league. When the 49ers defeated the Denver Broncos 55–10 in 1990 at the Superdome in New Orleans, the franchise had won its fourth Super Bowl. Quarterback Joe Montana, the MVP in the 1982, 1985 and 1990 Super Bowls, and wide receiver Jerry Rice, the MVP in the 1989 Super Bowl excelled for the 49ers as did the franchise's head coaches Bill Walsh and George Seifert.[18]

The NFL's player incomes and team payrolls continued to increase during the 1990s. According to one study, between 1993 and 1997 the Dallas Cowboys, New York Giants and Washington Redskins each spent more than $200 million for player salaries. Although the three clubs led the NFL in total salary expenditures, on average the San Francisco 49ers at $3.2 million, Pittsburgh Steelers at

$3.3 million and the Green Bay Packers at $3.4 million had the lowest payroll expenses per win. However, in salaries per victory the Cowboys ranked seventh at $3.9 million, Giants fifteenth at $4.8 million and the Redskins thirtieth at $7 million in the league.[19]

Similar to Tables 4.1 for the AL, 4.2 for the NL and 4.3 for the NBA, Table 4.4 was designed to determine the relationship between the total payrolls and number of victories for thirty NFL teams in two recent nonconsecutive seasons, that is for 1997–1998 and 1999–2000. With this research, the author compares the respective payroll per win and rank columns in Table 4.4 to the effectiveness of payroll spending by team owners in the AL, NL, NBA and NHL. Despite the

Table 4.4
Team Payroll Per Win and Rank in the NFL, 1997–1998 and 1999–2000

Team	1997–1998		1999–2000	
	Payroll/Win	Rank	Payroll/Win	Rank
Oakland Raiders	12.27	1	4.98	24
Indianapolis Colts	11.80	2	3.55	30
Arizona Cardinals	8.40	3	9.15	6
Chicago Bears	8.00	4	8.06	8
San Diego Chargers	7.65	5	6.24	14
Dallas Cowboys	7.48	6	6.85	12
St. Louis Rams	7.00	7	4.00	28
Buffalo Bills	6.86	8	4.86	25
Baltimore Ravens	6.66	9	6.19	15
New Orleans Saints	6.16	10	17.53	1
Philadelphia Eagles	4.73	11	10.83	4
Cincinnati Bengals	4.64	12	12.39	2
Seattle Seahawks	4.61	13	5.78	21
New York Jets	4.57	14	6.11	16
Miami Dolphins	4.24	15	5.86	19
Tennessee Titans	4.13	16	4.31	27
New York Giants	4.02	17	7.44	9
Atlanta Falcons	3.85	18	10.49	5
Carolina Panthers	3.81	19	6.62	13
Washington Redskins	3.73	20	4.73	26
Minnesota Vikings	3.61	21	5.15	23
San Francisco 49ers	3.40	22	11.32	3
Kansas City Chiefs	3.37	23	5.82	20
New England Patriots	3.32	24	7.07	10
Tampa Bay Buccaneers	3.29	25	5.25	22
Detroit Lions	3.07	26	6.02	17
Jacksonville Jaguars	3.06	27	3.81	29
Pittsburgh Steelers	3.06	28	9.10	7
Denver Broncos	3.01	29	6.91	11
Green Bay Packers	2.59	30	5.88	18

Note: The Cleveland Browns are not listed in Table 4.4 because the club did not exist in 1997–1998. The two Payroll/Win columns are in millions of dollars. Rank is self-explanatory.

Source: "NFL Football: Team Payroll," at http://www.cnnsi.com cited 6 September 2001; *The World Almanac and Book of Facts,* 1999, 2001.

work stoppages and lockouts in the other sports leagues, since the 1987 strike the NFL and its players association have experienced labor harmony. The league and association cooperate when they mutually update their CBA every few years and in negotiations when they seek the input and participation of the league commissioner and team owners, player representatives and association officials. What does Table 4.4 reveal about the salaries and ranks of the NFL players and teams?

From the 1997–1998 to 1999–2000 seasons, the average payroll per win in the NFL increased by 46 percent or from $5.2 million to $7.6 million (Table 4.4). Ranked in first place as the most cost-inefficient team in 1997–1998 was the Oakland Raiders. Owner Al Davis paid the highest total payroll at $49.1 million, which converts to $12.27 million in player salaries for each of four wins. The Raiders' prominent players were quarterback Jeff George, running back Napoleon Kauffman, receiver Tim Brown and touchdown threat James Jett. Although the team won few games, these four players ranked fifth or better in various offensive categories within the AFC. Besides the Raiders, the other NFL clubs that compensated their players in excess of $40 million included the Dallas Cowboys at $44.9 million, San Francisco 49ers at $44.2 million, Kansas City Chiefs at $43.9 million, Buffalo Bills and New York Jets at $41.2 million each, New York Giants at $40.2 million and the Baltimore Ravens at $40.1 million. The small-market Carolina Panthers, which spent $26.7 million in salaries and ranked nineteenth in payroll per win at $3.81 million, had the lowest team payroll in the league. At 7–9 in the 1997–1998 season, the Panthers tied the Atlanta Falcons for second place in the Western Division of the NFC. All-Pro punt and kickoff return specialist Michael Bates, tight end Wesley Walls, quarterback Kerry Collins and running back Fred Lane led the Panthers to their .438 win-loss percentage. At 11–5, the small-market, cost-efficient Jacksonville Jaguars qualified for the playoffs as a wild card from the AFC's Central Division. Despite the effectiveness of quarterback Mark Brunell, the Jaguars lost to the Denver Broncos 42–17.

As a member of the NFC's Central Division, the small-market Green Bay Packers won thirteen games with a total payroll of $33.7 million in 1997–1998. That season, the Packers were the most cost-efficient team in the league at $2.59 million per win. The club's leader was quarterback Brett Favre, who ranked third in passing efficiency in the NFC. Besides Favre, running back Dorsey Levens and receiver Antonio Freeman also excelled on offense for the Packers. Green Bay aside, the other very cost-efficient teams based on payroll per victory were the Denver Broncos at $3.01 million, Pittsburgh Steelers and Jacksonville Jaguars at $3.06 million, and the Detroit Lions at $3.07 million. In other words, on average the five lowest-listed NFL teams in Table 4.4 spent $2.9 million in payroll per win, and the top five clubs expensed $9.6 million per victory to complete the 1997–1998 season.

In contrast to the Super Bowl XXXII runner-up Green Bay Packers, in 1997–1998 the small-market Indianapolis Colts won just three games in the

Eastern Division of the AFC with a total payroll that exceeded $35 million. Quarterback Jim Harbaugh, running back Marshall Faulk, wide receiver Marvin Harrison and kicker Cary Blanchard were competitive players on offense, but the Colts' defense failed to contain its opponents' passing and running strategies. Other than the inefficient Colts, in the regular season the small-market Arizona Cardinals, Baltimore Ravens, Buffalo Bills, New Orleans Saints and San Diego Chargers each won less than seven games and spent more than $6 million in player salaries for a victory.[20]

In the 1999–2000 season, the payroll of the Tennessee Titans and New England Patriots each exceeded $56 million, while the Denver Broncos and San Francisco 49ers each spent less than $46 million on player salaries. As players for the Titans, running back Eddie George, quarterback Steve McNair and defensive end Jevon Kearse received high salaries. As players for the Patriots, quarterback Drew Bledsoe, running back Terry Allen and wide receiver Terry Glenn earned a lucrative wage. Relative to their payrolls per win in 1997–1998, two seasons later the Oakland Raiders, Indianapolis Colts, St. Louis Rams, Buffalo Bills and Seattle Seahawks each won more games and their cost efficiency and ranks considerably improved from, respectively, first to twenty-fourth, second to thirtieth, seventh to twenty-eighth, eighth to twenty-fifth and thirteenth to twenty-first. Alternatively, due to higher salaries and/or fewer wins the New York Giants, Atlanta Falcons, San Francisco 49ers, Pittsburgh Steelers, Denver Broncos and Green Bay Packers each became less cost efficient when its payroll per win increased. Thus, these six clubs moved up in rank as depicted in Table 4.4. For example, the Steelers' record declined from 11–5 in 1997–1998 when the club ranked twenty-eighth in payroll per win to 6–10 in 1999–2000 when the team ranked seventh. The Broncos, meanwhile, fell from 12–4 in 1997–1998 and ranked twenty-ninth to 6–10 in 1999–2000 and ranked eleventh. In 2000, quarterback John Elway, the Broncos' five-time Super Bowl starter retired, and running back Terrell Davis injured himself. In total, the NFL teams experienced greater changes in ranks from one season to another than did the clubs in MLB and the NBA. This occurred because of the clubs' salary caps and the marginal scores in regular season games in which a last-minute field goal frequently determined who won.

Beyond the two seasons represented in Table 4.4, in 2000–2001 the Washington Redskins paid the highest NFL payroll at $92 million. Redskins quarterback Brad Johnson, running back Stephen Davis and cornerback Deion Sanders received inflated salaries. However, because it won eight games the club ranked seventh in payroll per victory at $11.5 million. The Arizona Cardinals at $18.4 million and the New York Giants at $4.7 million were, respectively, the least and most efficient teams in payroll per win during the 2000–2001 season. The Cardinals won six fewer games in 2000–2001 than in 1998–1999, and the Giants were victorious in four more games. Interestingly, neither team had a top-ten player in rushing and receiving yards, or in points scored as a kicker or non-kicker.[21]

At their respective position, in 1999–2000 Dallas Cowboy quarterback Troy Aikman at $16 million earned the league's highest salary, followed by New York Giants defensive end Michael Strahan at $12.4 million and Indianapolis Colts running back Edgerrin James at $10 million. Given the previous performances of these athletes, their salaries seem inflated. Aikman failed to make the Pro Bowl in 1998, and his twelve touchdown passes that year were his lowest tally since 1991. A veteran player for six seasons, Strahan did not win many accolades on defense in his first four years, and the Giants failed to make the playoffs in 1994, 1995, 1996 and 1998. Even though his salary was greater than what 1998 Super Bowl starters Jamal Anderson of the Atlanta Falcons and Terrell Davis of the Denver Broncos received, Edgerrin James was not an all-time great college player at the University of Miami. However, in 1999 sports agent Leigh Steinberg successfully negotiated James's seven-year $50 million contract with the Colts, which that year was a team desperate to fill its domed stadium in downtown Indianapolis.[22]

How did the Cowboys with Aikman, Giants with Strahan and Colts with James perform in the 1999–2000 season? After earning a wild-card berth in the Eastern Division of the NFC, the Cowboys were beaten by the Central Division's Minnesota Vikings 27–10 in the first round of the Playoffs. Aikman finished eighth in passing efficiency among quarterbacks in the NFC. With seven wins in the Eastern Division, the New York Giants failed to qualify for the NFC Playoffs, and Strahan was not selected to the NFL All-Pro team. After winning the Eastern Division of the AFC, the Indianapolis Colts were defeated by the Tennessee Titans 19–16 in the Divisional Playoffs. James was selected Rookie of the Year, led the NFC in rushing yards, and made the league's All-Pro Team. In short, James excelled as a running back and earned his $10 million salary. However, given their performances in the regular season the Cowboys' Aikman and Giants' Strahan were overpaid, respectively, at $16 million and $12.4 million.[23]

In June 2001, the NFL Management Council and players association agreed to extend the league's $67.4 million salary cap through 2006. This was the fourth extension of the basic CBA that was negotiated in 1993. According to sports analysts, the league had criticized the previous contract because it created little security for the high-salaried veterans to remain with their teams. With the contract's extension, any increases in the overall salary cap will be offset if player salaries plus signing bonuses exceed an average of 71.5 percent of the league's designated gross revenues in a three-year period. Thus, in 2005 players are eligible to receive an increase in salaries up to 65.5 percent of designated gross revenues. Furthermore, veterans will have a portion of their salaries paid from leaguewide funds instead of charging those costs against the total salary cap. After the owners and players ratify the extension, the NFL should have labor tranquillity for at least five to ten years. In sum, the NFL team payrolls realistically reflect the demand for the sport and impose less of a burden on owners than the payrolls in MLB and the NBA. Based on published reports, how do player salaries and team payrolls in the NHL compare with the compensation levels paid in the other sports leagues? This topic will be discussed next.[24]

NHL

The average salary of NHL players grew by 108 percent or from $572,000 in 1993 to $1,194,206 in 1999. The player salaries in the sport ranged from a low of $100,000 to a high of $8.5 million in 1993 and from $150,000 to $10.3 million in 1999. Based on the demand for, and entertainment value of professional ice hockey games in the United States, these salary amounts and ranges are less than the values that prevailed in MLB, and in the NBA and NFL. Nevertheless, as the salaries of players increased and the valuation of franchises appreciated in the 1990s, the NHL's ticket prices increased at a much greater rate than inflation. That is, between 1990 and 2000 the average price per seat to attend an NHL game rose by 130 percent, or from $20 to $46 while the inflation rate increased by 35 percent. Besides ticket prices, the teams' payroll costs also increased in the league.[25]

Table 4.5 depicts the distribution of payroll per point and the respective rank of twenty-six NHL clubs for two recent nonconsecutive seasons. Essentially, the table shows which ice hockey teams were the least and most cost efficient at scoring points during the regular season based on each club's total payroll. According to the ratios and values in the columns, the mean payroll per point increased by 10 percent, or from $334,000 in the 1997–1998 season to $367,000 in the 1999–2000 season. In 1997–1998, the highest salaried hockey teams were the Colorado Avalanche at $43.8 million, New York Rangers at $43.7 million and the Philadelphia Flyers at $40.1 million. The Avalanche, who placed first in the Pacific Division of the Western Conference, was led on offense by center Peter Forsberg and goaltender Patrick Roy. While goaltender Mike Richter and defenseman Brian Leetch starred for the Rangers who finished fifth in the Atlantic Division of the Eastern Conference, left wing John LeClair and right wing Mark Recchi excelled for the Flyers who ended second in the Atlantic Division of the Eastern Conference. Because the Rangers failed to play for the Stanley Cup either season, center Wayne Gretzky was partially responsible for the club's mediocre performance and league-high payroll per point of $642,000 in 1997–1998 and $806,000 in 1999–2000. The other teams that restricted their payrolls to less than $20 million in 1997–1998 included the Calgary Flames at $17.1 million, Edmonton Oilers at $17.9 million, New York Islanders at $18 million and the Ottawa Senators at $19.6 million.

As portrayed in Table 4.5, in 1997–1998 the New York Rangers paid $642,000 per point and ranked as the least cost efficient among all NHL clubs, and the Boston Bruins spent $221,000 per point and ranked as the most efficient. Led by the aggressive play of Jason Allison and Dmitri Khristich, the Bruins finished the regular season second in the Northeast Division of the Eastern Conference. In the conference playoffs, the Washington Capitals defeated the Bruins in six

Table 4.5
Team Payroll Per Point and Rank in the NHL, 1997–1998 and 1999–2000

Team	1997–1998		1999–2000	
	Payroll/Point	Rank	Payroll/Point	Rank
New York Rangers	642	1	806	1
Vancouver Canucks	540	2	540	2
Tampa Bay Lightning	488	3	362	11
Colorado Avalanche	461	4	438	4
Florida Panthers	422	5	331	17
Philadelphia Flyers	449	6	449	3
San Jose Sharks	358	7	421	6
Carolina Hurricanes	352	8	333	15
Washington Capitals	351	9	282	23
Chicago Blackhawks	350	10	405	7
Toronto Maple Leafs	337	11	355	13
St. Louis Blues	322	12	272	24
Montreal Canadiens	312	13	381	9
Anaheim Mighty Ducks	301	14	424	5
Phoenix Coyotes	292	15	332	16
Detroit Red Wings	286	16	380	10
New Jersey Devils	262	17	307	21
Pittsburgh Penguins	260	18	344	14
Dallas Stars	259	19	402	8
Los Angeles Kings	258	20	359	12
Calgary Flames	255	21	303	22
New York Islanders	253	22	305	20
Ottawa Senators	236	23	233	26
Buffalo Sabres	234	24	320	19
Edmonton Oilers	223	25	246	25
Boston Bruins	221	26	330	18

Note: In the NHL, for the respective seasons Payroll/Point replaced Payroll/Win as an indicator of a team's payroll cost efficiency. Payroll/Point is measured in thousands of dollars. Rank is self-explanatory.

Source: "Hockey: Team Payroll," at http://www.cnnsi.com cited 6 September 2001; *The World Almanac and Book of Facts,* 1999, 2001.

games. Overall, 53 percent (14) of the NHL teams paid less than $321,000 per point, which was one-half of the sum that the Rangers spent in payroll for each point. In the 1997 Stanley Cup Playoffs, the Detroit Red Wings outscored the Philadelphia Flyers in four games.[26]

In the 1999–2000 season, 18 percent (5) of the clubs had total payrolls that exceeded $40 million, and 43 percent (12) spent below $30 million on player compensation. As it did in 1997–1998, the New York Rangers retained its top rank in payroll per point. As such, the Rangers rated as the NHL's most cost-inefficient club in 1999–2000. Meanwhile, the Ottawa Senators replaced the Boston Bruins as the most efficient team in the league when it paid player salaries of $233,000 for each point. In the regular season, the Rangers finished fourth in the Atlantic Division, the Senators second in the Northeast Division and the Bruins fifth in the Northeast Division. In the 1999 Stanley Cup Play-offs, the Dallas Stars defeated the Buffalo Sabres in four games.

Because of more points scored in the 1999–2000 season, the Florida Panthers fell in rank from fifth to seventeenth in payroll per point and finished second in the Southeast Division of the Eastern Conference. Pavel Bure, who scored 94 points, and Viktor Kozlov, who was fourth in the NHL with 53 assists, led the Panthers. Some hockey clubs lowered their payrolls and earned more points in 1999–2000. In Table 4.5, this is evident for the Washington Capitals, which declined in rank from ninth to twenty-third and the St. Louis Blues, which fell from twelfth to twenty-fourth. The Capitals were led by outstanding goalie Olaf Koizig and assist leader Adam Oates. For the Blues, the two key players were the NHL's MVP and outstanding defenseman Chris Pronger, and Roman Turek, a superior goalie who frequently shut out opponents.

In contrast to the Panthers, Capitals and Blues, when the annual payroll of the Anaheim Mighty Ducks rose by 84 percent, or from $19 million in 1997–1998 to $35 million in 1999–2000, the team's rank changed, respectively, from fourteenth at $301,000 per point to fifth at $424,000 per point. Likewise, in 1999–2000 the total payroll of the Dallas Stars rose by 46 percent from 1997–1998 and the club's performance fell by seven points. This result caused the Stars' rank to change from nineteenth at $259,000 per point to eighth at $402,000 per point. Indeed, the Stars paid an additional $143,000 more to earn a point in 1999–2000 than it did two seasons earlier.

In sum, 65 percent (17) of the NHL clubs paid more, 27 percent (7) spent less and 8 percent (2) expended the same amounts per point in 1999–2000 relative to 1997–1998. Thus, the majority of hockey teams became less cost effective in their distribution of players' salaries. This occurred in the other sports leagues as well. The final topic of this chapter looks at why a growing number of professional players in selected U.S. sports leagues are from foreign countries.[27]

FOREIGN PLAYERS

Since the late 1950s, the number of foreign players who were on MLB rosters has steadily increased. In proportions, there were 4 percent in 1958, 7 percent in 1968, 9 percent in 1978, 12 percent in 1988, 20 percent in 1998 and 25 percent in 2001. Indeed, during the 2001 season 216 major league baseball players were not born in the United States. Moreover, 93 percent (201) of these athletes emigrated from eight countries. Listed according to the number of players from each country, seventy-nine immigrated from the Dominican Republic, thirty-seven from Puerto Rico, thirty-three from Venezuela, fourteen from Mexico, eleven from Canada, ten from Cuba, nine from Panama and eight from Japan. The other 7 percent (15) of the athletes left Aruba, Australia, Curaçao, Colombia, England, Jamaica, Nicaragua, South Korea and the Virgin Islands. In a sample of teams, fourteen foreign players were hired by the Montreal Expos and ten each by the Kansas City Royals, New York Yankees and Philadelphia Phillies.[28]

The upward trend in the number of foreigners who play professional base-ball in the United States has occurred because of domestic and global business, cultural, economic and political reasons. First, amateur and sandlot baseball is popular and commonly played in many foreign nations. Some of the best youth sports teams and leagues in the world are located in Puerto Rico, South Korea and Taiwan. These organizations provide excellent training for baseball players to develop their basic skills and strategies. For example, from 1947 to 2000 in-clusive twenty-eight foreign teams won the Little League World Series in Williamsport, Pennsylvania. The representative countries included Taiwan, Chi-nese Taipei and Japan. Second, the international broadcasts of big-league games have expanded across the world, and especially in the Latin American and Pa-cific Rim countries. Because multifaceted entertainment and media companies such as AOL Time Warner Inc., News Corporation and Walt Disney operate and own MLB teams, baseball's broadcasting rights have expanded to many places in Asia, and in the Caribbean, Eastern Europe and South America. Thus, televi-sion exposure has created millions of professional sports fans even in remote areas of the world. Third, since there is no international players draft sports agents are encouraged and free to scout for talented athletes in various nations, and especially in countries that are friendly and at peace with America. Because of unenforceable global regulations, some home country and U.S. sports agents have illegally signed foreign players when the youths are only fifteen years old. Then, these youngsters are rewarded with a small financial bonus and provided some training by a professional club. Eventually, the sports authorities declare that the underage foreign baseball players are ineligible as free agents, which means they will be assigned and committed to play for minor league teams in the United States. Fourth, outstanding amateur and semi-pro players have an economic incentive to defect from poverty-stricken countries such as Cuba, Mexico and Nicaragua. However, to curtail the exodus of its best athletes and restore a flagging national baseball program, the Cuban government does not allow players to work illegally abroad. Indeed, Fidel Castro's government pro-hibits Cuban players who are considered flight risks from participating in in-ternational tournaments. Furthermore, some Caribbean nations have adopted repatriation agreements with Cuba, which makes it difficult for defectors to ob-tain residency in an underdeveloped country before seeking emigration to the United States. Because of the language barriers and the other adjustments needed to live in another country and adapt to its culture, many talented foreign ath-letes struggle in the United States and never fulfill their potential as players. Since the game rules and league structures may vary by country, in the late 1990s how did baseball in the United States differ from the sport as established in five selected countries—Australia, Cuba, Dominican Republic, Japan and South Korea?[29]

In Australia, the eight teams in the Australian Baseball League each play fifty-four games per season, which opens in late October and ends in mid-February. A board of directors manages the league, and amateurs and professionals are eligible to play. The competition level is equivalent to A and AA minor leagues in the United States. The games are generally played on rugby or soccer oval fields because there are few single-purpose baseball stadiums that exist in the country. Players may use aluminum bats during games. Minor league pitcher Robb Welch and infielder Shea Hillenbrand are Australians.

In Cuba, two leagues each consist of eight teams that play a ninety-five-game schedule that begins in late November and concludes in late March. In 1998, the player's average salary was $9 per month. Some players ride a bicycle or take a bus to the ballpark and then return to state-sanctioned jobs after the game and when the season ends. Equipment shortages such as a deficient number of baseballs, bats and uniforms are a constant problem in the Cuban leagues, and games are frequently delayed or canceled because of electricity blackouts. The Boston Red Sox's Luis Rolando Arrojo and the New York Yankees' Orlando Hernandez are Cubans.

In the Dominican Republic, a six-team winter league season lasts from November to January, and a twenty-nine team summer league season exists from early June to late August. Winter league teams employ top minor league prospects from the Dominican Republic and the United States, and the summer league teams consist of teenage prospects signed by MLB clubs. Baseball game rules are identical to those in the United States. The Boston Red Sox's Pedro Martinez and Ramon Martinez, and the Chicago Cubs' Sammy Sosa are natives of the Dominican Republic.

In Japan, two six-team leagues exist from early April to late September. Each team consists of twenty-eight players, and the club's rosters may contain up to two each foreign pitchers and other position athletes. During games, players frequently sacrifice bunt in the first inning because Japanese teams tend to play conservatively for a score. The Detroit Tigers' Hideo Nomo and the Seattle Mariners' Ichiro Suzuki are Japanese. As the 2001 AL batting champion, hits and stolen base leader, Suzuki is a national hero in Japan and immensely popular with Mariner fans. His clever radio advertisements for two Seattle restaurants appealed to Japanese tourists as well as to Mariner fans who did not speak Japanese.[30]

In South Korea, baseball is an emerging and growth sport because the dominant game is soccer. Yet, an eight-team baseball league thrives from mid-April to early September. American rules are followed, and a designated hitter bats for each team. The players wear batting helmets, which display small advertisements that promote the team's respective owners. The former Los Angeles Dodgers' pitcher Chan Ho Park was born in South Korea. Besides the athletes from the five countries, other prominent foreign players in MLB and their nations are the Colorado Rockies' Larry Walker who is from Canada, the New York Yankees' Bernie Williams from Puerto Rico and Mariano Rivera from Panama, and the Montreal Expos' Vladimir Guerrero from the Dominican Republic.[31]

At the 2001 MLB All-Star Game, 40 percent (8) of the players were of Latin descent. If the Red Sox pitcher Pedro Martinez had been healthy, and if one of the best infielders in baseball, the Cleveland Indians' Roberto Alomar, had been selected as the AL second basemen, then one-half of the starting lineups in the game would have been Latin. Martinez and Alomar are current stars and potential candidates for the Hall of Fame in Cooperstown, New York.

The first dark-skinned Latin-American baseball player in the big leagues was Cuban Minnie Minoso, who made his debut in 1949 for the Chicago White Sox. Minoso is also a worthy candidate for the Baseball Hall of Fame. In thirteen seasons, he collected approximately 2,000 hits, drove in eighty or more runs eight times and one-hundred or more runs four times, scored in excess of ninety runs ten times, led the AL in stolen bases three times, achieved a lifetime .391 on-base average and made seven All-Star teams. In short, Latinos have made a major contribution to baseball since Minnie Minoso broke into the major leagues. Two years prior to Minoso's first MLB game, the Cleveland Indians' Larry Doby became the AL's first black player. Then, before Doby's entry Jackie Robinson had joined the NL Brooklyn Dodgers. Besides MLB, the NBA and NHL contain numerous foreign players.[32]

In the NBA, there are several non-U.S. players who are skilled at their positions. Some are star performers such as the San Antonio Spurs' Tim Duncan who is from the Bahamas, Dallas Mavericks' Dirk Nowitzki from Germany, Sacramento Kings' Predrag Stojakovic from Yugoslavia and Vladie Divac from Serbia, and the Toronto Raptors' Hakeem Olajuwon from the Federal Republic of Nigeria. In a recent draft, three seven-foot Chinese players were selected to be the first representatives from their country to perform in the NBA. Because of Commissioner David Stern's marketing savvy and perseverance, the NBA broadcasts games in 200 countries, which has made the sport popular and well-followed around the globe. In the NHL, numerous players are from Canada, Eastern Europe, Russia and the Scandinavian countries such as Norway and Sweden. These athletes played ice hockey as youths and vigorously competed in this national sport within their countries. As professional hockey progresses in the United States and plateaus in Canada, only the most skilled foreign players will be qualified to compete for the NHL teams.

SUMMARY

This chapter describes how the compensation of selected players and composition of team payrolls varied during two nonconsecutive seasons in each of the five sports leagues. The growth in salaries depicts how franchise owners rewarded players as the demand to attend and watch professional sports games has increased in the United States and abroad. The measure of a team's efficiency with respect to total salaries and victories—payroll per win in MLB, and in the NBA and NFL, and payroll per point earned in the NHL—were calculated and tabled for each club in the respective leagues between 1996 and 2000. Then, all league teams were ranked in each year according to how effectively the total payroll contributed to regular season wins and postseason playoffs, titles and championships. The reasons why clubs changed ranks from one season to another, as well as which teams were least and most cost efficient, were also discussed.

In general, the payrolls per win increased for 93 percent (28) of the MLB clubs, 79 percent (23) of the NBA teams, 77 percent (23) of the NFL franchises and 65 percent (17) of the NHL teams. Because of the changes in payrolls and wins or points earned, these ninety-one teams achieved a higher rank, say from ninth to fifth, from one season to another. However, this meant that the clubs became more cost inefficient because each win or point amounted to more expenditure for player salaries. After this analysis was completed, the extent and influence of foreign players on U.S. professional sports teams in MLB and in the NBA and NHL were discussed.

In Chapters 1 through 4, the content focused on the growth, infrastructure and development of professional sports leagues and franchises, on the strategies of owners and on the financial rewards to players and the payroll costs of teams. These chapters, therefore, dealt with the internal components of the professional sports industry because team owners and players are directly influenced by and relate to leagues. On the other hand, Chapter 5 examines the contributions and operations of the media, which is an external component of the leagues but an institution within the sports industry. After Chapter 5, one chapter on fans and another on government is presented followed by the Conclusion, Appendix, Selected Bibliography and Index.

NOTES

1. For a discussion of the general and specific topics that exist in Collective Bargaining Agreements between leagues and player associations or unions, see Michael E. Jones, *Sports Law* (Upper Saddle River, NJ: Prentice-Hall, 1999), 68–77.

2. Ibid.

3. From their research, the authors derive two primary conclusions about how much and wherewithal athletes are compensated. First, at the margin the value of a salary reflects the amount of additional operating income that a player earns for the franchise owner. Second, the leagues' authority to monopolize a professional sport largely determines the exorbitant salaries that players receive for the services they contribute to a team. See James Quirk and Rodney D. Fort, *Hard Ball: The Abuse of Power in Pro Team Sports* (Princeton, NJ: Princeton University Press, 1999), 82–87.

4. Ibid.

5. The author attributes the enormous escalation in player salaries to four primary reasons. They are: first, the growth in the entertainment and leisure industry that is fueled by economic affluence; second, the growth in radio and television broadcast revenues paid by stations and networks to professional sports leagues and teams; third, the expansion of free agency that has given players more bargaining power with respect to the leagues; and fourth, the growth in the economic power of each league to be a monopoly supplier of a sport. For further details, see Thomas J. Kruckemeyer, *For Whom the Ball Tolls: A Fan's Guide to Economic Issues in Professional and College Sports* (Jefferson City, MO: Kruckemeyer Publishing, 1995), 99–103.

6. Ibid.

7. In reference to the disparities that exist in the gross gate receipts and in the television and radio revenues between small- and large-market clubs, Kansas City Royals President Joe Burke remarked, "I don't think in the future this market will allow us to continue to sign free agents at the top of the scale. We'll never get the revenue to compete for free agents with New York, Philadelphia and the West Coast teams." See Mike Dodd, "Soaring Player Salaries Threaten Small Markets," *USA Today* (12 December 1990), 25. For a discussion of how advertisers have treated slugger Barry Bonds after his single-season home-run record performance in 2001, see Mark Hyman, "The Trouble With Barry," *Business Week* (15 October 2001), 100; Gary Peterson, "Bonds Has Giants in Pickle With Arbitration," *Charlotte Observer* (12 December 2001), 3C. See various editions of *The World Almanac and Book of Facts* (Mahwah, NJ: World Almanac Books, 1950–2001) for the performance statistics on leagues, coaches, managers, players and teams.

8. Based on the average annual values of multiyear contracts, the top salary in MLB increased from $2.5 million in February 1999 to $25.2 million in December 2000. See "Baseball: Salary Progression Chart," at http://www.cnnsi.com cited 21 March 2001.

9. See "Baseball: Final 2000 Payroll Figures," at http://www.cnnsi.com cited 21 March 2001; Hal Bodley, "Major League Baseball Salary Report," at http://www.usatoday.com cited 19 May 1999; *The World Almanac and Book of Facts*, 1999, 2001.

10. As of 1999, the Anaheim Angels' first baseman Mo Vaughn had the highest average salary in the AL at $13.3 million followed by the Baltimore Orioles' outfielder Albert Belle at $13 million. In 1998, Vaughn had played for the Boston Red Sox. There he batted .337, slugged 40 home runs and accumulated 205 hits. Belle, meanwhile, batted .328, clouted 49 home runs, scored 113 runs and batted in 152 runs for the Chicago White Sox. For a partial list of players' contracts that averaged $12.5 million or more a season, and which originated from 1999 to 2001, see "Baseball: Highest Salaries," at http://www.cnnsi.com cited 21 March 2001.

11. Baseball payrolls are listed by average annual values as of 31 August 2001 in "Baseball: Final 2000 Payroll Figures," at http://www.cnnsi.com cited 21 March 2001. For the division titles, playoffs and championship series in each league for the 2000 season, see *The World Almanac and Book of Facts*, 2000, 2001.

12. In 2001, Alex Rodriguez hit .318, which was the seventh highest batting average in the AL. He led the league with 52 home runs and 133 runs scored, and placed second in hits with 201 and third in runs-batted-in with 135. For the final leaders' statistics, see Bernie Wilson, "Henderson Gets 3,000th Hit in Gwynn Farewell," *Charlotte Observer* (8 October 2001), 5C.

13. See "Who Wants to be a Millionaire?" at http://www.cnnsi.com cited 4 April 2001; Scott McCartney, "Why a Baseball Superstar's Megacontract Can be Less Than It Seems," *Wall Street Journal* (27 December 2000), B1, B3; Jay Weiner, "Good For A-Rod, Bad for Baseball," *Business Week* (25 December 2000), 59; "Misdirected Priorities," at http://www.cnnsi.com cited 14 December 2000.

14. For a list of coaches' salaries and each basketball team's 1997–1998 payroll and cap room, see "NBA: Team Payrolls," at http://www.usatoday.com cited 19 May 1999. Various payroll data are also available in "Basketball Team Payrolls," at http://www.ixquick.com cited 8 September 2001.

15. Ibid.

16. Player salaries and team payrolls are reported for each professional sports league. For example, see "Baseball: 1998 Team Payrolls," at http://www.usatoday.com cited 19 May 1999; "Basketball Team Payrolls," at http://www.ixquick.com cited 8 September

2001; "Football Team Payroll," at http://www.ixquick.com cited 8 September 2001; "Hockey: Team Payroll," at http://www.cnnsi.com cited 6 September 2001.

17. When the NBA salary cap increased from $3.6 million in the 1984–1985 season to $35.5 million in the 2000–2001 season, the average player's salary rose from $330,000 to $4.2 million. See Chris Grandstaff, "Webber Signs 2nd-Largest Contract," *Charlotte Observer* (22 July 2001), 13H.

18. According to sports analysts, during each decade since 1950 the NFL's greatest quarterbacks were the Cleveland Browns' Otto Graham and Detroit Lions' Bobby Layne in the 1950s, the Baltimore Colts' Johnny Unitas and Green Bay Packers' Bart Starr in the 1960s, the Pittsburgh Steelers' Terry Bradshaw and Dallas Cowboys' Roger Staubach in the 1970s, the San Francisco 49ers' Joe Montana and Miami Dophins' Dan Marino in the 1980s, and the Green Bay Packers' Brett Favre and Denver Broncos' John Elway in the 1990s. See Pat Sutherland, "Favre Last QB From Great Era," *Charlotte Observer* (25 November 2001), 6F.

19. In 1990, the NFL Players Association compiled salary information for its membership although the organization did not function as a union. See "Bang For the Buck," *Street & Smith's SportsBusiness Journal* (2–8 November 1998), 18.

20. Each NFL team's average and median salary, as well as the total payroll for the 1999 season, are reported in "NFL: Team Payroll," at http://www.cnnsi.com cited 6 September 2001.

21. See "Football Team Payroll," at http://www.ixquick.com cited 8 September 2001.

22. In August/September 1999, the weekend *Wall Street Journal* applied computer models developed by financial experts to determine which NFL player will earn the most money at each position for the season. See Sam Walker and Jonathan B. Weinbach, "All-Stars of '99," *Wall Street Journal* (3 September 1999), W1, W14.

23. *The World Almanac and Book of Facts,* 2001. In the 2001–2002 NFL season, the New York Giants' Michael Strahan established a league record with 22.5 sacks. For this achievement, Strahan was selected the Associated Press Defensive Player of the Year. See "Strahan Selected AP Defensive Player of Year," *Charlotte Observer* (17 January 2002), 2C.

24. See "Give Peace a Chance," at http://www.cnnsi.com cited 5 June 2001; "Kumbaya," at http://www.cnnsi.com cited 6 June 2001; Don Banks, "Tip O' the Cap," at http://www.cnnsi.com cited 21 March 2001.

25. For the percentage changes in the average player's salary; in the average fan's ticket prices in 1999 for MLB and in 1999–2000 for the NBA, NFL and NHL; and in the NHL salary growth from 1993 to 1999 inclusive, see "NHL Hockey Player Salaries," at http://www.sportsfansofamerica.com cited 18 July 2001; Don Muret, "NHL's Average Cost Up 5.5%; Bruins Top the List," at http://web4.infotrac.galegroup.com cited 18 October 2001; "The Cost of Sitting," at http://www.cnnsi.com cited 4 April 2000; "Ticket Price Comparison," at http://www.ixquick.com cited 15 October 2001; Dan Bickley, "Pro Sports May be Pricing Fans Out of Stadiums," at http://www.azcentral.com cited 24 June 2001; John Helyar, "Sports: Watching Football in Person Now Costs Even More," at http://www.proquestmail.com cited 19 July 2001.

26. See "NHL Team Payroll," at http://www.cnnsi.com cited 6 September 2001.

27. Ibid.; *The World Almanac and Book of Facts,* 1998–2001.

28. See Peter Gammons, "International Pastime," *Boston Globe* (27 March 1998), F2; "Foreign Legions," at http://www.cnnsi.com cited 4 April 2001.

29. Stefan Fatsis, "Cuba, Si. Stardom, No," *Wall Street Journal* (17 August 2001), W4.

30. Susan G. Hauser, "Japanese Baseball Stars Turn Seattle Radio Bilingual," *Wall Street Journal* (10 July 2001), A16; Steve Fainaru, "Serious Defects," *Boston Globe* (27 March 1998), F4; Gordon Edes, "Treasure Island," *Boston Globe* (27 March 1998), F3; Larry Whiteside, "Making Inroads Near the Outback," *Boston Globe* (27 March 1998), F8; Dan Shaughnessy, "Improved Grip?" *Boston Globe* (27 March 1998), F7.

31. In South Korea, the typical admission price to a baseball game in 1998 ranged from $3.50 to $5.75. When admitted, a customer was allowed to bring in food, beverages and hot dogs. However, peanuts and popcorn are not popular food with Korean fans. For further information about baseball in the City of Seoul, see Kevin Paul Dupont, "Pitching Change," *Boston Globe* (27 March 1998), F6.

32. To win a position in MLB, the unwritten rule is that Latin players must be far superior to American players. An explanation of this rule was discussed in Allen Barra, "An International Game," *Wall Street Journal* (13 July 2001), W6.

Chapter 5

Media

To successfully market a team as a brand to consumers in various local, regional, national and international areas, each sports franchise within the professional sports leagues must compete for exposure and recognition with other popular entertainment and leisure activities. Historically, the primary media that broadcast and publicize sports events and news, which besides games, leagues and teams also include coaches, managers, owners and players, have been a combination of newspapers, magazines, radio and television. As applied to the marketing of a professional sports team, each media type or medium has unique advantages and limitations. In the United States, the majority of local newspapers publish a sports section that contains specific information and statistics such as box scores, notes from the court, team standings and related articles and commentary about professional athletes, coaches, division and conference rivalries, owners, and recently completed and upcoming scheduled games. As a form of printed communication, newspapers have high believability and are flexible, timely and generally well-received by readers. A daily newspaper, however, can have a short life span and may exhibit poor reproduction quality. The *Charlotte Observer*, for example, contains data, statistics and informative articles that primarily feature updates about the games, players and seasons of the (former) NBA Charlotte Hornets and NFL Carolina Panthers, and secondarily about the events of the minor league baseball's AAA Charlotte Knights, East Coast Hockey League' Charlotte Checkers, and the local high school and university sports programs. To improve the newspaper's circulation, in recent editions *Observer* journalists have frequently focused on controversial and newsworthy issues such as player tragedies and rule violations, a team's losing streak, owner misdeeds and voter preferences to finance a new arena.[1]

Newspapers aside, there are popular nationwide magazines such as *ESPN The Magazine, Sport, Sports Illustrated* and *Street & Smith's SportsBusiness Journal* that provide statistics and in-depth, special-interest stories about games, leagues, managers, owners, players and teams. As advantages, sports magazines have credibility and prestige, good pass-along readership, high demographic and geographic selectivity, and a short to medium shelf life. Nevertheless, relative to newspapers, sports magazines are a mid-to-high cost medium that requires a lengthy advertisement purchase lead-time.[2]

To attract listeners and improve the station's ratings on the radio, there are experienced, knowledgeable and opinionated analysts and commentators who broadcast sports programs. These individuals may announce home and away games, conduct pre-game and post-game interviews of coaches, players and team executives, and schedule daily or weekly talk shows to excite fans and to entertain the general public. Compared with newspapers and magazines, radio sports broadcasts are a low-cost medium that penetrate local and regional mass markets. However, radio is solely an audio presentation that caters generally to a fragmented, inattentive and uninformed audience. To overcome this shortcoming, the once-hot, now-matured Entertainment Sports Programming Network (ESPN) introduced a twenty-four-hour radio sports station to mirror the success of its cable television network and in March 2002 debuted its made-for-television movie, *A Season on the Brink: A Year With Bobby Knight and the Indiana Hoosiers.*[3]

Besides newspapers, magazines and the radio, a lucrative, modern and vitally important medium—cable, network and satellite television programming—communicates all aspects of sports to a geographically dispersed and vast audience. For the viewers of professional sports programs, television combines motion, sight and sound. Moreover, similar to radio programs, television broadcasts have excellent mass-market coverage and a low cost per exposure. Nevertheless, television's disadvantages include high clutter, immense absolute costs and minimum audience selectivity. Later in this chapter, the innovative programs that various television executives and the sports leagues have jointly created and implemented are discussed.

Although direct mail and outdoor advertising are also media outlets, each has limited application for the professional sports leagues and team owners. In general, these communication channels are flexible in content, message transmission and quality. As to their specific advantages, direct mail is a personal medium that can be audience selective, while outdoor ads, such as billboards, have low message competition, small absolute costs and high repeat exposure. Applied to the sports industry, the disadvantages of direct mail are its relatively high cost per exposure and the image of "junk mail." Outdoor ads, meanwhile, possess minimal audience selection and are not considered a creative communication channel by marketers.

Libraries and movies are other traditional mediums that are appropriate for professional sports leagues and franchises. Although these media types are not necessarily convenient or optimally located in metropolitan areas, respectively, for readers and viewers, sports fans have the opportunity to visit their local public and school libraries to study the history of, as well as to collect information and statistics about, professional sports events, players and teams. Popular movies such as *The Field of Dreams* or *The Natural* create fantasies and adapt story plots and themes to sports heroes, legends and personalities that entertain all generations. In sum, since the early 1900s one or more media types have benefited from, and contributed to the development, growth, popularity and prosperity of professional sports in America.

Especially since the 1980s, the proliferation of personal computers, as well as the applications of e-commerce activities, information systems and interactive technologies, have markedly changed the business, infrastructure, marketing and operation of professional sports organizations. Because of its capability, flexibility and low absolute and relative costs, the Internet and online programming have gradually supplemented the traditional media such as newspapers, magazines and the radio to become the most accessible, convenient and up-to-date source of entertainment and information for sports fans. Single-purpose and sports World Wide Web sites such as cnnsi.com, ESPN.com, mlb.com, nba.com, nfl.com and nhl.com are each accessed daily by thousands of computer users from their homes and workplaces. Many of these users are diehard or casual fans who want to learn about recent game results, player and team performances, and to obtain other information like the history of sports leagues and teams, news features, player trades, season schedules, ticket prices and the costs of clothing and merchandise. In short, by 2005 the Internet will be the most useful source of sports information for avid fans and the general public.

With the primary and secondary media types identified, this chapter has two overriding objectives. First, it discusses how the multifaceted U.S. media industry interacts with, reports on and strategically promotes the five professional sports leagues and their member franchises. Second, it exposes how entrepreneurial broadcasters, league officials and team owners have jointly exploited the business opportunities to expand professional sports events and information to market areas in the United States and externally, in other nations. Lastly, the final portion of the chapter focuses on the recent innovative technologies in cable, network and satellite television programming, and how each technology has provided sports league executives and team owners with more options to create entertainment value, fun and utility for their respective audiences and markets.

HISTORY OF SPORTS MEDIA

Newspapers

The legendary editor and publisher, William Randolph Hearst, created the first professional sports section within a local newspaper, the *New York Journal* in 1895. Ten years later, other newspapers such as the *Commercial Advertiser, St. Louis Globe* and *Washington Post* published daily or weekly articles and commentary that touted the merits and social amenities of big league baseball. Thus, prior to sports magazines and the radio, television and other media, newspapers were the common source to find qualitative and quantitative data and other information about professional games, leagues, seasons and teams. Especially in the large U.S. East Coast cities where professional sports franchises existed such as Boston, New York, Philadelphia and Washington, D.C., fans could read about the past and recent performances of leagues, players and teams in their local newspapers.[4]

In addition to a record of home attendance, highlights of games and league standings, by the 1930s newspaper sportswriters and statisticians collected, organized and reported a variety of interesting player and team performance characteristics. Game scores and a team's errors, hits, home runs and win-loss percentages aside, these statistics included the batting averages of hitters and earned run averages of pitchers in baseball, the points-per-game and rebounds-per-game of players and teams in basketball, the number of touchdowns scored and total yards gained from passing and running of players and teams in football, and the assists, goals, points earned and shutouts in ice hockey games. Indeed, with these numbers and statistics sports analysts and fans could reasonably measure the abilities and achievements of their favorite hometown players and those on rival teams, and the progress of all league teams. Yet, other than the AL and NL in Major League Baseball (MLB), before the 1950s the characteristics of NBA, NFL and NHL events did not get sufficiently reported in newspapers and other media types for fans to read about and analyze their sport's games, leagues, players, seasons and teams. Because of this oversight, between the 1870s and 1940s MLB benefited more than the other professional sports leagues from media articles about interleague competition, player performances and team successes.[5]

As providers of updated information, local newspapers directly and intentionally seek to boost the demand for specific sports and franchises in a market area. For business and personal reasons, many sportswriters tend to be biased about which athlete, local team and sport to extol or critique. Because newspaper companies maximize operating revenues from subscriptions, generally the performances of the most controversial and skilled players on a team are highlighted and reported in the sports section. In other words, based on the image of the franchise in the community, when a player is perceived as lazy or a team endures a slump during the regular season, he or she and the team may be absolved, condemned or ignored by the local newspaper's columnists, editors and journalists. For the most part, a sportswriter frequently allows hometown players and teams some slack time to recover when a downward trend in performance occurs. Actually, during a losing streak the hometown sports franchise may benefit if the local newspaper gives encouragement and publishes articles as to why fans in the market area should support the efforts of the club's coaches and players despite a dismal performance. As press coverage expands, therefore, the cash inflows to the team owner increase from gate attendance and other stadium sales.

As stated earlier in this chapter, newspaper reporters generally prefer one or more players or teams to others in the professional sports leagues. It is the competitiveness and success of a team within its division and conference that largely determines which sport receives the most favorable or unfavorable local press coverage and reports. Because of market demand and tradition, within the majority of U.S. sports communities and metropolitan areas the NHL and its clubs are the least documented and promoted in the news. Indeed, the articles and performance statistics on professional baseball, basketball and football have always received the largest share of lineage in the sports section of local newspapers. Since the 1960s, however, city newspapers have become marginally less important as a medium, because more convenient and timely sources of information have emerged to furnish fans with facts and performances about their hometown and rival professional sports players and teams.

Radio

By the early 1920s, an alternative medium to newspapers, the radio, had penetrated the demographic markets in the United States to become a viable communicator of sports events. A celebrity sportscaster and entertainer, Graham McNamee, announced the first baseball game on the radio directly from the Polo Grounds in New York. He also broadcasted the 1921 World Series in which the NL New York Giants defeated the AL New York Yankees in eight games. Three years later, Hal Totten became the first announcer to report daily baseball games from a ballpark on station WMAQ in Chicago. Throughout the 1920s and early 1930s, the radio broadcasts of sports events, particularly MLB games, expanded across the nation's East and Midwest. Neophyte sports fans, who were unfamiliar with professional baseball rules and team strategies because they lived in remote and rural areas of the United States, eagerly listened to games on the radio rather than wait and read about the outcome in the local newspapers. Undoubtedly, to hear a broadcaster describe a home run hit by the New York Yankees' Babe Ruth or a steal of second base by the Detroit Tigers' Ty Cobb were dramatic moments that enticed individuals and families to tune in games on the radio and cheer for their favorite players and teams. Thus, newspapers and the radio enhanced and contributed to the business of sports.[6]

In 1933, the revenue from local baseball broadcast rights totaled $18,000 or approximately $1,100 for each of the sixteen MLB teams. Despite the macroeconomic instability that resulted from the U.S. stock market crash and Great Depression, in 1934 the Ford Motor Company of Dearborn, Michigan, committed more than $100,000 to sponsor the World Series on multiple radio networks. That Series was a competitive and thrilling professional sports event. It concluded when the NL St. Louis Cardinals defeated the AL Detroit Tigers in seven games. The Cardinals were sparked by Hall of Fame pitcher Dizzy Dean, home-run leader James A. Collins, and base-stealing champion and defensive ace Pepper Martin. Hall of Fame catcher Mickey Cochrane, pitcher Tommy Bridges and slugger Hank Greenberg led the Tigers. These players and teams generated excitement for fans as the radio broadcasts of games expanded the professional sports industry in America.[7]

Television

The first televised baseball game was broadcast in 1939 on W2XBS in New York City. Walter "Red" Barber announced a doubleheader between the NL Brooklyn Dodgers and NL Cincinnati Reds from Ebbets Field in Brooklyn, New York. As a result of broadcasting the sport on television, the annual cash inflows from local baseball broadcast rights amounted to $885,000 or about $55,300 per team in 1939. Thirteen years later, when the broadcast restrictions on games were suspended by the U.S. Department of Justice, the total baseball broadcast rights for the regular season, All-Star and World Series games surged to $5.4 million or $260,000 per team.

The first NFL game was televised in 1939 from Ebbets Field. Transmitted to one thousand television sets in New York by the National Broadcasting Company (NBC), the Eastern Division's Brooklyn Dodgers played its rival, the Philadelphia Eagles. In 1951, the NFL Championship Game between the American Conference's Cleveland Browns and National Conference's Los Angeles Rams was televised by the DuMont Network which paid $75,000 for the coast-to-coast rights. One year later, economists estimated that the twelve NFL teams shared $769,000 in local and national broadcast revenues, which equaled $70,000 per franchise. Then, on November 12, 1953, Judge Allan K. Grim of the U.S. District Court in Philadelphia upheld the league's policy of blacking out home games. In 1956, the Columbia Broadcasting System (CBS) became the first network to broadcast some NFL regular season games to selected television markets across the nation.[8]

To further increase each club's revenues from broadcasts, in 1958 NFL Commissioner Bert Bell delegated to the team owners the right to stop play for television time-outs. After he watched the NFL's Western Conference champion Baltimore Colts beat the Eastern Conference winner New York Giants 23–17 in the first sudden death overtime, Bell realized professional football's enormous appeal to a televised audience as an alternative to the game's broadcasts on the radio. When Pete Rozell replaced the late Bert Bell as the NFL commissioner in 1960, it was obvious that the league could increase its exposure and profits from the telecast of games throughout the United States. To this end, a bill that legalized single-network television contracts passed the U.S. House of Representatives and the Senate and was signed into law by President John F. Kennedy on September 30, 1961. For $4.6 million, CBS contracted to televise the NFL's regular season games in the 1962–1963 season. Then Commissioner Rozell created NFL Properties, which became the licensing unit of the league. Because of its expansion in the media, the NFL had approached baseball as the most publicized professional sport in America and a staunch competitor to MLB for fans.[9]

After 1963, the NFL successfully negotiated deals to broadcast its sport. For example, CBS submitted a winning bid of $14.1 million per year for football's regular season television rights and $1.8 million for the league's championship games in 1964 and 1965. The network then reacquired the television rights for $19 million per season and the championship games for $2 million each in 1966 and 1967, with an option to renew in 1968. When negotiations concluded, in 1969 Rozell approved a proposal from the American Broadcasting Corporation's (ABC) Roone Arledge to air "Monday Night Football," which expanded regularly scheduled games to prime time television. In short, this agreement allowed ABC the right to televise thirteen NFL regular season Monday night games in 1970, 1971 and 1972.[10]

Besides the television agreements and commitments that extended to MLB and the NFL, in the early-to-mid-1950s local and national sport broadcasts emerged as a viable revenue source for the franchises in the NBA and NHL. Then, the annual broadcast revenues for each NBA team totaled $130,000 and for each NHL club $132,000. By 1971, a national contract with ABC netted $5.5 million for the NBA, or approximately $324,000 per team. This value excluded local rights, which were not reported by the league at that time. In professional hockey, each NHL franchise received approximately $150,000 from the league's contract with CBS in 1970 and at least $200,000 in local rights revenues. From the 1950s to 1970s, it appeared that the growth in broadcasting rights and cash inflows had resulted in impressive financial returns for the NBA and NHL franchises. Yet, in 1971 each MLB team earned $1.6 million and each NFL club $1.7 million from radio and television broadcasts, which dwarfed what the NBA and NHL franchises collected from their television contracts. In sum, it was radio stations in the 1920s through 1940s and then television networks in the 1950s through 1970s that had established strategic alliances and business partnerships with the major sports leagues to provide national coverage of regular season and championship games and, thus, more broadcast revenues for the respective franchises. After the 1970s, these relationships continued to expand and generate more income for the sports leagues and wealth for the team owners and players.[11]

Beginning in the mid-to-late 1990s, the professional sports leagues and broadcast industry, which included cable, digital, network, satellite and television companies, and other programming and media businesses, jointly collaborated on several strategic deals. One goal of the media was to increase the exposure and entertainment value of professional sports to fans and households in the United States and other countries. During the 1990s, high-level meetings and negotiations occurred between executives of the various sports leagues and officials of the broadcast industry. From a decision-making perspective, there were significant business and operating risks and specific issues to be compromised and resolved before agreements were signed to broadcast games to areas using the latest high-tech and electronic equipment and processes. A sample of the relevant newsworthy events and transactions that involved the professional sports leagues and broadcast industry from 1997 through 2001 are described and summarized. In the discussion, the reader will detect the trends and short- and long-term strategies that were pursued during the five-year period by decision makers within the professional sports leagues and various broadcast companies. This topic begins with the deals concluded by the NBA and NFL in 1997.

SPORTS AND MEDIA BUSINESS

1997

The NFL's broadcast rights fees negotiated with the television networks steadily increased from $200 million in 1970–1973 to $4.4 billion in 1994–1997. When the latter four-year contracts with ABC, ESPN, NBC, Turner Network Television (TNT) and the Fox network expired in late 1997, six television companies prepared to bid for the rights to broadcast the league's regular season games and playoffs. In total, media industry analysts estimated the deal to be valued at $7 billion, which is a 59 percent increase above the 1994–1997 contracts. Thus, even though the television ratings of the NFL had marginally declined throughout the mid-to-late 1990s, some networks realized that football broadcasts guaranteed a mass audience, which included young males who are a cohort group that advertisers attempt to reach with beverage commercials. Furthermore, the television networks exploit the NFL and other sports leagues to carve out identities and promote nonsports programming, and thereby avoid the expenditures necessary to develop costly prime time shows. In turn, with extensive broadcast rights the NFL is able to create new programming such as highlight shows to air on Saturday mornings, which are broadcast to expose children and teenagers to the apparel and merchandise offered for sale by the league. Lastly, as another strategy the television networks are motivated to shift some football games from Sunday afternoon to weekday prime time slots to disperse the inventory of its sports programs.[12]

While negotiating for a contract with the league, some eminent television executives stressed that professional football was a diluted sport because during the early-to-mid-1990s five different networks had broadcast regular season games on four different days during various weeks. Moreover, the executives claimed that the broadcasts of games had resulted in operating losses, which totaled in the hundreds of millions of dollars for their companies. While they negotiated with the networks in early 1997, NFL representatives held discussions with the league's players union and requested that this group cooperate and extend the Collective Bargaining Agreement (CBA) through the 2004 season. With a renegotiated CBA and an agreement with the union, the league would be positioned to conclude a long-term and more profitable contract with the networks. Meanwhile, for its expenditures on commercials the third-party advertisers wanted more value per dollar from the networks and the NFL. With ad rates exceeding $350,000 for a thirty-second spot, many advertisers were wary of committing additional resources to professional sports, and especially during the NFL's regular season games. In short, these were business strategies that the NFL and media industry focused on and successfully pursued in 1997.[13]

Despite a 40 percent decline in professional basketball ratings on the telecasts of regular season games since the mid-1990s, and expecting that the Chicago Bulls' Michael Jordan would retire before 2000, in November 1997 the NBA signed a four-year, $2.6 billion contract with two television partners. For exclusive rights to regular season, playoff and championship games, General Electric's NBC paid $1.7 billion, and Time Warner Inc.'s Turner Sports budgeted $900 million. The new contract doubled the value of the former agreement and extended the league's eight seasons with NBC and fourteen with Turner Sports, which had broadcasted NBA games each season on its TBS and TNT stations. Because of the NBA's decline in popularity, the executives from rival networks refused to bid higher for the rights than did NBC and Turner Sports. Indeed, in 2001 NBC reported operating losses that exceeded $300 million from its current contract with the NBA.[14]

As a result of the multibillion-dollar contract signed in 1997, the television networks were permitted to show more NBA games, sell any excess advertising time, and retain total control of the broadcast and cable rights of the league. Besides the broadcasts of eight more playoff games, the contract authorized NBC to air an additional seven regular season games each year, while Turner Sports extended its telecasts from seventy-one to eighty regular season games and to forty playoff contests. NBC Sports President Dick Ebersol said that the increment in regular season and postseason games would provide about $300 million in new advertising revenue for the networks during the contract's life. Before the new deal was finalized, NBC had charged $400,000 for a thirty-second spot during the NBA Playoffs and $100,000 for spots during the regular season. However, because of these fees some observers predicted that the deal would generate $100 million less in profits for NBC than did the former four-year, $750 million agreement with the NBA. Although he preferred not to discuss net profits, in 1997 Turner Sports President Harvey Schiller claimed that the recent contract would provide a positive financial return on investment for its parent company, which was Time Warner Inc., and now AOL Time Warner Inc.[15]

From the NBA's perspective, the new television agreement was expected to strengthen its partnerships with NBC and Turner Sports, as well as to present the league as a viable organization from which to broadcast commercials. Moreover, the deal underlines the turnaround in the NBA from the early 1980s when the league struggled to find a network to broadcast its games and when its championship series was shown on taped delay. In sum, financial benefits and synergy result for each group when professional sports leagues and television companies agree to conduct business and negotiate deals to broadcast games throughout the world. Besides the contracts in 1997, another group of transactions with the media industry in 1998 increased the brand awareness of teams and improved the entertainment value of the professional sports leagues.

1998

For the first year since 1965, the NBC network did not televise an NFL game. To fill this void, in January 1998 the Walt Disney Company's ABC network and its ESPN cable unit acquired a portion of the NFL's television rights through the 2005 season for $9.2 billion. Based on the contracts, ABC paid a total of $4.4

billion, or $550 million per year, to air Monday Night Football, and ESPN spent $4.8 billion, or $600 million a year to show games on Sunday night. Moreover, to telecast Sunday daytime games CBS agreed to pay the NFL $4 billion, or $500 million per season, to broadcast the league's AFC games. Finally, the News Corporation's Fox Broadcasting Network shelled out $4.4 billion to televise games played by teams in the NFC. Thus, the record eight-year television contracts with the four networks will earn the NFL approximately $17.6 billion in gross revenues.[16]

Even though the NFL's television ratings in 1997 were the lowest in twenty-seven years, the contracts with the four networks negotiated in 1998 were guaranteed for five years. Then, after the contracts expire the league has the option of reopening negotiations for a better deal from the networks. In January 1998, NFL Commissioner Paul Tagliabue praised the $17.6 billion television agreement. In brief, Tagliabue said small-market franchises such as the Cincinnati Bengals, Green Bay Packers, Indianapolis Colts, Kansas City Chiefs, Tennessee Titans and San Diego Chargers would surely benefit from the contracts because the revenues from national television rights are split equally among the league teams. Furthermore, the commissioner stated that the deal benefits football fans because the amount of money negotiated by the league with the networks will make it unlikely that pay-per-view for games would be introduced on television.[17]

To collect their fees for the NFL broadcasting rights package, the four networks developed different business strategies. The ABC network proceeded to charge advertisers a 6 percent surcharge for a thirty-second commercial spot during the broadcasts of Monday Night Football games. Furthermore, ABC requested that its 211 affiliate stations each contribute approximately $50 million in cash to the network. Alternatively, ESPN, ESPN2 and ESPN Classic Sports planned to expand their pre-game and post-game shows and other sports programs, to devote about seven hundred hours to football programs during the 1998–1999 season, and to increase their thirty-second advertisement fees by 15 percent for commercials on Sunday Night Football. The ESPN programmers also pressured some of their affiliated cable companies for future fee increases that totaled more than $1 per subscriber in the late 1990s. For ad buys, ESPN suggested that its cable operators charge $60 per 1,000 viewers for NFL regular season games. To partially offset the higher fees charged to advertisers, ESPN offered cable companies 10 percent more ad spots during games, and 26 percent more spots in its studio and in NFL-related programming. However, the majority of cable firms preferred not to raise rates on their customers who had recently balked at spending more money for sports programs. Thus, ESPN sought additional slots for game advertisements from the league. However, to prevent an excessive number of interruptions during play, the NFL and other sports leagues restrict how many ad minutes can be imbedded into games. Finally, in September 1998 ESPN's World Wide Web site was upgraded to incorporate a Disney-designated sports store, a third-party-produced content theme, a speedier access technology and a trademark address titled ESPN.com.[18]

The ABC and ESPN networks aside, in 1998 the CBS and Fox networks implemented innovative strategies after their contracts with the NFL commenced. For example, to increase the cash inflows from the broadcasts of AFC games on Sundays, CBS raised the price of thirty-second ads by 10 percent. The network also requested that its affiliated station owners contribute $40 million to partially offset the cost increase of the new NFL contract. Because of the station owners' limited budgets, CBS feared that some advertisers would shift their expenditures from professional football games to cheaper alternatives such as movies, other sports events or prime time drama programs. Meanwhile, to raise more revenues from broadcasting NFC games on Sundays, Fox initiated an 8 percent increase for thirty-second advertisements. Furthermore, in mid-1998 the network revamped its foxsports.com Web site, tripled the number of online employees devoted to sports programming, and opened an administrative bureau at its headquarters in Los Angeles, California. Besides these strategies, Fox also introduced three Internet innovations. First, the network created Game-Tracker, which featured real-time drive charts of games and an array of offense and defense statistics. Second, the network developed Sports Online, which provided regional Web sites that included notes, records, schedules and statistics of key teams. The network's third innovation was Sports Store, which offered "NFL on Fox" hats, mugs, shirts and other clothing and merchandise items. In part, Fox initiated these online activities to be competitive with and reclaim market share from the two Internet industry leaders, ESPN's SportsZone.com and CBS's SportsLine.com.[19]

Other than the $17.6 billion NFL deal with the four networks, in July 1998 the NBA also renewed its contract with TV Azteca to broadcast sixty games each in Mexico during the 1998–1999 and 1999–2000 seasons. Moreover, the agreement required that TV Azteca generate on-site commentary for several regular season games, All-Star Weekend and the NBA Final Playoffs. The Mexican television network also committed resources to produce a thirty-minute basketball magazine program that highlighted many NBA celebrities and captured the best game moments in NBA history. In Mexico, these programming initiatives were adopted to increase youth participation in American-style basketball and to promote NBA games on television. After 1998, several intriguing business strategies were activated that further aligned the professional sports leagues and the media industry. These occurred in 1999, 2000 and 2001.[20]

1999

In this year, two questions emerged that involved the business relationships between the professional sports leagues and various media companies. First, would the Internet either temporarily or permanently supplement or replace the television networks as the primary link to the vast audiences and markets that demand sports programming? Second, which of the professional sports leagues, if any, would experiment and then successfully develop programming outlets that ultimately earn sufficient advertising revenues to challenge the dominant cable and television networks such as ABC, CBS, ESPN, Fox, NBC, TBS and TNT? In November 1999, these questions were partially answered when NBA Commissioner David Stern launched NBA.com TV, the first twenty-four-hour cable/satellite television network created by a premier U.S. professional sports league. Although the NBA's investment was moderate at $10 million, the NBA.com TV network was initially offered for $150 per season to 3.3 million U.S. households via the DirecTV and Viewer's Choice digital cable systems. Basically, the network is formatted to resemble a financial news channel with a live announcer who reads news reports while team scores and player statistics from the league's Internet site, NBA.com, appear on the screen. Furthermore, the network's stations broadcast a variety of league games in progress and vintage games from the NBA's film archives. Other sports industry news and team performances would also be highlighted on the network. In late 1999, the NBA began to negotiate with foreign broadcasters to carry NBA.com TV on a global network. Apparently, Commissioner Stern was signaling to the league owners and foreign television networks that the NBA intended to broadcast its own games across the hemisphere.[21]

The NBA Entertainment (NBAE) operations were another segment of the league's media kingdom that was upgraded in 1999. Founded in 1982, the NBAE began as a multimedia product empire that encompassed audio CDs, books, cable and television programs, films, photographs and videos. With revenues that exceeded $150 million in 1998, the NBAE was a profitable business primarily because of its abundant and high-valued library of films, photographs and videos. In the long term, NBAE's goal is to build one of the Internet's most lucrative sports sites, which may strain relations with the other news and entertainment providers such as the CNN, Fox and MSN networks. According to Stern, "The one thing we have concluded is that continuing to build NBA.com, NBA.com TV and NBAE can only add future value to our league and teams."[22]

Since the late 1990s, Jerry Colangelo and other investors have co-owned four professional sports teams in Arizona. The franchises are the Arena Football League's Arizona Rattlers, MLB's Arizona Diamondbacks, NBA's Phoenix Suns and the WNBA's Phoenix Mercury. In 1999, Colangelo published his views on the symbiotic relationship that exists between professional sports and the media industry. In a recent edition of *Management Review,* Colangelo stated, "The media [radio and television industries] devour product as the channels and stations transmit twenty-four hours a day, every day of the year. That means the media need the entertainment value that sports bring and the guaranteed endless supply of entertainment. At the same time, the sports business needs the media, needs the exposure and the excitement and the rights fees the networks pay." Essentially, Colangelo had justified how and why the professional sports leagues and the media industry complement each other in their business and programming efforts.[23]

In 1999, the online sites for the defunct American Basketball Association, World Football League and World Hockey League were popular among sports fans. The interest in these organizations attracted hundreds of visitors a day to Web sites such as geocities.com and remembertheaba.com. At these sites, for example, visitors watched former players as they performed silly stunts while on a team's bench, participated in a fantasy league, and downloaded video clips of dramatic games and outstanding players and plays. The success of these Internet sites reflects the curiosity of and demand from hard core and casual sports fans for the facts and history about events. Furthermore, fans wanted to learn how the alternative leagues managed to exist for a while and how the failed organizations were operated and performed. The other years aside, in 2000 what business arrangements and other relationships developed between selected professional sports leagues and the media industry?[24]

2000

In late 1999, President Bill Clinton signed into law the Anti-Cybersquatting Consumer Protection Act. Basically, the measure was passed by Congress to protect U.S. copyright and trademark holders in cyberspace. Unfortunately, to circumvent the law, in early 2000 a small group of Internet start-up companies, headed by opportunistic and unscrupulous individuals, registered Web site addresses with names similar to the authentic sites of the professional sports leagues and their various teams. To illustrate, four authorized sites were named NFLtoday.net, NFLtoday.org, newyorkyankees.com and yankees.com. Consequently, in order to make a short-term and quick profit from online operations, the majority of the unethical entrepreneurs intended to sell their legally registered addresses to the professional sport leagues and/or team owners. Because of an unregulated Internet market, currently intellectual property rights as applied to cyberspace remain undeveloped in comparison to the well-defined rights that pertain to capital goods and physical assets. This legal deficiency and market failure especially distress sports leagues and teams who previously had made huge dollar investments to create their own brands, copyrights, domains, trademarks and other intellectual properties. Therefore, to protect their intangible assets, images and organizations' names several leagues and team owners have filed lawsuits against cybersquatters for trademark infringements. For sure, besides the enforcement of the Anti-Cybersquatting Consumer Protection Act other legislation must be passed to shield fans from these business predators and scam artists. Otherwise, those who prey on naive and uninformed sports consumers will likely abuse the unregulated Internet to market and sell phony and unlicensed sports clothing, equipment, memorabilia, merchandise and game tickets.[25]

For another innovation, during 2000 some ingenious sports team owners from each league exploited the Internet to increase their franchise's operating and non-operating revenues while they contributed money to charity organizations. Indeed, that year 50 percent of the clubs in the four major sports conducted at least one online auction. The average cash inflows from such sales were estimated at approximately $200,000 per franchise. Interestingly, a fraction of the team own-ers earmarked the proceeds from their online auctions to specified charities or community foundations. What specific types of Internet transactions involved the NFL, MLB, NBA and NHL?

In May 2000, the NFL launched an online auction to sell discarded player uni-form components and once-in-a-lifetime fantasy experiences to football fans. At the league's Web site, visitors were free to bid on players' worn-out jerseys, helmets, pants, shoulder pads and sweat socks. Also, to participate in a rare experience successful bidders could win a ride on a team airplane or tour the franchise owner's suite at the club's stadium. Besides the NFL, MLB teams also auctioned off lifelong dreams to fans. High bidders, for example, won the right to participate in a pre-game batting practice session, shag ground balls in the in-field and fly balls in the outfield, sing the national anthem before a regular sea-son game, sweep the infield as a grounds crew member, snap pictures as the team photographer, or allow their children to entertain the crowd by dancing with a team mascot between innings. One ardent baseball fan successfully bid $999 to throw the opening pitch before a Chicago Cubs' game at Wrigley Field. On the Internet, teams also marketed memorabilia from soon-to-be-demolished and unoccupied ballparks and other facilities. At the former Milwaukee County Sta-dium, some fans made competitive bids to acquire the clubhouse mail box, ice cream machine, plastic and wooden seats, toilets, urinals, and the NL Brewers' dryer and washer.[26]

In the NBA, numerous items and properties have been auctioned off to col-lectors and fans from displaced arenas. At Boston Garden, the center-court lep-rechaun sold for $331,000, and the parquet-floor panels raised tens of thousands of dollars for the Boston Celtics. The Dallas Mavericks' owner Mark Cuban had planned to set up a Web site at shopping.yahoo.com to sell excess and unwanted property from the Reunion Center when the American Airlines Center opened in 2001. Pieces that were to be auctioned from the Reunion Center included ob-solete posters, game programs and tickets. In short, these transactions are a few examples that illustrate how opportunistic sports franchise owners have ex-ploited the Internet to increase cash inflows by selling their unused and out-dated assets, merchandise, property and other items to collectors and fans.[27]

In the summer of 2000, MLB's Seattle Mariners became the first sports team to auction tickets online with prices determined by the market's demand and supply. In the initial auction, the Mariners offered 1,000 seats for sale at Safeco Field. At the club's Web site, mariners.com, fans could bid for one or more of these seats. If the bid matched the going price, the ticket was immediately sold to the buyer. Because of high demand, the value of field-level seats increased by 300 percent, or from $32 to $128. In contrast, the lowest-priced seats at $14 failed to sell out even though a $2 per ticket discount was awarded to the successful bidders. The Mariners' auction was a productive effort by a professional sports team to sell game tickets other than at the gate or on the telephone. In sum, the Mariners' ticket sales conclude the discussion of Internet deals and transactions that involved the sports leagues and teams in 2000. To continue, a number of e-commerce and media activities by sports franchise owners and leagues also occurred in 2001. These actions are described next.[28]

2001

To stimulate attendance at the home ballparks and increase operating revenues, in 2001 several sports teams other than the Seattle Mariners also aggressively sold regular season game tickets on the Internet. In MLB, the Arizona Diamondbacks, Chicago White Sox, Detroit Tigers, Oakland Athletics, Pittsburgh Pirates and San Francisco Giants launched online services to market a variety of general admission and premium seats at their stadiums. A portion of baseball clubs shared the revenues from online seat sales with a San Francisco-based technology provider, LiquidSeats, which became MLB's new media company. Although some tickets were sold above face value, which most clubs prohibited, in Seattle team officials concluded that those online sales were legal. In August 2001, the Seattle Mariners were given permission by the league to sell tickets on the Internet to ten postseason games if played at Safeco Field. In total, the tickets admitted the holder to the AL Playoffs and Pennant Series, and to the World Series.[29]

Other sports teams besides those in MLB also used online technology for ticket distributions in 2001. Located in Raleigh, North Carolina, the NHL Hurricanes provided team advertisements on wireless phones and hand-held devices, and the club offered $5 discounts on tickets to games at the Entertainment and Sports Arena. By clicking on a computer button to speak with a team customer service representative, the NHL Washington Capitals allowed visitors to access their Web site, washingtoncaps.com, to inquire about ticket availability and options on seat prices. In the NFL, visitors to the New England Patriots' site, patriots.com, were permitted to click a button that connected to a customer service salesperson who provided information about team auctions, merchandise at the pro shop, and regular season tickets at the club's new stadium in Foxboro, Gillette Stadium, which opened in August 2002. Essentially, these initiatives illustrate how the Hurricanes, Capitals and Patriots were creative when they marketed unsold tickets, merchandise and other items on the Internet.[30]

To increase its online traffic and boost e-commerce sales in 2001, each sports league overhauled its primary Web site. For example, the NHL outsourced its online advertising budget by establishing a partnership with the Chicago-based Ignite Media Company. According to the agreement, the company was assigned to market the league's site and to arrange sponsorships for the NHL, and for the Stanley Cup logo and All-Star Game. The NHL aside, Ignite Media also provided promotional services for the Arena Football League, NFL New York Giants, Ladies Professional Golf Association and the Professional Football Hall of Fame.[31]

Meanwhile, in November 2001 MLB decided to hire Robert A. Bowman. His responsibility was to overhaul baseball's Web site, mlb.com, and to reconstruct the league's Internet operation to make it profitable. The funds to operate the site were generated from advertising, e-commerce business, sponsorships and subscriptions. Because the majority of online content was expected to be accessed for free by visitors, the site included a variety of options such as auctions, fan contests, gift certificates to the mlb.com store, archived and live radio broadcasts of games, ballpark tickets and video highlights of player and team performances. According to Bowman, the established online competitors to mlb.com were cnnsi.com, ESPN.com and SportsLine.com. As such, in response to MLB's strategy these businesses each planned to upgrade their respective Web sites and online operations.[32]

In July 2001, the NFL announced that its Web properties would be operated and promoted by three independent entities: AOL Time Warner Inc., Sports Line.com Inc. and Viacom Inc. Based on contractual commitments concluded in 2001, the NFL and its three partners would share any revenues from the advertising and commerce conducted on the league's sites. From estimates, the NFL was expected to earn $110 million in cash during the five-year agreement, plus approximately $200 million in noncash values and an unknown amount from promotional opportunities across various platforms. For its contribution, Sports Line.com Inc. was assigned to produce and market the NFL.com and Superbowl.com sites. Furthermore, according to the contracts AOL Time Warner Inc. and SportsLine.com Inc. businesses were authorized to apply some NFL content in their own Web developments such as audio game webcasts and video clips. Finally, the contracts would not prohibit an NFL team from building, managing and operating its own web site for other purposes.

In a cross-marketing deal negotiated in 2001, Walt Disney's ESPN.com agreed to be the sole sports-news provider to Microsoft's MSN Web portal. According to the contract, after MSN users click on the site's sports channel, they will be forwarded to ESPN.com, which has MSN logos on its site that link users back to MSN's site. To promote the products of their companies, Microsoft and Walt Disney could collude and create advertising packages for the benefit of users. Essentially, for ESPN.com this deal expands its Web distribution. Two Microsoft technologies, Windows Media Player and Passport, were expected to be used by ESPN.com for the delivery of its services.[33]

To attract a wide array of viewers, in mid-2001 certain sports leagues formed business alliances with one or more cable, digital, and network or satellite television companies. DirecTV, the nation's largest satellite-to-home broadcaster implemented a network television advertising campaign. This project promoted DirecTV's NFL Sunday Ticket programming package, which costs $179 in access fees to watch up to thirteen out-of-market regular season football games from September through late December. "Brand tailing," which combines creative advertising and discount messages, was the technique DirecTV used to promote its brand and entice consumers to purchase subscriptions for the package. After the NFL settled a $7.5 million class-action lawsuit with consumers in May 2001 for unlawfully bundling its televised out-of-market games, the league said it would consider allowing consumers the right to choose smaller packages of individual Sunday out-of-market games rather than the entire program. DirecTV's deal with the NFL was scheduled to expire in 2002 after an ad campaign in 1998 cleverly portrayed former Denver Broncos quarterback John Elway, and then current quarterbacks Brett Favre of the Green Bay Packers and Troy Aikman of the Dallas Cowboys as groceries in a supermarket. Since 1999, DirecTV has placed additional ads to motivate consumers who subscribe for the opportunity to view additional programs without incurring fees.[34]

One week after they agreed to join an $850 million regional sports television network with YankeeNets LLC, in September 2001 two principal investors withdrew their 20 percent stake in the deal. The investors disapproved of how the control and structure of the network was concocted by Leo Hindery Jr., a cable industry executive. Basically, the contract allowed the AL New York Yankees to operate its own sports network, which would include games by the NBA New Jersey Nets and NHL New Jersey Devils. Based on its scheduled operations, in 2002 approximately 125 regular season Yankees games and seventy-five Nets games were to be telecast. After its current cable agreements expire in 2007, the Devils' games will be broadcast on the network. In part, the long-term success of the project depends on the demand from cable operators such as Cablevision Systems Inc. and AOL Time Warner Inc. who must pay for the service, and whether these and the other cable operators can charge higher prices to their subscribers for the programming. In New York, cable operators may decide to offer the YankeesNets LLC as a premium channel or not consider the product in its program portfolio. If the former decision occurs, the network's high fees may induce some cable customers to switch to satellite systems. If the latter decision happens, then sports enthusiasts with cable would be disappointed, not having the option to watch games played by the Yankees, Nets and Devils from their homes. Since the Yankees' games are prestige programming, it appears that the cable companies will include the network in its basic package of channels. In turn, when the three teams are not playing the network expects to broadcast classic games and offer regional sports, lifestyle and entertainment programming opportunities to retain its market share. In April 2002, however, the Yankees Entertainment and Sports Network LLC filed an antitrust suit and accused the Cablevision Systems Corporation of refusing to pay a $2 per subscriber fee for the Network's service.[35]

Each of the aforementioned Internet, cable, digital, network and satellite television alliances and deals entail business and operating risks. Therefore, because of economic uncertainty, world military and political conflicts, and overpriced programming services to view professional sports, in the short run the networks and other businesses expect an accounting loss. If the broadcast ratings continue to decline for professional sports games, and average attendance remains static or diminishes, then the television networks will retrench. This means that in the future, the leagues will receive proportionately less operating revenues and financial returns from their contracts with the networks and from their online investments in technology and in other media systems. Therefore, beyond 2002 the Internet and television broadcasts will assume an increasingly critical but risky role in the advancement and business success of the professional sports leagues in America.

Sports Team Media Markets

A franchise's media revenues largely depend on the club's entertainment value, success and tradition, and the demand for the respective sport in its geographic market area. The player and team performances aside, there are a few relevant economic and demographic factors that affect the demand for a sport in a market. They are a metropolitan area's total population, population density and growth, amount of discretionary or household income, and consumer buying power. In large metropolitan areas, therefore, there are more households that subscribe to local newspapers and sport magazines, as well as fans that watch sports on television and listen to games on the radio, than in small or medium-sized metropolitan areas.

To partially measure the total revenues of each sports franchise, *Financial World* reported the media income of all clubs in MLB, and in the NBA, NFL and NHL from the 1990 to 1996 seasons inclusive. For those seven seasons, the values of the media income and respective ranks of the top and bottom two teams in each sports league were documented and contained in the magazine. Therefore, to highlight the differences between the media revenues earned by the two top and bottom teams in each league, their values and ranks are discussed next. (To be consistent, the media income of each sport's expansion franchises and relocated teams are placed in parentheses and described separately because those clubs played less than seven years at their particular hometown sites from the 1990 through 1996 seasons.)

In MLB, the AL New York Yankees at $59.3 million and the NL New York Mets at $38.7 million ranked first and second in media revenues per season, and, respectively, the AL Kansas City Royals at $16.3 million and the AL Milwaukee Brewers at $15.8 million placed twenty-fifth and twenty-sixth. (In contrast, from the expansion years of 1993 to 1996, the NL Florida Marlins in Miami and the NL Colorado Rockies in Denver averaged, respectively, $15.2 million and $12.2 million per season in media income.) In the NBA, the Los Angeles Lakers at $27.1 million and the Phoenix Suns at $21.9 million had the highest average annual media income, and the Indiana Pacers at $12.2 million and the Washington Wizards at $11.7 million had the league's two lowest incomes. (For the NBA's expansion teams, in 1996 the Toronto Raptors received $17 million in media money and the Vancouver Grizzlies $14.5 million.) Regarding the NFL clubs, in media revenues the Chicago Bears and Dallas Cowboys each averaged more than $39 million per season and the Atlanta Falcons and Indianapolis Colts each less than $36.2 million from the 1990 through 1996 seasons. (For the other NFL clubs that existed less than seven seasons, the expansion Carolina Panthers and Jacksonville

Jaguars each averaged less than $19.5 million in media revenues for two seasons, that is, in 1995 and 1996. The Panthers and Jaguars aside, in the 1995 and 1996 seasons the average media revenues were $42.3 million for the relocated Cleveland Browns, now Baltimore Ravens, and $43.1 million for the relocated Los Angeles Rams, now nicknamed the St. Louis Rams.)

In the NHL, the Boston Bruins at $10 million and New Jersey Devils at $9.4 million ranked first and second in average media cash inflows, respectively, and the St. Louis Blues at $3.4 million and Hartford Whalers at $3.3 million placed seventeenth and eighteenth in the league. (Meanwhile, in media inflows per season the expansion Anaheim Mighty Ducks averaged $5.1 million in 1994–1996, Tampa Bay Lightning $4.7 million in 1993–1996, Florida Panthers $4.5 million in 1994–1996, and the Ottawa Senators $4.2 million and San Jose Sharks $3.7 million in 1993–1996. Furthermore, the relocated Minnesota North Stars, now the Dallas Stars averaged $3.4 million in 1993–1996, the Quebec Nordiques, now the Colorado Avalanche, averaged $3.7 million in 1995 and 1996, and the Winnipeg Jets, now the Phoenix Coyotes, averaged $4.6 million in 1996.)[36]

Consolidated by sports league and ranked accordingly, from 1990 to 1996 inclusive the average media revenues per season for each team were $37 million in the NFL, $23.4 million in MLB, $15.9 million in the NBA and $5.1 million in the NHL. In short, the values from *Financial World* reflect two facts. First, the information confirms that the majority of large market teams in the major sports leagues generally averaged more revenues from local and regional media companies during the seven seasons than did the clubs located in small-to-medium-size markets. Second, the results show that in their respective market areas the NFL teams earned the highest average operating inflows, and the NHL clubs the lowest revenues from the broadcasts of their games on radio and television and from the other media outlets like billboards and direct mail.

To reveal how the media industry interacts with and influences the professional sports leagues, and to compare how the media income is distributed among each league's franchises, a total of three business and demographic statistics were collected from reputable sources in U.S. cities and/or metropolitan areas in which clubs were located during a recent strike- and lockout-free season. The statistics include the number of radio and television stations in each city, the population of the Consolidated Metropolitan Statistical Area (CMSA) or the Metropolitan Statistical Area (MSA), and the average daily circulation and number of leading newspapers in each city. Besides that data, Table 5.1 was created. It ranks, according to the number of television households (TV HH) the Designated Market Area (DMA) of the 103 U.S.-based franchises that existed during the 1997 season in MLB and the 1997–1998 season in the NBA, NFL and NHL. Because of irreconcilable intercountry differences on how to measure the geographic boundaries and distances of a DMA, CMSA and MSA, the ten Canada-based sports franchises were excluded from Table 5.1. Those teams not listed are the Toronto Blue Jays in the AL, Montreal Expos in the NL, Toronto Raptors and Vancouver (now Memphis) Grizzlies in the NBA, and the Calgary

Table 5.1
Number of Teams in Ranked Designated Market Areas, by League, in 1997

DMA	Rank	TV HH	AL	NL	League NBA	NFL	NHL	Total
New York	1	6.75	1	1	2	2	3	9
Los Angeles	2	5.00	1	1	2	0	2	6
Chicago	3	3.14	1	1	1	1	1	5
Philadelphia	4	2.65	0	1	1	1	1	4
San Francisco-Oakland-San Jose	5	2.29	1	1	1	2	1	6
Boston	6	2.16	1	0	1	1	1	4
Washington, D.C.	7	1.92	0	0	1	1	1	3
Dallas-Fort Worth	8	1.89	1	0	1	1	1	4
Detroit	9	1.78	1	0	1	1	1	4
Atlanta	10	1.67	0	1	1	1	0	3
Houston	11	1.64	0	1	1	1	0	3
Seattle-Tacoma	12	1.51	1	0	1	1	0	3
Cleveland-Akron	13	1.46	1	0	1	0	0	2
Minneapolis-St. Paul	14	1.44	1	0	1	1	0	3
Tampa-St. Petersburg	15	1.43	0	0	0	1	1	2
Miami-Ft. Lauderdale	16	1.38	0	1	1	1	1	4
Phoenix	17	1.28	0	0	1	1	1	3
Denver	18	1.19	0	1	1	1	1	4
Pittsburgh	19	1.14	0	1	0	1	1	3
Sacramento-Stockton-Modesto	20	1.12	0	0	1	0	0	1
St. Louis	21	1.10	0	1	0	1	1	3
Orlando-Daytona Beach-Melbourne	22	1.04	0	0	1	0	0	1
Baltimore	23	.98	1	0	0	1	0	2
Portland	24	.97	0	0	1	0	0	1
Indianapolis	25	.95	0	0	1	1	0	2
San Diego	26	.92	0	1	0	1	0	2
Charlotte	28	.84	0	0	1	1	0	2
Greensboro/Raleigh-Durham	29	.82	0	0	0	0	1	1
Cincinnati	30	.80	0	1	0	1	0	2
Kansas City	31	.79	1	0	0	1	0	2
Milwaukee	32	.79	1	0	1	0	0	2
Salt Lake City	36	.78	0	0	1	0	0	1
San Antonio	38	.64	0	0	1	0	0	1
Buffalo	40	.63	0	0	0	1	1	2
New Orleans	41	.62	0	0	0	1	0	1
Jacksonville	54	.52	0	0	0	1	0	1
Green Bay-Appleton	70	.39	0	0	0	1	0	1

Note: DMA is the Designated Market Area. It is a geographic viewing area composed of counties in which commercial metropolitan television stations achieve the largest audience share. Rank is self-explanatory. TV HH is the number of television households in millions within a DMA. The Canadian teams are excluded from Table 5.1 since counties and DMAs are not bounded entities in Canada. Until the Entertainment and Sports Arena was constructed in Raleigh, the Carolina Hurricanes played the 1997 and 1998 seasons in Greensboro.

Source: For DMA ranks by television households, see "Media Profile," at http://www.neilsen media.com cited 8 October 2001. For the location and number of teams, see *The World Almanac and Book of Facts* (Mahwah, NJ: World Almanac Books, 1997–1999).

Flames, Edmonton Oilers, Montreal Canadiens, Ottawa Senators, Toronto Maple Leafs and Vancouver Canucks in the NHL. In the aggregate, therefore, these data and statistics are reasonable measurements to evaluate and judge how the media industry contributed to the capacity, demand and success of each sports league and to the location, operating income and performance of specific league franchises. Simply put, based on the information and statistics collected the following discussion is a rough approximation of the media's impact on selected professional sports leagues and teams in the late 1990s.[37]

Table 5.1 lists thirty-seven U.S.-based DMAs that contained 103 franchises within the five sports leagues in 1997. The table includes twenty-six MLB (thirteen each in the AL and NL), twenty-seven NBA, thirty NFL and twenty NHL clubs. Based on the TV HH column, 47 percent (48) of the teams were located in the ten largest DMAs and the remaining 53 percent (55) in the twenty-seven medium-to-small DMAs. Furthermore, the top ten DMAs represented 50 percent—29.26 million—of the total television households listed in the table. Therefore, even though TV HH in first-ranked New York exceeded tenth-ranked Atlanta by 5.08 million, from a media perspective the forty-eight clubs that resided within the first to tenth DMAs had greater marketing advantages and more exposure than those ranked below tenth, or from Houston to Green Bay-Appleton.

Because of a 1997 CMSA population of approximately twenty million, New York contained 12 percent of the total television households for the thirty-seven DMAs listed in Table 5.1. Moreover, New York City was the headquarters of thirteen television and 117 radio stations, and its top three daily newspapers controlled 2.4 million subscriptions. Relative to teams that existed in the smaller DMAs, from 1990 to 1996 inclusive the majority of the nine franchises located in the New York DMA earned above-average revenues from their media sources. Even mediocre clubs such as the NBA New Jersey Nets and NHL New Jersey Devils received adequate media income for games that were broadcast by New York's radio and television networks. Meanwhile, teams in low-ranked DMAs such as the NFL Bills and NHL Sabres collected insufficient media revenues from Buffalo's twenty-three radio and eight television stations. Since the fortieth-ranked Buffalo DMA represented only 1 percent or 630,000 of the total television households in Table 5.1, on average the Bills received annual media cash inflows of $36.9 million and the Sabres $4.7 million during the 1990 through 1996 seasons. However, even though each club's media income was below its respective league averages, an MSA population of 1.17 million supported the Bills and Sabres who collectively appeared in five NFL and NHL playoff series during the early 1990s. By league, how did selected teams perform and rank in media income with respect to their DMA location in 1997?

In the AL, the TV HH ranged from 6.75 million in New York to 790,000 plus in thirty-first-ranked Kansas City and thirty-second-ranked Milwaukee. (Before rounding TV HH to .79, there were approximately 791,800 television households in Kansas City and 790,660 in Milwaukee.) With less than thirty-eight radio and thirteen television stations, from 1990 through 1996 the AL Brewers in Milwaukee placed last (excluding expansion franchises) in average media income at $15.8 million per year, while the Royals in Kansas City earned $16.3 million per year from twenty-nine radio and seven television outlets. Since moving to the NL's Central Division in 1998, and because of more revenues from their new stadium—Miller Ballpark—in Milwaukee, the Brewers' media income has likely increased but the club continues to flounder in performances. For example, in the 2001 season the team finished in fourth place and twenty-five games behind the Houston Astros who were the NL Central Division champions. The Royals, meanwhile, placed fifth in the AL Central Division and trailed the Division Champion Cleveland Indians by twenty-six games in the final standings. How did the media income vary for selected teams who competed in the NL?

Between 1990 and 1996, the Cardinals who were located in the twenty-first-ranked St. Louis DMA, the Padres in the twenty-sixth-ranked San Diego DMA, and the Reds in the thirtieth-ranked Cincinnati DMA each earned at least $1 million more in media income, on average, than did the Pirates in the nineteenth-ranked Pittsburgh DMA. In part, this occurred because in the early to mid-1990s the total number of radio and television stations in St. Louis and Cincinnati each exceeded those in Pittsburgh. Also, St. Louis and San Diego each had a larger population and similar newspapers in circulation relative to the population and number of newspaper subscriptions in Pittsburgh. With one more professional sports team located in Pittsburgh than in Cincinnati or San Diego, and the same number of clubs as in St. Louis, the Pirates had to share media exposure within its DMA with the established NFL Pittsburgh Steelers and NHL Pittsburgh Penguins. However, because it currently plays home games in a new ballpark—Heinz Field—in Pittsburgh, and even with below-average team performances, the Pirates will collect more cash inflows from its media contracts and perhaps eventually close the gap in team revenues with its small market competitors such as the Cardinals, Padres and Reds. Nevertheless, in the 2001 season, while the Pirates struggled to a sixth-place finish in the NL Central Division, the Cardinals placed second and Reds fifth in the Central Division, and the Padres ended its season fourth in the Western Division.

From 1990 through 1996, the average annual media income of the large-market NL Los Angeles Dodgers at $28.7 million and the Chicago Cubs at $26.2 million trailed that of the New York Mets at $38.7 million. In 1997, the total population of the CMSA for Los Angeles was 15.5 million and for Chicago 8.6 million. In their respective DMAs, the Dodgers' home games were available to be broadcast on a total of ninety-one radio and television stations, while the number of stations for the Cubs' home games totaled forty. With approximately 2 million more TV HH than in the third-ranked Chicago DMA, Los Angeles was a superior media market to exploit by the Dodgers and the five other professional sports teams that performed within the counties adjacent to that Southern California city.

In regard to the MLB franchises, during the early-to-mid-1990s there were four interesting developments that involved specific DMAs and the distribution of media revenues. First, even with significantly fewer TV HH and less total radio and television stations, in the AL the average media revenues of the Boston Red Sox exceeded those of the California (now Anaheim) Angels, Chicago White Sox and Oakland Athletics. The revenue differences between the Red Sox and the other three clubs occurred, in part, because the latter three teams co-existed with other professional baseball teams in their respective DMAs. Second, despite approximately 700,000 more TV HH and twenty-eight total radio and television stations located in tenth-ranked Atlanta than in twenty-third-ranked Baltimore, the NL Braves and AL Orioles each averaged about $22.9 million in media money per season from 1990 through 1996. In Baltimore, a state-of-the-art ballpark—Camden Yards—opened for the Orioles in the early 1990s, while the perennial Eastern Division champion Braves played at outdated Fulton Stadium, which had few marketing amenities for the advertisers and broadcasters who represented the radio and television networks in the Atlanta area. Third, for each season during 1990–1996 the NL Dodgers earned $8 million more in media revenues in the Los Angeles DMA than did the AL Angels in nearby Anaheim. Apparently, the radio and television stations in the Los Angeles area preferred to advertise and conduct their broadcasts and media promotions before, during and after games at Dodger Stadium rather than at Edison International Field in Anaheim. Fourth, the data indicate that between 1993 and 1996 the average annual media revenues for the expansion Florida Marlins in the sixteenth-ranked Miami-Ft. Lauderdale DMA was $23.9 million and $22.8 million for the expansion Colorado Rockies in the eighteenth-ranked Denver DMA. Those values exceeded the media incomes of MLB clubs in larger DMAs such as the Phillies in the fourth-ranked Philadelphia DMA, Giants in the fifth-ranked San Francisco-Oakland-San Jose DMA, and the Astros in the eleventh-ranked Houston DMA. Although four professional teams each was located in the Miami-Ft. Lauderdale and Denver DMAs, in 1997 the Marlins and Rockies each attracted strong media support, respectively, from fifty and forty-three radio and television stations in their market areas.

Based on Table 5.1, in 1997 Washington, D.C., was the highest ranked DMA without an MLB club. With its CMSA population of 7.16 million and its 1.92 million TV HH, sixty-one radio and five television stations, and approximately 800,000 newspapers in circulation per day, since the 1980s the nation's capital has been viewed as an obvious place for MLB to relocate an existing team or an expansion franchise. Because of the potential revenue losses from the violation of its territory by a competitor, Orioles' owner Peter Angelos has periodically threatened to file a lawsuit against the league if a team is approved to play in the larger city and DMA forty miles south of Baltimore. Other than the Washington, D.C., area, from a media perspective the twentieth-ranked Sacramento-Stockton-Modesto DMA with 1.12 million TV HH, the twenty-second-ranked Orlando-Daytona Beach-Melbourne DMA with 1.04 million, the twenty-fourth-ranked Portland DMA with .97 million, and the twenty-fifth-ranked Indianapolis DMA with .95 million TV HH are also prime locations for a relocated or expansion baseball team. Since 1998, when the Tampa Bay Devil Rays joined the AL and the Arizona Diamondbacks the NL as expansion franchises, there seems to have been no interest by Commissioner Bud Selig or the league owners to add one or more new franchises in MLB. The twenty-six baseball clubs aside, how did the media incomes of selected NBA teams vary by DMA?

In the NBA, there were twenty-seven franchises (excluding the Toronto Raptors and Vancouver Grizzlies) located in twenty-five DMAs in 1997. For various business, economic and demographic reasons, NBA clubs did not exist in three medium-sized DMAs. They were fifteenth-ranked Tampa-St. Petersburg, nineteenth-ranked Pittsburgh and twenty-first-ranked St. Louis. Why were these three areas each an inferior market for one or more professional basketball franchises? There are several reasons. First, with suitable NBA clubs such as the Heat in Miami and Magic in Orlando, the eighty-eight radio and twenty-seven television stations in the Tampa-St. Petersburg area had effectively committed their company's resources to the broadcasts of games played by the AL Tampa Bay Devil Rays, NFL Tampa Bay Buccaneers and NHL Tampa Bay Lightning. Second, in the 1970s Pittsburgh and St. Louis each hosted professional basketball teams that were, respectively, the Pittsburgh Condors/Pipers and the St. Louis Spirits. Both clubs experienced attendance and financial problems and terminated operations as members of the failed American Basketball Association. Third, in 1997 Pittsburgh and St. Louis were each the current home city of three long-standing MLB, NFL and NHL teams. Regarding the market areas that ranked below the St. Louis DMA, there were the Baltimore, San Diego, Raleigh-Durham, Cincinnati, Kansas City, Buffalo, New Orleans, Jacksonville and Green Bay-Appleton DMAs. Apparently, each lacked either the required TV HHs, radio and television stations, newspapers in circulation, or the MSA population to sustain an NBA franchise.

For the league, the Los Angeles Lakers at $36.5 million, Phoenix Suns at $32.5 million and the New York Knicks at $30 million earned the highest media incomes in 1996. That year, because of their superior entertainment value each club attracted an abundant amount of cash inflows from the media companies in their respective DMAs. To broadcast the Lakers' games, in the second-ranked Los Angeles DMA there were seventy radio and thirty-three television stations that served a CMSA population of 15.5 million. In 1996, even the inferior and underachieving NBA Los Angeles Clippers received $19 million in media money.

The Los Angeles DMA aside, rather than publish articles about the NFL Cardinals and NHL Coyotes in the seventeenth-ranked Phoenix DMA, the *Arizona Republic* promoted the Suns to its 380,000 subscribers, as did many of the fifty-eight radio and television stations in the area. Meanwhile, in 1996 and 1997 the Knicks competed for media revenues with eight other professional teams in the New York DMA. Nevertheless, the club's share of broadcast revenues exceeded the amounts earned by single-city NBA teams such as the Bulls in Chicago, 76ers in Philadelphia, Warriors in San Francisco and Celtics in Boston. Besides the AL Yankees and NL Mets, the NFL New York Giants and New York Jets who shared Giants Stadium in East Rutherford, New Jersey, also averaged more than $37 million per year from the media outlets in the New York DMA.

Because the media revenues of the expansion Toronto Raptors and Vancouver Grizzlies are excluded, in 1996 the Jazz at $15.6 million in the thirty-sixth-ranked Salt Lake City DMA, the Kings at $15.8 million in the twentieth-ranked

Sacramento-Stockton-Modesto DMA, and the Wizards at $16.2 million in the seventh-ranked Washington, D.C., DMA received the least media revenues for the twenty-seven NBA franchises listed in Table 5.1. Because of the insufficient TV HH that failed to tune in and watch the Jazz at the Delta Center, and given the Kings' and Wizards' poor team performances at, respectively, the ARCO Arena in Sacramento and the MCI Center in Washington, D.C., these three franchises earned below-average media revenues in the early-to-mid-1990s. (If ranked among the twenty-seven NBA teams for the expansion year of 1996, the Raptors at $17 million and Grizzlies at $14.5 million also received below-average amounts from the home game broadcasts, respectively, at the SkyDome in Toronto and the Bear Country at GM Place in Vancouver.)

If the league owners approve expansion or a franchise relocation after 2002, a site within the Raleigh-Durham DMA in North Carolina, the Nashville DMA in Tennessee, or the Columbus DMA in Ohio rate as three choice locations to place an NBA team. As DMAs, Raleigh-Durham ranked twenty-ninth, Nashville thirtieth and Columbus thirty-fourth, according to a Nielsen Media Research study for the 2001–2002 Broadcast Season. By 2001, the population, TV HH and number of radio and television stations in each area were measured as follows. In Raleigh-Durham, the MSA population was 1.1 million, and the area contained 939,000 TV HH and thirty-nine radio and television stations. The Nashville MSA included 1.2 million residents, 879,000 TV HH and forty-five radio and television stations. Finally, Columbus's MSA population exceeded 1.4 million, and there were 809,900 TV HH and thirty-seven radio and television stations located in its DMA. Interestingly, the DMAs in Raleigh-Durham, Nashville and Columbus ranked higher than those listed in Table 5.1 for Buffalo, New Orleans, Jacksonville and Green Bay-Appleton. In sum, the high-ranked DMAs that surround Boston, Chicago, New York, Philadelphia, San Francisco-Oakland-Modesto and other large U.S. cities where NBA franchises currently exist, are not ideal places to locate another professional basketball franchise even though these areas represent lucrative media markets. Next, the DMAs and media revenues of selected NFL clubs are discussed followed by the same topics for certain teams in the NHL.[38]

In 1997, thirty NFL teams were dispersed within twenty-eight DMAs. If the second-ranked Los Angeles and thirteenth-ranked Cleveland-Akron areas are included, in Table 5.1 there are nine DMAs that did not host an NFL franchise. Because a proportion of each club's media income is redistributed to other league members, from 1990 to 1996 inclusive the average annual media revenues per team varied less in the NFL than in the other sports leagues. If the media dollars of the relocated Baltimore Ravens and St. Louis Rams and the expansion Carolina Panthers and Jacksonville Jaguars are omitted, on average the Chicago Bears at $39.7 million and Dallas Cowboys at $39.5 million earned the most income from their media markets in the early to mid-1990s. In 1997, the Chicago DMA ranked third and the Dallas-Fort Worth DMA eighth in TV HH. Furthermore, each DMA contained at least forty radio and television stations and a CMSA population that exceeded 5 million. Evidently, during the seven regular seasons—1990 to 1996—the two teams benefited from the millions of dollars in media revenues since the Bears made the NFL playoffs in the 1990, 1991 and 1994 seasons and the Cowboys won Super Bowls in the 1992, 1993 and 1995 seasons.

Because of its ample demographic characteristic and strong tradition as a sports area, the league placed the expansion NFL Browns in the Cleveland-Akron DMA in 1999. That year, there were approximately 3 million residents and 1.50 million TV HH in the area, where a total of thirty-seven radio and television stations broadcast their programs. However, due to employment losses from the relocation of manufacturers, from 1997 to 2001 the Cleveland-Akron DMA fell from thirteenth to seventeenth in rank when it was surpassed by the growth of TV HH in the Miami-Ft. Lauderdale, Minneapolis-St. Paul, Phoenix and Tampa-St. Petersburg DMAs. Also, during the latter 1990s the MSA population in Cleveland marginally declined while it rose in the other areas.

The Houston Texans began its first season as an expansion NFL club in 2002. One year earlier, the eleventh-ranked Houston DMA included more than 4.4 million residents, 1.83 million TV HH and fifty-four radio and sixteen television stations. Because of factors like the construction of a new stadium, a local base of avid football fans, the franchise's ownership commitment and wealth, and the area's population growth and widespread radio and television markets, Houston's DMA overwhelmed the other potential expansion areas such as Columbus, Orlando-Daytona Beach-Melbourne, Portland, Raleigh-Durham, Sacramento-Stockton-Modesto, Salt Lake City and San Antonio. According to published reports, several well-heeled ownership groups and celebrities from California had competed with Houston representatives for the opportunity to join the NFL and place an expansion team in Los Angeles. However, because of financial disagreements, internal bickering and organizational controversies, these groups failed in their efforts to secure the franchise despite the media power of the second-ranked "City of Angels."

Given these four areas' media infrastructure and the location of current teams, after 2002 the DMAs in Columbus, Ohio; San Antonio, Texas; Memphis, Tennessee; and Las Vegas, Nevada, appear to be viable sites for an NFL team. Columbus is the home of the expansion NHL Blue Jackets, San Antonio of the NBA Spurs who are a former league champion, and Memphis of the NBA Grizzlies who relocated from Vancouver in 2001. With an MSA population of 1.1 million, in 2001 Memphis was the forty-first-ranked DMA. That area included 655,200 TV HH and a total of thirty-nine radio and television stations. Meanwhile, with an MSA population that exceeded 400,000, the Las Vegas DMA ranked fifty-first because of its 580,000 TV HH and thirty-seven total radio and television stations. Currently, the Green Bay-Appleton and Jacksonville DMAs each has a smaller media market and fewer TV HH than Columbus, San Antonio, Memphis or Las Vegas.

In 1997, twenty NHL clubs occupied seventeen U.S.-based DMAs. Twenty-five percent (5) of the professional hockey franchises were located in the two top-ranked media areas, which were the New York and Los Angeles DMAs. If the Canada-based hockey teams are excluded, in the early to mid-1990s the four highest average media incomes per team were earned by the Boston Bruins at $10 million, New York Islanders at $9.4 million, and the Detroit Red Wings and New York Rangers each at $6.8 million. In the meantime, the Hartford Whalers at $3.3 million, St. Louis Blues at $3.4 million, New Jersey Devils at $4.5 million and the Pittsburgh Penguins at $4.6 million received the lowest average media revenues for the NHL teams based in the United States. The Whalers, Blues and Penguins played in inferior DMAs with respect to media power. These areas had smaller populations, less TV HH, and fewer radio and television stations than did the Bruins, Devils, Islanders, Red Wings and Rangers. Except for the Penguins who won Stanley Cups in 1991 and 1992, the performances of the Whalers, Blues and Devils were marginal at best. Evidently, for business and demographic reasons, in 1997 there were no franchises located in the tenth- through fourteenth-ranked DMAs, which ranged from Atlanta to Minneapolis-St. Paul. Yet, the Hurricanes played in the twenty-seventh-ranked Hartford-New Haven DMA and the Sabres in the fortieth-ranked Buffalo DMA.

Because of the composition and growth in TV HH, each year after 1997 the DMA rankings changed and the sports leagues responded by expansion. Besides a new NFL team in Houston and MLB expansion clubs in Phoenix and Tampa Bay, between 1998 and 2000 three franchises joined the NHL. They were the Predators who chose to locate in the thirty-third-ranked Nashville DMA in 1998, the Thrashers in the tenth-ranked Atlanta DMA in 1999, and the Blue Jackets in the thirty-fourth-ranked Columbus DMA in 2000. Indeed, in 2001 the five highest ranked U.S.-based DMAs without an NHL team were eleventh-ranked Houston, twelfth-ranked Seattle-Tacoma, seventeenth-ranked Cleveland-Akron, nineteenth-ranked Sacramento-Stockton-Modesto, and twentieth-ranked Orlando-Daytona Beach-Melbourne. Consequently, because of their media potential, TV HH and other amenities these five areas are prime DMAs in which to relocate the struggling Canadian hockey clubs such as the Edmonton Oilers, Ottawa Senators and Vancouver Canucks. The population of Montreal at 3.4 million and Toronto at 4.7 million, plus the broadcast markets in those cities, are justifiable reasons for the NHL to allow the Canadiens and Maple Leafs to remain in Canada at least in the short term or until their financial condition deteriorates due to economic conditions.

Between 1997 and 2001, five team moves and six league expansions affected given DMAs. Based on the Nielsen Media Research Local Universe Estimates for the 2001–2002 Broadcast Season, which lists the DMAs by TV HH, in team movements the NBA Grizzlies relocated from Vancouver to forty-first-ranked Memphis in 2001, and the NFL Oilers left eleventh-ranked Houston for Memphis in 1998 and then moved to thirtieth-ranked Nashville in 1999. In the NHL, the Jets, now Coyotes, moved from Winnipeg to sixteenth-ranked Phoenix in 1996 and the Whalers vacated the twenty-eighth-ranked Hartford-New Haven DMA for the twenty-seventh-ranked Raleigh-Durham DMA in 1997.

The relocation of franchises aside, six sports league expansions occurred in DMAs. In MLB, the Devil Rays joined the AL in fifteenth-ranked Tampa-St. Petersburg in 1998, and the Diamondbacks entered the NL in seventeenth-ranked Phoenix. The NFL Browns expanded in thirteenth-ranked Cleveland-Akron in 1999. As stated before, in the NHL the Predators opened in thirty-third-ranked Nashville in 1998, the Thrashers in tenth-ranked Atlanta in 1999, and the Blue Jackets in thirty-fourth-ranked Columbus in 2000. In total, from 1997 through 2001 the number of franchises increased by 7 percent or from 103 to 110. Furthermore, the number of DMAs that hosted one or more professional sports teams enlarged by 8 percent or from thirty-seven in 1997 to forty in 2001. In sum, there are five medium-sized U.S. MSAs and media markets without a major league team in any sport. These areas are the Hartford-New Haven, Greenville-Spartanburg-Ashville, Grand Rapids-Kalamazoo-Battle Creek, Norfolk-Portsmouth-Newport News and West Palm Beach-Fort Pierce.

SUMMARY

This chapter described how the media industry cooperated and interacted with the professional sports leagues and their member franchises in the United States since the late 1800s. Three interrelated topics were discussed and analyzed. First, the historic linkages and relationships between league teams and the various media types such as magazines and newspapers, and radio, television and the Internet were examined. The research indicates that each media type has contributed to and promoted the business, and the formation, development and growth of the five sports leagues as highlighted in the chapter. Second, the newsworthy and significant events, incidents and transactions that involved the respective sports leagues and teams, and specific media companies were identified each year from 1997 through 2001. It appears that, especially in the late 1990s several media agreements and company alliances impacted and influenced the marketing, and operations of the professional sports leagues and the majority of their franchises. Third, the Designated Market Areas that contained a sports franchise in 1997 were tabled and ranked according to the number of television households. Then, the areas were compared based on their metropolitan populations, number of radio and television stations and the volume of local newspapers in circulation. These statistics provided evidence why teams located in large-market areas generally earned more operating revenues from their media sources than did the clubs that existed in small-to-medium markets. This concludes Chapter 5.

Prior to this discussion of how the media industry affects professional sports, Chapters 1 through 4 looked at the five prominent U.S. professional sports leagues and their member franchises, team owners and players. Thus, Chapters 1 through 5 form the basis for Chapter 6, which focuses on how and why sports fans are a vital component to the growth and progress of the professional sports industry. The identification of different types of spectators, and the sports league teams that have the most and least devoted fans are two topics examined. Based on studies and other facts and information, the reader will realize why an increasing number of prominent sports analysts, commentators, editors and journalists contend that fans are underappreciated and often ignored by leagues, players and franchise owners who struggle to make their teams competitive, entertaining and fun to watch and support.

NOTES

1. Since the late 1990s, the *Charlotte Observer* has published a plethora of articles about the gunshot death of the Carolina Panthers' running back Fred Lane, the automobile accident and demise of the Charlotte Hornets' Bobby Phills, the courtroom trial of the Charlotte Hornets' owner George Shinn, and the voters' defeat of a June 2001 referendum to build a $190 million taxpayer-subsidized arena for the franchise. For information about these and other interesting sports-related topics, see the newspaper's archives at http://www.charlotteobserver.com.

2. For a discussion of the advantages and disadvantages of the major media types as applied to the professional sports industry, see Matthew D. Shank, *Sports Marketing: A Strategic Perspective,* 2nd ed. (Upper Saddle River, NJ: Prentice-Hall, 2002).

3. Since 2001, ESPN's ratings have decreased 14 percent and its cable operators dispute the recent 15 percent increase in annual fees for ESPN Classic programs. To examine ESPN President George W. Bodenheimer's strategy to enhance revenues, see Tom Lowry, "ESPN's Full-Court Press," *Business Week* (11 February 2002), 60–61; Bruce Orwall, "ESPN Adds Entertainment Shows to Its Playbook," *Wall Street Journal* (6 March 2002), B1, B4.

4. See Frank G. Menke, *The Encyclopedia of Sports,* 5th ed. (Cranbury, NJ: A. S. Barnes, 1975); Benjamin G. Rader, *American Sports: From the Age of Folk Games to the Age of Spectators* (Englewood Cliffs, NJ: Prentice-Hall, 1983).

5. Beginning with the formation of the NL in the late 1800s and the AL in the early 1900s, MLB has been studied by several prominent historians. The sport's glorious and grievous era was explored by Harold Seymour, *Baseball: The Golden Age,* 2nd ed. (New York: Oxford University Press, 1989). For a summary of the important developments in the professional sports industry, see Rich Burton, "From Hearst to Stern: The Shaping of an Industry Over a Century," at http://proquest.umi.com cited 24 September 2001.

6. From business and financial perspectives, the radio broadcast of professional sports games was an important event. For radio's contribution to baseball, see Frank G. Menke, *The Encyclopedia of Sports,* 127.

7. The total revenues from local and national broadcast rights in MLB, and in the NBA, NFL and NHL were extracted from various tables. See Ira Horowitz, "Sports Broadcasting," in Roger G. Noll, ed., *Government and the Sports Business* (Washington, DC: The Brookings Institution, 1974), 275–323.

8. For the chronology of professional football from 1869 to 2001 inclusive, see the *NFL 2001 Record & Fact Book* (New York: National Football League, 2001), 278–289 "NFL Football: From the Beginning," at http://www.cnnsi.com cited 1 June 2001; "National Football League," at http://www.nfl.com cited 1 August 2001.

9. *NFL 2001 Record & Fact Book,* 278–289.

10. Ibid.

11. See Ira Horowitz, "Sports Broadcasting," 289–291.

12. In 1997, numerous newspaper articles publicized the ongoing negotiations between the NFL and the television networks for the league's television rights. For comments on this topic, see Stefan Fatsis and Kyle Pope, "TV Networks Rush to Splurge on NFL Deals," *Wall Street Journal* (15 December 1997), B1, B8.

13. Sports analysts agree that the NFL players on the richest teams would be the biggest beneficiaries of a new television contract. For this viewpoint, see Stefan Fatsis, "NFL Players May Help Get Fatter TV Deal," *Wall Street Journal* (2 January 1997), 3, 4; Kyle Pope, "Networks' Big Play for NFL May End in Fumble," *Wall Street Journal* (5 February 1998), B10.

14. See "NBA New TV Deal Worth Twice as Much," at http://www.austin360.com cited 12 November 1997.

15. At least two articles discussed the business ramifications of the contract between the television networks and the NBA. See Stefan Fatsis and Kyle Pope, "NBC Agrees to Pay About $1.5 Billion to Renew Contract to Air NBA Games," *Wall Street Journal* (11 November 1997), B8; Kyle Pope and Stefan Fatsis, "NBC, Turner Sports May See Less Profit Showing More Games in New NBA Pact," *Wall Street Journal* (12 November 1997), B9. For the negotiation and settlement between the NBA and television networks over broadcasts rights after 2001, see "Report Says ABC, ESPN Will Take Shot at NBA Rights," *Charlotte Observer* (5 December 2001), 4C; Stefan Fatsis and Bruce Orwall, "Broadcast Bounce: NBA's Pact With AOL, Disney Puts Most Games in Cable's Court," *Wall Street Journal* (17 December 2001), B6; "Sources: TV Deal Nets About $700 Million a Year," *Charlotte Observer* (11 January 2002), 4C; "Air Ball," *Wall Street Journal* (23 January 2002), A20; "NBA Switching Channels to ESPN, TNT, ABC," *Charlotte Observer* (23 January 2002), 4C; Joe Flint, "NBC Enters Arena Football Pact as NBA Arrangement Nears End," *Wall Street Journal* (6 March 2002), B9.

16. See Stefan Fatsis and Kyle Pope, "NFL Scores Nearly $18 Billion in TV Rights," *Wall Street Journal* (14 January 1998), B1, B13; Josh Dubow, "It's a Wonderful World for NFL's TV," *Charlotte Observer* (14 January 1998), B1.

17. In his January 1998 State of the Game address in San Diego, California, NFL Commissioner Paul Tagliabue discussed the league's television agreements, expansion and the employment of minority head coaches. See Tom Pedulla, "Tagliabue: TV Deals a Start," *USA Today* (26 January 1998), 14C.

18. The advertising budgets, marketing implications and long-term strategies in sports programming are interesting to analyze. For these topics, see Leslie Cauley, "To Pay the NFL, ESPN Plans a Blitz of Football Shows," *Wall Street Journal* (17 August 1998), B1, B4; Stefan Fatsis and Suzanne Vranica, "NFL's Marketing Thrust Goes on Display," *Wall Street Journal* (21 November 2001), B11; Stefan Fatsis, "The New Game in TV Sports," *Wall Street Journal* (21 January 2002), B1, B3; Tom Lowry, "ESPN's Full-Court Press," 60–61; Vanessa O'Connell, "Super-Bowl Spots Aren't Easy Sell for Fox," *Wall Street Journal* (21 January 2002), B5; Elliot Spagat, "Dallas Mavericks Owner Bets Big on HDTV," *Wall Street Journal* (7 March 2002), B5, B6; Joel Millman, "Young Maverick Sits on Sidelines But Stars in Ads," *Wall Street Journal* (27 February 2002), B1, B3.

19. See David Sweet, "Fox and ESPN Bolster Sports Web Sites," *Wall Street Journal* (3 September 1998), B8; Rebecca Quick, "For Sports Fans, the Internet Is a Whole New Ball Game," *Wall Street Journal* (3 September 1998), B9.

20. Since 1983, live NBA games have been broadcast in Mexico. For more information about the television contract and extent of the programming, see "TV Azteca and the NBA Extend Broadcast Partnership," at http://www.nba.com cited 29 August 1998.

21. In 1999, the NBA was at the forefront of a larger movement by the professional sports leagues to generate more original information, programming and game statistics. For insights regarding this strategy, see Sam Walker, "NBA Set to Launch 24-Hour Television Network," *Wall Street Journal* (24 September 1999), B7.

22. The NBA licenses its game broadcasts and produces many of its own entertainment properties. For the league's television programming and a list of its Web sites, see Anthony Bianco, "Now It's NBA All-The-Time TV," *Business Week* (15 November 1999), 241–242.

23. Professional sports franchise owner Jerry Colangelo commented on the synergy between the sports and media industries. See Jerry Colangelo, "Sports and the Media," at http://proquest.umi.com cited 24 September 2001.

24. To access the Web sites that discuss the failed sports leagues, see David Sweet, "It's Never Over, Yogi: Dead Sports Leagues Live Again Online," *Wall Street Journal* (30 September 1999), B1.

25. See Eric Fisher, "Cybersquatters Blitz Professional Leagues," at http://www.info trac.com cited 18 July 2001.

26. Online auctions present fans with the opportunity to interact with their favorite sports stars. When this occurs, charities may benefit as well. For more details, see David Sweet, "Sports Teams Find Revenue in Online Sales," *Wall Street Journal* (22 May 2000), A35A.

27. Everything from dirt to toilets has been sold from obsolete stadiums to help defray the construction costs of new facilities. See David Sweet, "Fans Line Up for Stadium Pieces on Web," *Wall Street Journal* (26 October 2000), B14.

28. See Mark Hyman, "Take Me Out to the Ticket Auction," *Business Week* (28 August 2000), 14.

29. Based on consumer demand, various Safeco Field tickets were sold at a discount or premium on the Seattle Mariners' Web site. For this event, see "Cyber-Scalping?" at http://www.cnnsi.com cited 15 August 2001.

30. Throughout 2001, various sport teams continued to use the latest computer and online technology to spur ticket sales and to entice wireless customers and Web-savvy sorts. For this activity, see David Sweet, "Sports Teams Use New Technology to Sell Tickets," *Wall Street Journal* (10 January 2001), B6.

31. See Rich Thomaselli, "NHL Markets Web Site," at http://proquest.umi.com cited 24 September 2001.

32. Tom Lowry, "Take Me Online to the Ball Game," *Business Week* (9 April 2001), 92; Chris Gaither, "Major League Baseball to Charge for Web Broadcasts," at http://proquest.umi.com cited 27 September 2001.

33. See Anna Wilde Matthews, "NFL Nears Web-Properties Deal With AOL, Viacom, SportsLine," *Wall Street Journal* (9 July 2001), B4; Bruce Orwall, "ESPN.com to be Sole Provider of Sports News to Microsoft's MSN," *Wall Street Journal* (7 September 2001), B2.

34. Vanessa O'Connell, "DirecTV Dishes Up New Marketing Push," *Wall Street Journal* (30 July 2001), B9.

35. The Yankees generally lead all MLB teams in local broadcasting rights. The developments and pitfalls of the Yankees' Entertainment and Sports network are discussed in three articles. See Stefan Fatsis, "Yankees Holding Company Set to Form a Sports Network Valued at $850 Million," *Wall Street Journal* (11 September 2001), B4; Idem., "Two Major Players in Yankees Network Pull Stake of 20%," *Wall Street Journal* (18

September 2001), B12; "Yankees to Form Own TV Network," at http://www.cnnsi.com cited 20 June 2001; "YES Sports Channel Files Anitrust Suit Against Cablevision," *Wall Street Journal* (30 April 2002), B7; "Yankee-Panky," *Wall Street Journal* (29 March 2002), W15.

36. From 1990 to 1996 inclusive, *Financial World* published the media incomes of franchises in MLB, and in the NBA, NFL and NHL. See James Quirk and Rodney Fort, *Hard Ball: The Abuse of Power in Pro Team Sports* (Princeton, NJ: Princeton University Press, 1999), 189–192.

37. For the rank and number of television households in fifty Designated Market Areas as of January 1998, see "Media Profile," at http://www.nielsenmedia.com cited 8 October 2001. The Consolidated Metropolitan Statistical Area and Metropolitan Statistical Area populations, the number of television and radio stations by city, and the daily circulation of city newspapers in millions are reported in various editions of *The World Almanac and Book of Facts* (Mahwah, NJ: World Almanac Books, 1950–2001).

38. The ranks and number of television households for more than 299 Designated Market Areas are available in two reports. See "Nielsen Media Research Local Universe Estimates for the 1997–1998 Broadcast Season," at http://www.nielsenmedia.com cited 8 October 2001; "Nielsen Media Research Local Universe Estimates for the 2001–2002 Broadcast Season," at http://www.nielsenmedia.com cited 1 October 2001.

Chapter 6

Fans

During the history of professional team sports, each league franchise has initially established a market and then broadened its fan base to improve local radio and television revenues and increase attendance at its games to sell more apparel, food and merchandise at the arena or stadium. For data and information about markets, league officials and team owners have consulted with various research companies. These organizations have studied and determined who sports fans are, where they live, which sport they prefer to support, and how they allocate their household budgets and time on leisure activities. In 2001, the Gallup Organization conducted a survey of U.S. consumers to measure the proportion of fans that had identified with each professional sport. The individuals that were polled had four choices to select from in the survey's questionnaire. That is, those sampled could respond as: yes a fan, somewhat of a fan, not a fan or no opinion. The survey results were insightful. Expressed in percentages, the proportion of choices in baseball were yes a fan 35 percent, somewhat of a fan 14 percent, not a fan 51 percent, and no opinion 0 percent. The percentages in basketball were 30 percent, 8 percent, 62 percent and 0 percent; in football 54 percent, 9 percent, 37 percent and 0 percent; and in ice hockey 24 percent, 7 percent, 69 percent and 0 percent, respectively. Essentially, the Gallup study indicated that by a wide margin professional football at 54 percent had the highest proportion of fans, and ice hockey at 24 percent scored the lowest. For the second choice, which was somewhat of a fan, professional baseball at 14 percent received the largest response and ice hockey at 7 percent earned the smallest. As to the third choice, which was not a fan, professional ice hockey at 69 percent placed first and football at 37 percent ranked fourth for the sports evaluated. Finally, there were no respondents that chose the fourth choice, which was no opinion.[1]

Other results of the survey show that from 1998 to 2001 inclusive the proportion of fans devoted to professional baseball had declined from 47 percent to 35 percent and to basketball from 36 percent to 30 percent. Alternatively, the fan proportion had increased from 45 percent to 54 percent in professional football.

(The Gallup Organization excluded professional ice hockey in its 1998 study of sports fans.) In short, for various demographic, economic and sports-specific reasons Gallup's study revealed that the majority of fans increasingly preferred professional football, but since the late 1990s had expressed less interest in professional baseball and basketball.[2]

In another Gallup poll conducted in early 2001, the respondents were asked to choose their favorite sport to watch as either game spectators and/or television viewers. Those who were questioned selected professional football first at 28 percent, then basketball second at 16 percent and baseball third at 12 percent. (The percentage of respondents who favored professional ice hockey was not reported in the research.) Yet, the survey indicated that 56 percent of the respondents said they were fans of major league baseball. According to the results, the "national pastime" appealed to fans because of interleague play, the leagues' championship playoffs and the wild-card system. However, a large portion of the baseball fans commented that the rapid rise in players' salaries was the sport's biggest drawback. In fact, 79 percent of them recommended that the league impose a salary cap to control player salaries and restrict team payrolls. The two Gallup polls, in sum, reflect fans' preferences for each sport studied.[3]

Other well-regarded research firms have focused on the profile of fans and how intensely fans were involved with the professional sports leagues and teams. For example, in 2000 and 2001 Scarborough Sports Marketing Inc. published a series of studies that investigated the characteristics, demographics and interests of professional sports fans. To interpret the results, Scarborough's studies revealed that fans of the AL and NL in MLB tended to be married males aged thirty-five to fifty-four. Generally, these fans had attended college and owned their homes. Furthermore, the majority of baseball fans were Internet savvy because 50 percent or more of them spent at least five hours a week involved with online programs. While connected to the Internet, they devoted their efforts to specific sports-related activities such as surfing the Web for information to update game scores and accessing various sites to shop for league and team products. Because the sport is considered important to their social well-being, baseball fans are prime targets for teams' marketers who offer to sell them game and season tickets, sports clothing and related merchandise and memorabilia. Furthermore, according to the studies NBA fans had moderately different profiles than those in MLB. Professional basketball groupies are likely to be single males aged eighteen to thirty-four. They lead an active lifestyle and rent an apartment or house. This group, whose average income is $57,000 a year, prefers to scan the Web for news and shop and purchase items while online. Between 1999 and 2000, from various Web sites over 4 million NBA fans had bought clothing with the teams' logos displayed. In total, this data and information about sports fans are useful to know for franchise owners. That is, from the studies each team can identify who their online customers are and then sell the products and services that appeal to this segment of the professional sports market.[4]

In comparison, Scarborough determined that the profiles of NFL fans are marginally distinct relative to the attributes and habits of households that were attached to MLB and the NBA. Hard-core football fans are typically males aged eighteen to thirty-four, whose annual household income exceeds $50,000. Two-thirds of the football addicts own their home and a computer, and approximately 25 percent of them use the Internet to monitor the scores of games played in professional football. To increase the clubs' cash inflows, some NFL franchise owners purchase software programs to contact these fans online and then attempt to electronically sell them single-game and season tickets, team clothing and various merchandise. NHL fans tend to be married males aged twenty-five to fifty-four, who have attended college and currently earn $50,000 or more a year. Similar to their counterparts, on average professional ice hockey fans own a cell phone, personal computer and video game system. They regularly access the Web to check sports scores and to shop for and purchase clothing that displays an NHL logo. In total, based on the data provided from the research accomplished by Scarborough Sports Marketing Inc. and by the other firms that sample the marketplace, to expand franchise market sales and revenues the professional hockey teams should also maintain contact with their fans via the Internet by installing online programs and promoting the sport.[5]

In 1999, a New York research organization based in Rochester, Harris Interactive, identified fans by their interest level in each professional sports league. In its surveys, the company differentiated fans as Diehard/Avid, Casual/Championship, Non-Fan or Anti-Fan. Reported by sports league, the NFL at 38 percent had the highest proportion of Diehard/Avid fans while MLB had 22 percent, NBA 15 percent and the NHL 9 percent. In Harris Interactive's classification of fans, the Diehard/Avid types have a "high level of interest" in a sport. On the other hand, the Casual/Championship types occasionally view regular season events. Moreover, they tend to follow up on the scores of regular season games and generally watch sports contests on television, or listen to the radio during the conference playoffs or league championship series. Within this category, the largest proportion of fans at 49 percent identify with MLB, and at 46 percent the NBA, at 43 percent the NFL and at 33 percent the NHL. In contrast, a Non-Fan rarely attends a team's home or away games and prefers to watch television programs other than sports events. Ranked in percentages by sport, 40 percent of the Non-Fans claim they are indifferent to the NHL, 31 percent to the NBA, 23 percent to MLB and 15 percent to the NFL. Regarding the last type, the Anti-Fan is the least represented of the four categories. This group adamantly opposes the radio and television broadcasts and competitiveness of professional sports events. In each league, the percentage distribution of an Anti-Fan is 10 percent for the NHL, 7 percent for the NBA, and 5 percent each for the NFL and MLB.[6]

In sum, the Harris Interactive studies indicate that the majority of fans were foremost identified as the Casual/Championship type, and then respectively, the Non-Fan, Diehard/Avid and Anti-Fan types. To apply and benefit from Harris's research results, the sports team marketers and owners should implement marketing strategies to upgrade their fans' interest levels to preferably the Diehard/Avid or Casual/Championship types. This can be achieved in several ways. Franchises could enhance and upgrade the entertainment value of home-town sports events, make games and sports a real and meaningful experience for spectators, encourage the teams' coaches, owners and players to bond with fans during the regular season and off-season, and promote the history and tradition of the organization in the local community and regional area.[7]

Since the early 1990s, the growth in fan loyalty attributed to the majority of the professional sports has been dormant in the United States. One reason for this is because of higher admission prices and the escalation of other costs to attend games by individual fans and families. These issues are discussed in the next sections of Chapter 6.

TICKET PRICE STRATEGY

A long-standing dilemma and sensitive topic that has negatively affected professional sports leagues, their franchises and especially fans are the inflated ticket prices at games and the higher retail prices of apparel, food and merchandise that is sold at an arena or stadium. The team owners maintain that ticket, clothing, food and merchandise prices must be periodically increased to improve the clubs' short- and long-term competitiveness within a division, conference and league. That is, professional sports team executives argue that because higher prices provide more gate and stadium revenues, their teams can bid for rookies and talented free agents and also offer lucrative contracts to retain the superior and veteran players on the current season's roster. The strategy to raise prices and win more games has been realized by some but not all of the professional sports franchise owners. Therefore, to explore how ticket prices at regular season games have changed in each sport and thereby impacted fans, leagues and teams, Table 6.1 was developed. With the AL and NL combined to represent MLB, this Table lists in four columns the average ticket prices for each league from 1998 through 2001, which is four recent seasons. Thus, what does the absolute and relative dif-

Table 6.1
Average Ticket Price, by League, 1998 to 2001

League	1998	1999	2000	2001
MLB	$13.59	$14.91	$16.67	$18.86
NBA	$42.50	$48.37	$51.27	$50.10
NFL	$42.81	$45.63	$49.35	$53.64
NHL	$42.79	$45.70	$47.69	$49.86

Note: The average ticket prices represent the 1998, 1999, 2000 and 2001 seasons in MLB. The NBA, NFL and NHL seasons are represented from 1998–1999 to 2001–2002 inclusive.

Source: "Fan Cost Index—League Averages," at http://www.foxsports.com cited 29 November 2000; "The Price of the Pastime," at http://www.cnnsi.com cited 29 March 2001; Chris Isidore, "Prices Going, Going … Up," at http://www.cnnfn.com cited 11 August 2001; "TMR's Fan Cost Index," at http://www.teammarketing.com cited 18 October 2001.

ferences in ticket prices presented in the table denote about fans, sports leagues, and the revenues and pricing strategies of their respective teams?

From the 1998 to 2000 seasons inclusive, the sports leagues' average ticket prices increased by 16.4 percent or from $35.42 in the 1998 season to $41.24 in the 2000 season. Ranked from high to low in percentages, during this three-season period the average ticket prices rose by 22.7 percent in MLB, 20.6 percent in the NBA, 15.3 percent in the NFL and 11.4 percent in the NHL. Furthermore, except for the NBA, the spectator prices in each league rose higher from the previous season, that is from 2000 to 2001. That season, on average MLB teams charged the least at $18.86 per game and NFL clubs the most at $53.64. Fans who watched the AL Red Sox play in the smallest ballpark in baseball, which was 33,871-seat Fenway Park in Boston, paid the highest price at $36.08 a game, while spectators who rooted for the AL Twins at the 48,678-seat Metrodome in Minneapolis paid the lowest at $9.55. To attract more fans at home games, in 2001 three MLB franchises trimmed their ticket prices. The teams that reduced prices were the AL Mariners by 2.4 percent at 47,000-seat Safeco Field in Seattle, the AL Tigers by 3.7 percent at 40,000-seat Comerica Park in Detroit, and the NL Expos by 5.7 percent at 46,500-seat Olympic Stadium in Montreal. Because of a few high-valued ticket options and inflated player salaries, the other twenty-three baseball clubs either raised or maintained their ticket prices in the 2001 season. The largest percentage increases per team were 82 percent by the NL Pirates at 38,127-seat PNC Park in Pittsburgh, 54 percent by the NL Brewers at 43,000-seat Miller Park in Milwaukee, and 43 percent by the NL Reds at 52,953-seat Cinergy Field in Cincinnati. Meanwhile, in 2001 the NL Astros held their average prices constant at 42,000-seat Enron Field in Houston, the NL Dodgers at 56,000-seat Dodger Stadium in Los Angeles, the NL Rockies at 50,381-seat Coors Field in Denver, and the AL Orioles at 48,876-seat Camden Yards in Baltimore. Evidently, ticket prices in MLB generally increased the most from 2000 to 2001 for clubs that opened the season in new stadiums (except for the Reds), but remained the same or declined for teams that focused on improvements in attendance at their home ballparks.[8]

During the latter 1990s and in 2000, surprisingly more fans attended professional baseball games even as the league's average ticket prices increased. For example, when prices rose by 22.7 percent from 1998 through 2000 in MLB, the total regular season attendance incrementally expanded by 3.4 percent, or from 70.3 to 72.7 million spectators. This occurred partly because of U.S. economic conditions and the sports market enthusiasm and momentum from the previous expansions in Phoenix and Tampa Bay. This was evident when MLB attendance rose by 11.6 percent, or from 63 million in 1997 to 70.3 million in 1998. At a national press conference, Commissioner Bud Selig gloated, "MLB is pleased to note that our ticket prices remain by far the best value among the major professional sports leagues, and most forms of entertainment."[9]

Nevertheless, a dilemma existed for the Diehard and Casual/Championship fans, but not for the affluent baseball addicts who love the game and sport. That is, while the U.S. Consumer Price Index had increased by 31 percent from 1991 to 2000, the average MLB ticket price nearly doubled from $8.64 to $16.67 per game. Furthermore, during this period the players' average salary rose by 158 percent, or from $851,492 in 1991 to $2.2 million in 2000. If MLB's average ticket prices and team payrolls continue to spiral upward after 2002, it is unlikely that the sport's total attendance will continue to increase, or that communities and local taxpayers will be willing to fund new ballparks when team owners earn excessive amounts of revenues and players make extravagant salaries. Thus, rather than travel to the ballpark, more fans will watch regular season games and the playoffs and championship series on cable and network television stations or subscribe to pay-per-view programs to avoid the payments for high ticket and stadium prices. For instance, at the 2001 NL Championship Series games between the Atlanta Braves and Arizona Diamondbacks at 50,062-seat Turner Field, where tickets cost $50 or more and parking $20, the gate attendance averaged 39,900 a game which equaled about 80 percent of the stadium's capacity. At a post-game interview, Commissioner Selig said to reporters, "It [low attendance] does surprise me," and words to the effect that he [Selig] was not sure why Turner Field had 10,162 vacant seats.[10]

Because of the sluggish demand for professional basketball in the United States and the moderate growth in player salaries, the NBA's average ticket price rose marginally by 16.2 percent, or from $20 in the 1981 season to $23.24 in the 1991 season. Since the early 1990s, however, the league's average admission prices to regular season and postseason games have soared. Fans paid $48.37 a seat in the 1999 season, which was a 108 percent increase from the 1991 season, and a 14 percent rise from the 1998 season (Table 6.1). Then, in the 2000 season each NBA seat price averaged $51.27, which was 6 percent greater than in the 1999 season. The Knicks, in the 2000 season, charged the highest average price in the league at $91 a ticket for spectators to see games at 19,763-seat Madison Square Garden in New York City, while the Bucks' fans paid the lowest price at $33 to attend games at 18,600-seat Bradley Center in Milwaukee. The Trail Blazers charged spectators, on average, $70 a seat at 19,980-seat Rose Garden in Portland, which was a 35 percent increase from the 1999 season. The three other NBA teams that significantly inflated their general admission costs in the 2000 season were the Heat who raised prices by 25 percent to $58 at 19,600-seat American Airlines Arena in Miami, the Suns by 14 percent to $52 at 19,023-seat America West Arena in Phoenix, and the 76ers by 13 percent to $50 at 20,440-seat First Union Center in Philadelphia. Interestingly, the ticket price increases resulted in higher revenues for the four teams since attendance in the 2000 regular season declined by less than 1 percent in Portland, 4 percent in Miami and 5 percent in Phoenix. In Philadelphia, the regular season attendance rose by 5 percent because the 76ers, led by guard Allen Iverson and center Dikembe Mutombo, won the Eastern Conference title and challenged the Western Conference's Los Angeles Lakers for the NBA Championship.

Alternatively, to boost attendance and therewith the sale of clothing, food and merchandise at their hometown arenas for the 2000 regular season, 24 percent

(7) of the NBA clubs lowered their average ticket prices. Ranked from the largest percentage price cut to the smallest, the teams were the Warriors by 12 percent to $42 at 19,596-seat Arena in Oakland, the Mavericks by 8 percent to $37 at 18,187-seat Reunion Arena in Dallas, the SuperSonics by 4 percent to $62 at 17,072-seat KeyArena in Seattle, and the Nets by 3 percent to $57 at 20,049-seat Continental Airlines Arena in New Jersey. The three other franchises that reduced their average ticket costs were the Nuggets by 3 percent to $37 at 19,099-seat Pepsi Center in Denver, the Celtics by 1 percent to $50 at 18,624-seat FleetCenter in Boston, and the Timberwolves by 1 percent to $39 at 19,006-seat Target Center in Minneapolis. In short, the owners of these seven franchises experimented by reducing prices to sell more game tickets and expand the clubs' operating revenues from the respective arenas.

Because of fan apathy and the national recession, which decreased the demand for regular season game tickets, the average NBA ticket price declined by 2.3 percent, or from $51.27 in the 2000 season to $50.10 in the 2001 season. Fifty-five percent (16) of the basketball clubs cut prices. The teams with the largest discounts included the Portland Trail Blazers who lowered ticket costs by 36 percent, Seattle SuperSonics by 32 percent, Detroit Pistons by 20 percent and the Washington Wizards by 14 percent. In contrast, eleven NBA franchises raised the cost of admission in 2001. The Dallas Mavericks, who began the season in a new arena, boosted game tickets by 56 percent and the Sacramento Kings by 12 percent. The New York Knicks charged the highest average price at $89.80 a seat and the Detroit Pistons the lowest at $31.90. Meanwhile, the Charlotte Hornets kept their average ticket prices constant at $34.80 per spectator. (The percentage changes for the Vancouver [Memphis] Grizzlies were not computed in the survey.) Given the new price levels in the 2001 season, the NBA ranked second to the NFL and within $1 of the NHL in average ticket costs per fan. If the strategy of deflating average prices succeeds in the NBA, perhaps the owners of clubs in MLB, as well as in the NFL and the NHL, will consider discounts or reductions in ticket prices for the 2003, 2004 and 2005 seasons.[11]

Even though ticket prices to regular season games increased throughout the 1990s in the NBA, its total attendance increased by 22 percent, or from 16.8 million spectators in 1990 to 20.5 million in 1995. Then, total gate attendance marginally declined by 2.4 percent to 20 million in 2000. The league's per game attendance followed a similar trend. It rose by 13 percent, or from 15,000 a game in 1990 to 17,000 in 1995, and then fell by 1.8 percent to 16,700 in 2000. Because of lower prices, the NBA's total regular season and per game attendance was expected to improve in the 2002 season and thereafter. This prediction was based on the fan appeal of young and energetic superstars such as Allen Iverson of the Philadelphia 76ers, Jason Kidd of the New Jersey Nets, Kobe Bryant of the Los Angeles Lakers, Paul Pierce of the Boston Celtics, Tim Duncan of the San Antonio Spurs, Tracy McGrady of the Orlando Magic and Vince Carter of the Toronto Raptors. These men generate excitement at games and attract spectators with their spectacular athleticism. Furthermore, the well-publicized return of former Chicago Bulls legend Michael Jordan, who plays guard and small forward for the Washington Wizards, will boost attendance at many arenas throughout the league.

In the NFL, the average ticket price per game increased approximately 7 percent to $45.63 in the 1999 season, 8 percent to $49.35 in the 2000 season and 9 percent to $53.64 in the 2001 season (Table 6.1). At $81.89 a ticket in the 2000 and 2001 seasons, the Redskins charged spectators the highest admission prices in the league to attend games at 80,116-seat FedEx Field in Landover, Maryland. (The Redskins did not raise ticket prices in the 2001 season.) On the other hand, at $39.05 per fan in those two seasons the Lions had the lowest prices in the NFL to watch games at the 80,311-seat Pontiac Silverdome in Detroit. When 76,125-seat Invesco Field at Mile High in Denver and 65,000-seat Heinz Field in Pittsburgh opened in 2001, respectively, the Broncos increased their average ticket prices by 67 percent to $77 and the Steelers by 53 percent to $62. The Broncos and Steelers aside, there were other football teams that implemented above-average price increases at their stadiums. The three NFL clubs with the highest percentage price jumps were the Dolphins who raised per game tickets by 25 percent to $57 at 75,192-seat Pro Player Stadium in Miami, the Giants by 22 percent to $56 at 79,466-seat Giants Stadium in New Jersey, and the Colts by 18 percent to $54 at 56,127-seat RCA Dome in Indianapolis. In short, due to excess demand and higher team payrolls these franchises improved their cash inflows and operating revenues to compete for a division title and conference championship and to play in a Super Bowl.[12]

To implement a different strategy, because of the teams' poor performances and declines in home-field attendance the Arizona Cardinals lowered prices by 5 percent to $38 at the 73,273-seat Sun Devil Stadium in Phoenix, and the Falcons cut prices 3 percent to $39 at the 71,228-seat Georgia Dome in Atlanta. Furthermore, based on the expected attendance and revenue per seat at their stadiums, nine NFL clubs did not change ticket costs in the 2001 season. Besides the Redskins at $81.89, the other seven teams that ranked from the highest to the lowest in prices included the San Diego Chargers at $58.55, Cincinnati Bengals at $56.21, Oakland Raiders at $51.74, San Francisco 49ers at $50, New England Patriots at $47.77, Buffalo Bills at $46.06 and Chicago Bears at $42.70.

Despite the steady escalation of ticket prices, the NFL's total regular season attendance rose approximately 8 percent, or from 13.9 million spectators in 1990 to 15 million in 1995. Five years later, the league's total attendance reached 16.4 million, which represented a 9 percent increase from 1995. If measured by games, between 1990 and 1995 the teams' per game attendance remained constant at 62,000, then gradually increased by 7 percent to 66,000 in 2000. Apparently, from the 1996 through 2000 seasons the league had benefited from expansion when the Carolina Panthers joined the Western Division of the NFC and the Jacksonville Jaguars entered the Central Division of the AFC. In the 1996 season, the Panthers won the Western Division title but were outplayed by the Central Division's Green Bay Packers for the NFC Championship. The Jaguars, meanwhile, qualified as a wild-card team but lost to the Eastern Division's New England Patriots in the AFC Championship game.

Since 1998, the NHL's average ticket prices for regular season games have also increased. Per seat, those costs rose by 6.8 percent to $45.70 in the 1999 season, by 4.4 percent to $47.69 in the 2000 season, and by 4.6 percent to $49.86 in the 2001 season (Table 6.1). That year, 60 percent (18) of the league teams increased ticket prices, 13 percent (4) lowered per game prices and 27 percent (8) kept their prices constant. With 2,036 club-level seats in its new arena, in the 2001 season the Dallas Stars imposed a 3.5 percent increase in per game tickets, which raised the team's average ticket price to $76 per spectator. The Stars aside, the NHL franchises that initiated the biggest percentage changes in prices at their home-town arenas were 17 percent to $53 at 18,500-seat Kiel Center by the St. Louis Blues, 16 percent to $45 at 19,700-seat MCI Center by the Washington Capitals, and 11 percent to $45 at 28,000-seat Ice Palace by the Tampa Bay Lightning. In the 2001 season, the four NHL clubs that dropped their per game ticket costs were the Hurricanes by 6 percent to $39 at 19,000-seat Entertainment and Sports Arena in Raleigh, the Thrashers by 3 percent to $50 at 18,750-seat Philips Arena in Atlanta, the Oilers by 1 percent to $35 at 16,437-seat Edmonton Coliseum in Canada, and the Flames by 1 percent to $33 at 20,000-seat Canadian Airlines Saddledome in Calgary. In short, each NHL franchise owner decided whether to adjust ticket prices from the 1998 through 2000 seasons based on expected attendance and performance, as well as the club's payroll.

The NHL's average attendance for the twenty-one teams that played 840 regular season games equaled 14,700 in 1990. That year, the highest priced tickets belonged to the Los Angles Kings that charged spectators between $10 and $200 per game. In comparison, the price range for the Calgary Flames was between $8 and $28 in 1990, which then were the lowest prices in the NHL. Five years later, twenty-six hockey teams participated in 1,066 games, and league attendance expanded by 8.8 percent to 16,000 spectators per contest. When league tickets averaged $34.79 per seat in 1995, the Boston Bruins charged its fans $45 and the Edmonton Oilers its spectators $20.68, which were the most and least expensive seat costs per team. In 1999, NHL attendance per game equaled 16,376, which was a 2.4 percent increase from 1995.

In sum, during the 1990s the NHL's total regular season attendance had fluctuated. It rose modestly from 1990 to 1995, despite moderately higher ticket prices, and grew slowly after 1995 when ticket prices increased by 32 percent from the 1995 to 1999 seasons inclusive. Then, the league's pricing strategy changed. To offset a potential decline in attendance and to keep fans from switching their loyalties and expenditures to other professional sports leagues, from 1999 through 2001 the average annual NHL ticket price rose less than 5 percent. If the entertainment value and popularity of professional ice hockey games continue to improve in the U.S. vis-à-vis the other sports, then the fan enthusiasm, attendance and gate revenues at NHL games will rise after 2002. As discussed next in this chapter, besides average ticket prices per season the total expenditures paid by families to attend games are an important economic factor that partially determines whether selected teams will succeed in the professional sports industry.

FAN COST INDEX: LEAGUES AND TEAMS

For teams in the U.S. professional sports leagues, ticket prices are approximately 50 to 70 percent of the total cost for a family to attend a regular season game. Other expenditures that a family might incur before, during and after a game include parking fees and payments for beverages, food, clothing, miscellaneous merchandise, and team programs at the arena or stadium. Since 1989, a Chicago-based company named Team Marketing Reports (TMR) has published a Fan Cost Index (FCI) that estimates the total cost for a four-person family to attend a game in MLB, and in the NBA, NFL and NHL. Annually, TMR surveys each league franchise and its respective arena or stadium concessionaires to determine a weighted average price of adult and children tickets, as well as the representative costs of beer, hot dogs, soft drinks, team caps, game programs and parking. To avoid cost distortions, the survey excludes luxury suite sales and the price levels that apply to less than 200 seats in the facility. Furthermore, the prices charged by the Canadian-based teams are converted to U.S. dollars at the market exchange rate by TMR to determine the FCIs for the respective franchises in MLB, NBA, NFL and NHL.

Despite these money adjustments, some critics claim that TMR's yearly survey and its estimated FCI are flawed measurements of affordability and of the amounts of money a family typically spends at sports events. Essentially, there are four reasons why the FCI is a vulnerable statistic. First, in its annual survey TMR does not consider the special family discount programs that exist to purchase game tickets and team merchandise, and it ignores other price options offered to groups by the clubs. Four deals that the FCI exclude, for example, are the Value Package and Bank One Family Day in Milwaukee, and the Family and Youth Nights in Denver. Second, some families will not necessarily buy the quantity of beverages and hot dogs, or obtain the number of caps and programs, or pay the parking fees as stipulated in the FCI. Third, a percentage of the dollar costs provided for the survey by the clubs and the venue's concessionaires are estimates, which may be inaccurate and/or outdated prices. Fourth, the FCI is not adjusted for differences in the arrangement and comfort of the arena or stadium seats, for the taste of the beverages and food, for the quality of the caps and programs, and for the parking conveniences. These factors will vary at each facility and between each team. Nevertheless, despite these imperfections in TMR's survey, the publication of the FCI attracts a reasonable amount of media coverage and is a yardstick of sorts to measure the total cost for a family to attend each team's games within the various sports league markets. As such, to examine each league's FCI during four recent seasons, Table 6.2 was constructed. It presents the FCIs from the 1998 through 2001 seasons in MLB, and from the 1998–1999 through 2001–2002 seasons in the NBA, NFL and NHL.[13]

Table 6.2
Fan Cost Index, by League, 1998 to 2001

League	1998	1999	2000	2001
MLB	$113.68	$121.36	$131.88	$144.98
NBA	$240.26	$268.56	$281.72	$277.19
NFL	$244.98	$258.50	$279.82	$303.33
NHL	$238.97	$254.48	$264.86	$274.66

Note: The Fan Cost Index includes the estimated costs of four average priced tickets, soft drinks and hot dogs, and two beers, game programs and adult-sized caps, and parking. The seasons are listed as indicated in Table 6.1.

Source: See Table 6.1.

In the 2001 season, a typical four-person family spent an additional $58.35 to attend an NFL game than it paid in the 1998 season (Table 6.2). Ranked after the NFL in dollar expenditures for those seasons, the incremental family costs per game increased by $36.93 in the NBA, $35.69 in the NHL and $31.30 in MLB. In percentage growths, from 1998 through 2001 the largest increase in family expenses at games occurred in MLB at 27.5 percent, and then in the NFL at 23.8 percent, the NBA at 15.4 percent and the NHL at 14.9 percent. Because of higher operating costs, the majority of teams that played in new or recently renovated arenas or stadiums experienced the largest percentage increases in FCIs during the four-season period. In MLB, for example, the FCI increased by 53 percent or $57 per family when the Detroit Tigers began to compete in 40,000-seat Comerica Park in 2000. That year, the other large percentage boosts in FCIs were 46 percent or $51 a family for the San Francisco Giants at 40,800-seat Pacific Bell Park, 40 percent or $55 a family for the Seattle Mariners at 47,000-seat Safeco Field, and 35 percent or $41 a family for the Houston Astros at 42,000-seat Enron Field.

In the 2001 season, MLB's FCI increased by 10 percent or from $131.88 to approximately $145 per household. It ranged from a maximum of $214 for a family to watch the Red Sox compete at 33,847-seat Fenway Park in Boston to a minimum of $80 a family to see the Expos play at 46,500-seat Olympic Stadium in Montreal. In MLB, the FCI also rose by 47 percent for the Pirates who moved into 38,365-seat PNC Park in Pittsburgh and by 29 percent for the Brewers who played its season at 43,000-seat Miller Park in Milwaukee. When the FCIs of teams declined because of lower ticket prices and/or other stadium costs, families spent less money. In 2001, this occurred at the Montreal Expos' games in Olympic Stadium, Seattle Mariners' games at Safeco Field and Houston Astros' games at Enron Field. The MLB clubs aside, what FCI changes were realized for teams in the NBA?

Due to significantly higher team ticket prices in the 2000 season, the FCI increased by 32 percent for the Trail Blazers at the Rose Garden in Portland, 24 percent for the Suns at the America West Arena in Phoenix and 23 percent for the Kings at the ARCO Arena in Sacramento. Although their venues were not upgraded in 2000, each team's payroll costs had dramatically risen when the respective franchise owners signed high-priced free agents and rewarded their veteran players with new contracts. In turn, the owners shifted all or some of the higher payroll costs to spectators who attended hometown games. Conversely, in the 2000 season 31 percent (9) of the NBA clubs experienced a decrease in their FCI. This happened primarily because of lower prices for tickets, clothing, food or merchandise at the teams' arenas. To illustrate, the three largest FCI percentage declines occurred for the Dallas Mavericks at 9.1 percent, Golden State Warriors at 8.8 percent and Seattle SuperSonics at 7.7 percent.

Due partly to lower ticket prices in the 2001 season, the NBA's FCI declined by 1.6 percent or from $281.72 to $277.19 per family. Relative to specific teams, the FCIs fell for 62 percent (18) of the clubs, which included the Portland Trail Blazers by 31 percent, Seattle SuperSonics by 18 percent and the Detroit Pistons by 14 percent. Conversely, because of a new arena in Dallas, higher prices raised the index for the Mavericks by 45 percent. For other franchises in 2001, the New York Knicks had the highest cost per family at $460.70, and the Charlotte Hornets reported the lowest at $198.20. Because the franchise relocated from Vancouver in 2001, an FCI was not reported for the Memphis Grizzlies, and one team, the Denver Nuggets, kept its FCI constant at $235.44 from the 2000 to 2001 season. Consequently, although the league's FCI declined by less than 2 percent, the NBA experienced the first league-wide decrease in family costs since the FCI was initially published in 1989 by TMR.

The NFL's FCI increased by 8.4 percent or from $279.82 in 2000 to $303.33 in 2001. That year, for a family it ranged from $442 a game to watch the Redskins compete in Landover, Maryland, to $228 at a Falcons game in Atlanta. By team, the largest positive changes in the index at 65 percent and 47 percent were because of higher ticket and stadium prices at, respectively, 76,125-seat Invesco Field at Mile High in Denver for the Broncos games and at 65,000-seat Heinz Field in Pittsburgh for the Steelers contests. In contrast, due to lower game costs per family in 2001 the FCI fell for four NFL teams. It dropped by 3.4 percent for the Cardinals at 73,273-seat Sun Devil Stadium in Phoenix, by 3 percent for the Falcons at 71,228-seat Georgia Dome in Atlanta, by 2.2 percent for the Chargers at 71,000-seat Qualcomm Stadium in San Diego, and by 1 percent for the Seahawks at 72,500-seat Husky Stadium in Seattle, where beer is not sold at home games. What costs changed for families at the home arenas in professional ice hockey?

In the NHL, the percentage growth rates of family expenditures at professional hockey games declined from 6.5 percent in 1998–1999 to 4.1 percent in 1999–2000, and then to 3.7 percent in 2000–2001. That year, the league's average cost per family rose approximately $10 to $274.66 per game. If the thirty NHL franchises in the 2001 season are included, the FCIs ranged from $386 to watch a Stars game in Dallas at the American Airlines Center to $188 for a family to see the Flames compete in Calgary at the Canadian Airlines Saddledome.

When the 2001 season began, four NHL clubs had experienced double-digit increases in their index. The four percentage changes, teams and arenas were, respectively, 32 percent to the Stars games, 15 percent to the Blues games at 18,500-seat Kiel Center in St. Louis, 14 percent to the Penguins games at 17,181-seat Civic Arena in Pittsburgh, and 11 percent to the Capitals games at 18,130-seat MCI Center in Washington, D.C. Evidently, these teams raised ticket prices and other costs for spectators to offset higher player expenses and/or to pay for arena improvements.

In sum, the FCIs for 23 percent (7) of the NHL clubs declined in the 2001 season because of either uninspired team performances, apathetic fan support, and/or minimal changes in average ticket prices and arena costs. Thus, affordability improved for a family to view games of the Flyers in Philadelphia at 17,380-seat First Union Center and of the Red Wings in Detroit at the 19,275-seat Joe Louis Arena. Also, family cost reductions occurred to support the Black Hawks in Chicago at 20,500-seat United Center, the Blue Jackets in Columbus at 18,500-seat Nationwide Arena, the Mighty Ducks in Anaheim at 16,223-seat Arrowhead Pond, the Predators in Nashville at 17,500-seat Gaylord Entertainment Center, and the Oilers in Edmonton at 16,437-seat Edmonton Coliseum.

This concludes the analysis of how family costs have changed in each league from the 1998 to 2001 seasons inclusive. The next topic of this chapter examines to what extent fans are emotionally and psychologically attached to professional sports, leagues and teams.

SPORTS LOYALTY INDEX

In addition to the impact of higher average ticket prices and total family costs to attend regular season games, there are other market forces and human impulses and idiosyncrasies that influence how fans relate to and why they support specific professional sports, leagues and franchises. Each year Brand Keys Inc.'s founder and president, Dr. Robert K. Passikoff, conducts a nationwide survey of sports fans to determine their emotional relationship with teams in the major leagues. Based on a series of questions to sports fans, the Brand Keys' marketing survey achieves three major purposes. That is, it identifies and quantifies the specific owner, player and team characteristics that attract spectators to the hometown arena or stadium; that create radio and television sports addicts; and that sell the products and services of companies whose banner appears on the clubs' scoreboard. Passikoff's annual scientific survey results in the publication of a Sports Loyalty Index (SLI), which is a computer output that ranks teams based on four factors—drivers—that collectively measure the intensity of support by sports fans. In the model, some of the factors are directly linked to a team's win-loss record on the field, court or ice, while other factors are not closely related to a club's performance. The model's four variables are defined as follows.[14]

Discussed in descending order, the first and most important factor is *pure entertainment value*. This driver includes a team's qualities such as excitement, persistence, and dramatic performance to achieve victories and a winning season. The second factor in the model is *authenticity*. It measures to what degree fans perceive players to be passionate about and proud of the game, sport and the host city team. The factor ranked third is *fan bonding*. This driver reflects the players' personalities and skills that are foremost admired and recognized by spectators. In Passikoff's model, the fourth and least important factor is the franchise's *history* and *tradition* within its respective league. In total, these four factors are each incorporated in a questionnaire, which is completed by sports fans. The results are statistically measured and weighted to create an Index number for each professional sports franchise. According to analysts at Brand Keys Inc., to increase fan loyalty and improve financial performance franchise owners must accomplish three tasks. That is, the owners should focus on the application of brand management techniques to differentiate the sport, implement strategic advertising and promotional activities that express one or more of the drivers, and apply metrics to assess whether the values of potential team sponsors contribute to or undermine spectator loyalty. If an owner successfully implements these tasks, the team will be well respected by its fan base and score high on the SLI.[15]

For the five sport leagues—AL, NL, NBA, NFL and NHL—Tables 6.3 to 6.6 were prepared. The tables depict the ranks of the top five or more professional teams—in descending order—and the bottom five or more teams—in ascending order—that received SLI scores for the years 1999, 2000 and 2001. Occasionally, two or more teams tied in rank during a year. Accordingly, each club and its rank are listed separately in the tables for that year. For example, in 2001 the Atlanta Braves, Colorado Rockies and Boston Red Sox tied for fourth place and the Minnesota Twins, Montreal Expos and San Diego Padres tied for and ranked sixteenth in MLB (Table 6.3).

In total and by league, the rankings indicate which sports franchises had earned the most and least loyalty from their fans based on survey questions that quantified each team's pure entertainment value, authenticity and fan bonding, and its history and tradition. Furthermore, the rankings denote the relative differences in fan support for two or more clubs that were located in the same metropolitan area. For a list of teams, index values and ranks per year and by leagues, see the Brand Keys Inc.'s Web site, which is the *Source* entered below the tables.

In MLB, from 1999 through 2001 the most ardent baseball fans enthusiastically supported the New York Yankees and Cleveland Indians in the AL and the Houston Astros and Atlanta Braves in the NL (Table 6.3). Except for the Astros, during various seasons the other three clubs attained a reputable history and tradition to compete for and win division titles and league championships. Furthermore, each season the Braves, Indians and Yankees, and since 1999, the Astros seem to provide pure entertainment value for spectators because they employ managers and players who are admired and recognized by baseball fans, respectively, in Atlanta, Cleveland, New York and Houston, and throughout the nation.

Table 6.3
MLB Loyalty Index Ranks, by Team, 1999 to 2001

Team	1999	Year 2000	2001
Top Five Ranks			
New York Yankees (AL)	1	2	1
Cleveland Indians (AL)	1	1	2
Houston Astros (NL)	2	3	3
Atlanta Braves (NL)	3	4	4
St. Louis Cardinals (NL)	4	-	-
Colorado Rockies (NL)	-	5	4
Boston Red Sox (AL)	-	-	4
Seattle Mariners (AL)	-	-	5
Bottom Five Ranks			
Florida Marlins (NL)	30	30	20
Anaheim Angels (AL)	29	29	19
Minnesota Twins (AL)	28	27	16
Montreal Expos (NL)	27	-	16
Los Angeles Dodgers (NL)	26	-	-
Tampa Bay Devil Rays (AL)	-	28	18
San Diego Padres (NL)	-	26	16
Baltimore Orioles (AL)	-	26	17
Chicago Cubs (NL)	-	26	-

Note: Teams that tied in rank are assigned the same numeric. For example, in 2000 the San Diego Padres, Baltimore Orioles and Chicago Cubs tied for twenty-sixth place in fan loyalty. A hyphen (-) appears if the team was not ranked in the top or bottom five that year. The AL is the American League and NL the National League.

Source: See the "Sports Loyalty Index," at http://www.brandkeys.com cited 24 October 2001.

When the expansion NFL Houston Texans, led by Head Coach Dom Capers begins its first season at 69,500-seat Reliant Stadium in August 2002, a portion of the Astros' fans will likely shift their loyalty to the Texans. After failing to win NL pennants in 1997, 1998, 1999 and 2001, eventually the Astros will fall in rank from third place in the SLI and be surpassed by the Braves, and perhaps by the Cardinals, Mariners, Red Sox or Rockies.

Given the franchise's long-standing history and tradition in the Boston area, it is a surprise that the Red Sox was not ranked among the top three baseball teams in fan loyalty. From 1999 through 2001, *The Sporting News* rated Boston as a superior sports city relative to Cleveland, Houston and Seattle but inferior compared with Atlanta, Denver, New York and St. Louis. Historically, some fans and local newspapers in Boston have been critical of the Red Sox's owners, and particularly the coaches and players for not defeating the Yankees and other teams to earn Eastern Division and AL titles and to win a World Series. It is reasonable to assume that the popularity and support from Massachusetts' fans for the NHL Boston Bruins, NBA Boston Celtics and the NFL New England Patriots, who are based in nearby Foxboro, have hindered the Red Sox and prevented the club from ranking above fourth in the SLI. Moreover, in a recent survey of professional athletes the Red Sox had the toughest fans, the Yankees had the most knowledgeable, loudest and scariest fans, and the best groupies followed the Astros. Furthermore, the athletes that were polled voted the St. Louis Cardinals' fans as the most loyal in MLB.[16]

According to Table 6.3, during one or more years a large proportion of the hometown baseball spectators are not emotionally attached to or excited about the Florida Marlins, Anaheim [formerly California] Angels, Minnesota Twins and the other six clubs listed in the bottom five of the leagues. Except for the Los Angeles Dodgers in 2000 and 2001, for the majority of regular seasons the other eight teams were not competitive within their respective divisions. Because of inconsistent and lackadaisical performances, apparently fans did not perceive that these teams' coaches, general managers, owners and players were proud of their sport or committed to win in their host cities. Fans especially regarded some players as aloof and vain, and as underachieving athletes who fail to emotionally bond with spectators at their home games. Nonetheless, throughout the 1990s the Orioles' Cal Ripken, Padres' Tony Gwynn and Cubs' Sammy Sosa were excellent players and well-respected role models for their clubs. If MLB downsized and eliminated the most deficient franchises after the 2002 season, the Anaheim Angels, Florida Marlins, Minnesota Twins, Montreal Expos and San Diego Padres would likely be the most eligible organizations to be folded, or alternatively, merged with another franchise and relocated to another site. Otherwise, the Baltimore Orioles, Chicago Cubs and Los Angeles Dodgers are unlikely teams to be terminated in MLB. Similarly, in the short run the Tampa Bay Devil Rays is a recent expansion franchise that will be permitted to exist despite the club's poor attendance and inept record as a member of the AL's Western Division.

Measured as sports metropolitan areas, in 2001 *The Sporting News* rated Los Angeles-Anaheim second, Miami-Ft. Lauderdale eighth, Minneapolis-St. Paul fourteenth and San Diego thirty-fifth. Although each ranked in the top forty as quality sports places, perhaps these areas and Montreal have a surplus of professional teams. Consequently, in each area the hometown sports fans preferred to support the inferior or superior clubs in the NBA, NFL and NHL, or to attend local college games. In the aforementioned survey of professional athletes, Montreal fans were voted as the dumbest in MLB. The players that participated in the survey, however, did not overwhelmingly support or critically denigrate the other bottom-ranked baseball clubs, which are listed in Table 6.3. In the next section, a table is presented that displays the distribution of fan loyalties for the top and bottom franchises in the NBA for 1999, 2000 and 2001.

In professional basketball, from 1999 to 2001 inclusive the highest ranked clubs that were most appreciated by their fans included the Indiana Pacers, Los Angeles Lakers and Phoenix Suns (Table 6.4). In 2000, the San Antonio Spurs placed fifth in the SLI. One year later, the Milwaukee Bucks replaced the Spurs, who moved to second place and one rank ahead of the Philadelphia 76ers and one place below the Los Angeles Lakers. In contrast, the other clubs that were

Table 6.4
NBA Loyalty Index Ranks, by Team, 1999 to 2001

Team	1999	Year 2000	2001
Top Five Ranks			
Chicago Bulls (EC)	1	4	-
Phoenix Suns (WC)	2	2	4
Los Angeles Lakers (WC)	3	1	1
Indiana Pacers (EC)	4	3	4
New Jersey Nets (EC)	5	-	-
San Antonio Spurs (WC)	-	5	2
Philadelphia 76ers (EC)	-	-	3
Milwaukee Bucks (EC)	-	-	5
Bottom Five Ranks			
Washington Wizards (EC)	29	29	23
Los Angeles Clippers (WC)	28	28	-
Dallas Mavericks (WC)	27	27	-
Orlando Magic (EC)	26	-	-
Toronto Raptors (EC)	25	-	-
Golden State Warriors (WC)	-	26	22
Denver Nuggets (WC)	-	25	21
Atlanta Hawks (EC)	-	-	20
Vancouver Grizzlies (WC)	-	-	19

Notes: See Table 6.3. In 2001, the Indiana Pacers and Phoenix Suns tied for fourth in rank and the Chicago Bulls dropped below fifth place and were not listed as indicated by a hyphen (-). The EC is the Eastern Conference and WC is the Western Conference.

Source: See Table 6.3.

in the top five ranks but noticeably down in fan appreciation from 1999 to 2001 were the Chicago Bulls and New Jersey Nets. Intuitively, the six top-rated teams in 2001 had dynamic and motivated players such as Jalen Rose and Reggie Miller for the Pacers, Kobe Bryant and Shaquille O'Neill for the Lakers, Jason Kidd and Penny Hardaway for the Suns, Glen Robinson and Ray Allen for the Bucks, Allen Iverson and Tyrone Hill for the 76ers, and David Robinson and Tim Duncan for the Spurs. When these players hustled on defense and scored points on offense, their respective team's performances dramatically improved. In turn, this aroused fan loyalty among the franchises. As a result, attendance rose when these six teams competed to win division and conference titles, and the league Playoffs. Between 1999 and 2001, the Pacers, Lakers, 76ers and Spurs played in games for the NBA Championship. If Coach George Karl continues to develop the Bucks, before 2004 the club should win an Eastern Conference title and compete for the league championship. Because of player retirements and trades, and flawed coaching strategies, fans in Chicago and New Jersey were not equally enthused about the current play and future prospects of the Bulls and Nets. Therefore, in recent seasons these clubs have not been consistent contenders in their respective divisions.

Since the clubs ranked low in the SLI for two or more seasons, NBA fans were especially depressed about the entertainment value and authenticity of the Dallas Mavericks, Denver Nuggets, Golden State Warriors, Los Angeles Clippers and Washington Wizards. These clubs had few admirable or recognizable players, and their regular season performances placed them at or near the bottom of their respective division and conference. Hometown fans sensed that the players on the Mavericks, Nuggets, Warriors, Clippers and Wizards were not passionate about competing for titles and that the athletes displayed little pride or emotion to win games. Thus, each club's spectators had a minimal attachment to and sentiment for these franchises. The Atlanta Hawks and Vancouver [now Memphis] Grizzlies joined the five bottom-ranked NBA teams in 2001. Unless each club's entertainment value and authenticity improves in the Atlanta and Memphis areas, respectively, the attendance and fan interest for the Hawks and Grizzlies will decline even further. If this occurs, eventually the hometown fans will become disillusioned and completely abandon their relationship with the two franchises.

Beyond the 2001 season, at least three of the NBA teams listed in the bottom five ranks of Table 6.4 have the potential to attract enthusiastic and loyal fans within their market areas. For example, the Mavericks' Mark Cuban is a wealthy and dedicated owner, and the club's star players, who are Steve Nash, Michael Finley and Dirk Nowitzki, have signed long-term contracts. Furthermore, All-Star Tracy McGrady is a skilled player who scores 20 points a game or more for the Magic, as does Vince Carter for the Raptors. Both players are committed to their teams and communities, and fans appreciate their passion for the game and sport. Therefore, the Mavericks, Magic and Raptors will likely improve their SLIs soon and not be ranked among the bottom five teams in the league.

Meanwhile, in 2001 the Grizzlies relocated from Vancouver, Canada, to Memphis, Tennessee, where fans are excited and eager to attend games and support the city's first professional basketball franchise since 1975 when the American Basketball Association's Memphis Sounds folded its operations. Likewise, besides the average sports fan, the return of Michael Jordan in the 2001 season excited politicians and other dignitaries in the Washington, D.C., area about the Wizards, who placed last in the SLIs during 1999, 2000 and 2001 for NBA teams.

According to an article published in *The Sporting News*, since 1997 Atlanta, Los Angeles, Oakland and Washington, D.C., each has improved its image and status as a sports city. This growth in prestige is expected to increase the entertainment value of and fan support for the Hawks, Clippers, Warriors and Wizards in their home arenas. Except for Orlando and Vancouver, in 2001 the bottom five franchises placed no lower than twentieth as sports cities in *The Sporting News* article. In regard to two NBA clubs not listed in Table 6.4, a survey of professional athletes revealed that the New York Knicks fans were the toughest, scariest and most knowledgeable, and the Sacramento Kings fans tended to be the loudest. The MLB and NBA teams aside, which professional football clubs ranked in the top and bottom five of the SLIs?[17]

Table 6.5
NFL Loyalty Index Ranks, by Team, 1999 to 2001

Team	1999	Year 2000	2001
Top Five Ranks			
Jacksonville Jaguars (AFC)	1	1	1
Green Bay Packers (NFC)	2	3	3
Atlanta Falcons (NFC)	3	-	-
New York Jets (AFC)	3	2	5
New York Giants (NFC)	4	-	3
San Francisco 49ers (NFC)	4	-	4
Minnesota Vikings (NFC)	-	4	2
Indianapolis Colts (AFC)	-	5	3
Buffalo Bills (AFC)	-	5	-
Bottom Five Ranks			
Carolina Panthers (NFC)	31	31	22
Oakland Raiders (AFC)	30	29	21
Cincinnati Bengals (AFC)	30	30	23
Philadelphia Eagles (NFC)	28	28	19
Miami Dolphins (AFC)	27	-	-
New Orleans Saints (NFC)	-	27	-
Chicago Bears (NFC)	-	-	20
Pittsburgh Steelers (AFC)	-	-	19

Notes: In 2001, the Philadelphia Eagles and Pittsburgh Steelers tied in rank at nineteenth, and the New Orleans Saints placed above the bottom five in 1999 and 2001 as indicated by a hyphen (-). The AFC is the American Football Conference, and NFC the National Football Conference.
Source: See Table 6.3.

In the NFL, from 1999 to 2001 inclusive nine teams appeared within the top five of the SLIs (Table 6.5). Generally, diehard fans in Jacksonville and in the other high-ranked cities have made a long-term commitment to their hometown football team and its coaches, general managers, owners and players. These fans are dedicated and involved with their teams. That is, they make financial commitments and invest in team-related activities and assets such as the purchase of a personal seat license and a season ticket, lease of a club seat, or the rental of a deluxe luxury suite at the stadium to entertain clients for business purposes or to party with family and friends for social reasons. Their hometown team, in turn, plays hard and smart in each game to satisfy the fan base that had remained committed even during mediocre and below-average seasons.

Because they appeal to their high identification spectators, the top-ranked teams in Table 6.5 were the most revered by fans of the sport. As the only professional sports franchise in northern Florida, the regular season ticket holders that attended the Jacksonville Jaguars' home games were the most passionate fans in the league since the club ranked first in the SLIs from 1999 through 2001. After it won four games in 1995, the team earned wild cards in 1996 and 1997 and competed in AFC playoff games in 1998 and 1999. Even though the win-loss percentages of the Jaguars have deteriorated since 1999, the Jacksonville area fans bond with the Jaguar players and appreciate and revel in the entertainment value that the club provides to the inhabitants of northeast Florida.

According to Table 6.5, the Indianapolis Colts, Minnesota Vikings and New York Giants are also beloved by their hometown fans, and each improved its SLI ranks from 1999 to 2001. Since 1999, each of these clubs has qualified for a wild-card spot or the conference playoffs. Quarterbacks Peyton Manning of the Colts, Jeff George then Daunte Culpepper of the Vikings, and Kerry Collins of the Giants are exceptional offensive players who organize the play patterns to pass and run for touchdowns, which generates excitement for their fans. In recent seasons, these players had the leadership qualities and skills to potentially propel their teams to a Super Bowl championship.

Alternatively, after 2000 the fan loyalty ranks marginally decreased below fifth for the Buffalo Bills and from second to fifth for the New York Jets. Both clubs experienced player injuries, the loss of free agents and coaching breakdowns. From their fans' perspective, the entertainment value of the Bills and Jets diminished, and the teams' coaches and players failed to establish and project a winning attitude. To place in the NFL's top four in fan loyalty, the Bills and Jets must recommit to be division and conference champions and appeal to their spectators for support at home games. Otherwise, the clubs' fans will switch their allegiance to professional teams in the other sports leagues such as the Sabres in Buffalo and the Islanders, Knicks, Mets, Rangers or Yankees in New York.

Based on Table 6.5, from 1999 through 2001 eight NFL teams appeared at least once in the bottom five ranks of the league. A large portion of local fans attended the games of these four each AFC and NFC clubs for social interaction with friends and other people, not for the pure entertainment value of the sport or team. Such spectators were soothed by the atmosphere of the games, by the events and promotions that occurred before, during and after the competition, and by the feelings of camaraderie that the games created. For example, rather than focus on the hometown teams' effort and struggle to win, the metropolitan area fans who attended games in New Orleans and the other cities preferred to participate in tailgate parties, to watch the cheering squad and scoreboard displays during time-outs and between plays, and to view pre-game and half-time activities.

During 1999, 2000 and 2001, low fan identification was especially evident for the Carolina Panthers, Cincinnati Bengals, Oakland Raiders and Philadelphia Eagles, and to a lesser extent, for the Chicago Bears, Miami Dolphins, New Orleans Saints and Pittsburgh Steelers. Some of these teams had less than three All-Pro players per season on their rosters. And, the teams' star players earned a below-average salary with respect to the best athletes who played on other NFL clubs. Other inferior teams in this category had controversial coaches and owners, miscreant players who were involved in criminal acts or who bitterly complained to the press when they were benched, and fans that refused to travel long distances to attend a home game. Casual fans that attended regular season games played by the Bears, Bengals, Eagles and Panthers were not overwhelmed with the drama and excitement of a team victory. Finally, in Chicago, New Orleans, Miami and Oakland there are affordable, fun-filled nonsports entertainment activities on Sundays that perhaps attracted potential football spectators.

To increase fan involvement within their broadcast markets, each of the bottom eight franchises listed in Table 6.5 need to highlight and reinforce the entertainment benefits of their teams, particularly at home games and also during the off-season. Furthermore, the respective coaches and players need to adopt a passion for winning games while the owners apply effective marketing principles to promote and tout their team's commitment to be a league champion. Lastly, the coaches, owners and players should establish strong community affiliations and regularly interact with local media officials such as the city newspaper editors and reporters, and with the hosts of sports programs who broadcast from the areas' radio and television stations.

Ranked as sports cities by *The Sporting News*, in 2001 Oakland placed second, Philadelphia fourth, Miami eighth, Chicago thirteenth, Pittsburgh fifteenth, Charlotte twenty-third, Cincinnati twenty-fourth and New Orleans twenty-eighth. Apparently, in some of these cities the NFL fans were more attached to and involved with various amateur and collegiate football programs, and with professional baseball, basketball and hockey events and teams in the areas. Or, because of the Athletics in Oakland and Giants in San Francisco, the Flyers and Phillies in Philadelphia, the Heat and Panthers in Miami, the Bulls and White Sox in Chicago, and the Penguins and Pirates in Pittsburgh, many mainstream football fans were not associated with their respective NFL teams. In Charlotte, it is rumored that there are thousands of "fair weather" sports fans that relocated to North Carolina for employment or retirement purposes, and therefore are not strongly attached to or identify with the NFL Panthers or (former) NBA Hornets. Similarly, Cincinnati and New Orleans are small markets, and historically, the Bengals and Saints have been inferior football clubs who struggle to win one-half of their regular season games. These reasons, in part, explain the low ranks and weak fan loyalties of the eight NFL franchises listed at the bottom of Table 6.5.[18]

In the NHL, from 1999 through 2001 seven teams appeared at least once in the top five of the SLIs, which measured how loyal fans were to the host city ice hockey franchises (Table 6.6). During their years as top five teams, the index rankings especially improved for the Dallas Stars, New Jersey Devils, Philadelphia Flyers and Toronto Maple Leafs, stabilized for the Detroit Red Wings and worsened for the Boston Bruins and Buffalo Sabres. The Stars won a Stanley Cup in 1999 and so did the Devils in 2000. During one or more seasons, the best teams in Table 6.6 each had excellent players such as Sergei Samsonov for the Bruins, Jere Lehtinen for the Stars, Scott Stevens for the Devils, Mark Recchi for the Flyers, Curtis Joseph for the Maple Leafs and Nicklas Lidstrom for the Red Wings. In the 1999 season, the Stars, Devils, Flyers, Maple Leafs and Red Wings placed first or second in their respective divisions. Because of the success

Table 6.6
NHL Loyalty Index Ranks, by Team, 1999 to 2001

Team	1999	Year 2000	2001
Top Five Ranks			
Boston Bruins (EC)	1	3	4
Detroit Red Wings (WC)	2	1	2
New Jersey Devils (EC)	3	2	1
Buffalo Sabres (EC)	4	-	-
Dallas Stars (WC)	5	4	3
Toronto Maple Leafs (EC)	-	5	4
Philadelphia Flyers (EC)	-	-	5
Bottom Five Ranks			
Los Angeles Kings (WC)	26	-	-
Anaheim Mighty Ducks (WC)	25	26	25
Chicago Blackhawks (WC)	24	25	24
Florida Panthers (EC)	23	-	-
Vancouver Canucks (WC)	22	22	21
Atlanta Thrashers (EC)	-	24	23
Tampa Bay Lightning (EC)	-	23	22
Nashville Predators (WC)	-	23	22

Notes: In 2000, the Nashville Predators and Tampa Bay Lightning tied in rank at twenty-third and the Buffalo Sabres fell in rank above fifth as indicated by the hyphen (-). The EC is the Eastern Conference, and WC the Western Conference.

Source: See Table 6.3.

at qualifying for the playoffs, and due to the outstanding attitudes and efforts of the coaches and players, each club provided authenticity, entertainment and excitement for its spectators. In turn, the fans became involved with and followed the team's progress during the regular season and playoffs. Thus, many local residents and out-of-town visitors attended the home games and perhaps a few of the away games of the top seven clubs. According to a survey of professional athletes, in 2000 the Philadelphia Flyers had the toughest and scariest fans, while the most knowledgeable and loyal fans identified with the Toronto Maple Leafs. Meanwhile, the marginal decline in spectator loyalty for the Boston Bruins and Buffalo Sabres occurred, in part, when each team slumped and the players failed to adequately bond with fans that attended home games or watched the clubs perform on television.

From 1999 to 2001 inclusive, the least loyal fans in the NHL supported the Anaheim Mighty Ducks, Chicago Blackhawks and Vancouver Canucks. Evidently, diehard fans in Anaheim, Chicago and Vancouver preferred to be identified with MLB, NBA or NFL teams that were located in their respective cities or metropolitan areas. The Mighty Ducks and Canucks have never competed for a Stanley Cup, and the Blackhawks' last appearance in a league's championship game was in 1992. Besides the Mighty Ducks, Blackhawks and Canucks, the Atlanta Thrashers, Nashville Predators and Tampa Bay Lightning were not fan-friendly franchises. However, the Thrashers and Predators are recent expansion clubs that will eventually attract more loyal fans if the players provide dynamic performances, victories and entertainment value for their spectators, especially at home games.

To collect relevant information about fan demographics and psychographics, the Predators use customer relationship management technology. That is, to increase fan loyalty the Predators combine new technology such as the Internet and turnkey client server hardware with modern marketing principles in advertising, pricing, promotion and product development. For example, the data from a computer software program revealed that the Gaylord Entertainment Center fans in Nashville did not enjoy the band that played between scheduled breaks at Predator games. Furthermore, the computer program indicated that ice hockey spectators in Nashville were attracted to golf, which inspired the Predators to offer coupons for a free round of golf to fans at home games. In sum, when their teams are not triumphant the marketers of the Predators and other low-ranked sports franchises such as the Thrashers need to apply radical marketing methods to boost fan support, increase attendance and expand the sales of arena apparel, food and merchandise.[19]

As an expansion team since 1992, the Lightning has rarely qualified for the NHL playoffs. In Tampa Bay, the ice hockey club and MLB Devil Rays have received far less fan support and media attention than the NFL Buccaneers have. Besides qualifying for the playoffs to compete for a division title and to market their brands, the Lightning and other inferior NHL teams would benefit from creative advertising and promotional strategies. These activities require marketing investments by the team owners and commitments from the players who must set high standards so they can perform to the expectations of the hometown fans. Otherwise, these and the other NHL clubs will struggle for media and spectator support in their respective Designated Market Areas.

Because of various strategies implemented in the late 1990s, the Florida Panthers and Los Angeles Kings have moderately expanded their fan bases. Each team plays in a top-ten sports city that has experienced robust employment, population and per capita income growth, and that appeals to the interests and needs of well-educated and professional people who have earning power. After raising their teams' payrolls in recent years, the Panthers and Kings have succeeded to qualify for playoff spots. Skilled players such as Pavel Bure and Viktor Kozlov of the Panthers and Bryan Smolenski and Ziggy Palffy of the Kings were fun to watch as sports fans in southern Florida and California gradually shifted their attention to ice hockey and flocked to the Panthers' games at the National Car Rental Center in Sunrise, Florida, and to the Kings' home games at the Staple Center in Los Angles. In sum, Table 6.6 reveals the seven best and eight worst professional ice hockey franchises that sport fans were either fervently devoted to or avoided from 1999 through 2001.

In the top five U.S. sports metropolitan areas, from 1999 to 2001 inclusive the fans' loyalty was passionate for the Yankees, Giants, Jets and New Jersey

Devils in the New York area, for the 49ers in the Oakland-San Francisco-San Jose area, for the Lakers in the Los Angeles-Anaheim area, for the 76ers and Flyers in the Philadelphia area, and for the Stars in the Dallas-Fort Worth area. Alternatively, fans were less loyal to the Islanders and Knicks in the New York area, to the Warriors and Raiders in the Oakland-San Francisco-San Jose area, to the Angels, Clippers, Kings and Mighty Ducks in the Los Angeles-Anaheim area, to the Eagles in the Philadelphia area, and to the Mavericks in the Dallas-Fort Worth area. In total, these five metropolitan areas were the home base of at least eight professional baseball, basketball, football and/or hockey franchises that ranked in the top and bottom five of the SLIs from 1999 through 2001.

Placed between the top and bottom five or more teams listed in Tables 6.3 to 6.6, there were the remaining franchises in each sports league. Interestingly, not ranked in the top five teams were the Chicago Cubs and New York Mets in MLB, Boston Celtics and Sacramento Kings in the NBA, Baltimore Ravens and Tennessee Titans in the NFL, and the Colorado Avalanche and Montreal Canadiens in the NHL. Although the Ravens, Titans and Avalanche have a short history and tradition in Baltimore, Nashville and Denver, respectively, each club exhibits strong fan identification and employs recognized players who bond with fans in each of the communities. Apparently, for these three teams one or more of the drivers that comprise the SLI model were measurably deficient. In turn, that failure negatively impacted the three franchises' entertainment value and fan identification in their host cities from 1999 through 2001. Because the Cubs, Mets, Celtics, Kings and Canadiens have not won league championships in recent seasons, their SLIs were inferior to those of franchises that ranked in the top five of the respective leagues.

SUMMARY

This chapter discussed the behaviors, characteristics, preferences, profiles and roles of fans as related to the professional sports leagues and teams. The results of research studies performed by the Gallup Organization, Scarborough Marketing Inc. and Harris Interactive Inc. were summarized. These companies examined how and why fans, as spectators, root for and support selected professional sports, leagues and teams based on economic, demographic and sports-specific factors and other information. Each study identified the various types of fans and their interests in games played by MLB, NBA, NFL and NHL teams. After the research studies were reviewed, the differences in the ticket price strategies of the leagues were presented in dollar amounts for four seasons. The changes in team ticket and stadium prices throughout the 1990s and in 2000 and 2001 indicate when and why selected franchise owners in each league decided to increase their cash inflows and operating revenues in order to invest in coaches, managers and players, and attempted to become more competitive and win division and conference titles and league championships.

After discussing several franchises' ticket price reforms, a table was created that contains the Fan Cost Indexes of the professional sports leagues during four recent seasons. Based on the table, the leagues' indexes were compared with those of numerous teams in each sport. The comparisons primarily focused on the clubs with the highest and lowest indexes. Furthermore, the discussion included the teams that experienced the smallest and largest changes in operating costs from one season or year to the next because of inflated player salaries, the opening of a new arena or stadium and other factors.

In the final section of the chapter, the application of a Sports Loyalty Index established the ranks of the top and bottom five or more teams in each league based on the clubs' entertainment value, authenticity, fan bonding and their history and tradition. The highest and lowest rated teams and their rankings for three years appeared in four tables that were discussed. This information highlighted how fans feel about, and relate to their respective professional sports team in one or more of the leagues.

Essentially, this chapter explained why sports fans are a unique market that each professional team seeks to dominate and exploit. The creation, development and implementation of effective strategies to penetrate and expand that market are an ongoing effort of the franchise owner and his or her executive staff. The research models and surveys, league and team ticket price reforms, and the Fan Cost and Sports Loyalty Indexes are basic and important updated information about the behaviors, beliefs and interests of fans and spectators.

The next chapter will look at the relationship and role of government to the professional sports industry. Why is government attracted to and involved with professional sports? Has the government improved the structure, conduct and performance of the various leagues and franchises? These are two questions that are documented and explored in Chapter 7.

NOTES

1. Besides fan loyalty for professional baseball, basketball, football and ice hockey, the Gallup Organization reported spectator preferences for auto racing, college football and figure skating, and for professional golf, tennis and wrestling. In 2001, college football at 44 percent and professional wrestling at 12 percent had, respectively, the highest and lowest proportion of fans per sport. In response to choosing "Not a Fan," the outcomes varied from 85 percent in professional wrestling to 46 percent in college football. For further results of the survey, see "Gallup Poll Topics A-Z Sports," at http://www.gallup.com cited 15 October 2001.

2. Ibid.

3. In the Gallup poll, the respondents picked the New York Yankees and Atlanta Braves as their favorite MLB teams and Babe Ruth, Mickey Mantle and Hank Aaron as the greatest players of all time. For a summary of the surveys on sports teams and players that was published in *ADWEEK* Southeast, see Mark Dolliver, "Many Really Don't Care If They Ever Come Back," at http://web2.infotrac.galegroup.com cited 15 October 2001.

4. Scarborough Sports Marketing Inc. measures local consumer and national lifestyle characteristics by interviewing adults in seventy-five U.S. markets, which include all professional sports markets. Furthermore, Scarborough has a supplemental database that focuses on Internet users. In one study performed in 2001, the highest

percent of Internet-savvy baseball fans lived in Cleveland, Atlanta and Boston. The U.S. cities with the lowest percentage of baseball fans that use the Internet were Flint, Michigan, Salt Lake City, Utah, and Charleston, West Virginia. For some reason, on its Web site Scarborough did not report the percentage of Internet-savvy fans that follow the NBA, NFL and NHL. See "Sports," at http://www.scarborough.com cited 16 October 2001.

5. Ibid.

6. For the study of how Harris Interactive categorized fans by sports league, see "Grading FanAtics," at http://web2.infotrac.galegroup.com cited 15 October 2001.

7. Ibid.

8. Besides the sources listed in Table 6.1, for ticket price information and specific cost data see Chris Isidore "Prices Going, Going ... Up," at http://www.cnnfn.com cited 11 August 2001; "The Price of the Pastime," at http://www.cnnsi.com cited 29 March 2001; "Baseball Ticket Prices," at http://www.cnnsi.com cited 5 April 2000; "Ticket Price Comparison," at http://www.ixquick.com cited 15 October 2001; "The Cost of Sitting," at http://www.cnnsi.com cited 4 April 2000; Stefan Fatsis, "Baseball Ticket Prices Are Outta Here," *Wall Street Journal* (3 April 1998), W6; Dan Bickley, "Pro Sports May be Pricing Fans Out of Stadiums," at http://www.azcentral.com cited 24 June 2001; "Money Matters," at http://www.cnnsi.com cited 1 April 2001; Kyle Noone, "1, 2, 3 Strikes You're Out," at http://www.myprimetime.com cited 15 October 2001; Mel Antonen, "Baseball Fans Pick Up Tab," *USA Today* (22 January 1998), 3C; Sam Walker, "Shaq, Jack and You," *Wall Street Journal* (18 January 2002), W1, W7. Although the ticket price and cost data occasionally overlap, in part, this group of articles provides a comparison of the recent price behavior of teams in each sports league.

9. "Bud Means Business," at http://www.cnnsi.com cited 22 November 2000; "Play Ball," at http://www.cnnsi.com cited 28 August 2000.

10. See Stan Olson, "Hey Bud, Empty Seats Show a Problem," *Charlotte Observer* (22 October 2001), 7C. Other issues and problems in professional sports were documented by Dan Bickley, "Costas: Allure of Sports Fading," at http://www.azcentral.com cited 25 June 2001; Idem., "Fed-Up Fans Worry Pro Sports Teams," *Charlotte Observer* (27 June 2001), 21A; Idem., "Race Question Colors Sports," at http://www.azcentral.com cited 24 June 2001; Allen Barra and Andrew Albanese, "Who's Watching?" *Wall Street Journal* (2 June 2000), W9; Jonathon Eig, "Why So Few Fans Are Asking for Pencils at Today's Ballparks," *Wall Street Journal* (10 July 2001), A1; Don Hudson, "Replays Don't Have to be Instant," *Charlotte Observer* (28 July 2001), 1B; Sam Walker, "Full Count and Empty Seats," *Wall Street Journal* (12 October 1999), B1, B4.

11. Team Marketing Report publishes the annual average ticket prices and other detailed price information for each professional sports team. The 2001 survey results for basketball franchises were reported in "NBA Posts First League-Wide Decrease in 11 Year History of Fan Cost Index," at http://www.teammarketing.com cited 29 October 2001.

12. The NFL's average ticket prices per team for the 1998, 1999 and 2000 seasons were available at the Web site of Team Marketing Report. For the 2001 average prices, see "NFL Ticket Prices Jump 8.7%, Panthers About 4.1%," *Charlotte Observer* (9 September 2001), 2H. In 1998, the best stadium deals from brokers, scalpers and box offices in professional football were discussed by Sam Walker, "How to Tackle the NFL's Hottest Tickets," *Wall Street Journal* (4 September 1998), W1, W4. For NFL ticket prices in 1994, see John Helyar, "Sports: Watching Football in Person Now Costs Even More," at http://www. proquestmail.com cited 19 July 2001.

13. There are other readings that examine the Fan Cost Indexes of teams. See Ray Waddell, "Ticket Price Hikes a Major Factor in Higher Fan Cost Index for MLB," at http://web4.infotrac.galegroup.com cited 18 October 2001; Idem, "NBA's Popularity, Salaries Cited for Fan Cost Increase," at http://web4.infotrac.galegroup.com cited 18 October 2001; Don Muret, "NHL's Average Cost Up 5.5%; Bruins Top the List," at http://web4.infotrac.galegroup.com cited 18 October 2001; David M. Carter, "Take Me Out to the Ball Game, James," *Business Week* (13 March 2000), 142; "Fan Cost Index— League Averages," at http://www.foxsports.com cited 29 November 2000.

14. Robert Passikoff, "N.Y. Yankees Aside, Winning Isn't Only Key to Fan Loyalty," *Brandweek* (6 November 2000), 32–33. The Sports Loyalty Indexes contain team rankings for 1999, 2000 and 2001. See "The Brand Keys Sports Loyalty Index," at http://www.brandkeys.com cited 1 November 2001. The Web site contains only the ranks and not the indexes of the top and bottom five teams in each sports league. Thus, the ranks and indexes are not reported for the other league clubs in Chapter 6.

15. For the determinants of fan loyalty in professional sports, see Matthew D. Shank, *Sports Marketing: A Strategic Perspective,* 2nd ed. (Upper Saddle River, NJ: Prentice-Hall, 2002), 274–275. According to Professor Shank, loyal fans endure all of the team's successes and hardships. Even during losing seasons, the fans continue to prefer their team to the other clubs. In his textbook, Shank lists the Fan Loyalty Indexes for the MLB teams in 1997.

16. Several sources published and discussed the best sports cities and fans in the United States. See Bob Hille, "TSN's Best Sports Cities," *The Sporting News* (30 June 1997), 14–23; Idem., "New York, New York," at http://www.sportingnews.com cited 9 August 2001; "New York Voted Best Sports City; Charlotte 23rd," *Charlotte Observer* (8 August 2001), 1C; "How'd We Do That," at http://www.sportingnews.com cited 9 August 2001; "The Criteria," at http://www.sportingnews.com cited 9 August 2001; "The Rest of the Best," at http://web2.infotrac.galegroup.com cited 22 October 2001; Steve Walentik, "Cityscape," at http://ehost.com cited 22 October 2001; Ken Garfield, "Lousy Sports Town? That's Good," *Charlotte Observer* (14 November 2001), 1E, 8E; E.M. Swift, "The Truth Hurts," *Sports Illustrated* (30 October 2000), 29; Rick Bonnell, "Charlotte Not Elite, But Not Bad," *Charlotte Observer* (5 July 1998), 2H; Tom Sorensen, "Fans Here Follow Trend, Not Team," *Charlotte Observer* (5 December 2001), 1C; Tommy Tomlinson, "Glitzy We Ain't; Genuine We Truly Are," *Charlotte Observer* (20 January 2002), 1B; Sam Walker, "Real Fans: They're Back," *Wall Street Journal* (21 December 2001), W11. *Sports Illustrated* polled professional athletes to see how fans view the competition. For the results, see "Field Notes," at http://ehostvgw3.epnet.com cited 12 July 2001.

17. See Bob Hille, "New York, New York," at http://www.sportingnews.com cited 9 August 2001; Idem., "TSN's Best Sports Cities," 14–23.

18. Ibid.

19. In 1999, the Oakland Athletics and St. Louis Cardinals implemented fan loyalty programs. Fans furnish basic demographic information at the ballpark and receive a loyalty card, which they swipe at kiosks in the stadium every time they attend a game. When the card is exchanged, fans earn points toward rewards such as coupons for free soda, free parking and a chance to win a trip to the World Series. For further details on the programs, see Charles Waltner, "CRM: The New Game in Town for Professional Sports," at http://proquestmail.com cited 29 October 2001; Sarah Lorge, "The Fan Plan," at http://proquestmail.com cited 29 October 2001.

Chapter 7

Government

Since the early 1900s, well-meaning politicians and other decision-makers within the U.S. federal government and numerous state, county and city governments have intervened in and generally supported the business and operations of the professional sports leagues and their member teams. The consequences of this involvement are reflected by the public legislation, policies and rules that apply to the business, economics and finance of professional team sports.

Besides the judicial decisions that have evolved from court cases, periodically the U.S. Congress and various government agencies and departments have decided to approve laws, ordinances and regulations that relate to the use of public debt to subsidize the construction and/or maintenance of sports arenas and stadiums. Other matters that concern professional sports and government are league expansion and team relocation, labor standards and antitrust, local and national broadcast rights, and the taxation of team assets and investments. In 1922, for example, Supreme Court Justice Oliver Wendell Holmes held that MLB owners were exempt from the federal antitrust laws and therefore immune from any collusive monopolistic business practices. Essentially, Justice Holmes had ruled that professional baseball was a sport and not interstate commerce. Besides that ruling, federal statute 15 U.S.C. Section 1291 was enacted in 1966. This act exempted sports league mergers from antitrust oversight. In addition to the economic effects on leagues and franchises, the statute dramatically impacted the welfare of communities, sports fans and the general public. As a result, the organization, infrastructure and outlook of professional team sports changed when agreements were reached to link the American and National Football Leagues in 1969, American and National Basketball Associations in 1976, and the World Hockey Association and National Hockey League in 1979. In short, historically the U.S. courts and government entities have provided the professional sports leagues and member franchises with sufficient liberties and privileges to conduct their business operations for profit in the United States and to provide entertainment value for sports and nonsports fans within America's market economy.[1]

As expected, the interaction and relationship between the sports leagues, their franchises and the public have concerned the economists who have studied the professional sports industry's behavior, conduct and performance. Since the 1970s, there are two controversial issues that economists have thoroughly researched. The first issue is how local and regional businesses, communities, fans and governments are affected by abrupt franchise movements. The second concern is whether the federal government or another public-sector entity should overrule, or at least monitor the leagues' decision process to allocate and relocate teams. Rather than unjustifiably prohibit team moves or outright micromanage the business of professional team sports, some academic researchers and public policy experts have suggested three enforceable government policies to deal with team relocation decisions and intraleague disparities in market power and wealth. First, they advocate that the government should require each sports league to equitably redistribute broadcast revenues each season among its member teams. Second, they state that the government should disallow or severely restrict how owners allocate franchise costs to players and then depreciate those costs for tax purposes. And third, they conclude that the government should urge each professional sports league to expand whenever an entrepreneur or group commits to invest a sufficient amount of capital to own and operate a franchise within a geographic or market area. In part, economists and other experts have recommended these and other policies to improve the utilization of resources that are allocated by the sports leagues and to remove the competitive imbalances that exist between the small- and large-market teams within a division or conference of a league. To date, U.S. government decision-makers have primarily treated the suggestions proposed by academicians as unnecessarily idealistic, impractical, theoretical or unworkable.[2]

Team relocation and league expansion matters aside, a related business and social policy issue that has interested economists and spurred abundant research is the use of taxpayer subsidies to construct, and the government ownership of, sports facilities that provide economic benefits primarily to franchise owners and team players. In 1971, 70 percent (53) of the arenas and stadiums in the United States occupied by AL and NL teams in MLB and by clubs in the NBA, NFL and NHL were publicly owned, while 24 percent (18) of them were privately owned. The remaining 6 percent (5) of the facilities were operated to benefit the sports programs affiliated with the nation's colleges and universities. To determine the economic and social returns of taxpayer expenditures on professional sports arenas and stadiums, several eminent economists have documented and studied the distribution of the dollar benefits that have resulted from local governments' direct and indirect subsidies, which amounted to approximately $23 million a year in the early 1970s. In general, the research indicates that the economic and social benefits from publicly owned arenas and stadiums had accrued disproportionately to middle and upper income citizens in a community.

Furthermore, the studies revealed that the three primary beneficiaries of tax-payer assistance are the respective team owners, players and then the fans who attend games at the subsidized facility.[3]

In response to business opportunities presented by politicians throughout the 1970s and early 1980s, numerous professional sports franchise owners bargained with and convinced government officials, who represented cities, counties, districts, states, and the federal government to provide subsidies such as cash and loans for the construction, and perhaps operating costs of a hometown arena and/or stadium. During those years, the total amount of public funds that were contributed by various governments for sports venues varied according to leagues and teams. To illustrate, the owner of the NFL Buffalo Bills received $4.6 million in taxpayer subsidies for the construction of the 73,800-seat Ralph Wilson Stadium, which cost $22 million to build and open in 1973. Likewise, other football entrepreneurs benefited from the public subsidies of stadiums. They were, for example, the owner of the NFL Seattle Seahawks who pocketed $10.5 million of taxpayer money when the $67 million Kingdome was constructed in 1976, the NFL Minnesota Vikings who banked $2.2 million when the Metrodome was erected in 1982, and the NFL Indianapolis Colts who kept $10.7 million when the Hoosier Dome was built in 1984. Then, after an intense debate about the existing federal tax laws, the U.S. Congress passed the Tax Reform Act in 1986. Essentially, the act stipulates that if a facility is partially funded with the proceeds from the sale of state or local government bonds, the debtor must provide a favorable lease to the professional tenants, if any, that occupy the facility. Moreover, the legislation stipulates that any interest payments on debts have to be redistributed to local taxpayers since all facility-related revenues must eventually be replaced with general revenue sources. Therefore, based on the Tax Reform Act professional sports franchise owners had an incentive to apply their market power and prestige, and persuade politicians and taxpayers to finance the construction of new, or the renovation of obsolete facilities, which would ultimately result in additional income for the owners and inevitably higher salaries for the team players.[4]

From 1990 to 2001 inclusive, U.S. taxpayers contributed an estimated $6 billion to $10 billion toward the expansion of the professional sports leagues. That is, when new arenas and stadiums were built or upgraded, the entire or a significant portion of the facilities' cost was financed with public money. Indeed, various local, municipal and state governments issued bonds and other debt securities and also raised excise and property taxes for the construction of sports venues to discourage host teams from abandoning their sites, or to attract a league's expansion franchise. To identify and contrast to what extent U.S. cities, metropolitan areas and states financially supported the construction or renovation of sports arenas and/or stadiums from 1990 through 2001, a variety of studies performed by reputable experts were researched. These references provided sufficient information and statistics to list by the number and type of sports, the specific franchises that relied on public money for the construction of a hometown arena or stadium in the 1990s, 2000 and 2001. Initially, the four franchises each in the Atlanta and Denver areas are discussed and then the respective teams in three and two sports, and finally in one sport. As economists and others have documented, the taxpayer expenditures for arenas and stadiums principally benefited franchise owners, team players and fans. Nevertheless, government officials proclaimed that the fund allocations were justified to improve the economic growth rate of communities and secondarily, to increase the cash inflows and employment of local businesses.[5]

FOUR SPORTS

Atlanta: Braves/Falcons/Hawks/Thrashers

For the NFL Falcons, the 71,228-seat Georgia Dome was constructed with $214 million of taxpayer money when it opened in 1992. Then, five years later the city of Atlanta spent $50 million to convert the $207 million Olympic Stadium to the 50,062-seat Turner Field for the NL Braves. In addition to the Georgia Dome and Turner Field, a $20 million payment from Braves' owner Ted Turner, $130 million from the issue of revenue bonds and $62 million from the implementation of a 3 percent automobile rental tax financed the construction of the $215 million 20,000-seat Philips Arena for the NBA Hawks and NHL Thrashers, which was an ice hockey expansion team in 1999. If the cost and conversion of Olympic Stadium and the proceeds from the revenue bonds and car rental taxes are aggregated, the total subsidies to the four franchises were estimated to exceed $660 million. Because of the generosity of taxpayers, for many seasons the sports fans located in Georgia and elsewhere will have four professional teams to cheer for in the metropolitan Atlanta area. Recently, only the Braves have set regular season attendance records, while the other three clubs struggle to attract spectators and sponsors.[6]

Denver: Broncos/ Nuggets/Colorado Avalanche/Colorado Rockies

In the mid-1990s, a 1 percent, six-county sales tax was enacted in the Denver area to raise $168 million for the construction of 50,381-seat Coors Field, which is the $216 million home ballpark of the NL Colorado Rockies. Besides Coors Field, in 1999 the $169 million 19,000-seat Pepsi Center opened for the NBA Nuggets and NHL Avalanche. To finance this project, Denver taxpayers contributed significant moneys to subsidize and pay for the Center's construction outlays. The funding sources for the venue included an unknown amount of private loans, $2.3 million in construction sales tax rebates and $2.1 million in annual property tax exemptions. Furthermore, to raise $140 million for the Nuggets' and Avalanche's facility, entrepreneurial financiers sold debt securities based on the anticipated revenues from arena-naming rights, corporate sponsorships and luxury suite licenses. This asset-backed financing method lowered capital costs and allowed the center's owner, which was the Ascent Entertainment Group Inc., to have more operational flexibility with limited oversight from lenders and to use the facility's other income sources any way it wished. However, bond-rating agencies consider asset-backed funding of sports venues to be a risky investment because a team's financial condition cannot be isolated from its arena.[7]

After the NFL Broncos owner Pat Bowlen suggested he might sell the team, which implied that the new owners could decide to move the club, Denver voters approved funds to build a new stadium for the franchise in November 1998. Three years later, 76,125-seat Invesco Field at Mile High, which is owned by the Denver Metropolitan Football Stadium District, was opened for the Broncos. A sales tax was extended to pay for 75 percent or $273 million of the stadium's estimated $364 million construction cost, and Bowlen planned to contribute $91 million. In sum, the market value of the four Denver sports franchises significantly increased when Colorado's taxpayers provided approximately $600 million in subsidies to build the three facilities for its professional sports teams. The Atlanta and Denver franchises aside, in the 1990s there were five three-sport areas that introduced recently constructed arenas and/or stadiums for the home-town teams.[8]

THREE SPORTS

Chicago: Bulls/Blackhawks/White Sox

To thwart a relocation of the AL White Sox from the "Windy City" to the Tampa Bay-St. Petersburg area, during the early 1990s a 2 percent hotel tax was activated in Chicago to raise $150 million. This amount financed the construction of 44,321-seat Comiskey Park, which is owned by the Illinois Sports Facility Authority. The White Sox aside, rather than seek taxpayer assistance, the owners of the NBA Bulls and NHL Blackhawks decided to jointly spend $175 million to construct the 21,500-seat United Center in 1994. While in that arena, the Bulls won league championships from 1996 to 1998 inclusive.

Cleveland: Browns/Cavaliers/Indians

To finance the inauguration of the $173 million, 43,368-seat Jacobs Field in 1994 for the AL Indians, in spring 1990 Cuyahoga County voters extended the excise taxes on alcohol and cigarettes for fifteen years. Then, for the NBA Cavaliers, Cleveland area taxpayers funded 97 percent of the $155 million, 20,562-seat Gund Arena, which opened in 1994. Those funds were obtained from the sale of tax-exempt county bonds and from the excise taxes that county voters had approved in 1990. When the city of Cleveland was awarded an NFL expansion franchise for the 1999 season, Cuyahoga County further extended the taxes on alcohol and cigarettes to erect the $283 million, 73,000-seat Cleveland Stadium for the AFC's Central Division Browns. Besides money from the bonds and taxes, other funds were obtained when Browns owner Al Lerner secured sponsorship agreements with the Cleveland Clinic, CoreComm, National City Corporation and Steris Corporation who each had its name displayed above an entrance to the stadium. In total, the owners of the Cleveland Browns, Cavaliers and Indians received approximately $600 million in taxpayer subsidies to compete in their respective divisions and to provide entertainment for sports fans in the northeast Ohio area. In team performances, the Indians have won titles before capacity crowds at Jacobs Field while the Cavaliers at Gund Arena remain mediocre in attendance and within the Central Division of the Eastern Conference. Meanwhile, since its expansion year the Browns have failed to qualify for a wild card in the NFL playoffs.[9]

Phoenix: Coyotes/Diamondbacks/Suns

In 1992, the city of Phoenix's bonds and loans plus money from the franchises' owners were allocated to pay the $90 million in construction costs for the 19,000-seat American West Arena. The NBA Suns and NHL Coyotes play in the Arena, which is owned by the city of Phoenix and managed by the Phoenix Arena Development Corporation. In addition to taxpayer subsidies for the Arena, a .25 percent Maricopa County sales tax was passed to raise at least $300 million to build the 48,500-seat Bank One Ballpark, which opened in 1998. This stadium is the home field of the NL Arizona Diamondbacks, who won the 2001 league title and then the World Series by defeating the AL New York Yankees in seven games. Maricopa County commissioners approved the sales tax without the passage of a direct referendum from the city or county voters. As a result of the tax hike, however, two county commissioners were defeated in the next election, and one commissioner was assaulted and injured by irate citizens. Nevertheless, the city of Phoenix rejuvenated itself after the investments in the Ballpark. In the downtown area, street crime declined as new commercial and residential development surged. Furthermore, urban neighborhoods were revived in the central city because crowds returned to watch the Diamondbacks compete for titles each season or from late spring to early fall.

Despite the club's success in the NL West Division, unfortunately by 2000 the franchise had reportedly accumulated $38 million in operating deficits. This amount was $100 million below the initial profit projections the team had promised its investors in 1998. Besides a decline in corporate sponsorships and average attendance at games, the deficits occurred when owner Jerry Colangelo launched a spending spree for players. He signed to long-term contracts high-salaried free agents such as the 2001 Cy Young Award pitcher Randy Johnson from the AL Seattle Mariners and the AL Playoffs co-MVP pitcher Curt Shilling from the NL Philadelphia Phillies. In total, the Diamondbacks' owners committed $119 million to its free agents in 1998, which was one of baseball's highest amounts ever and enough cash to cover the entire payroll of the NL Montreal Expos for seven regular seasons. Accordingly, the construction of the Arena for the Suns and Coyotes and the Ballpark for the Diamondbacks cost Phoenix area taxpayers approximately $300 million to $400 million for spectators to watch the three clubs perform. In fact, those subsidies exclude any appropriations to the NFL Arizona Cardinals.[10]

Seattle: Mariners/Seahawks/Supersonics

When the $120 million, 17,000-seat Key Arena was upgraded in 1995 for the NBA SuperSonics, the sale of city bonds committed Seattle taxpayers to absorb 62 percent or $74 million of the Arena's renovation costs. The Key Arena subsidy, however, was surpassed in 1996. That year, more than $700 million in public funds was approved by the Washington State legislature for two sports venues. Built for the AL Mariners was the $520 million, 46,621-seat Safeco Field, which is owned by the Washington-King County Stadium Authority, and for the NFL Seahawks was the $300 million, 67,000-seat Seahawks Stadium, which is owned by King County. Despite the heated debate and widespread opposition from various Seattle and King County citizen groups, the legislators and voters narrowly approved a .5 percent county prepared food tax and an automobile rental tax to erect Safeco Field. Lottery games, sales taxes, and a hotel-motel tax partially pay for Seahawks Stadium. The Mariners owner, Nintendo Chief Executive Officer Hiroshi Yamauchi, invested $75 million of his own wealth to build Safeco Field and former Microsoft cofounder and Seahawks owner Paul Allen contributed $100 million to ensure that the Seahawks Stadium would be completed. After $100 million in cost overruns at Safeco Field, in 2000 the Mariners tightened its payroll, which resulted in the loss of free-agent superstars Ken Griffey, Jr., to the Cincinnati Reds and Alex Rodriguez to the Texas Rangers.[11]

Between 1990 and 1996, Washington State taxpayers assumed more than $800 million in debt and interest payments to observe their three major professional teams perform in Seattle area stadiums. Given this staggering burden on taxpayers, it is unlikely that the NHL will soon expand to or relocate a franchise in the state of Washington. In their respective leagues, recently the SuperSonics and Seahawks have not performed to meet the expectations of sports fans, while the Mariners emerged to challenge the New York Yankees for the AL championship in the 2001 season.

Tampa Bay: Buccaneers/Devil Rays/Lightning

For the AL Devil Rays, in 1998 $70 million of public funds was allocated to renovate 45,200-seat Tropicana Field, which was formerly named the Florida Suncoast Dome in 1990 and the Thunderdome in 1992. Furthermore, taxpayer money was set aside to build 66,300-seat Raymond James Stadium for the NFL Buccaneers and the 19,500-seat Ice Palace for the NHL Lightning, which was an ice hockey expansion team in 1992.

When the Florida Suncoast Dome was built in 1990, it cost taxpayers $138 million in construction expenditures. The Dome was sited in Tampa Bay to supposedly lure the AL White Sox from Chicago or the NL Giants from San Francisco, or to exist as a home ballpark if MLB approved an expansion franchise. Beginning in 1992, however, the Lightning occupied the stadium until the Devil Rays began to play there in 1998. As the property of the Tampa Sports Authority, the Buccaneers' stadium cost the public $265 million. Moreover, Florida sales taxes and the sale of city parking and county tourist bonds contributed 62 percent or $86 million of the total expenditures for the Ice Palace, which is owned by the Davidson Group.

As an aside, in 1996 Florida's Hillsborough County passed a .5 percent sales tax for community investment purposes. The construction of Raymond James Stadium absorbed 11 percent of the sales tax, and the other 89 percent was targeted for schools, fire and law enforcement personnel and equipment, and infrastructure developments. Indeed, the community investment tax and a state of Florida sales tax rebate funded the Stadium's construction. Even with the estimated $300 to $400 million in taxpayer subsidies for the two sports facilities, as of 2002 the three Tampa Bay teams had not won their league's championship. Undoubtedly, sports fans in the western Florida area are rooting for their teams to excel and win a Stanley Cup, Super Bowl or World Series.[12]

TWO SPORTS

Anaheim: Angels/Mighty Ducks

In 1996, the AL Anaheim Angels signed a thirty-five-year lease to play its home games at the 45,000-seat Edison International Field. Then, after thirty years of multiple uses, in the late 1990s the City of Anaheim spent $117 million to convert the Field to a baseball facility for the Western Division Angels.

Earlier in the 1990s, Anaheim taxpayers had contributed $120 million to construct 17,174-seat Arrowhead Pond for the NHL Mighty Ducks. To avoid local tax increases, before 2000 the Ogden Entertainment Company assumed the debt service on the city of Anaheim bonds that were issued to fund the Pond. Unfortunately, due to each team's inferior performances and woeful fan support, the home attendance and local broadcast rights at the Angels and Mighty Ducks games have not been sufficient to earn profits from the operations of the Field and Pond. In retrospect, it appears that the public's investments in these sports facilities have provided negative financial returns for the franchise owners and Anaheim taxpayers.

Baltimore: Orioles/Ravens

Camden Yards, the 48,800-seat home ballpark of the AL Baltimore Orioles, was opened in 1992 after Maryland taxpayers grudgingly assumed 96 percent or $201 million of the stadium's construction costs. The Maryland Stadium Authority owns $210 million Camden Yards and the $200 million, 69,300-seat Ravens Stadium, which was built for owner Arthur Modell's NFL Ravens when the club vacated Cleveland in 1996 as the Browns. The total construction costs of the two venues included more than $400 million in public money so that the Orioles and Ravens could each play in state-of-the-art stadiums that contained plenty of club seats, luxury suites and food and merchandise outlets. In their respective divisions and leagues, the Ravens have been more successful than the Orioles in recent years. Nevertheless, crowds flock to fill both stadiums for each team's home games.

Buffalo: Bills/Sabres

In 1992, Buffalo's City Council approved $2.4 million for taxpayers to finance the land development costs and other expenses for a future arena that would benefit the NHL Sabres. Four years later, funds from New York State loans plus city of Buffalo and county bond issues were used to partially finance the construction of the $127 million, 21,000-seat Marine Midland Arena—later named HSBC Arena—for the professional hockey franchise. Besides the Sabres, in 1997 the New York State legislature approved $63 million to renovate the 73,800-seat Ralph Wilson Stadium, which is owned by Erie County and the long-standing home field of the NFL Bills. The minor league baseball's AAA Buffalo Bisons aside, the owners of the Sabres and Bills have undoubtedly prospered from the public subsidies to improve Buffalo's two sports facilities for professional ice hockey and football fans in the western region of New York State.

Cincinnati: Bengals/Reds

Without NBA or NHL teams in the area to subsidize, in 1996 the legislators who represented Cincinnati's City Council and Hamilton County committed taxpayers to partially pay for two new stadiums. That is, one facility for the NL Reds and the other for the NFL Bengals. According to the agreement reached between the Bengals and officials of the governments, the county donated 12.5 acres of land for the stadiums but retained the option to build parking garages on a nearby street named Ft. Washington Way. Meanwhile, the city of Cincinnati controlled the rights to the future development of the stadiums and the use of the pads atop the parking garages, and agreed to equally split any revenues from the stadiums with the county for up to twenty years. Indeed, the Hamilton County sales tax was raised by .5 percent to provide a total subsidy that exceeds $700 million for the 42,000-seat Great American Ball Park, which will replace thirty-two year-old Cinergy Field in 2003 for the Reds, and for 65,600-seat Paul Brown Stadium that opened in 2000 for the Bengals. Due to the underestimation of costs for the stadiums, relocation of streets and utilities, land acquisition and removal of old structures, in 2000 city and county taxpayers were obligated for the cost overruns that occurred. Later, an audit revealed that there were insufficient fiscal controls on the project and that many work-change orders were hurried and then approved and unjustified. These problems could have been avoided if the stadiums' budgets had reflected expenditures and interest rate premiums for inflation, risk and construction delays.[13]

Other than the costs of the facilities, in recent seasons neither club has won division, conference or league titles. Perhaps, star players such as the Reds' outfielder Ken Griffey, Jr. and the Bengals' running back Cory Dillon will be inspired to excel and motivate western Ohio and eastern Indiana fans to attend home games and purchase season tickets, and apparel, food and merchandise at the new stadiums. Because of the huge payments on the debt balances, Cincinnati taxpayers are unlikely to approve additional funds to construct new facilities for an NBA or NHL team.

Dallas: Mavericks/Stars

In 2001, the 19,000-seat American Airlines Center opened. This facility is the home court of the NBA Mavericks and the host rink of the NHL Stars. Owned by the city of Dallas, the Center cost about $325 million to complete and each team contributed 25 percent or approximately $81 million to finance its construction. The teams' owners paid the remaining 50 percent or $163 million of the arena's construction costs. Meanwhile, the NFL Dallas Cowboys owner Jerry Jones wants to erect a new $500 million, 100,000-seat stadium complex to replace thirty-two-year-old, 65,600-seat Texas Stadium, whose lease expires between 2006 and 2008. Some viable and worthwhile locations for the stadium project include cities such as Arlington, Dallas, Grand Prairie and Irving, and a site in an undisclosed Denton County district. The city chosen would pay a portion of the stadium's costs, and according to plans, perhaps contribute money for land and infrastructure improvements to build a sports theme park complete with a gallery, hotel and museum. Admired for his vision by other NFL owners, Jones' strategy is to convince Cowboy fans in Dallas and the Denton area that a modern football facility is required for the team to succeed in the Eastern Division of the NFC and to win a sixth Super Bowl. Besides this formidable investment, in late 2001 Jones and his family launched the Dallas Desperados of the Arena Football League. The team began its first season in April 2002. In sum, even though the image and reputation of the Cowboys has diminished in recent years, Jerry Jones is committed to making the team a champion again with the cash inflows from a new stadium and sports complex.[14]

Los Angeles: Clippers/Lakers/Kings

After the AFC Raiders moved to Oakland and the NFC Rams to St. Louis in 1995, the negotiations between the league and Los Angeles officials failed to produce an expansion professional football team for the area. Rather, the NFL awarded an ownership group from Houston, Texas, an expansion team to begin play in August 2002. Yet, in the late 1990s the city of Los Angeles spent an estimated $70 million to purchase adjacent land to prepare for the construction of the $330 million, 19,000-seat Staples Center, which is owned by the Los Angeles Arena Company. The Center is the current home of the NBA Clippers and Lakers and the NHL Kings. The city's expenditures will be repaid from parking lot revenues and from real estate and sales taxes. Although the Los Angeles Coliseum requires substantial renovation to improve its infrastructure for a professional football team, the stadium is an enviable site for any NFL franchise that seeks to abandon its low-revenue home facility. To accomplish this strategy, the potential clubs and their inferior stadiums include the Colts' 56,127-seat RCA Dome in Indianapolis, Raiders' 63,132-seat Network Associates Coliseum in Oakland, and the Vikings' 64,121-seat Metrodome in Minneapolis.[15]

Miami: Heat/Florida Panthers

In the late 1990s, the NHL Panthers played in the $212 million, 19,500-seat National Car Rental Company Center, which was built primarily with public money derived from a 2 percent tourism tax levied in Broward County, Florida. Besides the Panthers, the NBA Heat also benefited from public assistance. That is, the government donated land valued at $35 million to the franchise, and southeast Florida taxpayers agreed to subsidize $6.5 million of the annual operating costs for the $175 million, 19,600-seat American Airlines Arena, which opened in 1999. However, after the city of Miami rejected Florida Marlins owner Wayne Huizenga's request for a publicly financed ballpark in 1995 and 1997, the franchise was sold in 1999 for $150 million to John Henry, who was a commodities trader from Boca Raton, Florida. After stiff opposition from groups such as the Urban Environment League and Sierra Club, Henry failed to obtain taxpayer subsidies for the construction of a $400 million stadium at Bicentennial Park on a thirty-acre site on Biscayne Bay to replace fourteen-year-old, 42,500-seat Pro Player Stadium. Formerly named Joe Robbie Stadium, it was constructed in 1987 for the NFL Miami Dolphins. In early 2002, Henry sold the Marlins for approximately $158 million to Jeffrey Loria, the former owner of the NL Montreal Expos. Alas, without more revenues from a lucrative stadium deal, the Marlins' future in Miami is uncertain.[16]

Minneapolis-St. Paul: Minnesota Timberwolves/Wild

Five years after its construction for $104 million in 1990, the privately owned, 19,000-seat Target Center was sold by owners Harvey Ratner and Marv Wolfensen for $54.6 million to the city of Minneapolis that raised the cash from the sale of city bonds. The deal was completed to ensure that the NBA Timberwolves would not relocate from the Minneapolis-St. Paul area. Furthermore, in 2000 the 18,800-seat Xcel Energy Center opened in St. Paul for the NHL Wild, an NHL expansion team. The $130 million arena was built entirely with public funds. On the other hand, the owners of the AL Twins and NFL Vikings have not persuaded Minnesota's legislators and taxpayers to finance the construction of new stadiums for their clubs. The Twins and Vikings, meanwhile, play in the 48,600-seat Metrodome, which was built in 1982 with $55 million of public money. Due to each club's small market and low television rank, the future of these franchises in the Minneapolis-St. Paul area is at risk.

Nashville: Predators/Titans

To provide a modern facility for professional basketball and/or hockey teams, in 1995 the city of Nashville issued $144 million of general obligation bonds to build a 17,500-seat ice hockey arena, the Gaylord Entertainment Center. Then, in 1997 the expansion NHL Predators was placed in Nashville. Two years later, the 67,000-seat Adelphia Coliseum opened for the NFL Titans who had relocated after the 1996 season from Houston to Memphis as the Oilers. The Coliseum was financed with $290 million of public money, and Nashville taxpayers contributed an additional $24 million for land and infrastructure improvements. Thus, because of the Predators and Titans the residents of western Tennessee have entertainment options other than minor league baseball and country music performances and shows.

Oakland: Raiders/Golden State Warriors

To lure the NFL Raiders from Los Angeles, in 1995 the city of Oakland and Alameda County agreed to improve the twenty-nine-year-old, 63,100-seat Oakland/Alameda County Stadium—renamed Network Associates Coliseum—from the proceeds of a bond issue that financed the $225 million renovation. Then, to discourage the NBA Warriors from relocating to another city, in 1996 $121 million of taxpayer subsidies was allocated by the Oakland Coliseum Authority to upgrade the thirty-year-old, 19,600-seat Oakland Coliseum Arena, which was renamed the Arena in Oakland in 1997. Besides the Raiders and Warriors, what about the status of MLB's Oakland Athletics? Without additional club seats and luxury suites in the Network Associates Coliseum or the construction of an elaborate ballpark, the AL Athletics will continue to lose its free agent superstars such as Jason Giambi who signed a $125 million long-term contract with the New York Yankees in 2001.

St. Louis: Blues/Rams

The city of St. Louis became the host site for the expansion NHL Blues in 1967. Twenty-seven years later, the $170 million 19,200-seat Kiel Center Arena—renamed the Savvis Center—opened for the team after St. Louis' taxpayers spent $35 million for site preparation and garages and $60 million of the Arena's construction costs. The Blues aside, to attract the NFL Rams from Los

Angeles, in 1995 the city government allocated approximately $219 million of public money to build the $300 million, 66,000-seat Trans World Dome for the Rams. Because of these two sports, more than $300 million of eastern Missouri taxpayer money was committed to the construction of the hockey and football facilities. In June 2001, the state and local government officials and St. Louis Cardinals agreed to finance a $646 million redevelopment project that includes a new 50,000-seat ballpark to be built near thirty-six-year-old, 49,600-seat Busch Stadium. But, in 2002 the Missouri General Assembly refused to approve the ballpark's construction in downtown St. Louis. The team's owners and private developers will pay 66 percent of the development and stadium construction costs and 100 percent of its maintenance and operating costs. Euphoric because the modern ballpark will be completed by the 2006 regular season, Cardinals Chairman William O. DeWitt Jr. said that the team would remain in the St. Louis area through 2039.[17]

San Diego: Chargers/Padres

In 1997, the city of San Diego spent $60 million and the NFL Chargers' owner $18 million to renovate 71,000-seat Qualcomm Stadium, which was built in 1967. Since the stadium was constructed and reconfigured for spectators to view football games, for several years the NL Padres have lobbied the city of San Diego for a new publicly financed ballpark. After Proposition C was passed in late 1998 and the team's stadium lease expired in 1999, the city and Padres owner John Moores decided to jointly finance a new $411 million commercial district that will include a hotel and offices, shops, restaurants and a 42,000-seat ballpark, which will be opened in 2003 or 2004. Proposition C permits the city to contribute $275 million and Moores $115 million to the project. Furthermore, the Proposition stipulates that the Padres are required to remain in San Diego through 2024. In short, because of the financial obligations for the Padres' new ballpark, taxpayers in San Diego would not welcome the relocation of an NBA or NHL franchise to the area. Thus, it appears that the Chargers and Padres will play in San Diego for many years beyond 2002.[18]

ONE SPORT

After they approved a local sales tax increase of .5 percent in January 1991, the city of Arlington's taxpayers paid 74 percent of the stadium's cost or approximately $141 million to erect 49,100-seat The Ballpark, which opened in 1994 for the AL Texas Rangers. One year later, because of the high-level support from Governor Tommy Thompson, the Wisconsin State legislature passed a .1 percent multicounty sales tax to collect almost 64 percent or $160 million of the cost to build a ballpark for the AL—now NL—Milwaukee Brewers. After construction delays that increased the stadium's cost to approximately $400 million, the 43,000-seat Miller Park opened in the 2001 season for the Brewers.

In 2000, the NL Astros began its season at 42,000-seat Enron Field (now Minute Maid Park) in Houston and the AL Tigers at the 40,000-seat Comerica Park in Detroit. Automobile rental and hotel taxes that varied between 1 percent and 5 percent in Houston and Detroit paid for 68 percent or $180 million of Enron Field's construction costs and 38 percent or $115 million of Comerica Park's expenditures. Enron Field replaced the thirty-five-year-old, 54,300-seat Astrodome and Comerica Park superseded the eighty-eight-year-old, 52,500-seat Tiger Stadium. Finally, after assured of state funding, in 2001 the NL Pirates opened its regular season in the $262 million 38,000-seat PNC Park in Pittsburgh. The facility was built even though voters in eleven counties that surrounded Pittsburgh rejected a sales tax in 1997. When this occurred, Pittsburgh's Mayor Tom Murphy convinced the legislators in Harrisburg, Pennsylvania, to fund the Pirates' ballpark. Interestingly, in the long term it is uncertain whether the new baseball stadiums in Milwaukee and Pittsburgh will generate enough revenues for the small-market Brewers and Pirates to compete with the large-market clubs such as the NL Astros, Braves, Cubs, Dodgers, Giants, Mets and Phillies.[19]

In the NBA, between 1990 and 2001 three sports facilities were constructed partially with taxpayer subsidies. Each transaction was unique. First, in 1993 taxpayers in San Antonio were levied a .5 percent sales tax by the government that provided $186 million to erect the 20,557-seat Alamodome, which is the home court of the NBA Spurs. Second, in 1995 the city of Portland spent $34 million of taxpayer money for infrastructure improvements to the $262 million, 21,538-seat Rose Garden, which is where the NBA Trail Blazers play home games. Third, in 1999 the city of Indianapolis and Marion County jointly set aside $107 million of public money to partially finance the construction of the $183 million, 18,345-seat Conseco Fieldhouse for the NBA Pacers in downtown Indianapolis. The Fieldhouse replaced historic Market Square Arena, the place where the Indiana High School Final Basketball Tournaments were held. In total, the subsidies for the Alamodome, Rose Garden and Conseco Fieldhouse amounted to at least $325 million.[20]

In the NFL, during the mid-1990s an estimated $60 million to $80 million of public funds were spent for land and business relocation costs in Charlotte, North Carolina, where the 73,250-seat Ericsson Stadium was privately built for $248 million. As the home field of the expansion NFL Carolina Panthers, this open-air, grass-field facility has abundant restrooms, numerous beverage and food outlets, wide concourses and excellent seats for spectators. Likewise, in 1996 the expansion NFL Jaguars received a total subsidy of $124 million from the sale of city bonds, state of Florida rebates and lodging taxes for the renovation of the 73,000-seat Jacksonville Municipal Stadium, which was renamed the ALLTEL Stadium in 1998. The stadiums in Charlotte and Jacksonville aside, the construction of the 20,444-seat CoreStates Center—renamed First Union Center—in Philadelphia was privately financed for $210 million by the owners of the NBA 76ers and NHL Flyers. Lastly, in 1996 $100 million of taxpayer money was provided to renovate twenty-five-year-old, 65,352-seat Veterans Stadium for the NFC's Eastern Division Eagles.

Other than the dual-purpose arenas that are the homes of NBA and NHL teams such as the American Airlines Arena in Dallas, American West Arena in Phoenix, the Pepsi Center in Denver, the Staples Center in Los Angeles and the United Center in Chicago, during the 1990s taxpayer money was allocated to pay for establishing professional ice hockey arenas in the United States and Canada. Those allocations included $138 million for the 18,176-seat Entertainment and Sports Arena in Raleigh for the Hurricanes, which had relocated from Hartford, Connecticut, in 1997 as the Whalers; and approximately C$300 million for the 18,500-seat Corel Center in Ottawa for the Senators, which was an expansion franchise in 1992. Wake County bonds, funds from the state of North Carolina and city taxes paid for the Arena in Raleigh, and federal grants and government loans paid for the rink in Ottawa. There were other U.S. and Canadian single-purpose hockey arenas that were not described earlier in this chapter but which benefited from the private money of team owners. Those teams, facilities and their construction costs were the Maple Leafs' 18,800-seat Air Canada Center in Toronto for C$265 million, the Canucks' 18,422-seat General Motors Place in Vancouver for C$160 million, and the Blue Jackets' 18,138-seat Nationwide Arena in Columbus, Ohio, for an unknown amount.

After 2002, several professional sports teams are expected to be awarded public subsidies for the construction of new arenas and stadiums, and/or for land and infrastructure enhancements that surround those sports venues. First, in MLB a new ballpark in Boston will replace ninety-year-old, 33,800-seat Fenway Park for the Red Sox. The city of Boston and Massachusetts State taxpayers will likely be responsible for a portion of the construction costs. For example, one plan committed the city to contribute $140 million for land acquisition and site preparation plus $72 million for two parking garages, while the state would contribute $100 million for infrastructure costs such as roadway and subway improvements. To retire the city bonds issued for the stadium, there would be a parking surcharge on spaces that surround the ballpark on game days, as well as surcharges on general admission and luxury box tickets As of late 2002, the financial package was being negotiated between the city, state and team. Second, the cash from a commercial real estate tax has been discussed by New York City legislators to partially finance new ballparks for the AL Yankees and NL Mets that would vacate, respectively, seventy-nine-year-old, 55,000-seat Yankee Stadium and thirty-eight-year-old, 55,200-seat Shea Stadium. The total cost of the ballparks for the two franchises was estimated at $1.6 billion in early 2002. Third, in December 2000 the Philadelphia City Council approved more than $1 billion to build two stadiums to replace thirty-one-year-old, 62,400-seat Veterans Stadium for the NL Phillies and NFL Eagles. In June 2001, the Phillies unveiled a scale model of its grass-surface 43,000-seat ballpark, which will be finished before the 2004 regular season ends. As one amenity, the Phillies' stadium will contain seventy-two luxury suites that generate more revenues for the team. Fourth, the District of Columbia Sports Commission seeks to collect more than $300 million from taxpayers to eventually place an expansion or relocated baseball team in the nation's capital.[21]

The partial or total cost of future arenas for NBA teams and of stadiums for NFL clubs may be paid by taxpayers that reside within various U.S. cities, districts, municipalities and states. For example, since 2001 there have been ongoing discussions between local governments and respective franchise owners to replace current NBA facilities such as twenty-two-year-old, 20,049-seat Continental Airlines Arena in New Jersey for the Nets and twenty-seven-year-old, 16,285-seat Compaq Center in Houston for the Rockets. One arena plan in the Houston area failed. In late 1999, Harris County voters in Texas rejected a proposal to build a $160 million downtown facility for the Rockets. Although Houston Mayor Lee Brown and Rockets owner Les Alexander sincerely supported the plan, arena opponents said the ballot issue was hastily thrown together, and it placed too much of a cost burden on taxpayers. However, in 1999 Bexar County voters in Texas agreed by a wide margin to partially fund the construction of the $176 million, 18,500-seat SBC Center for the Spurs. The increase in the county's hotel tax from 15 percent to 16.75 percent and the car rental tax from 10 percent to 15 percent supplemented the sale of county bonds valued at $147 million. Spurs' owner Peter Holt contributed $29 million for the state-of-the-art SBC Center which opened in 2002. In the deal, Bexar County receives 2.7 percent or $1.1 million of the $41 million in naming rights paid by SBC Communications Inc.[22]

Besides those events, a countywide vote is expected in Memphis to determine whether taxpayer money will be used to build a $250 million arena for the NBA Grizzlies that relocated from Vancouver in 2001. In mid-2001, the city of Memphis proposed to sidestep a referendum vote by using sales tax rebates, publicly backed bonds and automobile rental and hotel taxes. However, Chancery Judge Walter Evans ruled that government would be paying for a private project with few public benefits and, therefore, taxpayers have a right to vote on how their money is spent by the local government. Conversely, Memphis Mayor Willie Herenton believed the ruling should be overturned because sports arenas promote the economic development and growth of communities. Eventually, a new arena will be constructed in Memphis primarily with taxpayer subsidies.[23]

The NBA arenas aside, various newspapers and sports magazines have published articles that report how franchise owners and governments propose to collectively finance and build new NFL stadiums. The football facilities that are expected to be evacuated and replaced or upgraded include forty-four-year-old, 73,273-seat Sun Devil Stadium in Tempe for the Cardinals, thirty-one-year-old, 60,300-seat Foxboro Stadium for the Patriots, forty-five-year-old, 60,800-seat Lambeau Field in Green Bay for the Packers, forty-two-year-old, 70,140-seat 3 Com Park at Candlestick Point in San Francisco for the 49ers, seventy-eight-year-old, 64,944-seat Soldier Field in Chicago for the Bears, twenty-seven-year-old, 70,200-seat Louisiana Superdome in New Orleans for the Saints, and twenty-year-old, 64,121-seat Metrodome in Minneapolis for the Vikings.

To illustrate, first, in November 2000 the voters in Arizona's Maricopa County approved Proposition 302, which authorized $229 million for the construction of a stadium for the NFL Cardinals. Specifically, the proposition permits a thirty-year increase in hotel and car rental taxes, earmarks $96 million to promote tourism, and allocates $73 million for improvements to the Cactus League's spring training facilities and $27 million for the youth and adult recreation programs in the Phoenix area. To finance the football stadium, which is scheduled to open in Tempe in 2004, the Cardinals pledged $85 million. The club will also provide $10 million to upgrade the Fiesta Bowl. Second, Patriots' owner Robert Kraft, who purchased the franchise in 1994, paid for the construction of the $325 million, 68,000-seat Gillette Stadium in Foxboro that opened in 2002. The construction began after the city of Foxboro approved the stadium deal in December 1999 and the state of Massachusetts devoted $70 million for roads, highway ramps and other infrastructure investments. Essentially, this project means that the Patriots will remain in Foxboro for the long term and not relocate to another city such as Los Angeles, California, or Hartford, Connecticut. Third, in fall 2000 Brown County voters in Wisconsin enacted a .5 percent sales tax to repay $160 million in loans for the $295 million expansion and renovation of Lambeau Field for the NFL Green Bay Packers. The state of Wisconsin will spend about $10 million for road improvements and other infrastructure work around the stadium, and the team charged season ticket holders a one-time fee to raise $93 million for the three-year project. Furthermore, in spring 2001 NFL owners approved a $13 million, fifteen-year loan to the Packers to offset its operating costs. Meanwhile, as of mid-to-late 2002 the financial decisions on the other NFL stadiums such as in Minneapolis and San Francisco were not complete.[24]

In 2002, the NFL Texans will play regular season home games at the $310 million, 75,000-seat Reliant Energy Stadium in Houston. Rental car and hotel taxes have been assigned to fund 63 percent of the stadium's cost while owner Robert McNair and the Houston Livestock Show and Rodeo will fund the balance. Given its public subsidy, the team estimates $30 million to $50 million in annual net operating income, which represents a meager 5 percent return on McNair's investment. Nevertheless, even though the financial return is expected to be low and team performances to be inferior in the short-term, there are tax benefits and other cash inflows that will make this project economically profitable in the long term for McNair and the Livestock Show and Rodeo.[25]

Besides the 19,100-seat Continental Airlines Arena in East Rutherford where the New Jersey Devils play, in the NHL taxpayer subsidies may be provided to renovate current arenas or construct new ice hockey rinks for the Islanders in the New York City-New Jersey area and the Coyotes in Los Arcos, Arizona. In 1999, the Devils and Cablevision Systems signed a letter of intent to explore the development and construction of a $206 million, 18,500-seat arena to be built above the commuter rail station at the Hoboken Terminal station. The proposal includes $30 million from the state of New Jersey for infrastructure renovations to provide space for the arena and train station. An alternate plan is the construction, by 2004, of an $85 million, 18,400-seat publicly funded arena at the Meadowlands Sports Complex. After 2002, a new $300 million, 16,300-seat Long

Island Arena may replace the thirty-year-old Nassau Veterans Memorial Coliseum, which is the 16,300-seat home rink of the Islanders. Team owners Howard Milstein and Steven Gluckstern offered to pay the arena's estimated $300 million construction costs, assuming that $30 million from New York State taxpayers would be allocated by the local government to subsidize the renovation of the Coliseum. In 1999, the voters in the city of Scottsdale and two other Arizona cities approved Proposition 300, which established a stadium district to fund a $624 million redevelopment of the Los Arcos Mall. The construction of a $170 million, 18,000-seat arena for the Coyotes is included in the project. As of late 2002, the specific location, construction costs, and taxpayer subidies of these new hockey arenas are being discussed between team owners and various government officials.[26]

SUMMARY

Chapter 7 describes how and why numerous U.S. government entities have historically provided taxpayer subsidies and other financial assistance to various franchises in the professional sports leagues. When public funds are allocated by the federal and local, county and state governments to construct or renovate sports arenas and stadiums, there are economic benefits and costs to communities, fans, taxpayers and team owners and players. Therefore, because of the income distribution effects and potential inequities of the subsidies, economists and public policy experts have normally opposed the use of taxpayer money for social investments in sports facilities. In short, this chapter provides the subsidy amounts when available, and identifies the teams in each sport that have prospered from taxpayer largesse during the 1990s and in 2000 and 2001.

Furthermore, Chapter 7 discusses which sports franchises seek government funds for the construction or rehabilitation of arenas and stadiums. In general, because of the resistance from conscientious citizen groups, the urgency to invest in public projects such as schools and roads, and the inflated costs to build and maintain sports complexes, a growing proportion of cities and taxpayers have become reluctant to subsidize the construction of an arena or stadium for wealthy owners and players in the professional leagues. This ensures that, in the future, each league commissioner and team owner will be required to improve his or her business and negotiation skills to conclude deals with government officials for taxpayer financial assistance to construct a publicly owned arena or stadium.

NOTES

1. Antitrust action has been an effective government policy instrument to detect and eliminate monopolistic business practices. For a review of antitrust history and its precedents as applied to the professional sports industry, see Steven R. Rivkin, "Sports Leagues and the Federal Antitrust Laws," in Roger G. Noll, ed., *Government and the Sports Business* (Washington, DC: The Brookings Institution, 1974), 389–395; Thomas A. Piraino, Jr., "The Antitrust Rationale for the Expansion of Professional Sports Leagues," *Ohio State Law Journal* (November 1996), 1677–1729. For an analysis of how sports cartels

behave and operate because of the antitrust exemption, see Lance E. Davis, "Self-Regulation in Baseball, 1909–71," in Roger G. Noll, ed., *Government and the Sports Business*, 349–386; James Quirk and Mohamed A. El-Hodiri, "An Economic Model of a Professional Sports League," *Journal of Political Economy* 79 (March/April 1975), 1302–1319.

2. To resolve the economic problems in the sports industry and to make the operating rules of sports leagues more consistent with the public interest, see Roger G. Noll, "Alternatives in Sports Policy," in Roger G. Noll, ed., *Government and the Sports Business*, 411–428.

3. Taxpayer subsidies of sports facilities are a controversial business and financial topic that has been studied by various economists. For the research performed on this issue, see Benjamin A. Okner, "Subsidies of Stadiums and Arenas," in Roger G. Noll, ed., *Government and the Sports Business*, 325–347. Besides Okner's article, there are books that have reported how taxpayer subsidies impact the professional sports industry. For a sample of these volumes, see Roger G. Noll and Andrew Zimbalist, eds., *Sports, Jobs and Taxes: The Economic Impact of Sports Teams and Stadiums* (Washington, DC: Brookings Institution Press, 1997); Mark S. Rosentraub, *Major League Losers: The Real Cost of Sports and Who's Paying for It* (New York: Basic Books, 1997); James Quirk and Rodney D. Fort, *Pay Dirt: The Business of Professional Team Sports* (Princeton, NJ: Princeton University Press, 1992). For a discussion of the legal implications that result when team owners seek public funds for private arenas and stadiums, which is called the "stadium shell game," see Michael E. Jones, *Sports Law* (Upper Saddle River, NJ: Prentice-Hall, 1999), 115–129.

4. Public funds used for the construction and maintenance of professional sports facilities affects the distribution and incidence of economic benefits and costs for the households and teams located in a metropolitan area. For a discussion of this issue, see Dennis Zimmerman, "Subsidizing Stadiums: Who Benefits, Who Pays?" in Roger G. Noll and Andrew Zimbalist, eds., *Sports, Jobs and Taxes: The Economic Impact of Sports Teams and Stadiums*, 119–145; Jordan Rappaport and Chad Wilkerson, "What Are the Benefits of Hosting a Major League Sports Franchise?" *Economic Review* (First Quarter 2001), 55–86; Adam M. Zaretsky, "Should Cities Pay for Sports Facilities?" *The Regional Economist* (April 2001), 5–9.

5. In addition to the articles and books referenced earlier in Chapter 7, other relevant sources were consulted to obtain information about professional sports coaches, games, leagues, managers, owners, players, seasons and teams. These sources included James Quirk and Rodney D. Fort, *Hard Ball: The Abuse of Power in Pro Team Sports* (Princeton, NJ: Princeton University Press, 1999); Frank P. Jozsa, Jr. and John J. Guthrie, Jr., *Relocating Teams and Expanding Leagues in Professional Sports: How the Major Leagues Respond to Market Conditions* (Westport, CT: Quorum Books, 1999); *The World Almanac and Book of Facts* (Mahwah, NJ: World Almanac Books, 1950–2001); "Ballparks," at http://www.ballparks.com cited 1 November 2001. Each sport leagues' Web site was frequently accessed for player and team information. For example, see "Major League Baseball," at http://www.mlb.com cited 1 August 2001; "National Basketball Association," at http://www.nba.com cited 1 August 2001; "National Football League," at http://www.nfl.com cited 1 August 2001; "National Hockey League," at http://www. nhl.com cited 1 August 2001.

6. Ibid.

7. To examine the economic returns and risks from asset-backed securities that were issued to finance sports facilities, see Nancy D. Holt, "Pepsi Center Scores in Financing Game," *Wall Street Journal* (3 March 1999), B12.

8. Ibid.

9. M.R. Kropko, "Cleveland Browns Stadium Sponsors Get Four Gates," at http://sports.yahoo.com cited 8 July 1999; Mark Hyman, "From Tears to Cheers in Cleveland," *Business Week* (16 November 1998), 108–116; "Lerner Gets the Browns," at http://www.cnnsi.com cited 8 September 1998.

10. As a member of the NL West Division since 1998, the expansion Arizona Diamondbacks has been a success story. Nevertheless, the club is one of baseball's biggest financial losers. For more information about the franchise's financial status, see Sam Walker, "Arizona Baseball Team Is Losing More Than Fans," *Wall Street Journal* (22 September 2000), B1, B4; Idem, "The Price of Victory," *Wall Street Journal* (11 June 1999), B1, B4; Jon Talton, "Stadium Tax Gives Phoenix a 2nd Chance," *Charlotte Observer* (12 July 1998), 1D, 3D; Anne Brady, "Visions of Phoenix-Area Expansion Differ," *Wall Street Journal* (14 August 2000), B11A.

11. The concerns of baseball fans, citizens' interest groups, city officials and team owners about the construction costs at Safeco Field created tension in Seattle. For the facts of this dispute, see Jay Greene and Ken Belson, "The Mariners Catch a Tsunami," *Business Week* (25 June 2001), 98–99; Josie Karp, "Squabble in Seattle," at http://www.cnnsi.com cited 13 July 1999; "License to Sell," at http://www.cnnsi.com cited 12 July 1999; "Ballpark Financing," at http://www.mariners.org cited 8 June 1998.

12. For information about the NFL Tampa Bay Buccaneers' stadium, see "Raymond James Stadium," at http://www.ballparks.com cited 6 October 1998; "Introducing ... " at http://www.cnnsi.com cited 7 July 1998; "Major League Baseball," at http://www.mlb.com cited 1 August 2001.

13. The cost overruns of the NFL Bengals' stadium in Cincinnati prompted public criticism from numerous county officials and taxpayers. For whether this criticism was justified, see "Budget Runneth Over," at http://www.cnnsi.com cited 10 August 2000; "Bengals' New Stadium Receives Approval," at http://football.yahoo.com cited 3 February 1998; "Bengals Stadium Gets Cash Infusion," at http://www.cnnsi.com cited 16 February 2000;

14. Dallas Cowboys owner Jerry Jones is a successful entrepreneur and franchise proprietor. For his plans to revitalize the team, see "Planning Ahead," at http://www.cnnsi.com cited 11 June 2001; Daniel Fisher and Michael K. Ozanian, "Cowboy Capitalism," *Forbes* (20 September 1999), 170–178.

15. The vast Los Angeles complex, which includes the Staples Center, raises hopes for a downtown revival. See Stacy Kravetz, "A New Sports Home Rises," *Wall Street Journal* (23 September 1998), B12; Stefan Fatsis, "Staples to Attach Its Name to Arena in Los Angeles," *Wall Street Journal* (2 December 1997), B6.

16. John W. Henry purchased the NL Marlins from Wayne Huizenga. To ensure that his club would survive in southern Florida, Henry pursued several options for a new ballpark in the Miami area. For the obstacles Henry encountered to obtain government subsidies for the new facility and other ownership problems, see "A Brick Wall," at http://www.cnnsi.com cited 27 November 1999; "Owners Agree to Sale of Marlins," at http://www.cnnsi.com cited 14 January 1999; "Huizenga's Legacy," at http://www.cnnsi.com cited 13 January 1999. For Henry's sale of the franchise in 2002, see "Sources Say Marlins Owner Ready to Sell," *Charlotte Observer* (23 November 2001), 14C; "Sales of Marlins, Expos Imminent," *Charlotte Observer* (2 February 2002), 8C; Ronald Blum, "Expos Marlins Switches Approved," *Charlotte Observer* (13 February 2002), 6C

17. In 2002, Busch Stadium in St. Louis was the fourth oldest ballpark in the National League. The senior baseball facilities were Wrigley Field in Chicago, and then Dodger Stadium in Los Angeles and Shea Stadium in New York. See "Cardinals Agree to Deal

for New Stadium," at http://www.yahoo.com cited 1 November 2001; "Ballparks," at http://www.ballparks.com cited 1 November 2001.

18. After Proposition C was approved by voters in 1998, there was much controversy and legal opposition from various groups about the construction of a new ballpark in San Diego for the NL Padres. For a discussion of the vote and this debate, see Dara Akiko Williams, "Judge Rejects Effort to Put Ballpark Back on the Ballot," at http://sports.yahoo.com cited 28 February 2000; "Padres Ballpark Opponent Files Lawsuit," at http://sports.yahoo.com cited 16 February 2000; "Rain Delay," at http://www.cnnsi.com cited 28 June 1999; "Padres Get New Home in 2002," at http://www.cnnsi.com cited 4 November 1998.

19. For a description of the new ballparks for the NL Houston Astros and Pittsburgh Pirates, see "The Ballpark at Union Station," at http://www.ballparks.com cited 1 November 2001; "Sticker Shock," at http://www.cnnsi.com cited 20 July 1998; Stefan Fatsis, "Pittsburgh's Field of Dreams," *Wall Street Journal* (11 April 2001), B1, B4; "Model of Intimacy," at http://www.cnnsi.com cited 17 March 1998; Scott Thurm, "Stadium Jinx: What to Call Enron Field? 'Enron Folds,' Maybe," *Wall Street Journal* (4 December 2001), A1, A10.

20. For specific information about the current arenas for the NBA's Pacers, Spurs and Trail Blazers, see "Ballparks," at http://www.ballparks.com cited 1 November 2001. Located in downtown Indianapolis, Conseco Fieldhouse is the home arena of the Pacers. See Kathleen Johnston, "Pacers Lease Contains Financial Guarantees," *Indianapolis Star* (5 November 1997), 16; John Helyar, "An Unpalatial Arena Designed to Please Just Plain Folks," *Wall Street Journal* (10 October 1997), B1, B11.

21. The proposed taxpayer subsidies to construct ballparks for the Boston Red Sox and Philadelphia Phillies are discussed in several articles. For a sample of these publications, see "New Fenway," at http://www.cnnsi.com cited 1 November 2001; "House Speaker Ups Ante," at http://www.cnsnsi.com cited 23 May 2000; Meg Vaillancourt, "Menino Wants High Return on Investment in Fenway," *Boston Globe* (11 May 2000), C1, C17; "Phillies Unveil Plans for New Park," at http://www.cnnsi.com cited 28 June 2001.

22. Houston voters in Harris County rejected while San Antonio voters in Bexar County approved referendums to use tax money for the construction of new arenas for their respective NBA teams. See "Rockets Rejected," at http://www.cnnsi.com cited 3 November 1999; "Deal in Jeopardy," at http://www.cnnsi.com cited 30 August 1999; "Spurs Break Ground on New Arena," at http://www.cnnsi.com cited 23 August 2000; "Home Sweet Home," at http://www.cnnsi.com cited 3 November 1999; Sam Walker, "Building a New Arena? A Winning Team Helps," *Wall Street Journal* (25 June 1999), B1.

23. Two articles discussed the legal implications of public funding for a new arena in Memphis for the NBA Grizzlies. See "Memphis Arena on Hold," at http://www.cnnsi.com cited 11 July 2001; Woody Baird, "Shelby County Commission OKs New Arena for NBA," at http://sports.yahoo.com cited 12 June 2001.

24. The use of taxpayer money to construct or renovate football stadiums or provide infrastructure improvements for the NFL's Arizona Cardinals, New England Patriots and Green Bay Packers are considered public investment by government. See "Quarter of Possibilities," at http://www.cnnsi.com cited 16 November 2000; "Stadium Measure Narrowly Passes," at http://www.cnnsi.com cited 8 November 2000; Anne Brady, "Visions of Phoenix-Area Expansion Differ," *Wall Street Journal* (14 August 2000), B11A; "Patriots Plan New Stadium for 2002," at http://www.cnnsi.com cited 19 April 2000; "Helping Hand," at http://www.cnnsi.com cited 23 May 2001; "Taxing Proposition," at

http://www.cnnsi.com cited 13 September 2000; "Pack Asks for Green," at http://www.cnnsi.com cited 15 May 2000.

25. For the expansion plans and operations of the NFL Houston Texans and its stadium, see "Finally an Identity," at http://www.cnnsi.com cited 7 September 2000; "Building a Foundation," at http://www.cnnsi.com cited 19 April 2000; Andrew Zimbalist, "The NFL's New Math," *Wall Street Journal* (13 October 1999), A30.

26. For the profiles of past, present and future ice hockey rinks for the current teams in the NHL, see "Ballparks," at http://www.ballparks.com cited 1 November 2001.

Conclusion

American Sports Empire concludes by restating how interdependent and linked the prominent U.S. professional sports leagues and their member franchises are with respect to team owners and players, the media industry, fans and various government organizations. These mutual interrelationships underscore how, when and why the AL and NL in MLB, and the NBA, NFL and NHL have each expanded in membership and prospered since 1950 to become highly publicized, reputable and well-recognized institutions in America's culture and economy. Given this environment and overview, the purpose, scope and theme of each chapter in *American Sports Empire* is herewith highlighted and reviewed. After this is completed, the future roles of U.S. professional teams sports and leagues are assessed.

Chapter 1 reveals how each sports league emerged, developed, matured and revitalized itself throughout the twentieth century. As the leagues formed and developed, there were important characters, events, incidents and reforms that determined the composition and structure of the organizations. In turn, these factors influenced the growth in the number of franchises and games, and in the volume of regular season and postseason attendance for each league and its respective teams. For example, professional team competition in MLB began in the mid-to-late 1800s. Thus, by 1950 the two leagues and sixteen clubs in professional baseball had formally established the game rules and standards to dominate and overwhelm the other three professional sports in exposure and notoriety. Conversely, in 1950 American fans and the general public perceived the NHL as essentially a Canadian-based sport. As such, the league had received only minimal exposure from the U.S. media industry and lackluster support from the nation's fans and spectators who preferred to watch games played between the teams that existed in the AL, NL and NFL. Furthermore, before the NBA became a full-fledged organization in the late 1940s, professional basketball in America was a fragmented sport and less popular than big-league baseball or the NFL, which had struggled to organize itself into a single entity in the early 1920s. In short, by 1950 each sports league had been founded and was distinguished by its organizational title, and especially by fans and the media industry.

After the midpoint of the twentieth century, the four major professional sports grew in entertainment value and popularity when franchises proliferated across the United States and when the leagues signed moneymaking broadcast contracts with the preeminent radio stations and television networks in the nation. Thereafter, individuals and families who lived in rural and urban areas were exposed to one or more of the professional sports leagues. These households became fans who listened to the radio and watched on television as well-known players demonstrated their athletic skills and performed during games. Meanwhile, competitive rivalries developed among many of the professional teams, which were located in adjacent geographic areas and played in the same division or conference. In other words, rather than retrench or stabilize to maintain its membership, each league expanded after the early-to-mid-1950s. (The NHL, however, remained fixed at six teams until 1967 when six U.S.-based franchises joined the league.) However, as the seasons progressed several franchises within each sports league either folded or moved to sites in metropolitan areas that were located in the U.S. South, Southwest and West. To recap this strategy, in Chapter 1 there are tables that contain the years and sites of league expansions and team movements, which had occurred from 1950 to 2000 inclusive.

Besides the coverage of these activities and events, the issue of whether and to what extent competitive balance or parity existed in playing strengths between each league's teams is emphasized and discussed. To analyze this issue, for selected clubs in each league the average number of wins and win-loss percentages and the total number of postseason appearances are listed and tabled as indicators of team performance. Then, the distributions of the performance data are interpreted for each league to determine the degree of equality that prevailed among clubs from the 1990 to 2000 seasons.

In contrast to other studies that measure parity, the statistics derived for Chapter 1 indicate that the most evenly balanced leagues were the AL and NL, while the NBA ranked as the least balanced league. However, since the mid-1990s the dominant performances of large-market, teams such as the NL Atlanta Braves and AL New York Yankees have furthered widened the disparities in total payrolls and playing strengths among the various franchises in MLB. If and when professional baseball decides to contract in size after 2002, the small-to-medium-market clubs in Kansas City, Miami, Minneapolis, Montreal, Oakland, San Diego and Tampa Bay are each vulnerable sports organizations for the league to disband, merge or relocate to another site in a large market. Likewise, after 2002 any inferior clubs in the NBA and NHL are candidates for elimination or relocation, and especially the ice hockey franchises located in Canada. Fortunately, because of the league's liberal revenue-sharing policies and guaranteed multi-billion-dollar television contracts, only a few NFL franchise owners have threatened to relocate their teams or expressed severe short- or long-term financial problems.

Since the mid-to-late-1980s, each sports league and the majority of teams have been confronted with and distracted by business, operation and finance issues. That is, the leagues have experienced one or more of the following: an escalation in player salaries and team payrolls; flat or moderate growth in average game attendance; player misbehavior and rudeness to each other and fans during games and illegal activity elsewhere; a lethargic growth in its television ratings. Despite these conditions and problems, however, for each league the total cash inflows received at the teams' arenas or stadiums from apparel, food and merchandise sales, and the revenues from gate receipts, media broadcasts and corporate sponsorships have generally increased, particularly for the large-market franchises located in Chicago, New York and Los Angeles. Yet, because of higher operating costs and other expenses several of the small-market and a few of the mid-sized and large-market clubs in each league have periodically experienced financial shortfalls. As such, these teams played the regular season schedule with little hope or opportunity to excel in their divisions and qualify for the league playoffs. To overcome or prevent this situation from reccurring in the future, each league will be required to make some complex and hard-nosed business decisions if it wishes to remain competitive and a well-balanced organization in the marketplace. It will be necessary, therefore, for one or more leagues to terminate its underfunded small-to-medium-market franchises and dismiss their inept owners. Furthermore, some leagues will be forced to expand the amounts and types of revenues that are shared by their member clubs, establish lower minimum player salary levels and ceilings on total team payrolls, negotiate more lucrative broadcast contracts with the various cable, satellite and television networks, reform the player draft system, enforce the penalties for substance abuse violations, and increase the luxury tax rates to penalize the high payroll clubs for irrational and unjustified expenditures on superstar players. In sum, the cooperation and visionary leadership from the respective league commissioners and member team owners, and compromise from the players unions and sports agents will be necessary to adopt any significant reforms and implement strategies in the early-to-mid-2000s.

With these topics and issues aside, Chapter 1 proceeds to describe the creation, development and progress of the minor leagues in professional baseball and hockey, the NBDL in professional basketball, and the NFL Europe League in professional football. In retrospect, because of innovative and passionate franchise owners who invest in and promote fun-filled family activities at games, and who sell tickets, stadium food and teams' merchandise at reasonable prices, minor league baseball is perhaps the most popular sport in the United States. Since the mid-to-late-1980s, most of the minor league ballparks in America have been reconfigured and renovated to meet the standards adopted by MLB. Furthermore, the stadiums are located at sites whereby sports fans can attend games without experiencing traffic congestion and long walks from distant parking lots.

As a result, the attendance at regular season and postseason games has boomed as entrepreneurial owners and former MLB players have cleverly marketed their minor league franchises. Inevitably, because of these and other developments the positive growth trend in minor league baseball will continue in the twenty-first century.

In 2001, the NBDL launched its first season while the NFL Europe League celebrated its tenth. As player development organizations for the NBA and NFL, respectively, the franchises in these leagues will succeed if their cash inflows from gate attendance and television broadcasts are near break-even, and if the parent clubs continue to subsidize their operations. Meanwhile, because there are optional affiliations and contractual agreements with the NHL and other independent professional hockey organizations, the minor hockey leagues will experience moderate instability each season because many of the franchises are not well-established and profitable businesses at their current locations. For the reasons cited, despite periods of growth the NBDL and minor leagues in professional hockey are less financially secure than minor league baseball and the NFL Europe League. To be sure, each of these sports leagues consists of average, inferior and superior franchises that struggle to increase revenues and operating incomes during individual seasons and in the long term.

In part, Chapter 2 highlights a sample of prominent teams in each sport that organized and competed prior to 1950. During this period, some clubs succeeded while others performed poorly and either bankrupted and folded or relocated to another metropolitan area. As the seasons progressed from the early 1900s to the late 1940s, intense rivalries gradually developed when teams were placed in divisions and conferences of an emerging or established sports league. Because of league competitiveness and team rivalries, the general public became enamored with and identified the popular and successful coaches, managers and players. In turn, this inspired fans to enthusiastically support their hometown clubs that performed to win games. Eventually, these teams gained recognition and prospered as a professional sports organization in their community and within the market area. In short, by 1950 each league had its well-known championship clubs such as the New York Yankees and St. Louis Cardinals in MLB, Philadelphia Warriors and Washington Capitols in the NBA, Chicago Bears and Washington Redskins in the NFL, and the Boston Bruins and Toronto Maple Leafs in the NHL.

There are several tables in Chapter 2 that list the most successful professional sports franchises in each league for ten seasons from the 1950s to 1990s inclusive. To measure their success, the top-performing teams in each sport were identified and then ranked based on each club's ability to win divisions and conference titles, as well as a league championship such as the NBA Playoff, Stanley Cup, Super Bowl or World Series. The contributions of the coaches, managers and key players that represented the outstanding teams are also discussed in this section of Chapter 2. Overall, during the fifty seasons—1950 through 1999—the dominant teams by sport were the Montreal Canadiens in the NHL,

New York Yankees in the AL, Brooklyn/Los Angeles Dodgers and St. Louis Cardinals (tie) in the NL, Dallas Cowboys in the NFL and the Boston Celtics and Los Angeles Lakers (tie) in the NBA.

Because many of the outstanding coaches, managers and players remained with their organizations for several seasons, some teams formed dynasties and remained champions. For instance, the Canadiens won five consecutive Stanley Cups in the late 1950s and four each in the late 1960s and 1970s. Likewise, the Yankees won six World Series in the 1950s, two each in the 1960s and 1970s, and three in the 1990s. In each decade, other great clubs that excelled besides the aforementioned franchises included the NFL Cleveland Browns in the 1950s, NFL Green Bay Packers in the 1960s, AL Oakland Athletics in the 1970s, NHL Edmonton Oilers in the 1980s and the NBA Chicago Bulls in the 1990s. The Athletics, Cardinals, Dodgers and Yankees aside, during a series of seasons other superb MLB teams that played competitively and won pennants and World Series were the Atlanta Braves, Baltimore Orioles, Cincinnati Reds, Pittsburgh Pirates and Toronto Blue Jays.

To evaluate the performances of inferior teams, Table A.2 in the Appendix contains the clubs in each sport that failed to win divisions, conference titles or league championships during ten consecutive seasons, which are distributed each period in the table. If ranked by league, these teams were primarily members of the NFL, and then of the NHL, NL, NBA and AL. To identify the most recent dismal performers, in Chapter 2 a table was prepared that lists the average win-loss percentages or points earned, the number of wild-card and playoff appearances, and the estimated market values for the least successful teams of the 1990s. Because they existed for less than ten seasons from 1990 to 1999 inclusive, the expansion franchises in each league were excluded from the table, while the relocated teams were included and therefore could qualify as an inferior performer. Indeed, there were ten clubs in the NBA, three in the AL, and two each in the NL, NFL and NHL that failed to win titles and championships in the 1990s. The lowest win-loss percentages in each league belonged to the AL California/Anaheim Angels, NL Chicago Cubs, NBA Dallas Mavericks and NFL Phoenix/Arizona Cardinals. In the NHL, the Edmonton Oilers earned the least points per season in the 1990s.

The final portion of Chapter 2 explains how selected franchise owners in the sports leagues have devised strategies and implemented plans to improve the future performances of their inferior teams. Strategically, to expand its payroll and hire high-salaried free agents and extend the contracts of experienced players, a franchise's cash inflow must increase by a large amount. Usually, this will occur when a new taxpayer-subsidized arena or stadium is constructed for the club, when a team introduces and implements innovative marketing campaigns, and perhaps when a change in ownership commences. These productive actions and tactics are among the strategies that are illustrated and discussed to conclude Chapter 2.

When professional sports franchises economically flounder, stagnate or prosper, and teams consistently lose or win games and championships, it is the business acumen, communication ability, executive skill, and the leadership and vision provided by the owners that is partly responsible for the organization's failure, mediocre performance or success. To further explore that hypothesis, Chapter 3 applies the information about leagues as portrayed in Chapter 1 and teams as documented in Chapter 2 to examine the risks and roles of the various owners who control and operate at least one franchise within the major professional sports leagues. Initially, Chapter 3 describes how and why franchise ownership types have changed throughout the 1900s. That is, the chapter assesses why corporations and especially entertainment conglomerates and multimedia companies have increasingly replaced general and limited partnerships, private syndicates and single proprietorships as team owners. The ownership sales for a sample of franchises are discussed next. A table is presented that contains the average three-year pre- and post-sale performances of twenty-five teams, that is, five in each sports league that had experienced at least one ownership transfer since 1950.

In short, the tabled data about the effectiveness of the twenty-five owners are interpreted as follows. During the post-sale seasons, a higher proportion of AL and NFL clubs improved their win-loss percentages and won more titles after the new owners assumed control of the organizations. Conversely, on average the NL and NBA team performances worsened with new ownership and relative to the pre-sale seasons when the former owners headed the enterprise. In the NHL, the performances of two teams improved and two declined subsequent to the sale of the franchise to new owners. One club, the Montreal Canadiens, averaged ninety-two points per season and won two titles each in the three seasons before and after its sale in 1957. In total, while performing for new owners 44 percent (11) of the clubs averaged a higher win-loss percentage during the post-sale seasons, and 52 percent (13) experienced a lower performance. To explain why the differences occurred, for each of the twenty-five teams listed in the table the ownership changes are discussed in further detail relative to the franchises' pre- and post-sale performances and sales prices.

Besides cash flows and net earnings, operating income is an accounting value that various analysts use to measure the financial success of an organization. To determine how that value relates to sports team ownership, in Chapter 3 the average and total operating incomes for franchises that existed during the mid-1990s were researched, entered into tables and then interpreted. The data reveals that the average annual operating incomes within each professional sports league are positive for 85 percent (29) of the NFL franchises, 76 percent (22) of the NBA teams, 69 percent (20) of the NHL clubs, and in MLB, for 68 percent (11) of the NL and 47 percent (7) of the AL teams. Indeed, several teams in each league recorded values that were at or below $1 million per year. These estimates suggest that, if expressed in percentages, the investment returns for the respective team owners were moderate because of the financial and operating risks of the professional sports franchise business. Nevertheless, according to economists, because each league is a cartel the sales prices of most teams have historically increased by large amounts despite the clubs' unimpressive annual operating in-come values. For the financial wherewithal of selected owners and to comple-ment the tables in Chapter 3, Table A.3 in the Appendix was prepared. It lists and ranks the wealthiest team owners within each sports league as of 1993.

After the analysis of teams' operating incomes concluded, six relevant state-ments were framed as current sports business issues and then discussed. Basi-cally, these issues expose the motivation, philosophy and strategy of selected professional sports franchise owners within each league. As such, the statements include the recent ownership actions and decisions that involved team reloca-tion and league expansion, sports marketing programs, escalation of player salaries and team payroll costs, revenue-sharing reforms and ticket price infla-tion. In effect, the majority of owners apply their experiences and skills as busi-nessmen, and they compel their teams to compete for titles and championships even though some clubs are located in small-to-medium metropolitan areas that contain relatively few radio and television stations and an obsolete arena or sta-dium. In any event, the discussion of the six statements summed up Chapter 3.

The contributions of the owner, and his or her administrative staff, coaches and/or managers aside, each team's achievements in the regular season and in any postseason appearances are primarily dependent on the individual skills and collective teamwork of the players. Thus, the role of players who perform in a professional sport is the focus of Chapter 4. As the content is organized, the chapter first describes the legal rights and status of players before the 1970s. To that end, the elements included in a typical Collective Bargaining Agreement that exists between a professional sports league and a player association or union are identified and examined. After that information is explored, for each sports league there were tables presented that depict the relationship between the total payroll of each team and its performances in two nonconsecutive seasons that occurred from 1997 to 2000 inclusive. The ratio, payroll per win, was derived for each team and placed in the tables to measure how cost effective and efficient franchise owners were in winning games with respect to player salaries. Then, for the two nonconsecutive seasons referenced in each table the teams are ranked according to payroll per win to discover whether their efficiency changed rela-tive to the other league clubs. To an extent, the tabled ratios and ranks reveal how each owner's decisions about total team payroll influenced the players' per-formances in each of the seasons.

In general, the payroll per win ratio increased for 86 percent (12) of the teams in the AL, 100 percent (16) in the NL, 79 percent (23) in the NBA, 77 percent (23) in the NFL and 69 percent (17) in the NHL. Thus, based on the two non-consecutive seasons studied, these percentages indicate that MLB owners paid proportionately more money in player salaries for each win than did the own-ers in the other three sports. As expected, within each league the majority of teams changed their rank from season to season. To evaluate the tabled results, the least cost-efficient team ranked first or realized the highest payroll per win. Therefore, this club placed at the top of the table in that season. Conversely, the team with the smallest ratio ranked last. Therefore, it was the most cost-efficient club in its respective league that year and placed at the bottom of the table.

From one season to another, 57 percent (8) of the teams in the AL fell in rank, which means that their payroll per win declined and cost efficiency increased. To interpret the other leagues, if the rank improvements are expressed in percentages and the number of teams in parentheses, there were 57 percent (17) in the NFL, 38 percent (11) in the NBA, 38 percent (10) in the NHL and 31 percent (5) in the NL. In other words, based on percentages the most cost-effective owners existed in the AL and NFL, NBA and NHL, and then the NL. Given these results for the various seasons studied, in total the payroll per win increased, and cost efficiency decreased for the majority of franchise owners. This outcome likely depressed the operating incomes of the inefficient teams, and especially those located in small-to-medium markets such as the AL Tampa Bay Devil Rays, NL Cincinnati Reds, NBA Portland Trail Blazers, NFL Carolina Panthers and NHL Anaheim Mighty Ducks. Rephrased, for the sports leagues combined, the players' incomes rose proportionately more than the teams' wins.

To conclude Chapter 4, the focus switches from payroll per win to a discussion of the presence and influence of foreign ballplayers, especially in MLB. Besides identifying the home countries and leagues of foreign athletes, this section reveals their incentives and opportunities to play baseball in the United States. In the future, as MLB and the other professional leagues expand their media coverage and transmit radio and television broadcasts of games and other events into far-flung international markets, more skilled foreign ballplayers will try to emigrate from their nations to America and participate in professional minor and major league sports programs. Alternatively, if U.S. immigration policy tightens and visas are restricted because of security reasons, the proportion of foreign ballplayers that exists in MLB will fall below 25 percent by 2005.

Chapter 5 examines how and why companies in the media industry eagerly cooperate and conduct business with officials in the professional sports leagues and franchise owners. Historically, each medium such as magazines, newspapers, radio and television has provided its audience with sports statistics and other general and detailed information about games, league standings and the performances of teams and players during the regular season and postseason playoffs. Of the sports leagues researched, MLB received the most attention from the media industry prior to 1950 when daily newspapers in cities published box scores, the batting and fielding averages of players and various team-specific performance data. Furthermore, because of an inadequate interstate roadway system between the major cities in the United States before 1950, a high portion of fans listened to a play-by-play account of professional games when the events were announced on the nation's radio stations. Due to technological advancements after 1950, however, television gradually replaced the radio to become the dominant medium for the broadcasts of games as well as a significant revenue source for teams. In the 1990s, besides the television networks there were cable and satellite stations, as well as the Internet, which increasingly became reputable communication sources that exposed and promoted sports events, leagues, players and teams to audiences and markets throughout the world.

Since the mid-1990s, authorities in each professional league have concluded business deals with a variety of entertainment and media companies to raise more cash and operating income for member franchises and to maximize the growth of the sport. Chapter 5 illustrates some examples of the transactions that occurred among the various sports leagues and media companies from 1997 to 2001 inclusive. As reported, there were multibillion-dollar contracts signed when negotiated settlements came to fruition between selected leagues and ABC, AOL Time Warner Inc., CBS, ESPN, Fox, NBC, TNT or Turner Sports. Furthermore, a number of online experiments and innovations proved to be worthwhile ventures for several sports franchises. For example, some clubs' marketers established real-time auctions and sold clothing, game and season tickets, and a variety of other merchandise on the information highway. Other teams raised cash from the sales of players' equipment and from the components of abandoned arenas and stadiums. Undoubtedly, as desktop, lap, and notebook computers proliferate in homes throughout the world, the Internet will expand its role as a media and revenue source for the sports leagues. Indeed, the primary beneficiaries of this development will be those team owners who are most knowledgeable about software programs and the application of online marketing systems.

A study of media markets that serve as sports areas is also included in Chapter 5. Arranged according to the number of television households as of the 1997–1998 Broadcast Season, a table was created that lists and ranks each U.S. Designated Market Area (DMA) where at least one professional sports franchise was located in 1997. Then, the quantities of three variables—the population within the respective consolidated or metropolitan statistical area, and the number of radio and television stations and newspapers in circulation within the largest city of each DMA—were collected and used to analyze the teams. In total, this data revealed why the media revenues varied for the U.S.-based sports franchises that existed within the boundaries of small, mid-sized and large DMAs during 1997.

Due to the number of television households within their media markets, the first-ranked New York, second-ranked Los Angeles, third-ranked Chicago and fifth-ranked San Francisco-Oakland-San Jose Areas each contained five or more professional sports teams. Otherwise, there were six areas with four teams, eight areas with three teams, ten areas with two teams and nine areas with one team. In sum, the table in Chapter 5 includes thirty-seven DMAs, which were the home sites of 103 sports franchises in 1997. According to the distribution of teams within the DMAs, there were twelve teams in the AL, fourteen in the NL, twenty-seven in the NBA, thirty in the NFL and twenty in the NHL. Based on the tabled values and an assessment of the three variables, the top ten DMAs contained 46 percent (48) of the franchises and the majority of newspaper subscribers, population and television households. Thus, in 1997 these ten DMAs were the dominant sports areas in the United States.

As compiled by Nielsen Media Research, in the 2001–2002 Broadcast Season there were forty DMAs that geographically enclosed 110 professional sports teams. Relative to the 1997–1998 Broadcast Season, four years later a relocated club appeared in the thirtieth-ranked Nashville and forty-first-ranked Memphis DMAs and an expansion team in the ninth-ranked Atlanta, fourteenth-ranked Tampa Bay-St. Petersburg, sixteenth-ranked Phoenix, thirtieth-ranked Nashville and thirty-fourth-ranked Columbus DMAs. Grouped, the top ten DMAs in the United States remained intact as in the 1997–1998 Broadcast Season, but they contained proportionately fewer teams. That is, they contained 44 percent (49) rather than 46 percent (48) of the clubs. Furthermore, except for the NHL each league had added one franchise. Apparently, because of nonuniform demographic and geographic boundary measurements, the Nielsen Media Research did not rank the eight Canadian-based franchises in the 1997–1998 or 2001–2002 Broadcast Seasons.

Chapter 6, which profiles America's sports fans and how they feel about, relate to and support their favorite professional teams, includes four distinct topics. Initially, the chapter reviews the research performed by various for-profit marketing and media companies that, from survey data, studied the results of questionnaires to determine sports fans' emotions about and preferences for teams. After each company's research is highlighted and interpreted, a table reveals the average ticket prices for fans to attend games in MLB, and in the NBA, NFL and NHL during four recent seasons. These values are compared and analyzed because they partially reflect the pricing strategies of team owners in each league and the behavior of potential spectators who respond when changes in the admission cost to watch games are implemented. Subsequently, another table that contains the Fan Cost Indexes for each sports league is presented and reviewed in the chapter. Finally, based on previous surveys and index points each professional team is ranked according to specific characteristics, which in total measure the commitment, devotion and respect that fans have for their hometown sports franchises. Titled as Sports Loyalty Indexes by Brand Keys Inc., in Chapter 6 the ranks of the top and bottom five or more clubs in each league are portrayed in tables and then discussed. With that overview of Chapter 6, the specific topics about fans are summarized in the next four paragraphs.

Based on its public-opinion polls, the Gallup Organization determined that spectators' favorite sports to watch were regular season and postseason games in professional football. After that, competitive contests in basketball, baseball and ice hockey were preferred. A business research company, Scarborough Sports Marketing, discovered how fans of each sport differed with respect to their personal income levels, educational and marital statuses, computer experiences and online activities. A third reputable organization, Harris Interactive Inc., classified fans as primarily the Casual/Championship type and then as the Non-Fan, Diehard and Anti-Fan types. In total, the results of the well-documented studies from the three organizations provide qualitative and quantitative measurements and business statistics about fans that benefit the sports leagues and franchise owners. That is, this information is important to consider when the decision-makers in professional sports plan and implement their annual and long-term marketing and operation strategies to maximize the profits of their franchises while located within a specific-sized DMA.

In the 2001 season, the highest average ticket price per spectator was paid for admission to NFL games and the lowest for entry to MLB games. Generally, from the 1998 to 2001 seasons inclusive the majority of franchise owners substantially raised the ticket prices at home games if their teams planned to play their regular season schedule in a new arena or stadium. In recent years, this occurred for the AL Tigers at Comerica Park in Detroit, NL Brewers at Miller Park in Milwaukee, NBA Mavericks at the American Airlines Center in Dallas, NFL Redskins at FedEx Field in Landover, Maryland, and the NHL Kings at the Staples Center in Los Angeles. Furthermore, some franchise owners periodically increased home ticket prices to offset the inflated contracts of free agents and experienced veteran players even if the athletes had overachieved during the previous season. Apparently, the respective owners decided that the total payroll of the team must be enlarged in order to retain the quality players and to compete for and win a division, conference title and league championship. For example, in the late 1990s the NL Arizona Diamondbacks hired free agent pitchers Randy Johnson and Curt Shilling and won the 2001 World Series. In sum, economic theory suggests that although a team's attendance is expected to decrease because of higher ticket prices, its revenues from gate receipts may actually increase and thereby benefit the owner. As such, those spectators who decided to attend home games and root for their heroes and a team victory inevitably spent more money for tickets and perhaps for apparel, food and merchandise at the arena or stadium.

The Fan Cost Index (FCI) measures the estimated total cost for a four-person family to attend a regular season game of a professional team. Besides the payments for tickets, the FCI includes a typical household's expenditures to purchase assorted types of beverages, foods, game programs and hats, and to pay for parking fees. At $303.33 a family, in 2001 the NFL had the highest FCI and at $144.98 a family, MLB had the lowest. Within each sports league, the highest FCIs per team and place were $214 for the AL Red Sox in Boston, $197 for the NL Mets in New York City, $460 for the NBA Knickerbockers in New York City, $442 for the NFL Redskins in Landover, Maryland, and $386 for the NHL Stars in Dallas. Interestingly, for various economic and sport-specific reasons the NBA's FCI declined by 1.6 percent ($4.53) from the 2000–2001 to 2001–2002 seasons. This percentage change is the first decrease in an index of a major sports league since Team Marketing Report began to assemble and publish the FCIs in 1990.

As obtained from questionnaires issued and compiled by Brand Keys Inc., from 1999 to 2001 inclusive, the sports league teams that received the highest and lowest scores on the Sports Loyalty Indexes were ranked and tabled in Chapter 6.

The top-ranked clubs included the AL's New York Yankees and Cleveland Indians, NL's Houston Astros and Atlanta Braves, NBA's Los Angeles Lakers and Phoenix Suns, NFL's Jacksonville Jaguars and Green Bay Packers, and the NHL's Detroit Red Wings and New Jersey Devils. Based on their pure entertainment value, authenticity, fan bonding, and history and tradition, these franchises were the most revered and well-respected organizations in their respective leagues according to the surveys submitted by sports fans. Conversely, the two bottom-ranked teams in each league included the AL's Anaheim Angels and Minnesota Twins, NL's Florida Marlins and Montreal Expos, NBA's Washington Wizards and Los Angeles Clippers, NFL's Carolina Panthers and Oakland Raiders, and the NHL's Anaheim Mighty Ducks and Chicago Blackhawks.

Following Chapter 6's discussion of fans, Chapter 7 highlights when and why the U.S. federal and various city, county and state governments have authorized and provided financial assistance to benefit the professional sports leagues. First, the chapter succinctly clarifies how government legislation and policies affect sports fans, franchise owners and team players. According to economists, these groups are the chief beneficiaries of government largess, which is the cash from taxpayer subsidies. Second, the chapter then identifies those professional sports franchises in specific U.S. metropolitan areas that relied on public funds for the construction of an arena or stadium. Since 1990, the recipients of taxpayer subsidies included four teams each in the Atlanta and Denver areas, three each in the Cleveland, Phoenix, Seattle and Tampa Bay areas, two each in the Anaheim, Baltimore, Buffalo, Cincinnati, Dallas, Los Angeles, Miami, Minneapolis-St. Paul, Nashville, Oakland, St. Louis and San Diego areas, and one team each in several other areas such as Indianapolis, Raleigh, and San Antonio.

Nevertheless, because of underdeveloped projects for roads, housing, schools and other public assets, and due to the weak economies of various metropolitan areas, in the future selected local, state and federal politicians and a growing portion of taxpayers will be unwilling to finance the construction of sports facilities on behalf of sports franchises. In sum, except for land and infrastructure expenditures, the sports leagues and team owners should expect to absorb a higher proportion of the costs to buy or renovate arenas and stadiums in their DMAs.

In the twenty-first century, the AL and NL in MLB and the NBA, NFL and NHL will continue to operate and thrive as the preeminent organizations in professional team sports. To remain viable and progress, however, each league's future popularity and success will increasingly depend on the growth of its fan base and on the exposure provided by the media industry that broadcasts games and other sport events to domestic and international markets. Furthermore, the gap in operating incomes and performances between the small- and large-market teams within each league will narrow if the respective commissioners and self-interested owners and player unions initiate radical reforms that benefit all teams. For example, to provide opportunities the leagues' decision-makers may agree to modify the luxury tax rates on teams with exorbitant payrolls, to share a higher proportion of local and regional broadcast and/or gate revenues, to establish realistic minimums and caps on team payrolls, to restrict salary arbitration, and as a last remedy, to fold or merge the inferior franchises that are located in small-to-medium metropolitan areas.

Because of the escalation in ticket prices and family costs to attend regular season and postseason games, and the scarcity of broadcast revenues, after 2002 the growth rates of player salaries and team payrolls will plateau and then diminish relative to the values that were realized in the 1990s. Moreover, if the franchises' operating costs continue to inflate, large corporations will gradually replace partnerships and syndicates as the proprietors of MLB, NBA and NHL franchises. Eventually, due to economic and sports market conditions, corporate organizations will also be authorized to own and operate NFL clubs. Lastly, many well-meaning citizen groups and taxpayers will always ideologically and philosophically oppose the use of public money for the construction of sports arenas and stadiums. As a result, because of the future economic environment, each team owner, as well as local business leaders and government officials, will be forced to publicly debate and compromise about whether to use taxpayer subsidies and invest in sports facilities to be valuable asset in their communities.[1]

NOTE

1. Are professional sports franchises generally productive assets to a city or region? How does one identify and measure the economic and social benefits and costs of sports teams? Should the construction of sports arenas and stadiums be subsidized by taxpayers? In part, the future of professional sports leagues and the location of teams depend on the answer to these three questions. To illustrate, seven months after voters overwhelmingly defeated a June 2001 referendum to use taxpayer money for the construction of a downtown sports arena in Charlotte, North Carolina, and for other city projects, a new proposal emerged. That is, the chief executive officers of the Bank of America, Duke Energy and Wachovia Bank offered a total advance of $100 million in corporate funds to finance the construction of a $220 million arena. Meanwhile, before the proposal had surfaced, the NBA Charlotte Hornets owners George Shinn and Ray Woolridge had visited several cities such as Anaheim, Louisville, New Orleans, Norfolk and St. Louis to speak with business leaders and government officials about the relocation of their franchise and an arena for the club. If a deal was concluded and the NBA approved their relocation request, Shinn and Woolridge planned to move the Hornets before the 2002–2003 NBA season began. As expected, the details of the $100 million proposal received an inordinate amount of attention in Charlotte from various citizen and pro-arena groups, City Council, radio and television commentators, and journalists at the *Charlotte Observer*. Despite the referendum's failure in June 2001, however, the majority of local politicians and the media favored the proposal. In the *Observer*, articles appeared that touted the benefits of retaining the Hornets and building an arena for them somewhere in downtown Charlotte. Generally, the articles' authors noted how the players have participated in local public education and charity events, how the Hornets generated excess revenues from regular season games to subsidize other civic facilities such as the Cricket Arena where the

ECHL Checkers play its home games, and how the team makes Charlotte and Mecklen-burg County a more attractive place for residents, visitors and new business firms, and a convention site. In short, the pro-arena advocates claimed that the team made a positive contribution to the identity, quality and spirit of the area and its communities. Yet, small-to-medium markets such as the Charlotte metropolitan area lack the critical mass to con-sistently support more than one professional sports franchise. Consequently, in these areas the government tax base, media market, number of corporate home offices, and the pop-ulation are inferior to those factors in medium-to-large metropolises. Each sports league, therefore, is challenged to evaluate the economic, financial and social returns and risks in expansion and team relocation decisions. For more information about the Hornets' situ-ation prior to relocation to New Orleans, see Peter St. Onge, "Big Enough to Play?" *Char-lotte Observer* (13 January 2002), 1A, 6A; "Keep the Hornets," *Charlotte Observer* (13 January 2002), 2D; Lauren Markoe, "City Agrees to Consider Arena: Staff Analysis to Take 3 Weeks," *Charlotte Observer* (15 January 2002), 1A, 5A; Idem, "Poll Tilts in Favor of Arena," *Charlotte Observer* (9 February 2002), 1A, 10A; Tim Whitmire, Peter Smolowitz, and Rick Bonnell, "Hornets, Louisiana Near Deal," Charlotte *Observer* (17 January 2002), 1A, 6A; Rick Bonnell, "Hornets Sign Deal With New Orleans," *Charlotte Observer* (18 January 2002), 1A, 4A; Idem., "NBA Chief Picks Panel to Weigh in on Hor-nets Move," *Charlotte Observer* (26 January 2002), 1B, 4B; Lauren Markoe and Rick Bon-nell, "Council Backs Arena 8–3, in Appeal to NBA," *Charlotte Observer* (12 February 2002), 1A, 6A.

Appendix

Table A.1
Mean and Standard Deviation of Sports League Characteristics, 1990 to 2000

League	Wins		Win-Loss Percentage		Postseason	
	Mean	SD	Mean	SD	Mean	SD
MLB	867	51	.500	.03	2.4	2.1
AL	866	45	.500	.03	2.4	1.9
NL	867	57	.500	.03	2.4	2.2
NBA	441	93	.500	.11	6.4	3.2
NFL	88	16	.500	.09	4.4	2.3
NHL	907	87	n.a.	n.a.	7.5	2.3

Note: The three Mean columns represent the average wins, win-loss percentages and postseason games per league. The three SD columns are the standard deviations of each characteristic per league. SD measures, for each characteristic, the spread of the values from their respective means. The Mean and SD in Wins and Postseason for the NHL are measured in points and not games. The n.a. indicates not applicable.

Source: The World Almanac and Book of Facts (Mahwah, NJ: World Almanac Book, 1991–2001). The means and standard deviations were derived with a Microsoft Excel program.

Table A.2
Sports Teams Without Division and Conference Titles, and Championships,
by League, 1950 to 1999

Year	League	Teams
1950–59	AL	Boston Red Sox, Detroit Tigers, Philadelphia/Kansas City Athletics, St. Louis Browns/Baltimore Orioles, Washington Senators
	NL	Chicago Cubs, Cincinnati Reds, Pittsburgh Pirates, St. Louis Cardinals
	NBA	No teams without titles
	NFL	Chicago Cardinals, Green Bay Packers, Philadelphia Eagles, Pittsburgh Steelers, San Francisco 49ers, Washington Redskins
	NHL	Boston Bruins, Chicago Blackhawks, New York Rangers
1960–69	AL	Chicago White Sox, Cleveland Indians
	NL	Chicago Cubs, Philadelphia Phillies
	NBA	Cincinnati Royals, Detroit Pistons
	NFL	Chicago/St. Louis Cardinals
	NHL	Detroit Red Wings, New York Rangers
1970–79	AL	Washington Senators/Texas Rangers
	NL	Houston Astros, Montreal Expos, San Diego Padres, San Francisco Giants
	NBA	Detroit Pistons
	NFL	Atlanta Falcons, Buffalo Bills, Detroit Lions, Houston Oilers, New Orleans Saints, New York Giants, New York Jets, Philadelphia Eagles
	NHL	Detroit Red Wings, Los Angeles Kings, Minnesota North Stars, Pittsburgh Penguins, St. Louis Blues, Toronto Maple Leafs
1980–89	AL	Seattle Mariners
	NL	Cincinnati Reds, Montreal Expos, Pittsburgh Pirates
	NBA	Chicago Bulls, Cleveland Cavaliers, Indiana Pacers, Kansas City-Omaha/ Sacramento Kings, Portland Trail Blazers, San Diego/Los Angeles Clippers, Seattle SuperSonics
	NFL	Green Bay Packers, Houston Oilers, Kansas City Chiefs, New Orleans Saints, New York Jets, St. Louis/Phoenix Cardinals
	NHL	Colorado Avalanche/New Jersey Devils, Los Angeles Kings, Pittsburgh Penguins, Toronto Maple Leafs, Vancouver Canucks
1990–99	AL	California/Anaheim Angels, Detroit Tigers, Kansas City Royals
	NL	Chicago Cubs, New York Mets
	NBA	Cleveland Cavaliers, Dallas Mavericks, Denver Nuggets, Golden State Warriors, Los Angeles Clippers, Milwaukee Bucks, Minnesota Timberwolves, New Jersey Nets, Sacramento Kings, Washington Wizards
	NFL	Philadelphia Eagles, Phoenix/Arizona Cardinals
	NHL	Edmonton Oilers, New York Islanders, Winnipeg Jets/Phoenix Coyotes

Note: Year excludes the teams that were expansion franchises during the respective ten seasons.
Source: The World Almanac and Book of Facts, 1951–2001.

Table A.3
Net Worth of Team Owners and Estimated Franchise Values and Ranks, by League, 1993

League	Owner	Net Worth	Rank	Team	Value	Rank
AL	Hiroshi Yamauchi	1.4	6	Seattle Mariners	100	44
	Carl Pohlad	.9	9	Minnesota Twins	100	44
	Michael Ilitch	.9	10	Detroit Tigers	80	62
	Walter Haas	.6	13	Oakland Athletics	140	20
	Gene Autry	.3	22	California Angels	140	20
NL	Ted Turner	1.9	4	Atlanta Braves	100	44
	Wayne Huizenga	.6	15	Florida Marlins	80	62
	Drayton McLane	.4	18	Houston Astros	80	62
	O'Malley Family	.2	36	Los Angeles Dodgers	200	2
	Nelson Doubleday	.2	37	New York Mets	200	2
NBA	Paul Allen	3.2	1	Portland Trail Blazers	85	57
	Richard DeVos	3.0	2	Orlando Magic	85	57
	Ted Arison	2.5	3	Miami Heat	60	83
	Ted Turner	1.9	4	Atlanta Hawks	60	83
	George/Gordon Gund	1.5	5	Cleveland Cavaliers	100	44
NFL	Bob Tisch	1.1	7	New York Giants	150	11
	Jack Kent Cooke	.9	8	Washington Redskins	125	27
	Leon Hess	.8	12	New York Jets	125	27
	William Clay Ford	.6	14	Detroit Lions	115	38
	Hugh Culverhouse	.3	19	Tampa Bay Buccaneers	100	44
NHL	George/Gordon Gund	1.5	5	San Jose Sharks	35	106
	Michael Ilitch	.9	10	Detroit Red Wings	80	62
	Wayne Huizenga	.6	15	Florida Panthers	50	89
	Jeremy Jacobs	.5	16	Boston Bruins	75	70
	The Wirtz Family	.5	17	Chicago Blackhawks	75	70

Note: The Team Owner's Net Worth is in billions of dollars. Franchise Value is in millions of dollars. Teams may tie in rank according to franchise values.

Source: John Steinbreder, "The Owners," *Sports Illustrated* (13 September 1993), 64–87.

Selected Bibliography

ARTICLES

"Air Ball." *Wall Street Journal* (23 January 2002): A20.

Alm, Richard. "Sports, Media Find a Business Marriage Made for Profits." *Charlotte Observer* (9 August 1999): 10D.

Antonen, Mel. "Baseball Fans Pick Up Tab." *USA Today* (22 January 1998): 3C.

Badenhausen, Kurt, and William Sicheri. "Baseball Games." *Forbes* (31 May 1999): 112–117.

Bai, Matt. "A League of Their Own." *Newsweek* (11 May 1998): 68.

"Bang for the Buck." *Street & Smith's SportsBusiness Journal* (2–8 November 1998): 18.

Barnett, Gigi. "A Lot of Leagues of Their Own: Corporate American Spies the Future—Women's Team Sports." *Business Week* (3 March 1997): 54–55.

Barra, Allen. "An International Game." *Wall Street Journal* (13 July 2001): W6.

———. "Building a Contender." *Wall Street Journal* (22 February 2002): W4.

———. "Canada Hits a Cold Spell." *Wall Street Journal* (17 May 2002): W4.

———. "Fair Ball?" *Wall Street Journal* (13 April 2001): W12.

———. "Reality Check for the NHL." *Wall Street Journal* (1 March 2002): W7.

Barra, Allen, and Andrew Albanese. "Who's Watching?" *Wall Street Journal* (2 June 2000): W9.

Barrett, Wayne M. "Crying All the Way to the Bank." *USA Today Magazine* (January 1995): 59.

Beatty, Sally. "ESPN to Produce Made-For-TV Movie, Sports Soap Opera." *Wall Street Journal* (13 July 2001): B2.

Benson, Mitchell. "Sacramento Kings Count on a Troika in the NBA Playoffs." *Wall Street Journal* (19 April 2002): A1–A8.

Bernstein, Andy. "Rockin' the Cradle." *Sporting Goods Business* (12 May 1997): 54–55.

Bianco, Anthony. "Now It's NBA All-The-Time TV." *Business Week* (15 November 1999): 241–242.

Bickley, Dan. "Fed-Up Fans Worry Pro Sports Teams." *Charlotte Observer* (27 June 2001): 21A.

Bliss, Marjo Rankin. "Perko to Build Team in NBDL." *Charlotte Observer* (24 June 2001): 9H.

Blum, Ronald. "Cash Flow: Baseball Wants Some." *The Daily News* (Jacksonville, NC: 15 July 2000): 1C, 3C.

———. "Expos, Marlins Switches Approved." *Charlotte Observer* (13 February 2002): 6C.

Bock, Hal. "First Cabin at L.A. Forum $450 a Seat." *Charlotte Observer* (11 November 1990): C1, C14.

Bonnell, Rick. "Charlotte Not Elite, But Not Bad." *Charlotte Observer* (5 July 1998): 2H.

———. "Hornets Sign Deal With New Orleans." *Charlotte Observer* (18 January 2002): 1A, 4A.

———. "NBA Chief Picks Panel to Weigh in on Hornets Move." *Charlotte Observer* (26 January 2002): 1B, 4B.

Brady, Anne. "Visions of Phoenix-Area Expansion Differ." *Wall Street Journal* (14 August 2000): B11A.

Burton, Rick. "Apocalypse Soon: Pro Sports Teetering on Edge of an Abyss." *Street & Smith's SportsBusiness Journal* (2–8 November 1998): 30–31.

Carter, David M. "Take Me Out to the Ball Game, James." *Business Week* (13 March 2000): 142.

Catanoso, Justin. "Baseball Should Go Where the Money Is." *Business Week* (29 June 1998): 131.

Cauley, Leslie. "To Pay the NFL, ESPN Plans a Blitz of Football Shows." *Wall Street Journal* (17 August 1998): B1, B4.

"CBA Rises to Play Its 56th Season." *Charlotte Observer* (10 August 2001): 6B.

Chandler, Charles. "Panthers in NFL's Top 12 for Making a Profit." *Charlotte Observer* (16 April 2001): 1C.

Cone, Edward. "Boys and Their Toys." *Interactive Week* (5 June 2000): 34–41.

"Contentious Labor Situation Casts Cloud Over Season, Sport." *Charlotte Observer* (29 March 2002): 7C.

Craig, Susanne. "A Great Hockey Fight Rivets Nova Scotia and Two Old Gents." *Wall Street Journal* (23 January 2002): A1, A8.

"David Stern: This Time, It's Personal." *Business Week* (13 July 1998): 114–118.

Davis, Lance E. "Self-Regulation in Baseball, 1909–71." In Roger G. Noll, ed., *Government and the Sports Business*. Washington, DC: The Brookings Institution, 1974, 349–386.

Dodd, Mike. "Soaring Player Salaries Threaten Small Markets." *USA Today* (12 December 1990): 25.

Dodd, Scott. "For Stern, Prosperity in NBA Has Bred Power." *Charlotte Observer* (29March 2000): 1A, 13A.

Dubow, Josh. "It's a Wonderful World for NFL's TV." *Charlotte Observer* (14 January 1998): B1.

Dupont, Kevin Paul. "Pitching Change." *Boston Globe* (27 March 1998): F6.

Durston, Ellen. "Sports Xanadu." *USA Weekend* (14–16 December 2001): 14.

Edes, Gordon. "Treasure Island." *Boston Globe* (27 March 1998): F3.

Editorial. "Our Kind of Town." *Wall Street Journal* (20 July 2001): W15.

Eig, Jonathon. "Why So Few Fans Are Asking for Pencils at Today's Ballparks." *Wall Street Journal* (10 July 2001): A1.

Fainaru, Steve. "Serious Defects." *Boston Globe* (27 March 1998): F4.

Farrey, Tom. "Too Much of a Good Thing?" *Business Week* (11 May 1998): 70–71.

Fatsis, Stefan. "Baseball Ticket Prices Are Outta Here." *Wall Street Journal* (3 April 1998): W6.

———. "Can Iverson Pitch to the Mainstream?" *Wall Street Journal* (8 June 2001): B1.

———. "The 'Coolest Game on Earth' Tries to Match the NHL Type." *Wall Street Journal* (25 April 1997): B9.

———. "Cuba, Si. Stardom, No." *Wall Street Journal* (17 August 2001): W4.

———. "For Pro Football, Giant TV Pacts May Carry a Price." *Wall Street Journal* (15 January 1998): B1, B6.

———. "In the NBA This Season, Discontent Looms." *Wall Street Journal* (3 November 1997): B12.

———. "In Yankees–Cablevision Fracas, Consumers Will Lose." *Wall Street Journal* (20 March 2002): B1, B4.

———. "Muscling Out Supplemental Income." *Wall Street Journal* (30 November 2001): W14.

———. "NBA's Problems Mounting." *Wall Street Journal* (24 February 1998): W9.

———. "The New Game in TV Sports." *Wall Street Journal* (21 January 2002): B1, B3.

———. "New Leagues Go for Central Ownership." *Charlotte Observer* (27 July 1997): B1, B2.

———. "NFL Players May Help Get Fatter TV Deal." *Wall Street Journal* (2 January 1997): 3, 4.

———. "NFL's Television Partners Scramble for Ad Dollars." *Wall Street Journal* (29 August 2001): B13.

———. "121 Teams? Not for Long." *Wall Street Journal* (16 November 2001): W10.

———. "Pittsburgh's Field of Dreams." *Wall Street Journal* (11 April 2001): B1, B4.

———. "Ready or Not ... " *Wall Street Journal* (5 April 2002): W9.

———. "Save Our Expos!" *Wall Street Journal* (29 March 2002): W6.

———. "Staples to Attach Its Name to Arena in Los Angeles." *Wall Street Journal* (2 December 1997): B6.

———. "Two Major Players in Yankees Network Pull Stake of 20%." *Wall Street Journal* (18 September 2001): B12.

———. "Yankees Holding Company Set to Form a Sports Network Valued at $850 Million." *Wall Street Journal* (11 September 2001): B4.

Fatsis, Stefan, and Bruce Orwall. "Broadcast Bounce: NBA's Pact With AOL, Disney Puts Most Games in Cable's Court." *Wall Street Journal* (17 December 2001): B6.

Fatsis, Stefan, and Kara Swisher. "Group Led by AOL's Leonsis to Acquire NHL's Capitals and Other Sports Stakes." *Wall Street Journal* (13 May 1999): A8.

Fatsis, Stefan, and Kyle Pope. "NBC Agrees to Pay About $1.5 Billion to Renew Contract to Air NBA Games." *Wall Street Journal* (11 November 1997): B8.

———. "NBC, Turner Sports Are Kicking Off Serious Drive for New Football League." *Wall Street Journal* (29 May 1998): B8.

———. "NFL Scores Nearly $18 Billion in TV Rights." *Wall Street Journal* (14 January 1998): B1, B13.

———. "TV Networks Rush to Splurge on NFL Deals." *Wall Street Journal* (15 December 1997): B1, B8.

Fatsis, Stefan, and Suzanne Vranica. "NFL's Marketing Thrust Goes on Display." *Wall Street Journal* (21 November 2001): B11.

Feinstein, John. "Money Doesn't Buy Championships. But It Helps." *Wall Street Journal* (6 November 2001): A26.

Fisher, Daniel, and Michael K. Ozanian. "Cowboy Capitalism." *Forbes* (20 September 1999): 170–178.

Flint, Joe. "NBC Enters Arena Football Pact as NBA Arrangement Nears End." *Wall Street Journal* (6 March 2002): B9.

Flynn, Michael A., and Richard J. Gilbert. "The Analysis of Professional Sports Leagues as Joint Ventures." *Economic Journal* (February 2001): F27.

Fong, Petti. "Canada: Penny-Wise, Franchise-Foolish." *Business Week* (27 March 2000): 70.

"Football." *Charlotte Observer* (14 November 2001): 6C.

"Foul." *Wall Street Journal* (16 January 2002): A14.

Fowler, Scott. "The Original 'America's Team' in Town." *Charlotte Observer* (26 March 2002): 1C, 4C.

Frayne, Trent. "Too Many Teams, Too Few Players." *Maclean's* (4 January 1993): 64.

Gammons, Peter. "International Pastime." *Boston Globe* (27 March 1998): F2.

Garfield, Ken. "Lousy Sports Town? That's Good." *Charlotte Observer* (14 November 2001): 1E, 8E.

Garrity, Brian. "Sports Owners Look to Maximize Equity Value in Synergies." *The Investment Dealer's Digest* (30 November 1998): 9–10.

Grandstaff, Chris. "Webber Signs 2nd-Largest Contract." *Charlotte Observer* (22 July 2001): 13H.

Granitsas, Alkman. "China Sees Dawn of Big-Money Sports TV." *Wall Street Journal* (31 May 2002): B4.

Green, Ron Sr. "Drawing Crowds to Parks Now Major Fun for Minors." *Charlotte Observer* (4 September 2001): 5C.

———. "Once Man of the Hour, Shinn a Passing Thought." *Charlotte Observer* (24 September 2001): 2C.

Greene, Jay, and Ken Belson. "The Mariners Catch a Tsunami." *Business Week* (25 June 2001): 98–99.

Grover, Ronald. "Diamondbacks in the Rough—Again." *Business Week* (3 June 2002): 60.

———. "Why the NBA Can't Find the Hoop." *Business Week* (10 April 2000): 132.

Hauser, Susan G. "Japanese Baseball Stars Turn Seattle Radio Bilingual." *Wall Street Journal* (10 July 2001): A16.

Helyar, John. "A Team of Their Own." *Fortune* (14 May 2001): 190–197.

———. "An Unpalatial Arena Designed to Please Just Plain Folks." *Wall Street Journal* (10 October 1997): B1, B11.

———. "NFL Hopes Offshoot Scores in Europe." *Wall Street Journal* (12 March 1991): B1, B6.

Hille, Bob. "TSN's Best Sports Cities." *The Sporting News* (30 June 1997): 14–23.

Holt, Nancy D. "Pepsi Center Scores in Financing Game." *Wall Street Journal* (3 March 1999): B12.

Hoppes, Lynn. "Why Are You Selling the Magic?" *Orlando Sentinel* (13 January 2002): C1, C9.

Horowitz, Ira. "Sports Broadcasting." In Roger G. Noll, ed., *Government and the Sports Business*. Washington, DC: The Brookings Institution, 1974, 275–323.

Hudson, Don. "Replays Don't Have to be Instant." *Charlotte Observer* (28 July 2001): 1B.

Hyman, Mark. "And Then There Were 28 . . . " *Business Week* (11 October 1999): 98–100.

———. "Bronx Cheers in Montreal." *Business Week* (26 June 2000): 181.

———. "Down to Their Last Out." *Business Week* (28 January 2002): 88.

———. "The Egghead in the Owner's Box." *Business Week* (28 January 2002): 88.

———. "From Tears to Cheers in Cleveland." *Business Week* (16 November 1998): 108–116.

————. "How Bad Is the NBA Hurting." *Business Week* (7 May 2001): 123.

————. "How to Lose Fans and Get Richer: The NFL Masters the Playing Field That Matters." *Business Week* (26 January 1998): 70.

————. "The Jets: Worth a Gazillion?" *Business Week* (6 December 1999): 99–100.

————. "A League of Their Own." *Business Week* (15 June 1998): 66.

————. "The Owner's Box Gets Wired." *Business Week* (22 May 2000): 89–94.

————. "Play Ball—Even if No One Loves You." *Business Week* (25 March 2002): 84.

————. "Putting the Squeeze on the Media." *Business Week* (11 December 2000): 75.

————. "Take Me Out to the Ticket Auction." *Business Week* (28 August 2000): 14.

————. "The Trouble With Barry." *Business Week* (15 October 2001): 100.

————. "Up From the Dugout." *Business Week* (24 March 1997): 211.

————. "Where Beisbol Is the Stuff of Revolution," *Business Week* (15 May 2000): 28–30.

Hyman, Mark, and Jay Weiner. "The NBA: Why Push May Come to Shove." *Business Week* (25 May 1998): 77.

Hyman, Mark, and Paula Dwyer. "What Does This Town Need? New Senators." *Business Week* (14 May 2001): 54.

Jenish, D'Arcy. "The Troubled State of Sport." *Maclean's* (11 September 2000): 36–37.

Jensen, Jeff. "Pro Sports Catch on to New Media: Leagues See Profits as Content Providers for CD-ROMs, Online." *Advertising Age* (7 November 1994): 27.

————. "Shooting to Score on the Net." *Advertising Age* (3 April 1995): 24.

————. "Wayward Sport Leagues Rediscover Their Youth." *Advertising Age* (12 February 1996): S2.

Johnson, Roy S., and Rajiv M. Rao. "Take Me Out to the Boardroom." *Fortune* (21 July 1997): 42–48.

Johnston, Kathleen. "Pacers Lease Contains Financial Guarantees." *Indianapolis Star* (5 November 1997): 16.

Jones, J.C.H., and D.G. Ferguson. "Location and Survival in the National Hockey League." *The Journal of Industrial Economics* (June 1998): 443–457.

Jozsa, Frank. "New Arenas Aided NBA Teams in '90s." *The Business Journal* (Week of 14 July 2000): 41.

————. "New Arenas, Subsidized or Not, Pay Dividends in the NBA." *Street & Smith's SportsBusiness Journal* (10–16 July 2000): 36–37.

Kauffman, Bill. "A Diamond in the Rough." *Wall Street Journal* (1 September 2000): W13.

"Keep the Hornets." *Charlotte Observer* (13 January 2002): 2D.

"Kelly to Red Sox: Thanks, But No Thanks." *Charlotte Observer* (11 March 2002): 11C.

Kennedy, Sheila S., and Mark S. Rosentraub. "Public-Private Partnerships, Professional Sports Teams and the Protection of the Public Interest." *American Review of Public Administration* (December 2001): 436–459.

Klas, Mary Ellen. "Squeeze Play." *Florida Trend* (March 2002): 54–57.

Klein, Frederick C. "Baseball Makes a Move, Sort of, to Realignment." *Wall Street Journal* (17 October 1997): B13.

————. "Footing the Bill for New Stadiums." *Wall Street Journal* (14 May 1999): W11.

Kraker, Daniel, and David Morris. "Let Public Own Pro Teams." *Charlotte Observer* (4 December 1997): 22A.

Kravetz, Stacy. "A New Sports Home Rises." *Wall Street Journal* (23 September 1998): B12.

Kuper, Simon. "Marlins Seek a Place in the Sun." *Financial Times* (20–21 April 2002): XXII.

————. "New Jersey Outshines the Big Apple." *Financial Times* (20–21 April 2002): XXII.

"Leagues Merge After IHL Folds." *Charlotte Observer* (5 June 2001): 5C.

Lentze, Gregory. "The Legal Concept of Professional Sports Leagues: The Commissioner and an Alternative Approach From a Corporate Perspective." *Marquette Sports Law Journal* (Fall 1995): 65–94.

Levine, Alan M. "Hard Cap or Soft Cap: The Optimal Mobility Restrictions for the Professional Sports Leagues." *Media and Entertainment Law Journal* (Autumn 1995): 243–299.

Lippman, John, and Robert Frank. "Media Firms Discuss Sports Assets." *Wall Street Journal* (18 July 2002): 35.

Lopatka, John E., and Jill Boylston Herndon. "Antitrust and Sports Franchise Ownership Restraints: A Sad Tale of Two Cases." *Antitrust Bulletin* (Fall 1997): 749–791.

Lowry, Tom. "ESPN's Full-Court Press." *Business Week* (11 February 2002): 60–61.

———. "Small-Time Football, Big-Time Buzz." *Business Week* (22 October 2001): 128.

———. "Take Me Online to the Ball Game." *Business Week* (9 April 2001): 92.

Lowry, Tom, Ronald Grover, Lori Hawkins, and David Polek. "For the Love of the Game—And Cheap Seats." *Business Week* (28 May 2001): 46–47.

Markoe, Lauren. "City Agrees to Consider Arena; Staff Analysis to Take 3 Weeks." *Charlotte Observer* (15 January 2002): 1A, 5A.

———. "Poll Tilts in Favor of Arena." *Charlotte Observer* (9 February 2002): 1A, 10A.

Markoe, Lauren, and Rick Bonnell. "Council Backs Arena 8–3, in Appeal to NBA." *Charlotte Observer* (12 February 2002): 1A, 6A.

Matthews, Anna Wilde. "NFL Nears Web-Properties Deal With AOL, Viacom, SportsLine." *Wall Street Journal* (9 July 2001): B4.

McAdam, Sean. "Baseball OKs Contraction." *Charlotte Observer* (7 November 2001): 1C, 5C.

McCartney, Scott. "Why a Baseball Superstar's Megacontract Can be Less Than It Seems." *Wall Street Journal* (27 December 2000): B1, B3.

McFarland, John. "Cuban's Comments Draw Record Hit—$500,000." *Charlotte Observer* (9 January 2002): 4C.

McGraw, Dan. "Big League Troubles." *U.S. News & World Report* (13 July 1998): 40–46.

———. "NBA Finals Are No Slam-Dunk for TV." *U.S. News & World Report* (1 May 2000): 45–46.

McKay, Betsy, and Stefan Fatsis. "Pepsi Scores One on Coke, Gaining Sponsorship Rights to the NFL." *Wall Street Journal* (29 March 2002): B5.

Mehrtens, Cliff. "Canes, Hockey Fever Latest Rage in Raleigh." *Charlotte Observer* (29 January 2002): 1C, 7C.

———. "Charlotte Considers Options of ACHL." *Charlotte Observer* (17 April 2002): 8C.

———. "Checkers Not Lone Choice." *Charlotte Observer* (13 March 2002): 2C.

———. "Player Promotions a Fact of Life in Leagues Such as the ECHL." *Charlotte Observer* (27 January 2002): 10F.

Miller, D.W. "Scholars Call a Foul on Pro Sports Leagues." *The Chronicle of Higher Education* (13 October 2000): A28–29.

Millman, Joel. "Young Maverick Sits on Sidelines But Stars in Ads." *Wall Street Journal* (27 February 2002): B1, B3.

Moores, John. "Damn Yankees." *Wall Street Journal* (14 May 2002): A18.

Mushnick, Phil. "Less Is More." *TV Guide* (1 May 1999): 56.

"NBA Switching Channels to ESPN, TNT, ABC." *Charlotte Observer* (23 January 2002): 4C.

Newcomb, Peter, and Doug Donovan. "The Forbes 400: Jocks." *Forbes* (11 October 1999): 330–332.

"New Denver Center Is NBA's 2nd Chinese Player." *Charlotte Observer* (27 February 2002): 4C.

"New League Has NBA Backing, Player Interest." *Charlotte Observer* (15 November 2001): 4C.

"New York Goes Minor League With 2 Teams." *Wall Street Journal* (31 July 2000): B11A.

"New York Voted Best Sports City; Charlotte 23rd." *Charlotte Observer* (8 August 2001): 1C.

"NFL Ticket Prices Jump 8.7%, Panthers About 4.1%." *Charlotte Observer* (9 September 2001): 2H.

Noll, Roger G. "Alternatives in Sports Policy." In Roger G. Noll, ed., *Government and the Sports Business*. Washington, DC: The Brookings Institution, 1974, 411–428.

———. "Professional Basketball: Economic and Business Perspectives." In Paul D. Staudohar and James A. Mangan, eds., *The Business of Professional Sports*. Champaign: University of Illinois Press, 1991, 18–47.

O'Brien, Richard, and Mark Mravic. "Owners You Can Trust." *Sports Illustrated* (21 December 1998): 32–33.

O'Connell, Vanessa. "DirecTV Dishes Up New Marketing Push." *Wall Street Journal* (30 July 2001): B9.

———. "Super-Bowl Spots Aren't Easy Sell for Fox." *Wall Street Journal* (21 January 2002): B5.

Okner, Benjamin A. "Subsidies of Stadiums and Arenas." In Roger G. Noll, ed., *Government and the Sports Business*. Washington, DC: The Brookings Institution, 1974, 325–327.

Olson, Stan. "Hey Bud, Empty Seats Show a Problem." *Charlotte Observer* (22 October 2001): 7C.

———. "Owners, Players Should Settle Labor Dispute Fast." *Charlotte Observer* (23 September 2001): 3F.

Onge, Peter St. "Big Enough to Play?" *Charlotte Observer* (13 January 2002): 1A, 6A.

Orwall, Bruce. "ESPN Adds Entertainment Shows to Its Playbook." *Wall Street Journal* (6 March 2002): B1, B4.

———. "ESPN.com to be Sole Provider of Sports News to Microsoft's MSN." *Wall Street Journal* (7 September 2001): B2.

Orwall, Bruce, and Matthew Rose. "Disney Held Talks With Condé Nast, Hearst to Sell Fairchild Magazine Unit." *Wall Street Journal* (16 August 1999): B12.

Ozanian, Michael K. "Cowboy Capitalism." *Forbes* (20 September 1999): 170–178.

———. "How to Buy a Sports Team." *Financial World* (20 May 1996): 66.

———. "Selective Accounting." *Forbes* (14 December 1998): 124–134.

Ozanian, Michael K., and Kurt Badenhausen. "Baseball Going Broke? Don't Believe It." *Wall Street Journal* (27 July 2000): A22.

———. "Baseball's Owners, Deep in Debt, Can Avert a Strike." *Wall Street Journal* (17 July 2002): D12.

"Partners Agree to Sale of Red Sox." *Charlotte Observer* (21 December 2002): 4C.

Passikoff, Robert. "N.Y. Yankees Aside, Winning Isn't Only Key to Fan Loyalty." *Brandweek* (6 November 2000): 32–33.

Pedulla, Tom. "Tagliabue: TV Deals a Start." *USA Today* (26 January 1998): 14C.

Peirce, Neal. "Pittsburgh's Lesson for Uptown Arena Advocates." *Charlotte Observer* (16 January 1998): 15A.

Peterson, Gary. "Bonds Has Giants in Pickle With Arbitration." *Charlotte Observer* (25 December 2001): 3C.

Piraino, Thomas A., Jr. "The Antitrust Rationale for the Expansion of Professional Sports Leagues." *Ohio State Law Journal* (November 1996): 1677–1729.

"Pittsburgh's Field of Dreams." *Wall Street Journal* (11 April 2001): B1, B4.

Pope, Kyle. "Networks' Big Play for NFL May End in Fumble." *Wall Street Journal* (5 February 1998): B10.

Pope, Kyle, and Stefan Fatsis. "NBC, Turner Sports May See Less Profit Showing More Games in New NBA Pact." *Wall Street Journal* (12 November 1997): B9.

Prager, Joshua Harris. "Managing Cultural Diversity—On the Pitcher's Mound." *Wall Street Journal* (30 September 1998): B1.

Quick, Rebecca. "For Sports Fans, the Internet Is a Whole New Ball Game." *Wall Street Journal* (3 September 1998): B9.

Quirk, James, and Mohamed A. El-Hodiri. "An Economic Model of a Professional Sports League." *Journal of Political Economy* 79 (March/April 1975): 1302–1319.

———. "The Economic Theory of a Professional Sports League." In Roger G. Noll, ed., *Government and the Sports Business*. Washington, DC: The Brookings Institution, 1974, 33–80.

Rappaport, Jordan, and Chad Wilkerson. "What Are the Benefits of Hosting a Major League Sports Franchise?" *Economic Review* (First Quarter 2001): 55–86.

Raugust, Karen. "Sports Leagues Target Young Fans With Books." *Publishers Weekly* (24 February 1997): 34–35.

"Report Says ABC, ESPN Will Take Shot at NBA Rights." *Charlotte Observer* (5 December 2001): 4C.

Rivkin, Steven R. "Sports Leagues and the Federal Antitrust Laws." In Roger G. Noll, ed., *Government and the Sports Business*. Washington, DC: The Brookings Institution, 1974, 389–395.

Rosentraub, Mark S. "Teams Extort Public Subsidies." *ENR* (19 July 1999): 71.

Ross, Stephen F. "Break Up the Sports League Monopolies." In Paul D. Staudohar and James A. Mangan, eds., *The Business of Professional Sports*. Champaign: University of Illinois Press, 1991, 152–173.

Rowan, Roy. "Play Ball!" *Fortune* (4 September 2000): 310–326.

Rozin, Skip. "The Amateurs Who Saved Indianapolis." *Business Week* (10 April 2000): 126, 130.

"Sales of Marlins, Expos Imminent." *Charlotte Observer* (2 February 2002): 8C.

Salfino, Catherine. "Making the Pirates Walk the Plank: The Licensed Team Apparel Biz Strikes Back." *Daily News Record* (29 March 1993): 34–36.

Salfino, Catherine. "Mass Market Still Scoring Points for Pro Leagues: League Executives Say Teaming Soft and Hard Goods Heats Up Sales." *Daily News Record* (8 September 1995): 1–3.

Saporta, Maria. "Home Depot Founder to Buy Falcons for $545 Million." *Charlotte Observer* (7 December 2001): 1C.

Scott, David. "Hornets, Hurricanes Go Further to Draw Fans." *Charlotte Observer* (13 November 2000): 7D.

"Selig Hopes to Avoid Repeat of '94." *Charlotte Observer* (30 August 2001): 4C.

Shaughnessy, Dan. "Improved Grip?" *Boston Globe* (27 March 1998): F7.

Silverman, Rachel Emma. "How Much for Those Jets Tickets? That's It—Let's Just Buy the Team." *Wall Street Journal* (19 August 1999): B1.

Smith, Russ. "Amusement Parks." *Wall Street Journal* (29 March 2002): W15.

Sorensen, Tom. "Fans Here Follow Trend, Not Team." *Charlotte Observer* (5 December 2001): 1C.

"Sources Say Marlins Owner Ready to Sell." *Charlotte Observer* (23 November 2001): 14C.

"Sources: TV Deal Nets About $700 Million a Year." *Charlotte Observer* (11 January 2002): 4C.

Spagat, Elliot. "Dallas Mavericks Owner Bets Big on HDTV." *Wall Street Journal* (7 March 2002): B5, B6.

Spanberg, Erik. "Redskins Make Waves Here." *Charlotte Business Journal* (19 April 2002): 1, 55.

Starr, Mark. "The Best Boys of Summer." *Newsweek* (19 October 1998): 62–64.

Steinbreder, John. "The Owners." *Sports Illustrated* (13 September 1993): 64–87.

"Strahan Selected AP Defensive Player of Year." *Charlotte Observer* (17 January 2002): 2C.

Sutherland, Pat. "Braves' President Kasten Says Team Didn't Take Advantage of A. Jones." *Charlotte Observer* (2 December 2001): 3F.

———. "Favre Last QB From Great Era." *Charlotte Observer* (25 November 2001): 6F.

Sweet, David. "Fans Line Up for Stadium Pieces on Web." *Wall Street Journal* (26 October 2000): B14.

———. "Fox and ESPN Bolster Sports Web Sites." *Wall Street Journal* (3 September 1998): B8.

———. "It's Never Over, Yogi: Dead Sports Leagues Live Again Online." *Wall Street Journal* (30 September 1999): B1.

———. "Sports Teams Find Revenue in Online Sales." *Wall Street Journal* (22 May 2000): A35A.

———. "Sports Teams Use New Technology to Sell Tickets." *Wall Street Journal* (10 January 2001): B6.

Swift, E.M. "The Truth Hurts." *Sports Illustrated* (30 October 2000): 29.

"Tagliabue on the NFL Today." *Business Week* (25 October 1999): 160–162.

Talton, Jon. "Cities May be Sorry Places If Ballparks Strike Out." *Charlotte Observer* (10 May 1998): 1D.

———. "Stadium Tax Gives Phoenix a 2nd Chance." *Charlotte Observer* (12 July 1998): 1D, 3D.

Thurm, Scott. "Stadium Jinx: What to Call Enron Field? 'Enron Folds,' Maybe." *Wall Street Journal* (4 December 2001): A1, A10.

Tomlinson, Tommy. "Glitzy We Ain't; Genuine We Truly Are." *Charlotte Observer* (20 January 2002): 1B.

Vaillancourt, Meg. "Menino Wants High Return on Investment in Fenway." *Boston Globe* (11 May 2000): C1, C17.

Vrooman, John. "A General Theory of Professional Sports Leagues." *Southern Economic Journal* (April 1995): 971–991.

Walden, Michael L. "Don't Play Ball." *Carolina Journal* (Oct./Nov. 1997): 23.

Walker, Sam. "Arizona Baseball Team Is Losing More Than Fans." *Wall Street Journal* (22 September 2000): B1, B4.

———. "Building a New Arena? A Winning Team Helps." *Wall Street Journal* (25 June 1999): B1.

———. "Full Count and Empty Seats." *Wall Street Journal* (12 October 1999): B1, B4.

———. "How to Tackle the NFL's Hottest Tickets." *Wall Street Journal* (4 September 1998): W1, W4.

———. "NBA Set to Launch 24-Hour Television Network." *Wall Street Journal* (24 September 1999): B7.

———. "Need Help? Hire a Pro." *Wall Street Journal* (14 December 2001): W10.

———. "Play Ball, Pay Tax!" *Wall Street Journal* (1 June 2001): W1, W8.

————. "Poor, Poor Baseball." *Wall Street Journal* (7 December 2001): W8.

————. "The Price of Victory." *Wall Street Journal* (11 June 1999): B1, B4.

————. "Real Fans: They're Back." *Wall Street Journal* (21 December 2001): W11.

————. "Scoring in a Slow Economy." *Wall Street Journal* (7 September 2001): W1, W6.

————. "Shaq, Jack and You." *Wall Street Journal* (18 January 2002): W1, W7.

Walker, Sam, and Jonathan B. Weinbach. "All-Stars of '99." *Wall Street Journal* (3 September 1999): W1, W14.

Weiner, Jay. "Good For A-Rod, Bad for Baseball." *Business Week* (25 December 2000): 59.

Whalen, Jeanne, and Jeff Jensen. "PepsiCo Units Play the Ambush Game." *Advertising Age* (28 August 1995): 3.

Whiteside, Larry. "Making Inroads Near the Outback." *Boston Globe* (27 March 1998): F8.

Whitmire, Tim, Peter Smolowitz, and Rick Bonnell. "Hornets, Louisiana Near Deal." *Charlotte Observer* (17 January 2002), 1A, 6A.

Wilson, Bernie. "Henderson Gets 3,000th Hit in Gwynn Farewell." *Charlotte Observer* (8 October 2001): 5C.

Woellert, Lorraine. "Baseball Owners Could Bobble This Ball." *Business Week* (3 December 2001): 59.

Yang, Catherine. "Media Mergers: The Danger Remains." *Business Week* (29 April 2002): 96–97.

"Yankee-Panky." *Wall Street Journal* (29 March 2002): W15.

"YES Sports Channel Files Antitrust Suit Against Cablevision." *Wall Street Journal* (30 April 2002): B7.

Zaretsky, Adam M. "Should Cities Pay for Sports Facilities?" *The Regional Economist* (April 2001): 5–9.

Zimbalist, Andrew. "The NFL's New Math." *Wall Street Journal* (13 October 1999): A30.

————. "Not Suitable for Families." *U.S. News & World Report* (20 January 1997): 9.

————. "Why 'Yer Out!' Is a Bad Call for Baseball." *Business Week* (12 November 2001): 120.

Zimmerman, Dennis. "Subsidizing Stadiums: Who Benefits, Who Pays?" In Roger G. Noll and Andrew Zimbalist, eds., *Sports, Jobs and Taxes: The Economic Impact of Sports Teams and Stadiums*. Washington, DC: The Brookings Institution, 1997, 119–145.

BOOKS

Berry, Robert C., and Glenn M. Wong. *Law and Business of the Sports Industry*. Westport, CT: Praeger, 1993.

Bougheas, Spiros, and Paul Downward. *The Economics of Professional Sports Leagues: A Bargaining Approach*. Nottingham, England: University of Nottingham, 2000.

Costas, Bob. *Fair Ball: A Fan's Case for Baseball*. New York: Broadway Books, 2001.

Davidson, John, and John Steinbreder. *Hockey For Dummies*. 2nd ed. Foster City, CA: IDG Books Worldwide, Inc., 2000.

Downward, Paul, and Alistair Dawson. *The Economics of Professional Team Sports*. London and New York: Routledge, 2000.

Fowler, Scott, and Charles Chandler. *Year of the Cat*. New York: Simon & Schuster, 1997.

Gitlin, Todd. *Media Unlimited: How the Torrent of Images and Sounds Overwhelms Our Lives*. New York: Metropolitan Books, 2002.

Gorman, Jerry, Kirk Calhoun, and (Contributor) Skip Rozin. *The Name of the Game: The Business of Sports*. New York: John Wiley & Sons, 1994.

Halberstam, David, ed. *The Best American Sports Writing of the Century*. Boston: Houghton Mifflin Company, 1999.

Hollander, Zander, ed. *The Modern Encyclopedia of Basketball*. Old Tappan, NJ: Four Winds Press, 1969.

Jamail, Milton H. *Full Count: Inside Cuban Baseball*. Carbondale: Southern Illinois University, 2000.

Jones, Donald G., and Elaine L. Daley. *Sports Ethics in America: A Bibliography, 1970–1990*. Westport, CT: Greenwood Press, 1992.

Jones, Michael E. *Sports Law*. Upper Saddle River, NJ: Prentice-Hall, 1999.

Jozsa, Frank P., Jr., and John J. Guthrie, Jr. *Relocating Teams and Expanding Leagues in Professional Sports: How the Major Leagues Respond to Market Conditions*. Westport, CT: Quorum Books, 1999.

Kruckemeyer, Thomas J. *For Whom the Ball Tolls: A Fan's Guide to Economic Issues in Professional and College Sports*. Jefferson City, MO: Kruckemeyer Publishing, 1995.

Levinstein, Mark S. *Sports Law: Representing and Advising Athletes, Teams, Leagues, and Sports*. New York: Lawyer Media, Inc., 1998.

Maraniss, David. *When Pride Still Mattered*. New York: Simon & Schuster, 1999.

Menke, Frank G. *The Encyclopedia of Sports*. 5th ed. Cranbury, NJ: A.S. Barnes, 1975.

Mullin, Bernard J., Stephen Hardy, and William Sutton. *Sports Marketing*. Champaign, IL: Human Kinetics Publishers, 1993.

Noll, Roger G., ed. *Government and the Sports Business*. Washington, DC: The Brookings Institution, 1974.

Noll, Roger G., and Andrew Zimbalist, eds. *Sports, Jobs and Taxes: The Economic Impact of Sports Teams and Stadiums*. Washington, DC: Brookings Institution Press, 1997.

Pope, S.W., ed. *The New American Sport History: Recent Approaches and Perspectives*. Urbana: University of Illinois Press, 1997.

Quirk, James, and Rodney D. Fort. *Hard Ball: The Abuse of Power in Pro Team Sports*. Princeton, NJ: Princeton University Press, 1999.

———. *Pay Dirt: The Business of Professional Team Sports*. Princeton, NJ: Princeton University Press, 1992.

Rader, Benjamin G. *American Sports: From the Age of Folk Games to the Age of Spectators*. Englewood Cliffs, NJ: Prentice-Hall, 1983.

Riess, Stephen A. *Major Problems in American Sport History*. Boston: Houghton Mifflin Company, 1997.

Roberts, Randy, and James Olsen. *Winning Is the Only Thing: Sports in America Since 1945*. Baltimore: Johns Hopkins University Press, 1989.

Rosentraub, Mark S. *Major League Losers: The Real Cost of Sports and Who's Paying for It*. New York: Basic Books, 1997.

Schaff, Phil. *Sports Marketing: Its Not Just a Game Anymore*. Amherst, MA: Prometheus Books, 1995.

Schlossberg, Howard. *Sports Marketing*. Cambridge, MA: Blackwell Publishers, 1996.

Seymour, Harold. *Baseball: The Golden Age*. 2nd ed. New York: Oxford University Press, 1989.

Shank, Matthew D. *Sports Marketing: A Strategic Perspective*. Upper Saddle River, NJ: Prentice-Hall, 1999.

————. *Sports Marketing: A Strategic Perspective.* 2nd ed. Upper Saddle River, NJ: Prentice-Hall, 2002.

Staudohar, Paul D., and James A. Mangan, eds. *The Business of Professional Sports.* Champaign: University of Illinois Press, 1991.

The World Almanac and Book of Facts. Mahwah, NJ: World Almanac Books, 1950–2001.

Weiler, Paul C. *Leveling the Playing Field: How the Law Can Make Sports Better for Fans.* Cambridge, MA: Harvard University Press, 2000.

DISSERTATIONS

Dobbs, Michael E. "The Organization of Professional Sports Leagues: Mortality and Founding Rates, 1871–1997." Ph.D. diss., University of Texas at Dallas, 1999.

Grice, James J. "The Monopolistic Market Structure of Professional Sports Leagues." Senior Thesis diss., Colorado College, 1987.

Jozsa, Frank P., Jr. "An Economic Analysis of Franchise Relocation and League Expansion in Professional Team Sports, 1950–1975." Ph.D. diss., Georgia State University, 1977.

Rascher, Daniel A. "Organization and Outcomes: A Study of Professional Sports Leagues." Ph.D. diss., University of California at Berkeley, 1997.

Vincent-Mayoral, Roberto. "Competitive Balance in Professional Sports Leagues: Determinants and Impact." Honors Thesis, Coe College, 2000.

PUBLISHED GOVERNMENT DOCUMENTS

Gerena, Charles, and Betty Joyce Nash. "Playing to Win." *Region Focus.* vol. 4, no. 2, Fifth Federal Reserve District Economy (Richmond, VA: Spring 2000): 13–19.

MEDIA GUIDES

Hurricane Watch. Issue 3, Volume 5 (Raleigh, NC: Carolina Hurricanes Hockey Club, 2001).

NFL 2001 Record & Fact Book (New York: National Football League, 2001).

INTERNET SOURCES

"About the American Hockey League." http://www.monarchshockey.com cited 29 November 2001.

"Alberta Approves Lottery to Help Struggling NHL Teams." http://www.yahoo.com cited 19 June 2001.

"A's Settle Dispute With Authorities: Team Remains Up for Sale." http://yahoo.sports.com cited 2 December 1998.

"Bad Teams Often Have Something in Common—Bad Owners—NFL Insider." http://sports.yahoo.com cited 23 November 1999.

Badenhausen, Kurt. "NBA Owners Score Big." http://www.forbes.com cited 30 November 1999.

Badenhausen, Kurt, and William Sicheri. "Baseball Games." http://www.forbes.com cited 19 May 1999.

Baird, Woody. "Shelby County Commission OKs New Arena for NBA." http://sports.yahoo.com cited 12 June 2001.

"The Ballpark at Union Station." http://www.ballparks.com cited 1 November 2001.

"Ballpark Financing." http://www.mariners.org cited 8 June 1998.

"Ballparks." http://www.ballparks.com cited 1 November 2001.

Banks, Don. "Taking a Stand Against Violence." http://www.cnnsi.com cited 1 June 2000.

———. "Tip O' the Cap." http://www.cnnsi.com cited 21 March 2001.

"Baseball: Final 2000 Payroll Figures." http://www.cnnsi.com cited 21 March 2001.

"Baseball: Highest Salaries." http://www.cnnsi.com cited 21 March 2001.

"Baseball Hopes Its Next TV Deal as Sweet as NFL's." http://www.cnnsi.com cited 20 January 1998.

"Baseball: Largest Contract Packages." http://www.cnnsi.com cited 21 March 2001.

"Baseball: 1998 Team Payrolls." http://www.usatoday.com cited 19 May 1999.

"Baseball: Salary Milestones." http://www.cnnsi.com cited 21 March 2001.

"Baseball: Salary Progression Chart." http://www.cnnsi.com cited 21 March 2001.

"Baseball Ticket Prices." http://www.cnnsi.com cited 5 April 2000.

"Basketball Team Payrolls." http://www.ixquick.com cited 8 September 2001.

"Bengals' New Stadium Receives Approval." http://football.yahoo.com cited 3 February 1998.

"Bengals Stadium Gets Cash Infusion." http://www.cnnsi.com cited 16 February 2000.

"Bickley, Dan. "Costas: Allure of Sports Fading." http://www.azcentral.com cited 25 June 2001.

———. "Pro Sports May be Pricing Fans Out of Stadiums." http://www.azcentral.com cited 24 June 2001.

———. "Race Question Colors Sports." http://www.azcentral.com cited 24 June 2001.

Blum, Ronald. "MLB Owners OK Rules to Share Wealth." http://wire.ap.org cited 18 January 2001.

Bodley, Hal. "Major League Baseball Salary Report." http://www.usatoday.com cited 19 May 1999.

"Borrowing Some Bucks." http://www.cnnsi.com cited 26 May 2000.

"The Brand Keys Sports Loyalty Index." http://www.brandkeys.com cited 1 November 2001.

"A Brick Wall." http://www.cnnsi.com cited 27 November 1999.

"Bud Means Business." http://www.cnnsi.com cited 22 November 2000.

"Budget Runneth Over." http://www.cnnsi.com cited 10 August 2000.

"Building a Foundation." http://www.cnnsi.com cited 19 April 2000.

Burton, Rich. "From Hearst to Stern: The Shaping of an Industry Over a Century." http://proquest.umi.com cited 24 September 2001.

"Buyers Say ABC Getting $2 million for 30-Second Super Bowl Ads." http://sports.yahoo.com cited 22 September 1999.

"Cardinals Agree to Deal for New Stadium." http://www.yahoo.com cited 1 November 2001.

"Carolina Panthers." http://www.nfl.com cited 1 July 2001.

Colangelo, Jerry. "Sports and the Media." http://proquest.umi.com cited 24 September 2001.

Coleman, Joseph. "NBA Commissioner Sees More Globalization for Basketball." http://www.yahoo.com cited 11 November 1999.

"The Cost of Sitting." http://www.cnnsi.com cited 4 April 2000.

"The Criteria." http://www.sportingnews.com cited 9 August 2001.

Curran, John. "Nets Get Sweeter Lease." http://sports.yahoo.com cited 2 December 1998.

"Cyber-Scalping?" http://www.cnnsi.com cited 15 August 2001.

"Deal in Jeopardy." http://www.cnnsi.com cited 30 August 1999.

Deford, Frank. "Athletics 101." http://www.cnnsi.com cited 6 June 2001.

———. "Incompetent Owners Ruining Baseball." http://www.cnnsi.com cited 26 July 2000.

Dolliver, Mark. "Many Really Don't Care If They Ever Come Back." http://web2.info-trac.galegroup.com cited 15 October 2001.

"Economic Block: Baseball Panel Urges Increase in Revenue Sharing." http://www.cnnsi.com cited 1 December 2000.

"Equal Portions: NFL Owners Approve New Revenue-Sharing Plan." http://www.cnnsi.com cited 17 January 2001.

"Escrow Tax." http://www.cnnsi.com cited 15 April 2001.

"Expanding Their Borders." http://www.cnnsi.com cited 28 September 1999.

"Fair Ball: A Fan's Case for Baseball." http://www.amazon.com cited 2 July 2001.

"Fan Cost Index—League Averages." http://www.foxsports.com cited 29 November 2000.

"Fanatics." http://www.cnnsi.com cited 28 March 2000.

"Field Notes." http://ehostvgw3.epnet.com cited 12 July 2001.

"Finally an Identity." http://www.cnnsi.com cited 7 September 2000.

Fisher, Eric. "Cybersquatters Blitz Professional Leagues." http://www.infotrac.com cited 18 July 2001.

"Follow the Leaders." http://www.cnnsi.com cited 15 May 2001.

"Football Team Payroll." http://www.ixquick.com cited 8 September 2001.

"For Whom the Ball Tolls: A Fan's Guide to Economic Issues in Professional and College Sports." http://www.amazon.com cited 3 July 2001.

Forbes, Gordon. "Owners to Kick Around Realignment." http://www.usatoday.com cited 18 October 1998.

"Foreign Legions." http://www.cnnsi.com cited 4 April 2001.

Gaither, Chris. "Major League Baseball to Charge for Web Broadcasts." http://proquest.umi.com cited 27 September 2001.

"Gallup Poll Topics A–Z Sports." http://www.gallup.com cited 15 October 2001.

Georgatos, Dennis. "49ers Might Scrap New Stadium Plans." http://sports.yahoo.com cited 12 January 1999.

"Give Peace a Chance." http://www.cnnsi.com cited 5 June 2001.

Gloster, Ron. "A's to Stay in Oakland for at Least Two More Seasons." http://yahoo.sports.com cited 2 December 1998.

———. "Groups Looking Into Bid for Oakland Athletics." http://baseball.yahoo.com cited 29 October 1998.

"Good Luck Woody." http://www.buythejets.com cited 3 September 2001.

"Grading FanAtics." http://web2.infotrac.galegroup.com cited 15 October 2001.

Grover, Ronald. "Pro Basketball's Family Act." http://proquest.umi.com cited 30 August 2001.

———. "Superstars Could Make Super Owners." http://www.proquest.umi.com cited 30 August 2001.

Hall, Landon. "Building Boom Brings Millions of Fans Back to Minor Leagues." http://sports.yahoo.com cited 16 June 2001.

Hall, Steve. "HBO Explains How the Wacky ABA Revolutionized the Game." http://www.starnews.com cited 18 November 1997.

"Hands-On Approach." http://www.cnnsi.com cited 24 February 1998.

"Hard Ball: The Abuse of Power in Pro Team Sports." http://www.amazon.com cited 5 July 2001.

Harris, Hamil R. "ABA Returns With Black Ownership." http://proquest.umi.com cited 30 August 2001.

"Helping Hand." http://www.cnnsi.com cited 23 May 2001.

Helyar, John. "Sports: Watching Football in Person Now Costs Even More." http://www.proquestmail.com cited 19 July 2001.

"Hey You. You With the Website. You Want a Piece of This?" http://www.ecompany.com cited 7 November 2000.

"High Rollers." http://www.cnnsi.com cited 24 July 1999.

Hille, Bob. "New York, New York." http://www.sportingnews.com cited 9 August 2001.

"History 101: Chronology of How the Modern-Day NFL Came to Pass." http://www.cnnsi.com cited 1 July 2001.

"Hockey: Team Payroll." http://www.cnnsi.com cited 6 September 2001.

"Home Sweet Home." http://www.cnnsi.com cited 3 November 1999.

"House Speaker Ups Ante." http://www.cnnsi.com cited 23 May 2000.

"How'd We Do That?" http://www.sportingnews.com cited 9 August 2001.

"Huizenga's Legacy." http://www.cnnsi.com cited 13 January 1999.

"Interleague Overhaul." http://www.cnnsi.com cited 24 June 2001.

"Introducing ... " http://www.cnnsi.com cited 7 July 1998.

Isidore, Chris. "Prices Going, Going ... Up." http://www.cnnfn.com cited 11 August 2001.

————. "WNBA: Lovable Money Loser." http://www.cnnfn.com cited 21 August 2001.

Karp, Josie. "Squabble in Seattle." http://www.cnnsi.com cited 13 July 1999.

"Kings Co-Owners Buy Into Lakers." http://www.cnnsi.com cited 4 November 1998.

Kropko, M.R. "Cleveland Browns Stadium Sponsors Get Four Gates." http://sports.yahoo.com cited 8 July 1999.

"Kumbaya." http://www.cnnsi.com cited 6 June 2001.

"Legislators Seek to Halt Stadium Strong-Arming." http://www.cnnsi.com cited 14 January 1998.

"Lerner Gets the Browns." http://www.cnnsi.com cited 8 September 1998.

"Leveling the Playing Field: How the Law Can Make Sports Better for Fans." http://www.amazon.com cited 28 June 2001.

"License to Sell."http://www.cnnsi.com cited 12 July 1999.

"Life in Yonkers?" http://www.cnnsi.com cited 19 January 2000.

"Loan Closed Tuesday to Finance New Tiger Ballpark." http://baseball.yahoo.com cited 26 August 1998.

Longman, Jere. "Pro Leagues' Ratings Drop: Nobody Is Quite Sure Why." http://proquest.umi.com cited 27 September 2001.

Lorge, Sarah. "The Fan Plan." http://proquestmail.com cited 29 October 2001.

"Major League Baseball." http://www.mlb.com cited 1 August 2001.

"Maloof Family Gains Control of Kings." http://www.cnnsi.com cited 1 July 1999.

Matthews, Anna Wilde. "Sports Leagues Tightening Grip on Web Content." http://proquest.umi.com cited 24 September 2001.

"Media Ownership of Teams." http://www.resonator.com cited 20 November 2001.

"Media Profile." http://www.nielsenmedia.com cited 8 October 2001.

"Memphis Arena on Hold." http://www.cnnsi.com cited 11 July 2001.

Miller, Ira. "Bad Teams Often Have Something in Common—Bad Owners—NFL Insider." http://sports.yahoo.com cited 23 November 1999.

"Misdirected Priorities." http://www.cnnsi.com cited 14 December 2000.

"MLB Owners OK Rules to Share Wealth." http://wire.ap.org cited 18 January 2001.

"Model of Intimacy." http://www.cnnsi.com cited 17 March 1998.

"Mo' Money." http://www.cnnsi.com cited 6 April 2000.

"Money Matters." http://www.cnnsi.com cited 1 April 2001.

"More Power to Selig." http://www.cnnsi.com cited 20 January 2001.

"Mr. A's Owner." http://www.cnnsi.com cited 2 July 1999.

Muret, Don. "NHL's Average Cost Up 5.5%; Bruins Top the List." http://web4. infotrac.galegroup.com cited 18 October 2001.

Muret, Don, and Linda Deckard. "Teams Take Varied Approach to the Net." http:// proquest.umi.com cited 27 September 2001.

"Musical Chairs? NFL to Consider Realignment Plans." http://www.cnnsi.com cited 13 October 1998.

"The Name of the Game: The Business of Sports." http://www.amazon.com cited 26 June 2001.

"Naming Rights Deals." http://www.teammarketing.com cited 12 November 2001.

"National Basketball Association." http://www.forbes.com cited 30 November 1999.

———." http://www.nba.com cited 1 August 2001.

"National Football League." http://www.nfl.com cited 1 August 2001.

"National Hockey League." http://www.nhl.com cited 1 August 2001.

"NBA New TV Deal Worth Twice as Much." http://www.austin360.com cited 12 November 1997.

"NBA Posts First League-Wide Decrease in 11 Year History of Fan Cost Index." http://www.teammarketing.com cited 29 October 2001.

"NBA's Popularity, Salaries Cited for Fan Cost Increase." http://web4.infotrac. galegroup.com cited 18 October 2001.

"NBA: Team Payrolls." http://www.usatoday.com cited 19 May 1999.

"NBDL Background Information." http://www.nba.com cited 31 July 2001.

"NBDL Fact Sheet." http://www.nba.com cited 31 July 2001.

"New Fenway." http://www.cnnsi.com cited 1 November 2001.

Newcomb, Peter, and Doug Donovan. "The Forbes 400: Jocks." http://proquest.umi.com cited 10 September 2001.

"NFL Europe: The Adventure Begins." http://www.nfleurope.com cited 31 July 2001.

"NFL Europe: Commissioner Praises NFL Europe League." http://www.nfleurope.com cited 3 July 2001.

"NFL Football: From the Beginning." http://www.cnnsi.com cited 1 June 2001.

"NFL Owners Approve New Revenue-Sharing Plan." http://www.cnnsi.com cited 18 January 2001.

"NFL: Team Payroll." http://www.cnnsi.com cited 6 September 2001.

"NHL History." http://www.nhl.com cited 30 March 2000.

"NHL Hockey." http://www.infoplease.com cited 12 April 2000.

"NHL Hockey Player Salaries." http://www.sportsfansofamerica.com cited 18 July 2001.

"NHL Team Payroll." http://www.cnnsi.com cited 6 September 2001.

"Nielsen Media Research Local Universe Estimates for the 1997–1998 Broadcast Season." http://www.nielsenmedia.com cited 8 October 2001.

"Nielsen Media Research Local Universe Estimates for the 2001–2002 Broadcast Season." http://www.nielsenmedia.com cited 1 October 2001.

Noone, Kyle. "1, 2, 3 Strikes You're Out." http://www.myprimetime.com cited 15 October 2001.

"Owners Agree to Sale of Marlins." http://www.cnnsi.com cited 14 January 1999.

"Owners Not Pleased With Davis After Lawsuit Against NFL." http://www.cnnsi.com cited 24 May 2001.

"Owners Tackle Easy Issues, But Sleep on Tough Ones." http://www.cnnsi.com cited 1 November 2000.

"The Owners: Who Are These Guys?" http://www.resonator.com cited 20 November 2001.

Ozanian, Michael K., and Stephen Taub. "Adam Smith Faces Off Against Karl Marx." http://proquest.umi.com cited 18 October 2001.

"Pack Asks for Green." http://www.cnnsi.com cited 15 May 2000.

"Padres Ballpark Opponent Files Lawsuit." http://sports.yahoo.com cited 16 February 2000.

"Padres Get New Home in 2002." http://www.cnnsi.com cited 4 November 1998.

"Patriots Plan New Stadium for 2002." http://www.cnnsi.com cited 19 April 2000.

"Pay Dirt: The Business of Professional Team Sports." http://www.amazon.com cited 1 July 2001.

"Payrolls for Every MLB Team." http://www.augustasports.com cited 23 October 1999.

"Phillies Unveil Plans for New Park." http://www.cnnsi.com cited 28 June 2001.

"Phoenix Coyotes." http://www.phoenixcoyotes.com cited 27 January 2002.

"Planning Ahead." http://www.cnnsi.com cited 11 June 2001.

"Play Ball." http://www.cnnsi.com cited 28 August 2000.

"Price Check." http://www.cnnsi.com cited 27 October 1998.

"The Price of the Pastime." http://www.cnnsi.com cited 29 March 2001.

"Quarter of Possibilities." http://www.cnnsi.com cited 16 November 2000.

"Rain Delay." http://www.cnnsi.com cited 28 June 1999.

"Raymond James Stadium." http://www.ballparks.com cited 6 October 1998.

"The Rest of the Best." http://web2.infotrac.galegroup.com cited 22 October 2001.

"Rockets Rejected." http://www.cnnsi.com cited 3 November 1999.

"Sale of Royals to Glass Approved." http://www.cnnsi.com cited 18 April 2000.

"Sports." http://www.scarborough.com cited 16 October 2001.

"Sports, Jobs and Taxes: The Economic Impact of Sports Teams and Stadiums." http://www.amazon.com cited 30 June 2001.

"Sports Loyalty Index." http://www.brandkeys.com cited 24 October 2001.

"Sports Stadium Madness: Prevailing Wage Impact on Stadium Construction." http://www.heartland.org cited 16 February 1999.

"Spurs Break Ground on New Arena." http://www.cnnsi.com cited 23 August 2000.

"Stadium Measure Narrowly Passes." http://www.cnnsi.com cited 8 November 2000.

"The Stanley Cup." http://www.nhl.com cited 29 November 2001.

"Stanley Cup Dynasties." http://www.nhl.com cited 29 November 2001.

"Sticker Shock." http://www.cnnsi.com cited 20 July 1998.

"Survey Says." http://www.cnnsi.com cited 26 July 2000.

"Taxing Proposition." http://www.cnnsi.com cited 13 September 2000.

"The Taxman Cometh." http://www.cnnsi.com cited 24 January 2000.

"Team Values." http://www.forbes.com cited 7 September 1999.

Thomaselli, Rich. "NHL Markets Web Site." http://proquest.umi.com cited 24 September 2001.

"Ticket Price Comparison." http://www.ixquick.com cited 15 October 2001.

"TV Azteca and the NBA Extend Broadcast Partnership." http://www.nba.com cited 29 August 1998.

"2000 Inside the Ownership of Professional Sports Teams." http://www.teammarketing.com cited 20 November 2001.

Vertuno, Jim. "Nolan Ryan's Minor League Team Debuts $25 Million Stadium." http://sports.yahoo.com cited 16 April 2000.

Waddell, Ray. "NBA's Popularity, Salaries Cited for Fan Cost Increase." http://web4.
    infotrac.galegroup.com cited 18 October 2001.
————. "Ticket Price Hikes a Major Factor in Higher Fan Cost Index for MLB."
    http://web4.infotrac.galegroup.com cited 18 October 2001.
Walentik, Steve. "Cityscape." http://ehost.com cited 22 October 2001.
Waltner, Charles. "CRM: The New Game in Town for Professional Sports." http://
    proquestmail.com cited 29 October 2001.
"Who Wants to Be a Millionaire."http://www.cnnsi.com cited 4 April 2001.
Will, George. "Pay Dirt: The Business of Professional Team Sports." http://www.
    amazon.com cited 1 July 2001.
Williams, Dara Akiko. "Judge Rejects Effort to Put Ballpark on the Ballot."
    http://sports.yahoo.com cited 28 February 2000.
"World League Renamed NFL Europe." http://www.nfl.com cited 11 March 1998.
"Yankees to Form Own TV Network." http://www.cnnsi.com cited 20 June 2001.

INDEX

About the Author

FRANK P. JOZSA, JR. is Associate Professor of Economics and Business Administration at Pfeiffer University. He co-authored *Relocating Teams and Expanding Leagues in Professional Sports: How the Major Leagues Respond to Market Conditions* (Quorum Books, 1999). His publications have appeared in *Athletic Business*, the *Carolina Journal*, the *Charlotte Observer*, the *Wall Street Journal Review of Books*, *Street & Smith's SportsBusiness Journal*, and in the *Proceedings: International Conference on Sports Business*.